26.95

D0148472

No Longer Property of
Fr. Leonard Alvey Library
Brescia University

Managing With INTEGRITY

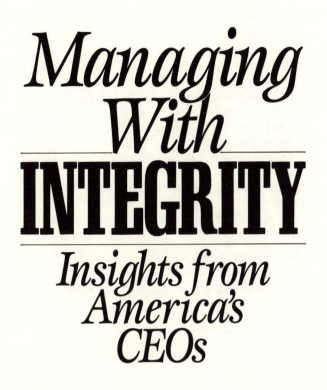

Managing
With
INTEGRITY

Insights from America's CEOs

CHARLES E. WATSON
Foreword by C. William Verity

PRAEGER

New York
Westport, Connecticut
London

BRESCIA COLLEGE LIBRARY
OWENSBORO, KENTUCKY

Copyright Acknowledgments

The author and publisher are grateful to the following for granting use of their material:

Our Credo and the Johnson & Johnson logo used by permission of Johnson & Johnson, New Brunswick, New Jersey.

Ford Company Mission and Guiding Principles and the Ford logo used by permission of Ford Motor Company, Dearborn, Michigan.

Our Principles and the Campbell Soup Company logo used by permission of Campbell Soup Company, Camden, New Jersey.

The Bristol-Meyers Squibb Pledge used by permission of Bristol-Myers Squibb, New York, New York.

Hilton's Corporate Mission used by permission of Hilton Hotels Corporation, Beverly Hills, California.

The Southland Creed, copyright © The Southland Corporation, used by permission of The Southland Corporation, Dallas, Texas.

Library of Congress Cataloging-in-Publication Data

Watson, Charles E.
      Managing with integrity : insights from America's CEOs / Charles
   E. Watson ; foreword by C. William Verity.
            p.   cm.
      Includes bibliographical references (p.   ) and index.
      ISBN 0-275-93865-4
      1. Business ethics.   2. Executives—United States—Attitudes.
   I. Title.
      HF5387.W38   1991
      658.4′094—dc20   90-48582

658
.4094
W337

British Library Cataloguing in Publication Data is available.

Copyright © 1991 by Charles E. Watson

All rights reserved. No portion of this book may be reproduced, by any process or technique, without the express written consent of the publisher.

Library of Congress Catalog Card Number: 90-48582
ISBN: 0-275-93865-4

First published in 1991

Praeger Publishers, One Madison Avenue, New York, NY 10010
An imprint of Greenwood Publishing Group, Inc.

Printed in the United States of America

The paper used in this book complies with the Permanent Paper Standard issued by the National Information Standards Organization (Z39.48-1984).

10 9 8 7 6 5 4 3 2 1

In loving memory to my mother, Iva Murphy Watson

85879

Contents

Foreword

At a time when standards of ethics in business, the professions, and government are being challenged in the media and in our universities, it is most uplifting to read *Managing with Integrity*.

For five years Charlie Watson has traveled the United States interviewing over 125 senior CEOs of American business and documenting their responses to difficult ethical questions. *Managing with Integrity* is full of examples of how courageous leaders in business have exhibited the highest qualities of character. I believe we all can be inspired and instructed by reading about deeds and philosophies of these business leaders.

All of us are constantly searching for values on which to build our lives or our companies. This book reveals how leaders forge success for themselves and their companies by doing right for right's sake; that it's not so much what you say but what you do and how you do it. They ignored their critics and, like Abraham Lincoln and more recently Ronald Reagan, they are content to let history judge their actions and their character.

In this splendid work by Charlie Watson we can learn from the experiences of 125 business leaders as they sought to lead their companies and add to the betterment of their communities. This is about people who lead by example, who create climates where employees can achieve the best that is within themselves, and who prove the importance and the value of service. *Managing with Integrity* is about those kinds of experiences which both instruct and inspire. This book will be of particular interest to those young people who seek values upon which to base their lives.

C. William Verity
Former U.S. Secretary of Commerce

Preface

Most efforts aimed at elevating morality in business have a record of limited success. The three most common approaches found are: (1) indoctrination in company codes of conduct and acceptable standards and practices, (2) clarification of personal values to sensitize learners to the ethical dimensions of business situations, and (3) instruction in ethical reasoning using any one of several models designed to guide people toward better decisions.

Mankind has long preferred legalistic codes to moral goodness. Codes are clear, fairly easy to understand and they allow one to know, in most situations, whether he is within the bounds of accepted standards. From a policy perspective codes are an excellent method of communicating to employees exactly where management stands and what it expects from them in areas where experience indicates trouble can arise. Thus codes are quite useful in saving people from making serious mistakes while protecting the interests of the company and others. But unless one is the kind of person, by belief and habit, who embraces the ideals codes and ethical standards attempt to advance in the first place, their impact will be limited.

The plain truth is that genuine goodness transcends legalistic righteousness. Moreover, whenever a person is motivated merely to adhere to a proscriptive code, there is always a tendency to take pride in how well one conforms. This inclination can easily crowd out one's finer impulses and blur his vision to many other worthy matters. Perfection is a laudable aim, but if pursued singlemindedly it can lead one to become unbearably self-righteous. The spotless life is insignificant if it fails to contribute to mankind's betterment.

One does well when he sets his sights far beyond the mere adherence to ethical codes of conduct and tries to live a useful life—one which is productive and significant. Anyone of wit and experience knows that ours is an imperfect world. There are morally objectionable realities in all situations and choices. While we shall probably not live perfect lives, we can still lead useful lives. A fundamental theme of this volume is this: the flawless life counts for very little if it has failed to produce something of lasting value—some useful service in the world, some measure of good. The possibilities for the person in business to do good while creating, producing and distributing goods and services are endless.

One school of thought believes that humans will answer the challenge of behaving more ethically if they confront their own attitudes and values. This is thought to occur in training situations where learners discuss and debate moral conundrums to a minute nicety. Unfortunately, discussions of such matters frequently fail to reach consensus. Rather than pressing still further into debate or permitting sharp disagreement to persist, those who are bent more on not offending and being accepted by others are frequently found to stop the discussion short and issue the familiar remark, "There is no correct answer here, for it's really just a matter of opinion." This is a conclusion so feeble as to render the entire process almost futile, but appealing to those who fancy themselves as being "open minded" and "tolerant" because it has such broad appeal. Calling right and wrong "a matter of opinion" discourages many from giving serious consideration to vexing issues worthy of consideration. The justification offered for such efforts runs something like this: "While we cannot seem to agree," trainers will say to learners at the conclusion of these sessions, "you will no doubt be more sensitive to ethical issues in the future." Apparently the expectation is that sensitized people will behave more ethically than those who are not—an unverified hypothesis.

History is lavish with instances where the quest for ethical living has rested on the application of intelligence alone and found expression in the development and use of decision making guides and models for moral reasoning. The ethical person in question strives to meet the ideal of living a life guided by reason alone and within the defined boundaries of right and wrong. This approach amounts largely to a highly intellectual process that weighs and evaluates conflicting alternatives in the light of procedures in logic and guiding principles. The sad truth is that in our world there are unethical aspects to all actions.

It is doubtful whether those efforts aimed at elevating the level of behavior from an ethical perspective by applying reason alone to moral dilemmas have made a lasting impact on practical persons. They certainly have not stirred much enthusiasm in, or significantly altered the behaviors of, ordinary people. Although consideration of borderline cases is important, and intelligent, rational discussion of them is interesting we do well to recognize why they provide limited possibilities for actually altering behavior toward the ethical and the useful. Several points deserve consideration.

Most of us go through lengthy stretches in our lives not having to face moral dilemmas of anywhere near the magnitude and complexity brought up for discussion purposes in the course of these attempts to teach people to think more ethically. Should a drug be permitted on the market which can cure terrible illness and relieve considerable pain and suffering even though some persons will die from unpredictable side effects? Should a plant be closed and many loyal employees put out of work because compliance with environmental laws would make the plant unprofitable? Few of us have to make choices this hard.

Whereas those who already have learned to delight in the good may find stimulation in pondering and debating difficult moral dilemmas, the claim that anyone else can be influenced meaningfully by such discussions is untenable. In fact, we have as much reason to believe that this experience may teach the uninstructed conscience little more than how to be shrewd. It was Aristotle's position, after his considerable experience with such matters, that before moral argument can be effective the soul of the listener must first have been conditioned by habits of the right kinds of likes and dislikes. The proposition that people who, in training settings, engage in thinking about hypothetical ethical conflicts will actually use like, high-minded approaches to solve real life problems has yet to be confirmed.

Each man leads his life answering to the pattern his vision beholds and his heart honors. A disturbing fact of our time is that we, particularly our nation's youth, have practically no vision of the greatness and the goodness which is alive in the world in general or in the world of business in particular. Our minds are regularly and continually pounded with only the wrongdoings and ill-schemes which are found out and reported—as they ought. But all this does very little good in lifting standards and elevating the levels of ethical conduct. Solid standards of conduct are useful and logical reasoning guides are helpful in sorting out complex issues. But these alone are not the end of the matter. Something more needs to be included in the equation which will stir the heart and strengthen the will.

Personality, of course, is not limited to intelligence alone. Emotion and will are to be counted in the equation also. These three factors form a triangle, perfectly balanced, around which life revolves. Each is essential and, although one may temporarily dominate, if any one of these factors is lacking, the personality to that measure is deficient. Unless guided by reason and focused by will, emotion is wild, erratic, unpredictable. Little beyond abstract theorizing is possible through intelligence by itself. It cannot guide until emotion desires some outcome and the will is quickened and concentrates one's energies to attain that end. And will, by itself, produces little more than frenzied efforts unless it is stirred by some deep longing from emotion and guided by reason to build a useful structure. The trick lies not solely with knowing what is right and good but also in suppressing the ego, with its unrelenting hunger for pride, and building a love for the good and the worthwhile.

Even the simplest mind can comprehend the idea that one's ability to handle tough choices is vastly improved once he has mastered ordinary ones and has become an ethical person by force of habit. To lift the level of one's ethical behavior and lead a useful life, the mastering of right living in ordinary circumstances is far more effective than occasionally discussing hypothetical abstractions. Mere clarification of personal feelings toward an issue will not lead someone to act ethically unless he first has developed a love of the good and is resolute enough to focus his efforts steadily toward it. The ideal, then, is to develop, using Aristotle's term, "settled habits" of right living—virtues—which shape the kind of person one is: one's character and, in turn, the kinds of situations one confronts and how one handles them. Moral theories may be useful in helping people to arrive at well reasoned decisions, but it is really moral habits, a way of living that gives them the vision and love of the good, that ultimately enable them to pursue these well reasoned decisions consistently.

We know very little about how to cause humans to love the good. Our need here exceeds our abilities. One encouraging hypothesis is that it is inherently appealing and attractive. Set before minds in the form of concrete examples, the good reveals itself in ways which tend to win over the heart in much the same way beauty appeals to the aesthetic senses. Still, this could be subject to the same criticism leveled against the values clarification approach discussed earlier. A glimmer of hope arises when we consider that Alfred North Whitehead confirmed the value of examples when he brilliantly stated, "Moral education is impossible apart from the habitual vision of greatness." Visions of greatness can provide a source of optimism and inspiration that both instruct and direct people toward worthy aims and thus worthwhile lives.

In our age of cynicism we seem to have developed disdain for looking toward old truths and simple stories of virtue. Unlike their counterparts a few generations ago, many younger Americans today have scarcely been exposed to examples of honesty, loyalty, friendship and patriotism and so forth for guidance in how to live. Without inspiring standards there is little hope for elevating the level of ethical conduct. Every person has a story in his or her life, much like the one of George Washington and the cherry tree, which reveals some positive aspect of character. These anecdotes can lose their value if they are, like a medal, pinned to the hero's lapel. But, they can also serve as valuable moral lessons from which any thoughtful person can profit. Samuel Johnson held the same idea in his thoughts when he wrote, "Examples as well as arguments propagate the truth." What most rings true in the minds and hearts of ordinary, intelligent people are not sophisticated ethical theories but concrete examples of decency and goodness from the lives of successful people.

By focusing on character and its development, it is possible to reach beyond the sterile domain and limited focus heretofore taken by ethics. When we realize that our actions are a function of our vision and that our vision is determined by the persons we are, we can begin to comprehend the value of this expanded perspective. It is best when the discussion of character unfolds largely, although not be treated exclusively, within the fabric of everyday realities—the continuities of life commonly experienced as opposed to infrequently encountered and indeterminable moral dilemmas. The aim here is to set forth for learners what might be labeled "visions of good"—what is so true that it is self justifying and so attractive that it wins men's hearts.

We have still not contended here adequately with the matter of man's will and the process of strengthening it to do what is right. Nor have we begun to do justice to the problem of genuinely winning his allegiance to the good. To look to religion for better answers and help in these matters is reasonable. To cast aside, arbitrarily, what has obviously been a major part of the human experience and a significant influence on the course of civilization is limiting.

The approach taken in this volume is to explain the various dimensions of character and the challenges each presents. Illustrations of exemplary character found in the world of business are cited to give greater meaning to the ideas presented and to give readers the hope and encouragement needed to work to develop good character in themselves.

This is not an unbiased analysis of business and its leaders. It is not an apology for business or an attempt to falsely portray what goes on in business. Those are other matters not dealt with here. This is a book that depicts the finest and most admirable choices and actions found in business. These are intended to provide uplifting, guiding visions of higher standards for the reader's own life.

The book is organized into five parts which present the main themes. The idea for the three central sections—to aspire, to adventure, and to serve—come from a businessman: William H. Danforth, founder and former chairman of the Ralston Purina Co. These words are inscribed on the base of his statue in Checkerboard Square, St. Louis, Missouri.

Part I examines the realities facing a person within the business setting. It uncovers many of the sources of our negative image of business. It introduces evidence that challenges the assertion that the ethical person can not succeed. It examines man's struggle to find meaning in his business life, his freedom to choose, and the difficulties associated with quality thinking within the context of business—a realm laden with many difficulties.

Part II discusses the influence of aspirations on the businessperson's character. Although rules and high ethical standards are an important dimension of character, there is something greater that needs to be a driving force in one's aspirations—a compelling desire to serve some worthy business purpose. And this section shows there are many worthy purposes to be found in the realm of business. In chapter 8 the profit paradox is presented. It says that those persons and organizations that aspire to serve worthwhile purposes are ultimately the most profitable and that the ordering of aspirations to embrace people, products, and profits, in that order, are the most competitive and thus the most successful.

Part III calls attention to the importance of daring and committing oneself boldly to a purpose or course of action. Every major decision seems plagued with uncertainty. The practical businessperson knows that he is always forced to act upon what his best judgment and what his beliefs tell him. One's best hope lies in living positively and boldly, while pursuing the worthwhile and making difficult decisions.

Part IV goes into depth with the overriding theme of this volume— the importance and value of service. It shows the incredible impact that serving can have on any ordinary life. It discusses the many ways business can serve others—employees, customers, communities—and contribute to technological and economic progress.

Part V puts all that has been said before into perspective from the viewpoint of the individual: What does character matter? This part, comprised of the one last chapter, examines the concept of success in business; it reports and discusses the dimensions of success that are most mentioned by those who are regarded as the most successful in the business world. After reading the book and thinking about the evidence and examples presented, the reader is challenged to decide whether he will try to manage with integrity himself, much as the scores of successful people depicted in the text who have done what's right and done well in business.

I am indebted to the 125 senior-level executives and CEOs who gave their time and shared their valuable views and experiences. It bears mentioning that I found these business leaders personable, easy to talk to, and genuine. They are men of goodwill who struggle hard and honestly to live decently and produce profitably in difficult circumstances where no easy answers are to be found.

C. William Verity of Armco, who later became U.S. Secretary of Commerce, was the first CEO to be interviewed. Dickinson C. Ross was instrumental in helping the study in its early stages by introducing me personally to his circle of friends and acquaintances on the West Coast, thus enabling the list of interviewees to grow and acquire the measure of stature needed to encourage others to participate. My colleague Prof. Harry F. Brooks was enormously helpful during the interviewing phase of the study; he gathered useful comments and examples in the interviews he conducted. Dr. D. Elton Trueblood, who needs no special introduction in theological and philosophical circles, provided many useful suggestions and insights. Charles T. Peers, Jr., became a much relied upon source of advice and reassurance during troubling times, and there were many.

I
REALITIES

I

REALITIES

1

The Ethical Realities of Business

Every age and every people has a character stamped upon it by the heros and visions it honors. One popular superstition that grips many lives in our time is the belief that success in business requires greed, deceit, and unfeeling ruthlessness. Accordingly, living a virtuous life is fully incompatible with profitable commercial activity. And too, this belief holds that one's advancement in the ranks of a business establishment can come only from unsavory actions. Plainly put, many believe that a truly good person cannot succeed in business.

If these assertions were true, the consequences would be a tragedy of colossal proportions. The 8 million men and women performing managerial and executive duties in our economy would be leading marred lives and the 84 million Americans who are employed in private enterprise would be tainted or corrupted merely through their participation in business. Although this perception of morality in the realm of business is widespread and goes largely unquestioned, an attentive study of successful people engaged in commercial activity shows that it does not tally with reality. Instead, success in business, as in all other honorable human endeavors, turns largely on adhering to the highest moral ideals and ethical standards our civilization honors. In Voltaire's words, "Men succeed less by their talents than by their character." Observes chairman and CEO Richard L. Gelb of Bristol-Myers Squibb, "To be successful you don't have to resort to all sorts of things; you can be successful and stand for the *right* sorts of things."

UNTRUE CHARACTERIZATIONS

The corrosive assumption that highly ethical behavior must be divorced from standard business practice can only bear bitter fruits to individuals and ultimately to our private-enterprise economy itself. So popular is this belief—that one must break the rules to gain success—that something on the order of a moral epidemic is clearly present. The fact that many of the third of a million men and women who graduate each year with bachelor's or master's degrees in business from U.S. colleges and universities embark upon their careers with the belief that their main objective in life should be to acquire and enjoy wealth and that it is all right to bend the rules in order to survive, profit, or move ahead evokes alarm.

This concept of what is acceptable in terms of morality in the business world is only part of a larger pattern of perceptions held by many others. Americans, in general, tend to believe that to get ahead in business one needs to be a little bit slick, slightly underhanded, somewhat sneaky, and quicker than the next person. The idea, they think, is to "get yours first" and "do in the other guy before he does you in." Nathan S. Ancell, cofounder and chairman of the board of Ethan Allen Furniture, summed it up when he remarked, "The American public thinks that businessmen generally are a bunch of thieves. And that comes from the perspective they've had with dishonest things that a few dishonest companies do." The careful observer can see examples daily of people willing to forge ahead in their quests for success acting as if this view were totally true. But this perception is only partially correct. It contains just enough truth to appeal to the cynicism of people, causing them to accept it. But, as Ancell observes, "I think it's a terrible, terrible distortion. I know lots of heads of lots of businesses that I've met over the years and most of those men are good, hard-hitting, genuine, solid, decent people who know that it's important to run a decent, honest business. They don't get very much publicity. As a matter of fact the notoriety and publicity of some dishonest companies spills over on the many good companies that don't deserve that notoriety."

Corporate America is able to withstand some amount of undeserved, adverse publicity. Its thoughtful and well meaning leaders actually welcome honest reporting of the dishonorable conduct and illegal practices of the few who bend or break the rules. And the business establishment can cleanse itself of unethical actions when they are infrequent, the exception to the norm. But business is at great risk when large numbers of inexperienced wealth seekers join its ranks with views of right and wrong far different from the time-tested truths civilized mankind looks to for order and stability and a just society. Business is hard pressed to survive, let alone flourish, without decent people who place high value on morality. In the extreme, economic freedom as we know it is at stake.

Marked by a mood of distrust, there is a great thirst today for the negative. Occasional reports of serious wrongdoing seem insufficient to quench it. Unfavorable news stories about business, many of them distorted beyond any standard of reason or fairness, are welcomed by a cynical public which is eager to reconfirm the belief that anyone connected with commerce is ill meaning and solely motivated by the lowest intentions and standards. Such reporting is unfair and harmful to people and their organizations. It erodes the public confidence and goodwill business works hard to earn. But there is a deeper tragedy. Biased and inaccurate reports and portrayals plant in the minds of many young people erroneous views of commercial enterprise and what is tolerable in business activity. Such views can cause them to accept as permissible conduct that our civilization regards as deplorable. As a consequence, many minds are prevented from even a fair consideration of what actually goes on within the world of business. Worse still, when these perceptions are accepted and acted on accordingly, lives can become misshaped.

Targets deserving criticism will be found in business. Human frailties in the face of the temptations found therein, as there are in any other human activity, will surface. Of course mistakes will occur. But the media, with its tendency to emphasize and report only the negative side of business, mislead the public, especially impressionable young people. Philip M. Hampton, of Bankers Trust of New York, says, "I think corporate America is much more ethical than the public gives it credit for being. Partly, I think, it's a function of, not necessarily bad, but terse reporting and the tendency to get toward the controversial side of a news story and the tendency to make business news stories sound a little more sensational than they really are. I think they try to make stories a little more controversial, which makes everything come out a little more as if it were a cold-hearted decision. In the situation, for example, where a decision has been made to spin off a business or lay off a thousand people the news stories will never state that the enterprise was saved and another ten thousand people are still working, and that the thousand laid off have a preferred right in coming back in, and that they have benefits while they are out and that things were done to rehabilitate those people and make them useful to another industry."

The media have demonstrated themselves not to be inclined to get stories to the public in an accurate and unbiased fashion. By taking statements out of context and reporting only part of what business figures have stated publicly, for example, the media have through carelessness, ineptness, or deliberateness, falsely reported what a number of business people in the public's eye actually said or meant to say. The following examples illustrate the sharp contrast between reality and the illusions created by outside writers and pundits.

John D. Rockefeller's statement at the University of Chicago that "God gave me money" has, taken out of context, created an image of this great man as being sanctimonious and arrogant. Actually, Rockefeller uttered this remark in complete humility. True to his strict Baptist upbringing, he devoutly believed that Providence had made him a trustee for his hundreds of millions of dollars, which were not to be kept but disbursed widely to do the utmost possible good.[1]

The remark, "History is bunk," attributed to Henry Ford, paints him as anti-intellectual, an ignoramus, indifferent to the world and its problems. Accurately quoted, however, Ford's remark was this: "History as sometimes written is mostly bunk. But history that you can see is of great value."[2] The automobile and his work in the present stirred Henry Ford's mind, but the past, history, captured his heart. He accumulated an incred-

ible amount of Americana, which he assembled into one of the world's
great historical restorations: his Greenfield Village. It depicts for visitors
today an era that Ford, more than any other man of his time, had changed
forever.

In testimony before Congress during his confirmation hearings, a
former president of General Motors, Charles E. Wilson, was being grilled
on the question of whether he, as a businessman, could be loyal to the interests of the United States if he were to become the Secretary of Defense.
Practically all readers are familiar with the statement, "What's good for
General Motors is good for the country," implying that, among other
things, the public interest is subordinate to the interest of a giant corporation. This is a misquotation. In actuality, Wilson said "For years I
thought what was good for our country was good for General Motors,
and vice versa," meaning that a strong and healthy United States was good
for business and that by putting the interest of the country first we all, including the nation's corporations, would benefit.[3] However, what stuck
was the "and vice versa," remark, which was taken out of context and recast into the infamous misquotation.

On the front-page of the 7 February 1969 *Wall Street Journal*, Fred
Hartley, then the president of the Union Oil Company, was accused of
callously saying, "I'm amazed at the publicity for the loss of a few birds."
In truth, Hartley never said such a thing at any time, anywhere and he
certainly did not say it before the Senate subcommittee, investigating an oil
spill in the Santa Barbara Channel, as some news media reported.
Subsequently *The Wall Street Journal,* the *New York Times*, and *Time*
Magazine all printed corrections.[4]

Ill-chosen expressions can easily linger on to haunt business leaders
and invite scathing criticism from their antagonists. The supreme example
of this occurred on 8 October 1882. William Henry Vanderbilt, riding on
his private car, was explaining to reporters that the New York Central
Railroad could not make a profit on a $15 fare between New York and
Chicago but was maintaining the route because of a fare war with the
Pennsylvania Railroad. Clarence Dresser, a free-lance writer, pressed
Vanderbilt with a baiting question, "Don't you run the train for the public
benefit?" In a momentary outburst Vanderbilt reacted. "The public be
damned! I'm working for my stockholders. If the public wants the train
why don't they pay for it?"[5]

This provided ammunition for the critics of capitalism who claimed it
epitomized the attitude of business moguls of the day and of all the other
builders who had fashioned the giant enterprises of an industrializing nation. Yet this was not at all an accurate reflection of Vanderbilt's opinion
or policy. He had worked hard to create harmony between the New York
Central and the public. Historical accounts reveal that he and his father,
Cornelius "Commodore" Vanderbilt, were neither always high-minded
nor always altruistic. Perhaps, selfishly they fully recognized the wisdom
of working for the public, never against it. It was Cornelius Vanderbilt
who had built the base of his fortune on a fleet of steamships operating on

the Hudson River by cutting fares and offering unheard of luxury to passengers, and thereby nearly driving his competitors out of business. The competitors later paid him to leave. "Serve the public, and ye make money," were the Commodore's words.[6]

To pinpoint errors in reporting and conclude that all news reports are inaccurate and that all people in the news media are always incompetent and ill-meaning would be unfair and untrue. Business, by its own actions, can rightfully be accused of creating a distasteful image of itself in the mind of the ordinary person. All men of depth and substance believe that wrongdoing ought to be denounced and arrested. And many bad situations in business have been spotted and responsibly reported in the news, ranging from ill-treatment of employees to outright fraud and from illegal stock trading to bribery and illegal payoffs. We might find comfort in the fact that these ill-schemes are in the news: to be newsworthy and reported the bad actions must be really out of the ordinary and not what goes on most of the time.

BUSINESS'S OWN BLUNDERS

People in business may do things that, although not necessarily immoral or unethical, are not praiseworthy either. These actions arouse suspicions about the motives of business people and about fair play among the organizations they serve. For instance, a major U.S. cigarette manufacturer severed a long-standing account it had with a leading advertising agency in 1989. It did this because that agency had put together an advertising campaign for a national airline and had run television commercials telling of the airline's new policy of banning smoking on all flights.

In their advertising many firms depict their competitors as less than completely honest, or as unresponsive to customers, or as purveyors of shoddy merchandise. In these advertisements the competition's brand of laundry detergent cannot remove stains or disgusting odors; the competitor's truck does not have the qualities a reasonable person would want; and the competitor's bank has tellers who are rude, loan officers who belittle customers and never lend money to ordinary people, and data processing equipment that hopelessly scrambles accounts and checking transactions. These advertisements seem to suggest that all their competitors are out to cheat the public.

One particular automobile in the U.S. market advertised through televised commercials emphasizing the fact it is built "on this side of the Atlantic," with the apparent suggestion that Americans ought to purchase products made by their countrymen. Viewers of the advertisement are told that "this car is built in North America." The automobile *is* made in America; but, as a matter of fact it isn't built in the United States of America; it is built in Canada by Canadians. There isn't anything wrong with cars built in Canada. Canadians build very good cars and trucks.

But the advertisements neatly skirt the fact that the car is made in Canada hoping to persuade U.S. citizens to buy this car because it is the patriotic thing to do.

A telephone-system advertisement depicts a business situation in which the competitor's telephone system fails and, because of the breakdown, the competitor's customer loses a major piece of business. The one responsible for selecting the system, the televised advertisement shows, is in serious trouble with higher-ups because of the failure and may even be fired. Besides suggesting that the competitors' products are defective this advertisement suggests to viewers that mistakes in the business world are dealt with harshly. Since it is bombarded daily with such negative messages, created by some of the ablest and most talented advertising people in the country, it is no wonder that the American public now holds negative images of business. Businesses have been their own worst enemy by creating these disturbing scenes and unfavorable images. In their single-minded efforts to sell their products, they have also sold Americans on the idea that business is a bad thing.

Authors of best-selling books on business and management travel about the world giving lectures on what is wrong with business today. Calling attention to shortcomings and problems that ought to be addressed, they at the same time feed on frustrations and aggravations that are exceptions to the ordinary, portraying these as typical and reinforcing the many negative images already in place. "When was the last time you bought a product that actually worked?" and "when was the last time you were treated like a human being when you purchased a product?" the lecturer fervently shouts to his audience. He captures the listeners' emotions with his cynical rhetoric and they laugh in agreement without much thought. Yet, the listeners will later get into automobiles that work, listening to radios or tape players that play beautifully, and go home to sleep on clean sheets washed in Brand X laundry detergent and enjoy many other products that perform admirably.

On the television and motion picture screens, business executives are generally portrayed as brutal and callous. They are shown as polluters, drug dealers, extortionists, adulterers, and murderers, who are eventually exposed and brought to justice by heroic figures. In earlier decades business people were portrayed as both good and bad, or having a mixture of good and evil. Now, however, they are regularly depicted as villains. In a Public Broadcasting System documentary, "Hollywood's Favorite Heavy," writer and producer Ben Stein asked script writers why they portrayed business executives as villains, as unscrupulous plunderers, and from time to time as murderers. Their answers varied, but in general they said that their story-line heros needed formidable opponents. Although they did not really know of any business leaders who really were criminals, still, because the public had that perception already, they reasoned, they could exploit it.

CONSEQUENCES

Many among us commit the logic error of *allness*. This is the act of assuming that all in a class or category are alike, having the same qualities of the few who are observed or heard about. The allness error in logic, with the constant portrayal of all business leaders as being evil and corrupt and the exposure of *only* the dishonest and unethical practices of a few, results in a number of undesirable outcomes. Each outcome is harmful, because each one lowers the expectations of what those in or entering the business world could become. One outcome is despair, the feeling of helplessness and hopelessness. This is typified by those who say, "Business is just plain corrupt, and those who prosper in it will do any-thing, without scruples, to get what they want. People are basically evil and that's something we just have to live with."

Another outcome is self-righteous moral superiority and smug-ness—the feeling of being better than other people. This feeling could be characterized by the attitude, "I would never think of being a part of that evil business world filled with unprincipled wealth seekers. I certainly would never do all those unfeeling, despicable things." This response can consume people, as they continue to look for even more wrongdoing as a way of justifying their own worth, instead of working toward worthwhile accomplishments. The tragedy is they can never seem to find enough evil in others to satisfy themselves, so their search intensifies. Many could profit from the words of Confucius: "When you see a good man, think of emulating him; when you see a bad man, examine your own heart." It is impossible to live a productive life when one is preoccupied with evaluat-ing the evil ways of others.

Still another outcome is the popularly held attitude captured in this familiar refrain: "Well, that's business and you just have to be a little bit underhanded to get ahead and profit. Besides, who is really to say what's right or wrong or what a worthy life involves? It's all relative and just a matter of opinion and my opinion is just as valid as anyone else's. So, I'll go ahead and play by my standards adjusting them to the situation and try to win all I can. After all, that's what everyone else is doing." Some of this attitude could be seen a few years ago when a well publicized Wall Street trader (he was later convicted of illegal insider trading) addressed the graduating class of the University of California's School of Business Administration. In his commencement speech he proclaimed, "Greed is all right. Greed is healthy. . . . You can be greedy and still feel good about yourself." The graduating class of MBAs cheered and roared with approving laughter.[7]

Although it is quite impossible to predict what the full impact of popular entertainment will be on a maturing mind, we can see that the negative depiction of business is making a considerable imprint upon young people's perception of what constitutes and leads to business suc-cess, as well as on what they feel is right or wrong. Fed by an unhealth-ful number of hours of television shows and movies, high-school students were once asked by Herb London, a dean at New York University, "If you ran a company, and in order to make a profit you had to endanger the lives of people, would you do it?" The unanimous response was yes, although one or two expressed reservations about endangering the lives of relatives or close friends. "I guess we get our ideas from what we watch on television," one student said.[8]

It should not be surprising, therefore, that in one recent poll 40 percent of college students admitted to cheating. In another study of dishonesty at a Midwestern university, the figure was 90 percent. CBS News reported that in a poll of college students at Rutgers University, two-thirds admitted to cheating. And 53 percent of college students polled by the *Daily Illini*, the student newspaper at the University of Illinois, answered yes to the question, "Do you think there is a general attitude on campus that cheating is okay as long as you don't get caught?" After its massive survey of research on the ethics of youth, the Josephson Institute of Ethics published a 1990 report with the alarming conclusion that young people in unprecedented proportions, "have severed themselves from the traditional moral anchors of American society—honesty, respect for others, personal responsibility, and civic duty."[9]

The negative image of business leaders has spilled over to practically everyone to some degree. Those who are furthest from the world of business and thus the least able to have a first-hand view are usually the most ill-informed and the most affected by the distortions. Typical of this ill-informed perspective are well-meaning people such as the one described by Donald Petersen of Ford, "At my church they are trying a forty minute educational period between the two services. They asked me to conduct one. I got this letter . . . [that] said, 'we're having a series of sessions in our education system where we're trying to help people come to grips with the everyday problem of life of having to compromise moral standards. Because of the needs of your role in business, we would like very much if you, since you obviously have so much experience . . . [in effect, at compromising your morals]' So I wrote him a fairly long, longhand response on his letter saying, 'you have the wrong man. I just disagree absolutely and totally with your premise.' "

A HIGHER STANDARD

Each man leads his life answering to the pattern his vision beholds and his heart honors. When we consider the many influences that currently shape these patterns, we see at once there is cause for alarm. A disturbing fact of our time is that we, particularly our nation's youth, have practically no vision of the greatness and goodness that is alive in the world in general or in the world of business in particular. Our minds are continually pounded with the wrongdoings and ill-schemes that are found out and reported—as they ought to be. But all this does very little good in lifting standards and elevating the levels of ethical conduct.

Alfred North Whitehead, perhaps the most eminent philosopher of the twentieth century, compressed an important truth into a few words when he observed, "Moral education is impossible apart from the habitual vision of greatness." Visions of greatness can provide a source of optimism and inspiration to direct people toward worthy aims and thus worthwhile lives. Something with hope in it needs to be identified that can lift sights, elevate expectations, and save people from venturing down paths that lead to miserable lives. In our age of cynicism we seem to have developed a disdain for old truths and simple stories of honesty, loyalty, friendship, and patriotism as guidance in how to live. Nevertheless, these visions of greatness are available to everyone.

Every person has a story in his or her life, much like the one of George Washington and the cherry tree, that reveals a positive aspect of character. These anecdotes can lose their value if they are pinned to the hero's lapel like a medal. But they can also serve as valuable lessons, from which any person can profit.[10] Samuel Johnson expressed this same idea when he wrote, "Examples as well as arguments propagate the truth." What most rings true in the minds and hearts of ordinary, intelligent people are not sophisticated, ethical theories but concrete examples of decency and goodness from the lives of successful people.

REALITIES: INSIDE AND OUTSIDE PERSPECTIVES

There is a perception that there are many easy paths to quick riches in business through cold-hearted and unscrupulous schemes. Those who hold this view will say that people in the business world may appear honorable and respectable but in truth their ethics and morality are swift casualties in the face of available temptations. This perception should not go unexamined.

Roughly a third of the American population is employed in private enterprise. It is fair to think that companies, in general, reflect society as a whole. If society were generally corrupt, then business would be generally corrupt also. But our experiences tell us that basically people are decent and responsible and law abiding. If they were not, our democratic institutions would crumble. People in America's companies are basically upright, too. Going more deeply into the matter, we should come to realize that democracy and economic freedom demand ethical conduct and cannot exist without it. In any free, democratic, capitalistic society—an economic arrangement that has proven itself to be the best the world has ever known—people in general must freely behave ethically; otherwise the economic system would collapse, so strong and tight would the laws and policing have to be just to maintain order and stability. Certainly in any aggregation of people, each one is not spotless, and our experiences tell us that there are always a few dishonest souls in any grouping. But the overriding majority must act ethically if a free-enterprise, market economy is to flourish.

Because economic freedom and economic performance require a high level of honesty in general, truth compels us to admit that unethical practices must be the exception to the norm if the system flourishes, as ours does. Richard E. Heckert, of Du Pont, observes that, "there are very few crooks in the system. Some of us aren't as bright as we'd like to be but we are not dishonest, by and large. I think, from my personal observations, and I've rubbed shoulders with a lot of CEOs of a lot of very large companies, these are the kinds of people that are tremendously admired all through their lives. They were achievers when they were kids. They did well when they were coming up through the ranks. They've earned their leadership and they're discharging their duties just as honestly as they know how to do it. They make mistakes. They try to correct them. Frequently, what you read in the paper has absolutely no relation to the facts in the matter, and you don't appreciate that until you're somebody that's being written about."

It is enlightening to learn what reasonably fair-minded critics from the outside find when they take the time to view for themselves at close range what goes on in business and how large organizations are run. Concerned with what he saw as misrepresentation by the news media, Hicks B. Waldron, of Avon, once complained to people from the *New York Times* that better balance was needed in business news reporting. It was his opinion that the press could not write a story without slanting it against big business.

The newspaper responded to his challenge. "We'll put a reporter on your tail for three weeks and he'll follow you around and chronicle, in diary form, what you do. And then he will write what you do, and that's what the public will see," they said.

Waldron asked, "You say you have a reporter who will write what he sees?"

"Yes," they said. So, the *New York Times* took its number one business reporter and assigned him to the Sunday magazine section. He was to follow Waldron around for three weeks.

At the end of two weeks he came to Waldron and said, "I'm exhausted. I can't keep the pace up." It had been a pretty normal couple of weeks as far as Waldron was concerned. The reporter said, "I am shocked and surprised at what you are doing to try to run this company."

Waldron said, "Well, Sonny [Kleinfield], that proves my point. Here you are, the number one reporter of the number one newspaper of the world; you followed me around for two weeks and you're shocked and surprised at how the system works. I win my bet."

Through a considerably longer period of experience in the business world, as a participant, the son of Robert E. Mercer, of Goodyear, was able to learn at firsthand how corporate America works. After graduating with a degree in journalism, he started working for a small-town newspaper in Findlay, Ohio. Not long after that, he thought of looking for another job. He found an opportunity in Akron with Goodyear. He told his father he had an offer and his father said, "Go ahead and take it." At the time Robert Mercer was at Kelly-Springfield, a Goodyear subsidiary. It would not create a problem of nepotism. But the son wasn't sure. He told his father, "I don't want to have anything to do with big business. I've studied enough about that and I've heard enough about it." He said, "I know that you, Dad, personally aren't like this, but big business is bad news. And they're out to take people. They have no feeling for environmental matters or for their own employees. It's a rotten mess."

"If you stay on the outside, you're just a young punk throwing rocks at something you don't know anything about," said the senior Mercer. "I'd get in there and really expose them."

That challenged the son's mind and he accepted the job offer with Goodyear. About six months later the senior Mercer was brought back to Akron as a vice president. The son was a bit upset with this turn of events and told his father, "One of us has to leave."

The senior Mercer said, "What's the matter?"

The son said, "This is really a great company. They're not out to rook people. They're concerned about the environment. They're concerned about their employees." He said, "This is a really great place to work."

Even though the original news accounts of alleged corporate misbehaviors may have been reasonably accurate, oftentimes the secondary reports of these news stories become distorted over time through re-telling. The results are disturbing. The average American is convinced that chemical companies dump toxic waste into waters regularly and with impunity, that unsafe products are foisted upon consumers deliberately by irresponsible firms, that defense contractors gouge the taxpayers of the country by selling the federal government $400 hammers and $600 toilet seats, and that all of these illegal and unethical actions are done in the name of profit, which is the sole purpose of business. There are clear-cut cases of wrongdoing; however, many other stories have been distorted beyond any reasonable standard of truth.

The Love Canal incident is a perfect illustration of this. The public's perception today is that the Hooker Chemical Company carelessly and irresponsibly dumped toxic waste, which later seeped through the grounds and lawns and into the basements of neighborhood homes, resulting in public outcries and health problems years later. True, Hooker Chemical did dispose of toxic wastes between 1942 and 1952, in an approved site located in an old canal. The dump site was excellent. It was large, and the walls were lined with thick, impermeable clay. When the site was nearly full, in 1953, the disposal of toxic wastes in the abandoned canal was stopped. It was capped with clay. The design to keep water out and prevent harmful seepage was working; grass and weeds grew on the surface. Even under current EPA standards the design would be classified as state-of-the-art. The only thing that would be different by today's standards would be monitoring wells around the perimeter to find out if some water were getting inside. The waste dump was designed by competent engineers and built properly and responsibly. Later, the City of Niagara Falls school board purchased the land from Hooker for a park area.

The deed of transfer from Hooker to Niagara Falls contains some very clear language specifying that that site had been used for the disposal of certain types of toxic chemicals. Company officials, in no uncertain terms, warned that the site *should never be disturbed.* The school board decided not to use Love Canal for a playground but instead chose to build a school. When the school board announced its intent, Hooker officials went to the city and the school board and publicly repeated why it should not be done. Regardless, construction began in 1954. Roads were built across the property. A drainage system was dug connecting ground water to the storm sewer system, which was drained into the Niagara River. In doing so the city disturbed the cap that Hooker had put over that site to keep water out.

The same newspaper that 20 years later tore the Hooker Chemical Company apart had carried those first public disclosures at the public meetings, with the request by Hooker that the original deed restrictions be honored. That newspaper had covered the 1953 hearings accurately. Yet, nearly twenty years later, the reporter from that newspaper chose not to refer to and report the factual background on Hooker's stance.[11]

Defense contractors have been the target of misleading, and hence unfair, charges by the press and politicians. In the case of the $435 hammer story, when the details became known, it was really a $22 hammer. But on the same invoice was a $413 charge for engineering service unrelated to the hammer. That detail never showed up in press reports.

The truth about the so-called $7,500 coffee pot and the $600 toilet seat brings sharply into view what actually occurred, as contrasted with what is popularly believed to be the case.

In the early 1970s Lockheed won a contract to build the original 80 C-5 aircraft. The Air Force insisted on a very tough specification for the coffeepots on the plane; they would have to withstand tremendous jolts when the aircraft landed. At the time, Lockheed executives said they thought the design specifications were unnecessarily high for the unit under the conditions it would be subjected to, but if that was what the Air Force wanted, okay, they'd go ahead and do it. Lockheed bought the coffeemakers, contracting for them to be built for between $1,200 and $1,500 for the first 80 C-5s. They were special installations. After that, the Air Force started to buy them for spares when some were damaged, and they'd order only one and two at a time. Because of that, the price in comparison was exorbitant. The Air Force was buying the coffeemakers, not Lockheed.

Some years later, Lockheed received a repeat order for 50 more C-5s—a $7 billion contract. Lockheed planners looked for every place they could to save money in building these planes and thought the specially designed coffee making devices was one of them. They sat down with the Air Force representatives and said, "Why do you need this kind of a coffeemaker?"

The coffeemaker is a huge installation in an airplane, much like the ones found in commercial airplanes. The units are big and have shock-resistant features and lock mechanisms to prevent the actual coffeepots from flying out in the event of a jolt. The Air Force agreed that it ought to use commercial airline specifications instead of the tougher standards it had used with the first 80 C-5s. In the meantime, the Air Force had in front of them a quotation from the supplier of coffeemakers (the company which subcontracted to produce large quantities for Lockheed earlier at $1,500) priced at $7,500 apiece. The higher price reflected the true cost associated with making the "over speced" coffeemakers in small production batches of 1–3 units. The Air Force decided not to buy these and instead go with commercial airline models which are less costly to produce. Now Lockheed is supplying coffee makers on the new C-5s, for about $3,000—a price that is considerably less than what the commercial airlines are buying them for; that story never came out either.

The toilet seats Lockheed made for the P-3 aircraft, were not toilet seats at all. They are shrouds that encompass a honey bucket. They are not flush toilets; they're rather crude. A plastic shroud covers them, and a common toilet seat fits on top, which Lockheed buys from a supplier for about $10. However, the whole unit, the specially molded shroud made for that airplane and the cover, was priced around $600.

The case of the Firestone 500 is yet another example of how news stories and later textbook writers have distorted public opinion. The following paragraph, written from 1978 news accounts, explains what most people have come to believe about a radial tire manufactured by Firestone.

Firestone Tire & Rubber Co. recalled 10 million radial tires [Firestone 500s], offering to replace them free of charge with its new 721 radial tires. The recall came after much prodding from the National Highway Traffic Safety Administration [NHTSA], which said that Firestone 500s were implicated in highway mishaps that had caused at least forty-one deaths and sixty-five injuries.[12]

The realities in this situation were far less sensational, but although they were made public, the press coverage they received was so sparse that the average person was never made aware of the full story. What is worth knowing is that, after the first recall in November 1978, at Firestone's request an engineering firm specializing in accident reconstruction and risk quantification, Failure Analysis Associates, conducted an exhaustive evaluation of the safety record of the Firestone 500. This is the same respected firm that the U.S. government brought in to study the C-5A cargo door failure, and it was also brought in to analyze a Kansas City hotel skywalk collapse.

In this study, Failure Analysis Associates went to Ford, General Motors, and Chrysler. It obtained the serial numbers of all the cars that had been equipped with Firestone 500 tires, along with the serial numbers of comparable cars equipped with other tires at this time. So its study covered the same number of convertibles, the same number of station wagons, the same number of four-door sedans, an so on. Then Failure Analysis Associates went to the states where there is a requirement that a policeman produce an evaluation of the car and the cause in an accident;

was it tire related? When a policeman does an appraisal of the causes of an accident, he is more likely to say it's tire related than is the case. It isn't deliberate error, but many times the officer will see an accident with a tire blown on the car and he'll say the tire was blown. It may be found out later that the tire was blown when it hit a railing. This, of course applies to Goodyear, Goodrich, or whatever. The analysis was massive. It demonstrated beyond any doubt that the Firestone 500 tires were safer than the average tire on the road at that time, not less safe.

Firestone 500-equipped cars were involved in 45,952 accidents during the four-year 1975–78, period. The police reports identified 91, or 0.2 percent, of those accidents as being tire associated. Cars equipped with other tires were involved in 407,820 accidents during the period. Police reports indicated that 1,275, or 0.31 percent, of those accidents were tire associated. In total, almost 500,000 accidents were studied.

Firestone 500-equipped vehicles were found in the study to have been less likely to be involved in any kind of tire-related accident. They were found less likely to be involved in tire-related injury accidents and less likely to be involved in tire-related fatal accidents than were identical vehicles equipped with other tires. The fact that 0.2 percent of the cars equipped with Firestone 500 tires were involved in tire associated accidents, compared with 0.31 percent of the cars equipped with other tires, was found by Failure Analysis Associates to be statistically significant. Its report states categorically, "In sum, Firestone's recalled 500 tire proved safer than the average of all other original equipment manufacturers' tires combined in the largest tire accident survey ever conducted."

The conclusions reached by Failure Analysis Associates and the data supporting those conclusions have appeared in the publications of the Systems Safety Society, the Society of Automotive Engineers, the American Society of Mechanical Engineers, and the American Society for Testing Materials. Its conclusions and the data from which they were drawn have not been questioned or challenged by any of the many thousands of scientists, engineers, and technicians who are members of the groups to which they have been presented.[13]

REASONS FOR HIGHLY PRINCIPLED BEHAVIOR

The paths to success in business are not at all what superficial thinking makes them appear to be. We hear a good bit about corrupting influences in the realm of commercial activity. But we should also see that these are not the only forces acting upon participants in the world of business and industry; there are also many positive forces, which encourage ethical behaviors. It is instructive to examine several here.

The Need to Build Something Useful

The normal, well adjusted person is generally inclined to contribute something of lasting value. He does so to achieve a sense of satisfaction. A deep, personal sense of accomplishment comes from producing something of genuine merit. Theologian and philosopher D. Elton Trueblood reminds us that we are made to make, to produce. In his later years Cornelius Vanderbilt seems to have derived his greatest satisfaction not from knowing he was the wealthiest American but from building successful steamship lines and railroads. As his biographer Arthur D. Howden Smith noted, Vanderbilt was a man of vision, a builder. And the public benefited from it.[14]

Frank Carlucci, of Sears World Trading (he later served as U.S. Secretary of Defense under President Reagan), explains: "I don't think it's human nature to just be driven by the profit motive. People that function properly have to have a broader goal. They have to feel they are contributing to society's betterment in some way; at least most people do." The implication here is obvious: people will not gain a sense of self-worth and genuine satisfaction unless their life's work has meaning. This strongly suggests a high ideal: careers directed at producing something of value—of real benefit to others—and not merely a handsome profit.

Profit Maximization Is Not the Only Purpose of Business

It is far from true to say that the owner's interests and expectations are the only ones considered in the decision-making processes in business. Seeing beyond superficial thought it is evident that a business will not be able to survive for very long if it neglects to satisfy its other constituents. Timm F. Crull, of the Carnation Company, states an important truth in a few sentences. "The company is run not only for its stockholders but for its customers and for its employees. It's really a three-legged stool. And if *all* three aren't equally protected and considered, it's not going to work." J. David Barnes, of the Mellon Bank, adds to the explanation of the matter with this observation: "I don't think there is a good chief executive officer in the country who would accept it [maximization of shareholders' wealth] as the be all [and] end all [of a business]. . . . Our perception is that the corporation has a number of legitimate, very probably very considerable number of legitimate constituencies—admittedly, one of them is the shareholder—and that the corporation's job is to really sort of ration and struggle with the balance of all these competing demands, none of which can be satisfied in the entirety. You know, the employees, presumably, their legitimate demand [is] to have the maximum highest pay. If you give in entirely to their demands, you make no money at all. Presumably, our customers have some very legitimate demands. . . . [There are] shareholders' demands. . . . One of the hard jobs of a chief executive officer is to . . . reconcile . . . and try to find a position

85879   658.4094   Brescia College Library
W337   Owensboro, Kentucky

that's a reasonable compromise between satisfying, as best you can, [the] interests of all these constituencies."

The Need to Feel Honorable and Ethical

A person who does not feel right about what he is doing will most likely not perform very well or give his best efforts for extended periods of time. Enthusiastic and sustained performance in an organizational setting necessitates that the job demands placed on the organization's employees be in keeping with prevailing ethical standards. To be sure, there can be many strong crosscurrents in the dynamics of business. Each constituent group wants the organization to meet its particular needs and demands, particularly stockholders, who are ever watchful of the most recent earnings report. But to go against the standards of decency the employees honor in order to cut expenses or generate added sales can lead to a loss of their commitment and support.

Conscientious leaders are careful not to overstep these limits of right and wrong, first, because they hold high standards themselves, and second, because they do not believe it is right to befoul the organizations their employees consider their occupational home. As Donald D. Lennox, of Navistar, mentions, "I say my job is to be responsible in an ethical manner that relates to all our stakeholders. And they are lenders, vendors, employees, and stockholders. And while the stockholders might have their money in the company, the employees have their lives in it. And it is these employees and their motivated efforts which are ultimately needed if success is ever to be achieved."

The ethical dimension cannot be ignored, as Charles W. Parry, of Alcoa, attests. "In point of fact, there isn't any top business manager in this country that operates his enterprise, be it a part of the corporation or the entire corporation, solely for the benefit of the shareholder. You just don't do that. The enterprise does things to further its goals. So, what are the goals of the corporation? They are obviously to serve, to profit, to grow. But, not at any cost."

Laws to Protect Individuals' Rights and to Advance the Public Interest

Without laws, individual rights and the public's interest can easily be neglected and harmed. Laws can put competing firms on an equal footing so that the ones that otherwise would, for instance, pollute to cut costs of operation and gain an advantage over more publicly spirited firms are unable to do so. Moreover, individuals and companies strive to do what is right and avoid illegal actions because they are wrong and because they invite unwanted troubles. In fact, because it is so highly regulated and watched over by all sorts of bureaus, agencies, consumer groups, and the like, business doesn't dare misbehave, lest it be exposed. William D.

Smithburg, of Quaker Oats, observes, "The average business people I know are some of the hardest working people and generally the most ethical. I shouldn't say more than others but certainly they are average human beings like everybody else. I think our system of laws and regulations tends to create a responsiveness on them [business people] that quite often doesn't exist in other parts of our society. Because we are all very heavily regulated, very public, our actions are shown in the market place everyday."

The corporate fishbowl discourages illegal or unethical practices. Corporations and their officers are under a spotlight all the time. "No one wants an EEO suit. No one wants to have his name in the paper that [some inspector] came in and made a surprise inspection and found [out some wrongdoing]," says J. Ray Topper of Anchor Hocking. Chicanery thrives in darkness; so the opportunity for villainy is rarely found in a well regulated and closely watched environment, even though the inclination for wrongdoing exists. The IRS does not call large companies in once in a while for an audit; it has a staff of people in their offices almost all the time. When officers of a large, publicly held company buy or sell stock, the SEC knows it every time. The Labor Department checks corporate records to make sure that employees are paid for the hours they work and that companies have equal opportunity programs. OSHA visits their plants, checking everything from fire extinguishers to ladders. And for every agency of the federal government, there's usually another in each state where the firm operates.

Social Forces and Pressures

Peer pressures and social forces within a group frequently help to elevate the ethical choices. In large organizations most major decisions are made by some form of group discussion, rather than by one person. John M. Henske, of Olin Corporation, tells us, "In all my experience, when it comes to the ethical considerations of a decision, a group of people are talking about doing something—what should they do?—it tends to rise to the higher level of ethics of the individuals, not to the basest level of any one individual. And because of that I think most large corporate decisions are actually more ethical than they would be if an individual made them on his own. There's a check and balance there that tends to pull you up. The things that an individual might try to get away [with] if he is doing it privately, the group won't try to get away with. I'm sure you'll find lots of exceptions to that but I honestly think psychologically it's true. And I think I've seen enough of it in business that people do things that will hurt the company that they'd rather not do because they conclude it's the right thing to do. And that group discussion helps elevate the ethics into a higher level."

If trust between group members is eliminated, a vital component of group cohesion, the force that holds a group together, is dissolved. Being trusted and predictable are among the top requirements for good standing in a group. Moreover, a person's standing within a group is also a function of the extent to which that person adheres to the norms and advances the purposes of the group. Being part of a group frequently requires honesty and integrity. John H. Bryan, Jr., of Sara Lee, observes, "The one that you know is making a judgment based on what's in the best interest of the institution, loyal to the institution and nothing for himself, that's usually the best evidence of that person's integrity. It's amazing how people around here shy away from the one that you know is making a decision, making a judgment that he thinks is going to serve him. Or, after he has been misleading a couple of times, he loses, he's gone, he gets out of the mainstream of business. Over time that's been the way it's worked out in American business and in companies."

Thousands of examples abound where straight, honest, ethical dealing with employees, customers, and the public have proven beneficial to the strength, productivity and, of course, to the profitability of a business. People would rather not trade with someone dishonest. In a survey of corporate leaders in the 1980s conducted by Lester B. Korn and the UCLA Graduate School of Management, respondents were asked, "What quality do you think most necessary for business success?" Of a list of 16 traits most responsible for enhancing an executive's chances for success, 71 percent of the respondents put "integrity" at the top.[15] Why would this be? The most logical explanation is that people will not work very long for, let alone support enthusiastically, higher-ups whose motives they doubt and whose aims are morally intolerable. Thus, to get to the top spots in an organization, integrity is a must. People will generally follow freely and enthusiastically those whom they trust, and understandably, they will try to avoid those whom they do not trust.

Ability to Influence

One's credibility and ability to influence others rests to a large measure on a good image built through ethical conduct. Certainly a mark of our current scene is public scrutiny. Public figures, up to and including the highest public servant of the country, have had to step aside when their credibility was seriously damaged by the perception of many others that they were less than completely honest and ethical. J. Ray Topper, of Anchor Hocking, explains how he sees the need to be ethical if he is to maintain credibility. "You . . . read of the terrible things that some companies do, and you just don't want a part of that. I think part of it is that I don't want my name in the paper saying I did something wrong. . . . For example, no way do I want to get caught DWI or even take a chance on it. After I write a nasty letter to the union, I don't want them to have anything on me. I want to be Simon Pure. I want to look them right in the eye and say, 'I do nothing unethically, including drinking while driving or unfair contracting or kickbacks or insider trading. Nothing.' "

Not Worth the Gamble

There is too much at stake for companies to risk not playing fair and not living within the rules. Particularly in large organizations, where exposure to practically everything eventually occurs, doing the right things and acting according to the highest ethical standards is the only sensible course. Fines and imprisonment are bad enough, but even though businesses can weather some financial setbacks, they cannot exist profitably and function effectively in society when their reputations are severely damaged and consumer and public confidence is greatly diminished. Edmund T. Pratt, Jr., of Pfizer, says, "We've got so much at stake, you don't dare *not* have a high standard. You can't afford to play fast and lose with all that's at stake in a General Motors, or a Pfizer, or an IBM."

Highly Principled Behavior is Smart Business

The well worn phrase "honesty is the best policy" contains a good bit of wisdom. Honesty assures a good night's rest; those who have a clean conscience sleep better and work harder, because they believe in the soundness of what they do. Honesty keeps the competitive advantage that one enjoys on the footing that is the most difficult to dislodge—the solid ground of superior competence and performance. A good reputation attracts good employees. Ethical dealings with employers, with customers, with suppliers, and with others in and outside the business community help to assure favorable relationships and fair dealings. Surely a good way to drive away customers is to treat them unfairly.

In the long run, one gains little advantage through chicanery and corrupt practices. Schemes are eventually exposed, prompting swift and strong countermeasures and retribution. The firm that mistreats its employees not only loses out on their best efforts and loyalty but usually suffers from the troubles they, in turn, are provoked into causing. Ill-treated suppliers find that it is uneconomical—that it's simply bad business to try to sell to those who try to cheat them or who are too slow in paying their bills. Angry inspectors and regulators and legislators, clearly, can make life difficult for businesses.

In order to exist for extended periods and to flourish a firm needs to be a positive, contributing member of society. Richard Heckert, of Du Pont, expresses this view: "Every decision involves giving up something to get something. . . . The real intelligent course involves being sure that you deliver the quality that the customer expects, not sacrificing quality to increase earnings. And if you make that call correctly, you may make a little less today but you're very likely to make more in the future. So I think when an individual's goals or a corporation's goals are very much out of line with society's goals, they're in trouble. . . . The fact is you can't be a large, successful corporation and be working against the public will; not for long."

"I'm a businessman, not a philosopher," said Elisha Gray II, the first chairman of the board of Whirlpool Corporation, "but I've never had any difficulty reconciling what I knew in my heart to be right . . . ethically and morally . . . with what I knew to be right from a business standpoint."

CHALLENGING THE MYTHS ABOUT BUSINESS

With the vast amount of news reports drawing attention to the negative aspects of business, distasteful images have been created about people who serve in corporate America, thus making it easy to conclude that a career in business carries the price of living a dishonorable life. No doubt a number of business people have stooped to despicable schemes and actions in their quests for profit and prestige. With only their actions in mind, we could be left without much hope that highly principled behavior and praiseworthy actions can bring business success. At best we may have only a nodding acquaintance of the many fine and decent things that go on daily in the business world and in the lives of the most successful people in business. Many of these discouraging myths should be called into question.

Myth: Extravagant Work Environments and Life-Styles

Ask the person in the street for his image of the working world and life-style of the typical successful executive and he'll describe something much like one sees depicted on the television screen. It's a world that seems like paradise. There's the huge salary. The art-filled office. The sleek limousines. The jets. The power. The prestige. In short, to the average person successful executives are "fat cats" who enjoy high living, as shown in the "lifestyles of the rich and famous." In former times cartoonists drew successful businessmen as overweight, wearing tuxedos and top hats, and sporting diamond stick pins, with $100 bills falling out of their pockets and smoking big cigars.

We can easily see that top corporate executives are well paid. Many of the leaders of the largest U.S. corporations have compensation packages (salary and stock) that exceed a million dollars annually; a few may even earn a few to several million dollars during particular years when their firms' success merits it. There are offices appointed with quality furniture and decorations much on the scale of the decor of many well decorated homes of upper-income families. There are corporate jets available for business travel, expense accounts, club memberships, and limousines. Some executives travel first class on commercial flights. But it would be grossly incorrect to think that their life-styles are as lavish and frivolous as popular thought depicts them. Peter Magowan, of Safeway, says, "We don't have some of the perks and things that some other businesses do. You don't see many of our people belonging to country clubs and driving fancy cars and traveling first class. We don't travel first class in our company." Moreover, even when business leaders do fly first-class or use corporate aircraft for business purposes, there are good reasons for it—peace and quiet and a bit more privacy for work which is done during the flight. Considerable time is saved, valuable time, through use of company jets and limousines. These are really tools that, although they may appear to be luxurious to the outsider, are available to afford privacy and peaceful surroundings for thought and discussion, saving energy and time.

Personal preferences vary; not all people of substantial wealth choose to live extravagantly. Newspaper accounts of one of America's wealthiest industrialists, John D. Rockefeller, said this: "He was not a man for yachts, polo ponies, and wild parties. His love of family was deeply rooted. He raised a good and simple family and some of the happiest moments of his life were spent in its midst."[16]

In a letter to his friend, the magazine publisher Arch Shaw, William K. Kellogg wrote, "I never had a taste for high living. I never cared to own a yacht. I have never desired to become extremely rich, although I have had a natural desire to make enough money to live on comfortably and to provide well for my family. But that's about as far as my ambition for wealth has ever gone."[17]

Top-level corporate executives today are more likely to have come up through the ranks; few own the companies they head. They are paid employees. Douglas D. Danforth, of Westinghouse, observes, "Most of the senior executives at Westinghouse, and I'm sure it's true at other companies, came from modest beginnings. I think most of our people had to work their way through college. And I think that when you do, you don't lose track of that era in your life. My living standard is about a third of what it could be. And I think most executives do that for a couple of reasons. One, it becomes superfluous after a while. You have two cars and a nice home. Few people "need" a mistress or a yacht or what have you; that's very expensive and very troublesome. And, the other thing is, at least in our case, we have four youngsters we did not want to grow up in an artificial cocoon. You can grow up in the country club set and be useless and actually deprive them of something we were fortunate enough to have, and that's, kind of, [not being so well off financially that you are sapped of the incentive to] dig it out one way or another, and we haven't done that. "

Myth: Business Must Push Shoddy and Unsafe Merchandise Off on a Naive Buying Public

Companies do not have to sell faulty merchandise to succeed. In fact, it's quite the reverse. If they did, they would be found out by an alert public; their sales would dry up; and their leaders would be apprehended, tried, and sent to jail, where they would belong for violating any number of laws. Similarly, a popular misconception of big business used to be that it could produce anything and create an enormous demand for it through clever advertising. Advertising can influence people but this belief gives it far more credit than it deserves. One doesn't have to look very long to find business fiascoes where the public simply did not want or like the product, despite the advertising done to entice buyers. The vision of Madison Avenue as having the power to sway the thinking of the buying public doesn't stand up to the myriad of examples to the contrary.

Hicks Waldron, of Avon, observes, "[the suggestion] that many of us are producing products which are cheap, low cost [and] high priced and forcing those products down the throats of consumers [is incorrect]. . . . the facts of the matter are that companies like Avon spend a hell of a lot of money in an effort to find out what's in the consumer's mind, maybe not even necessarily [what the consumer] should have but at least what that consumer perceives is his or her wants to enhance his or her quality of life. Business in general spends a hell of a lot of money trying to pull that out of the minds of people and put it out here and say, 'now how can we serve that [need or desire] profitably?' It's only those companies that work in this way that make it in the long pull."

There are literally millions of products on the market, and because nobody is capable of envisioning the thousands of ways and conditions under which each one of these might be used, from time to time, people will be injured accidentally. In some rare situations companies have knowingly put products on the market that, although under normal conditions perform correctly and are safe, malfunction or become unsafe under extreme, one-in-a-million conditions. Some corporate managements approach these situations using probability and profit and cost concepts and take the risk of having to pay off on lawsuits on the odd chance of a product liability claim.

Some argue that this calculating approach is just good business. Others think not; they do not believe business has to operate in this way to be successful. AT&T is a good case in point. They market a personal computer that is made by Ollivetti in Italy. It has not beaten IBM but it has done well. Although this computer was UL approved, one of AT&T's computer technicians, while experimenting with some ways of making various connections to it, found that it could be connected in such a way that the user might possibly suffer a shock. AT&T's vice chairman, Charles Marshall, recalls, "UL had already approved the whole wiring and we had 40,000 of them in a warehouse. We stopped shipping. We immediately went back through, at our own expense, and changed that, on every one of those. We went out to every customer's location and changed theirs even though Underwriters Laboratories said, 'You don't need to do that; the conditions that would cause them to do that is so strange.' We said, 'we don't care. We're just not going to put anybody who buys our product at any kind of risk. Our standards are that high, regardless of what yours are.' And it was an expensive project at the time, but we thought we had to do it."

When one surveys thoroughly and objectively the product complaints American consumers lodge, it is impossible to escape the realization that many of these consumers do things to and with otherwise good products that rightly should be labeled stupid. Products do not break down so much as they are broken down by ignorant and careless users. Moreover, the ethics of some consumers should be called into question. James Eiszner, of CPC International, explains, "We get all kinds of claims, for example, of mice that have 'crawled' into a Mazola Oil bottle and the plant has shipped out bad. Now, you know very well, you can't get a mouse into a Mazola bottle unless you sort of grease him up first and shove him in. All kinds of things [are supposedly found by consumers] in Skippy Peanut Butter. I know how we make Skippy Peanut Butter, and I can tell you there's no way they can get in there. I think perhaps the most outstanding example is the Gerber problem with glass shreds in the baby food last year, where some of the glass turned out to be fluorescent lightbulb pieces and others turned out to be regular lightbulb pieces and others turned out to be window glass. And all kinds of glass was found in Gerber baby food, none of which could have come from the Gerber plant."

Myth: To Be Successful One Must be Objective; One Cannot Let One's Heart Get in the Way

Upton Sinclair's book, *The Jungle,* depicted vividly the cruelty to which American workers were subjected a century ago. As a result of the American labor movement and progressive, educational efforts to enlighten and make humane American's work places, many deplorable management practices have vanished. Yet we still find, here and there, a lingering strain of insensitive and uncaring treatment erroneously justified by some managements as being "objective business decision making." A question that deserves attention is not whether managements ought to be concerned and humane in the treatment of employees—of course they should. The question is, how can they be sensitive and decent and humane when times are bad as well as when times are good? Happily, much of American management is not only sensitive to and sympathetic with this philosophy, but also can and do treat employees fairly at the same time they are forced by events to make difficult business decisions. In other words they do their level best to serve both ends: profit and people. William R. Howell, of J. C. Penney, observes, "There's a lot of evidence of the right way and the wrong way, I think, to go about the downsizing in corporate America. I happen to sit on Warner Lambert's board and [on] Exxon's [board], both of which went through major downsizing. And I saw the same kinds of concerns, the same line of questioning being asked by independent directors. 'Is this the right thing to do? Is this the right way to handle this? What has been the reaction from your people?' All those concerns represent to me, in my mind, a concern about doing what is right."

Balancing the concerns for healthy economic performance and tenderness toward employees is extraordinarily difficult when business survival demands layoffs. Certainly, from the individual's perspective being put out of work is terrible. It is distressing and painful. But sometimes pruning back a part of an enterprise enables the other parts to survive and flourish. And *how* that is done reveals one measure of a management's feelings and relationships with its employees. Hicks Waldron, of Avon, recounts a situation his company faced. "We did close a plant last year in the city [New York], our biggest one, oldest one. We took the proposition to our board. Hands went up as soon as the slide presentation was over, all asking, very first question, 'What happens to the people?' It wasn't 'Gee, can't you make more return on that investment?' which is what most outsiders would imagine what goes on inside the terrible thing called a boardroom. It was a concern for the people. Fortunately we were deeply concerned, and the next step of the presentation had to do with those people. It's very interesting, that when that project ended there wasn't one lawsuit. There were, maybe, two negative letters. To the contrary, there was very positive television coverage—interviews of our employees saying, 'Avon had class to the very end. And they are still a great company and I'm out of a job.' "

Myth: One Needs to Be Sneaky to Succeed

Honor, fairness, loyalty, and other admirable qualities can be pursued right along with profit and earnings. The pressures may be great, and from time to time the temptation to do something underhanded may present itself, but that does not mean it is smart business. Top companies owe a good measure of their success to the fact they have played the game fair and square. Because they have done so, other firms want to do business with them, and their employees sleep better at night and can give their loyalty without reservation and hesitation. The way the J. C. Penney Co. approached changing its merchandise mix (i.e., decided which products and product lines should be added, kept, or dropped) in the early 1980s is a good illustration of this. It would have been expedient to get out of some lines of business immediately, because the markets had stopped growing or were eroding. Moreover, there was considerable pressure on Penney's management from stock analysts, and from others interested only in company earnings and stock price levels in the short term to be more decisive and move quickly. But the company's managers looked at the situation not from just a profit-and-loss perspective but also from a humane and ethical perspective, trying as best it could to balance the interests of all concerned and thereby do the "right" thing. They dealt with the nine thousand associates (the store managers) who sold the various lines of Penney merchandise—paint, automotive, hardware, appliances, fabrics, and prepared foods—bringing them in on the decision and considering their welfare and interests. They did the same with all the suppliers and all the landlords where they had auto centers across the United States.

Myth: Business Has No Concern for the Environment

Firms do not need to pollute air, water, and land in order to control costs so profits can be earned. Business people can and generally do share the same concerns about protecting the environment as others in society do. "Business people," as William R. Timken, Jr., of The Timken Company, says, "don't want to breathe pollution any more than anybody else does. Businessmen are people and, therefore, have the same emotional drives that newspaper people have. They may end up coming to different conclusions over subjects because they see things from a different perspective."

Business does not have to be conducted in ways that harm the environment. Industry can go beyond that which is required and expected. The states that border the Mississippi River would like to have the Mississippi look prettier than it is, quite apart from what they're doing about real pollution. The problem with the Mississippi River is, by and large, untreated sewage coming in from cities. But the chemical companies and others along the river have adopted strict standards, and there's nothing going into the river from them. Monsanto Chemical has a plant in Muscatine, Iowa, and nothing comes out of it and into the Mississippi River that has any hazard to it. Monsanto put in all the required treatment plants except there was some water color which was not acceptable at a time when attempts were underway to improve the color in that part of the river. So, in response, Monsanto took care of that correcting the color of the water being discharged back into the Mississippi. Monsanto has an identical facility in Inchon, Korea. A question arose at corporate headquarters, "Should they or should they not adopt the color standards that were relevant to the Mississippi?" Nobody was going to get hurt; there would be no health risk. This debate went on by the hour among internal management and then subsequently with the board of directors. It was very expensive item to meet the color standards. The river that goes out behind the plant in Inchon is filthy. The most socially responsible thing one could do would be to put signs all around it to warn people to stay away from the water, and not to wash cloths in it as they do. After long and hard debates, Monsanto went ahead and adopted the Muscatine, Iowa, standards in Korea, at some considerable expense. In the boardroom, discussion on the matter was settled when the question was raised, "What's the right way to behave?"

Myth: Business Doesn't Stand for Decency or Promote
Wholesome Values

As individuals, most of the respect we are accorded is from how we conduct ourselves—what we stand for and what we will stand up for. Very little has to do with what we know, or what we are able to do, or what we possess or control. Just as it is important not to project a bad image through cold-hearted, thoughtless, and crude actions, it also is important to act in positive ways. The Procter & Gamble Company has a long-standing tradition for high standards of decency and good taste. Long ago that company established standards of decency and common sense for the radio and television programs in which Procter & Gamble would advertise. Script writers of Procter & Gamble-sponsored shows are told that any scene that contributes negatively to public morale is not acceptable. Also, the company's view is that religion and patriotism ought to be reflected in a positive fashion. If, for example, in a drama or a documentary, a character attacks some basic conception of the American way of life, then a rejoinder must be completely and convincingly delivered someplace else in that broadcast. Ministers, priests, rabbis and similar representatives are not to be cast as villains, or represented as committing a crime, or be placed in any unsympathetic, antisocial role. Men in uniform are not to be cast as heavy villains or portrayed as engaging in any criminal activity.[18]

Myth: Business Is a Bad Neighbor

A good neighbor is one who minds his own affairs and doesn't make a nuisance of himself, but is glad to help those who need it. A good neighbor actively works to improve the quality of life in the community. In any community there are those who need help in one form or other, and there are a multitude of possible projects and activities for improving the quality of life. America's economic system distinguishes itself from those of other countries through the role private business plays in community improvement and charitable activities. In other countries, government and the churches look after the needy and support community betterment efforts. In this country, a large share of these activities are headed or heavily supported financially by the business community.

Little doubt exists that some amount of community involvement is motivated by the self-serving desire to improve the firm's standing and reputation; it makes good business sense to spend time and resources on community and charitable activities because it is good public relations. . But a large part of what takes place in this realm goes unheralded and is hence unrecognized by the outside world. Support for the construction of cultural centers, for bond drives, for United Way campaigns, and for countless other worthwhile causes is frequently headed by business leaders and staffed by business people, who give freely of their time and talents. In addition to what they have to do in their companies, they spend hours at breakfast meetings, at lunches, on the telephone, and during evening hours and on weekends, in planning sessions and fund-raising activities and organizing efforts to get these jobs done. Surely if just public relations were the motivating force, organizations would not choose these means. Much better company image-building could be performed with considerable less time, trouble, and money simply through advertising. Why, then, do business people become involved in community activities? Because they understand the importance of healthy communities and because they genuinely believe in these causes. They gain great personal satisfaction from their efforts. In most large corporations we see a strong commitment to local communities and active efforts to educate their employees about the importance of serving community needs and participating in charitable activities. And top managements encourage and recognize employees' efforts in these activities. Heartwarming stories abound as to the many ways business and those in business have been charitable and been positive influences in mending and improving communities.

In 1986, two arson fires destroyed 400,000 volumes of the Los Angeles Central Library's 2.3 million volume collection. "Save The Books" was organized to raise $10 million to restore the collection. The program was a multifaceted fund raising campaign sponsored by Atlantic Richfield, which donated $500,000 to get the fundraising started and pledged to pay all administrative costs. The "homeless" library staff was provided office space at the ARCO Tower, across the street from the Central Library. Atlantic Richfield assigned a specialized team of employees from different departments to work on the project. A nine-minute multimedia slide show was made, focusing on the Central Library's key role in the community.

Atlantic Richfield's chairman, Lodwrick Cook, made an unusual electronic person-to-person appeal for funds in a four-minute video. Copies were delivered to 200 civic-minded persons in late December. By 6 February, 1987, "Save The Books" had raised more than $7.9 million. Atlantic Richfield pledged to continue to support this program until the full $10 million was raised.[19]

In September 1986 the Chicago area was flooded by heavy rains, leaving 1,800 homes damaged and entire communities under water. Over four hundred families were forced to evacuate their homes. In an effort to assist these victims, many of whom were Allstate employees, the Allstate Flood Assistance Program was developed.

Volunteers were given release time from work, and for 14 days, teams were mobilized and dispatched by company vans to the hardest-hit communities where they assisted in every aspect of the cleanup. An average of 1,200 meals were prepared each day by the Allstate cafeteria and loaded onto Red Cross food wagons for distribution. Food was delivered every day for two weeks.

As the floodwaters receded, a large tent at Allstate's headquarters and another at its warehouse were established as drop-off locations, to accommodate donations of appliances and furniture from Allstate employees and neighboring corporations. A temporary disaster relief policy was developed through Sears, Roebuck & Co. to replace uninsured household necessities and clothing at local Sears stores. The program was developed and implemented in only 19 days. During that time, about 280 volunteers assisted nine communities, serving over 14,000 meals to volunteers and victims and donating over 200 items to help 35 families begin their lives again.[20]

The Anheuser-Busch Urban League Scholarship Program has provided more than 500 black adults in St. Louis, Chicago, Newark, Columbus and Houston with a "second chance" to further their education through the community college system. The company has contributed more than $400,000 to the program since its inception in 1966.

More than 300 young people were hired for ten-week jobs during the summer of 1985, in 17 cities across the country, through a $400,000 project of Anheuser-Busch, Inc. In each community, primarily minority youth and young adult supervisors were hired by local nonprofit agencies, which oversaw their employment on community cleanup and social service projects under the title of Operation Brightside.[21]

Since 1986 Kmart stores, in conjunction with the Coca-Cola Co., has offered free booklets designed to help children use the telephone in case of an emergency. "The Coca-Cola Tele-Photo Phone Book: The Children's Emergency Phone Book" includes spaces for a child to write his or her name, address, and telephone number and important personal data, such as blood type, allergies and birth date. The small paper booklet includes pictures of various emergency-help providers, including phone operator, police, fire, doctor, and relatives. Also, there are spaces for commonly called numbers, such as the library, school, and neighbors. Other sections allow the children to paste in photos and phone numbers of their favorite friends.[22]

GOVERNING OUR OWN BEHAVIOR: SETTING AND LIVING UP TO HIGH ETHICAL STANDARDS

If a person cannot govern himself, then people cannot govern themselves. Freedom requires responsible living if it is to survive. People must govern their own behavior as individuals, as well as in business entities and professional and trade associations. History has many examples of idealistic men and women profoundly concerned with ethical conduct in their professions. Hippocrates, the Greek physician known as the Father of Medicine, who lived during the fifth and fourth centuries B.C., laid down one of the first professional codes of conduct, the Hippocratic Oath, which embodies the duties and obligations of physicians. Stonecutters and masons established professional codes and standards before the time of Christ. In 1727, in this country, Benjamin Franklin formed the Junto, a forerunner of modern-day civic clubs. It was dominated by businessmen having goals of "communityism", fellowship and service. Ethical issues were a significant focal point of that organization.

Today's business and civic organizations, such as the Rotary and Kiwanis clubs, have codes of ethical business conduct. The Junto, in Franklin's time, focused attention on many questions of the day, and among those that dealt with morality and business ethics was the following: Do you know of a fellow citizen who has lately done a worthy action deserving praise and imitation; or has lately committed an error, proper for us to warn him against and asked to avoid?

Professional and trade associations founded around and just after the turn of this century established professional standards and codes of ethical conduct. Today, most large companies have codes of ethical conduct. These are printed in the form of small pamphlets or booklets and distributed widely. The Ethics Resource Center was established in 1977 as a private, nonprofit organization working to strengthen public trust in business and government. The center provides a focal point for those concerned with the study, application, and advancement of ethical principles in all phases of American life. The ultimate aim of its work is to preserve and enhance economic and political freedom by strengthening the ethical values that support that freedom. Two of the projects carried out by the Ethics Resource Center include:

1. A 31-minute film/video, *A Matter of Judgment*, which dramatizes five ethical dilemmas—conflicts in aims and values. Through financial and creative support by IBM, McDonnell Douglas, Pennzoil, Sperry, Sun, Texas Instruments, and Vulcan Materials, this production dramatizes five short case studies or incidents useful for focusing discussion on ethics and how to resolve the problems of choices involving ethics.

2. A survey of ethics programs and practices within corporations to provide information for other companies to draw upon in fashioning their own ethical standards and practices.

When we see these efforts, or others like them, how impossible it is to believe that the business world would generally prefer to remain unbothered with ethical concerns, that its leaders think that doing right is at odds with doing well. Drawing on the fruits of his experience, Chairman and CEO Donald Petersen of the Ford Motor Company observes, "A working business career is totally compatible with a goal of living a completely moral life, whether you express it in religious terms or just technical terms. Completely compatible."

2

The Search for Significance

Each normal, well adjusted person wants to be loved, to feel secure, to feel significant. He wants to think that his life counts for something. But count for what? Many among us don't exactly know. Road signs along highways riddled by bullets, a commonplace sight, are indication of the depth and extent this vexing question holds for many. Among older, metal signs, whether they be to mark dangerous curves in the road, or to alert motorists to watch out for animals, or to indicate the distance to towns and cities up ahead, or to tell drivers to yield or stop, in many areas it's the exception to find one that does not have at least a few bullet holes in it, put there by any one of millions of perplexed souls who seem to be saying, "I was here and I wanted to be noticed but I did not know quite what to do."[1] Too often, and like the unknown passersby who spend bullets putting little holes in road signs, we also are baffled about how to feel significant; the little things we try quite often do not bring us happy answers.

LIVING WITH ONE'S SELF

Early in life each person discovers that he is an individual, that he is a distinct and separate creature with a mind and feelings and freedom of choice. And he becomes aware of the haunting fact, from which he never escapes, that he has a self. Each of us, having this self on our hands, is thereafter nagged by the questions, "Who am I?" and "How satisfied am I with me?" As age creeps up, each of us feels some measure of despair over our littleness, our physical limitations, our finiteness, and the inevitability of death. We are unwilling to settle for being the creature of dust we know, ultimately, that we are. The human spirit seeks more. But what? And how should we attempt to achieve it?

Around and within each person a battle of beliefs rages as to what will work and what will give him the happiness, the peace of mind, the contentment, and the sense of self-worth he desires. Few ideas are more infected with error and false notions than those about happiness and its sources. To the "have nots" in our world, and also to the "pampered and protected," born with every comfort money can buy, there is the belief that happiness is in having: having wealth, having power, having prestige, and having recognition and the approval of others. The automobile bumper sticker that says "He who dies with the most toys wins," captures this belief perfectly. And so, because many people seem to want just a few extra dollars, a say in what goes on, an important-sounding job, and a pat on the back, we can witness daily their pursuit of these aims as their ultimate purpose in life, following the advice given by popular self-help books with titles like *Looking Out for Number One; How to Work the Competition Into the Ground and Have Fun Doing It; Cashing In on the American Dream; You Can Have It All: The Art of Winning the Money Game & Living a Life of Joy; How to Make a Quick Fortune*, and *One Upsmanship*. Such titles have the simple and alluring theme: Follow the advice given here and you can have all that you desire, perhaps more. Your wishes will be fulfilled and you will be made happy.

For many Americans money becomes life's report card. Their main concerns are not merely to earn a livelihood and enjoy the rich and varied wonders and adventures the world has to offer; instead, we see much, if not most, human effort being directed at just "loading up" on loot, grabbing what can be gotten, the more the better. The primary aim of most business-school graduates today is to find the job that pays the most money so they can get on with the scramble to accumulate material goods. It appears that ideas and values like teamwork and community, and social and economic progress, have been replaced by the pursuit of wealth and the belief that money is the only thing that matters, or at least it's the thing that matters most. There are many who act as though the idea, "Profit isn't everything; its the only thing," were completely true and worthy of their full allegiance.

These current beliefs and values can damage not only individual lives but entire organizations, and they can even weaken the stability of economic systems. Greed, self-aggrandizement, and the attitude that the dollar is all important form the crucible in which unethical, destructive, and dehumanizing business dealings are hatched. Thomas L. Phillips, of Raytheon, captured this idea with the remark, "Some people just don't care about anything except themselves. I think they can be very destructive."

There are many appealing enticements to lure one into accepting the belief that success, happiness, and a sense of self-worth are things that can be reached simply through having the right possessions. The portrayal of wealth by popular business magazines as being *the* main determinant of success reflects a belief commonly held in many minds. Once each year *Forbes* magazine lists the 400 wealthiest people in America in rank order, starting with the billionaires and ending with multimillionaires.

It also publishes, annually, a listing of the world's wealthiest. Cover-page headlines which read, "The Richest Man in the World and 95 Also-Rans"[2] and "The Billionaires: Who they Are, How Much they Have, How they Got It"[3] are particularly revealing about the nature of the perception that wealth equals success. Once each year *Fortune* magazine presents a similar issue identifying over 100 people throughout the world who are worth more than $1 billion. It is questionable whether these people want to be identified and listed in these magazines, and it's also questionable whether they derive any great satisfaction from it. But to readers, wealth is seen as omnipotent.

Business textbooks in marketing, management, decision sciences, and finance, to name just a few fields, identify clearly and simply *the* purpose of business: to maximize profits and to maximize the wealth of those who own the business organization. It is a commentary on society that these attitudes and expectations largely go unexamined and unchallenged. The exceptional athlete who, before completing the requirements for a degree, leaves college to enter professional sports for millions of dollars is seen by many as doing the only sensible thing. "Why continue on with college? He'll make millions in sports; he'll never have to worry," people will remark. And this is exactly what they think: "With all that money what else is there? What else is there to worry about?" Whereas in the 1960s the preponderance of college students were concerned about finding a meaningful philosophy for living, today college is merely supposed to impart just enough of the right sorts of information to enable the graduate to secure an attractive employment opportunity and begin making money.

The American dream of success was once grounded in the concept of building: building a great nation, building successful enterprises, building better communities, building up our neighbors. An unpleasant reality that has descended upon our present age is that this dream has narrowed drastically to embrace primarily, perhaps only, individual success. As Dickinson C. Ross, of Johnson & Higgins of California, observes, "The pressure to succeed in our country, starting really at the educational level, focuses on you, an individual, and what you must do to get there. So little effort is made really to show that individual what the formula is to do it. It isn't just how much you learn individually and how much you yourself have to have every day in the way of vitality to beat your way to the finish line. It is stopping on the way to the finish to be sure that you're bringing some others along with you."

In his struggle to find happiness and satisfactory answers to the questions of who he is and what is his worth, the individual can easily become obsessed with his own self. This can take various forms. He can pamper and entertain it with amusements and diversions. He can indulge his self and feed it through extravagant purchases and consumption. He can polish and perfect it until it is pure and unblemished. He can mold it to the expectations of others and become a model person in their eyes. He can acquire vast amounts of knowledge so as to feel that he knows more than others, or accumulate great wealth and priceless possessions so as to feel that he owns more than others, or achieve a station in life where he can exercise considerable influence and power so as to feel that he has great control over others and hence is *more* important than they are. All these things he can do for his self, and then be overwhelmed with pride in what he has done through his efforts and accomplishments.

Each of these has a certain amount of appeal; each one brings about some amount of pleasure and happiness and, to an extent, relief from the burden of what to do with the self and its insistent, pestering search for significance. But the sense of self-worth and satisfaction one receives through any of these avenues is transitory. Pathetically, the person who chooses to reach success in these ways traps himself; the more he gets, the more he wants. Each attempt aimed at pleasing the self throws the person back on himself, making him even more self-conscious and eventually dissatisfied. He always sees one more rung on the ladder he climbs, beckoning for his reach. And as he grasps it, there is another one still. There is never quite enough of whatever he tries to acquire for his self. As he intensifies his efforts to reach for more, his attention becomes focused more intensely upon his self. As he becomes dissatisfied with his progress or what he has, he feels worthless. To escape this feeling, he becomes even more self-centered. A vicious circle develops, with little hope of stepping out of it.

The wisdom of the ancients saw this idea clearly and recognized the folly and destructive consequences of looking inward and trying to serve one's self. The seven deadly sins—sloth, anger, envy, greed, lust, pride, and gluttony—are self-serving through forms of escape or attempts to feed unbridled appetites of various types. It isn't that these are bad because they are harmful to other people; quite often they are not. They are seen as deadly sins because they kill off the individual, himself, as they are pursued. Thus they cause him to be less of the person he could otherwise become. They lead to a form of self-destruction.

A well-adjusted person does have a certain amount of self-awareness and is moderately self conscious. He is careful in exercising self-control as he masters his self and nurtures and develops it. He does this with temperance, guarding against over-concern with self and against becoming obsessed with self to the point that he pampers, feeds, unduly protects, entertains, or idolizes it. It is healthy psychologically to respect and love one's self, but not excessively. Eric Fromm points out that we must first be able to love ourselves if we are to become able to love others. This is healthy self-respect and thinking highly of one's self. But Fromm also shows us that excessive self-concern comes from inner self-hatred; people who feel worthless often become very selfish and self-centered.[4]

Luxury and Wealth

There really is nothing "wrong" or harmful to the self in the simple enjoyment of material possessions. No apology is necessary for experiencing the pleasures of good food and drink, fine clothes, a new automobile or boat, a well built home, a beautiful ornament or piece of jewelry, or a pleasant vacation. A certain level of wealth provides a person with the financial means and independence to relax, to travel, to expand his knowledge and abilities, and to pursue his interests outside his vocation. And considerable wealth permits one to support worthy causes that are believed in deeply. The Puritanical guilt some people are made to feel from having wealth and enjoying nice things creates anxiety, which is ultimately debilitating to the individual. Of course one ought to be concerned for the welfare of his less fortunate neighbors and work hard to help them better their lot. But there is no solid reason for people to heap guilt upon themselves if they consume sensibly and enjoy the good things available to themselves even though others have considerably less than they have. If a man is wealthy, that alone, is not sound cause to count him among the scoundrels of the earth.

A certain amount of gratification can be gotten from diversions and amusements and from having possessions and from consuming. But these pursuits do not produce the most satisfying happiness people are capable of reaching. If relied upon exclusively, they can unnecessarily constrict one's human possibilities. There is really a great deal more to life than the primitive experience and actions of having and consuming. A person cannot honestly find lasting value in his self through the act of consuming, because when he looks back on it all, he is inwardly disturbed by the realization that nothing *stands* as a reminder that he was once there. Even Epicurus, the Greek philosopher, came to admit that although they may not be the most intense, the highest and most lasting pleasures are spiritual and not physical ones.

The accumulation of possessions is far different and considerably less pleasure-giving than owning and enjoying. The man who orders three feet of leather-bound volumes to fill his bookshelves only because they match the carpets and draperies, possesses, but does not have and enjoy, the richness of their words and the meaning in them. A person may keep hidden a priceless fly rod or an expensive painting; he may possess these things, but that is not the same as using and enjoying them. When used this way, possessions do not give lasting pleasure to the person who accumulates them or to anyone else. At best they provide the person only with the knowledge these things are locked away. At worst this behavior leads to greed. Greed is wanting more than one can possibly need, use, or be able to enjoy and then craving for more still. Greed is a terrible curse, because, like an addiction, one is never satisfied with, nor can one possibly use and truly appreciate, that which one does have. Greed can easily trick us into thinking that we will find real satisfaction in having. The senselessness of greed is described in Ecclesiastes: "If you have money, you will never be satisfied, if you long to be rich, you will never get all you want. It is useless. The richer you are, the more mouths you have to feed. All you gain is the knowledge you are rich."

There appears to be little reason to feel guilty about being wealthy. Enjoying wealth and spending it sensibly and wisely for good and worthwhile purposes are not, in and of themselves, harmful. But being miserly and hoarding material objects or pursuing wealth just to satisfy the self is debasing to what one could be as a human being. The constant searching and calculating how best to serve one's self and to get what one wants in the form of wealth and possessions keeps that person from seeing what else is possible, from doing interesting, exciting, and worthwhile things, and from truly living. If a person is confined in his imagination and experiences to plotting just how to get what he feels he wants, in the immediate future, he is apt to miss the adventure and the excitement of discovering much about his self along the road.

Some things start large and only grow smaller, others begin small and only become larger. A life, however, can grow either way. But it will always tend toward its holder's dreams and ideals—what one honors. There can be no escape from it, each person honors something. It may be grand and significant or small and of little consequence. Nonetheless, each person holds some aspiration. And, large or small, it will determine his life's direction and, ultimately, whether he can rightly find value in what he does. The person whose ideal is the accumulation of belongings for the sake of having them rarely finds value in himself, because when he looks back at his life all he finds standing there is a pile of possessions.

Perfection and the Opinions of Others

The attempt to find significance through perfecting the self to a state of flawlessness most often reduces the person to a smug, self-righteous, unbearable bore who is arrogantly critical of all others. In his efforts to make something worthwhile of his self, this person is tripped into becoming self-absorbed and idolizing himself for his faultlessness. And because he has followed all the little rules to the letter, he expects others to be in awe of him.

There are also those who have insecure feelings about their own selves and these persons may live in ways to win the approval of others. It is their way of attempting to achieve a sense of personal identity and worth. But as they do they enslave their entire beings to the standards and petty likes and dislikes of others. The person of this type is driven to earn praise from others. It is his primary aim to please others. This person seeks not to be outstanding but to fit in. He lives as though he were directed by a radar set fastened to his head perpetually telling him what other people expect. All along the aim is approval for the self.

Again, there is nothing wrong or harmful with reasonable levels of effort to improve one's own quality and standards of behavior or with winning the approval of others. The tragedy with living exclusively to perfect one's own character or to secure another's approval is that it can also be debilitating. Although it can produce some satisfaction, the approbation of others is not the summit of the human experience. Surely, overconcern with winning approval from others is not healthy. It makes a person dependent on them for a sense of self worth.

Selfishness

In business organizations, the totally self-serving person may move ahead, but he is generally the exception to the way most achieve success. This type of individual may win out now and then, and seem to advance and meet with success from time to time, but sooner or later his methods and motivations wear thin and then he is cast aside by his colleagues, who have had enough of him and have become unwilling to tolerate his selfish methods any longer. Roy A. Anderson, of Lockheed, observed, "In this company it's pretty well known that those who try to push themselves up are going to run into difficulty because in trying to push themselves up they, many times, will damage somebody else. . . . We look for the types of people who just by pure talent and effort and dedication have the respect of their fellow employees, their peers. Those are the kind of people that we look for because they are going to follow that philosophy all the way through. . . . Those who try to push themselves forward or take advantage of other people, in the end, are not going to be the best leaders."

An overconcern for personal happiness and repeated attempts to grasp it, primarily through concentrating on financial betterment and the advancement of self-interest, are often ruinous. In the end, a sure way to fail ever to achieve a sense of importance for our lives and experience significance would be to pursue directly and attempt to acquire what most people perceive success to be: wealth, power and prestige. D. Elton Trueblood has pointed out that those whom we honor most in history have, strangely, been uninterested in whether they were personally happy. In Trueblood's words, "Concern for self poisons all situations and is ultimately self-defeating."[5] The person who makes as his supreme goals happiness, peace of mind, and a sense of personal importance will surely encounter disappointment. If one is ever to reach happiness he must forget it; it will elude those who make it their chief goal.

Happiness and a sense of self-worth come from within and depend on what one chooses to do with his life. It appears attractive to look inwardly at the self and attempt to serve it by feeding its many appetites. But fulfillment comes only to those who escape their self, not through denying it but by *forgetting* about it. The trick is to focus one's full attention and energies outward. We gain a sense of significance from our lives by losing them, by devoting them to a great ideal or cause that we can pursue in concrete ways. Only through living in this way is a person relieved of the burden of what to do with his self and its nagging demands.

SENSING ONE'S SELF

A person is capable of sensing his self on various levels, depending on his actions. The most elementary, or basic, level is *awareness of self,* which is just knowing he is a unique creature capable of experiencing pleasure and pain. At this level the individual experiences his self through amusements and diversions, through consuming and possessing material objects, and through rebelling and exercising his own freedom of choice. The sense of worth and lasting significance from these behaviors at this level is small and temporary. The person who becomes stuck at this level demands more and more—more amusements, more diversions, more possessions. As a result he becomes increasingly weary and indifferent to what he does and what he consumes. He thereby grows increasingly displeased with his self-worth. Lord Byron's tragic tale of Don Juan is an excellent account of what happens to a person stuck at this primitive level. Thinking of women as nothing but sex objects to fulfill his fantasies and insatiable sexual appetite, Don Juan, who was incapable of love, went from woman to woman and into and out of one sordid sexual encounter after another, never finding fulfillment and eventually destroying himself.

Another level is *regulating and understanding one's self.* It is achieved through learning from experiences, seeing one's errors and shortcomings, and tempering and adjusting one's behavior in light of them. It is laughing at one's self and allowing conscience and other's opinions to have an influence on behavior. And it is developing and shaping one's life and behavior. This level is concerned with self and at the same time with others; it is not totally self-centered. One's sense of security and social compatibility are addressed at this level.

Still another level is *accomplishing* tasks and developing one's own skills and abilities. This yields a sense of self-esteem and is gratifying to the healthy ego. There are trouble spots here worth mentioning. A sense of accomplishment can easily cause a person to forget about what he is doing and focus his attention on himself and the fact he is doing it and doing it so well. It can be a source of pride, but if the person looks inward too much and too long, it quickly becomes a source of pain because he will come to feel he must perform to certain levels to get what he wants from himself and others, and not because he truly finds fulfillment in performing well and usefully.

The highest level is *creating and contributing* one's talents without thought or expectation of material or social rewards, or even self-approval. This is the most difficult level, because one must actually forget, not consciously deny the self. By becoming so absorbed in creative efforts directed at a cause that one cares for more than oneself, the self is forgotten. In practice this level is rarely reached and then only for short periods, because as humans we really never do elude the burden of our self. This level yields the greatest height of human satisfaction, because at these moments the individual finds the whole breadth and depth of his being and can delight in the greatest levels of the human experience. The highest form of happiness is experienced by a person who is busy or going somewhere with a worthy purpose in mind, which he pursues wholeheartedly and without reservation or regret.

What a person chooses to do and how he approaches it determines how he experiences his self and ultimately the extent to which he experiences happiness through finding something of lasting and worthwhile significance. Happiness, it should be remembered, is not an end to be sought but instead is a by-product of worthwhile living. It is nevertheless a good to be desired. And, it is within the power of each human to experience. Clearly there is no set formula that will work for everyone for achieving a feeling of significance and enjoying the state of happiness one gets from it. Careful thought reveals that the only truly happy people in the world are those who do not labor under the absurdity that the chief purpose of life is to find happiness.

ACHIEVING SATISFACTION

Extensive examination of the lives of happy and unhappy people indicates four factors of major importance. By coming from the opposite direction, looking at the characteristics of happy people, it is possible to obtain a glimpse of what worthwhile living is. First is a well-integrated self, free from inner conflicts. Certainly every life will have problems, and every person will experience pain and frustration from the conflicting goals and demands he faces. But, the normal, well adjusted person is able to resolve these conflicts by relying on a set of established values that give guidance toward paths that do not cause himself lasting harm. Here the person has accepted these value guides and has confidence in their soundness because he fully believes that they provide best for the welfare and betterment of himself and others. In short, this person has consistent, well established values and habits, and he has the quality of character that enables him to rely upon these, knowing that they are good.

The second characteristic of happy people is an interest and concern for others, for their feelings and welfare. The self-absorbed person is inconsiderate of the rights and needs of others. The selfish person is rarely happy; he is too concerned about himself and his own ailments and problems. In fact, the more a person pays attention to his own ills, the sicker he becomes. The person who is interested in others is able to share in his neighbors' experiences of life. As human beings we are social animals. Each of us has a need to belong, to be part of something larger than ourselves. The fault finder and the gossip interact to carry misery from one person to another, so unhappy are they with themselves. The well adjusted, basically happy person delights in other people's good fortune, successes, triumphs, and joys. He derives no happiness, feeling of success, or sense of superiority in seeing the frailties or misfortunes of others. He delights at the sight of good in the lives of others and does not, as the self-centered individual does, look for the faults and frailties of others in order that he might feel self-righteous and superior to them by perceiving himself to be less flawed.

The third characteristic is worthwhile work, which draws upon one's best efforts and talents. Enjoyment of one's work, no matter what it may be, is one of the chief ingredients of happiness. This is work that the person enjoys because the truly likes performing it and not because it pays well, brings praise from others, is seen as glamorous or socially desirable, or is accorded great status. Philip E. Lippincott, of Scott Paper, advises young people who are thinking about their own future careers, "Don't do something because someone else has done it or it gives you some of the superficial things that you might like out of life. Really find something. You spend too much of your life engaged in whatever your life pursuit is. And, if you don't enjoy it and can't have fun out of it and don't experience the fulfillment of accomplishment when you have it, then get on to something else."

The fourth characteristic is loyalty in serving something greater than one's self. J. C. Penney, while in his nineties, observed, "Selfishness sometimes wins momentary material gains but the rewards that come through service will last longer and be more satisfying all around."[6] The people who seem to have the greatest vitality and zest for living, those who are impregnable to illness, those who are too busy to worry about or involve themselves with little things because they are so absorbed with big things, are the people who care more about some great cause than they do about their own comfort and well being. These people find the greatest sense of significance and self-worth and as a result, happiness. These people seem not to have gotten themselves hopelessly embroiled with the question, "What is the purpose of life?" but instead have found useful purposes for their lives and have busied themselves in pursuing these.

Sultans of oil rich sheikdoms or heirs to fabulous fortunes may have splendid opportunities come their way, and they may enjoy great amounts of material comfort. They may meet interesting and powerful people and find excitement in that. They may take pride in the rich and rare treasures they collect. They may enjoy what they have in their lives, but that does not mean that they will find significance in what they *do* with their lives. They may have all the vestments of comfort and security, the things which most people work to acquire and see as progress, but that does not mean that their minds rest easy and that they find value in what they have made of themselves and what they have done with their talents and abilities and possessions.

Significance is achieved through building something of lasting value, large or small, that benefits many others. It is easy for us to see and value only the seemingly biggest examples of building. And indeed, people like Charles Lazarus, who started Toys "R" Us, and Frederick W. Smith, who founded Federal Express, have built successful, giant sized organizations in our time. But even what many people see as merely small contributions—an improvement here or there, a brick well laid, an inspiring and uplifting word or act, a resolute adherence to a high ethical standard—these all build, too, and they form a small but nonetheless important part of the foundation upon which civilization stands. The business philosophy of Dean Witter—"We measure success, one investor at a time"—captures the flavor of this idea. The many millions of small things done well by ordinary people, when combined, produce a profound and lasting influence on the lives of millions of other people in succeeding generations and thereby leave a very large imprint upon human history.

3

The Freedom to Choose

A clear mark of maturity is to realize that many of the choices one is called upon to make are not easy, for a number of reasons. (1) The options possible are not always obvious or clear; considerable imaginative effort is needed to envision the many alternatives. (2) Each option open to us oftentimes carries with it profound implications; there are both positive and negative consequences associated with each choice. (3) There is always some amount of ambiguity with each choice; ambiguities abound in the nature of the situations encountered as well as in the consequences of each choice. (4) The implementation of the alternative chosen is not always easy; there are always hidden snags in implementing any course of action. Is it any wonder, then, that people are usually divided on what to do when it comes to important choices? It requires sober thought and courage to face these difficulties honestly and to struggle with unknowns and controversies, to choose as wisely as one's capabilities permit, especially where there are conflicting values, and then to accept the responsibility for what follows.

DIFFICULT CHOICES

Early in his career and while a plant manager at a Caterpillar Tractor operation in Decatur, Illinois, George A. Schaefer faced a difficult situation indicative of the many value conflicts found in business. One of the plant's employees, a man who had been with the company for 20 years, showed up one Sunday morning with a truckload of materials and tools that he had pilfered from the plant 10 years earlier. Because his conscience had begun to trouble him, he decided to return what he had taken. The plant guards let him through the gate. He explained what he was trying to do, and then proceeded to unload his truckload of stolen tools and materials. In sum, what had been taken amounted to a few thousand dollars. When Schaefer arrived for work on Monday morning, the question before him was, "What do we do with this guy?" There was an absolute divided house on the issue. The labor relations people and the head of the accounting department said, "He's reformed. He's got a good record. We shouldn't do anything. Keep him on the payroll." And, the manufacturing head, and the quality control and engineering people said, "No. He's got to be terminated. He stole from us and he should be terminated." What to do? It was a "gray area" call. An otherwise good employee had stolen company property 10 years before. It was bothering him, and he finally decided to do what was in his heart and mind, and that was to 'fess up and bring it all back and face the consequences.

Opposing concerns and interests are found at the center of most big decisions. The wise and thoughtful person recognizes and weighs each carefully before choosing. But that step is seldom easy. Charles W. Parry, of Alcoa, struggled with one such question, a decision regarding a plant expansion in Mexico that presented issues of cost, productivity, changing technology at the site, and the workers' health. Years earlier, Alcoa had built an aluminum smelting plant but over the years, that technology had become outmoded. A smelter is highly capital intensive; the investment in a plant is large, running into the millions of dollars. This plant was making an adequate return, but the profits weren't enormous. The process of smelting at this plant releases tar fumes. Under the constraints of the technology known at the time the plant was built, no practical way was available to collect those fumes, except possibly with a roof monitor system, which would have rendered the plant unprofitable and required its closing. Alcoa engineers eventually got around this difficulty by having individuals working within the environment of the electrolytic cells wear what is called a cool hat, a protective device that encloses the head and keeps recirculating air inside. It shields its wearers from the almost certainly carcinogenic fumes. The decision involved whether to use the same technology in the expansion of the plant. It was a difficult decision, because the workers in Mexico don't always follow the work rules and keep their cool hats on, irrespective of the many and repeated efforts to educate them with respect to the dangers involved and company attempts to enforce the safety rules. What should be done—close the plant, or expand it using the old technology?

THE RESPONSIBILITY TO CHOOSE

A fundamental necessity for the existence of an advanced civilization is for people to accept responsibility for their actions. Man achieves an increased level of dignity over other creatures when he holds himself accountable for his own behavior. The processes of child rearing and education are largely concerned with teaching children that there are consequences to every action. Maturity and good sense are evidenced when one comprehends the connection between cause and effect and regulates his actions to the betterment of both himself and others.

That humans are fully capable of connecting actions with outcomes in their minds before these events occur is rarely disputed. Those among us who demonstrate the greatest capacity for this are regarded as the most astute and wisest and are therefore held in esteem.

If people are going to live in any kind of social order there must be some method or system for governing their behavior. This may spring from one or more sources, ranging from self-regulation, to outside control. People may live together peaceably by means of despotic controls and rules and regulations that are policed by authorities, or by means of morals and virtues commonly accepted and honored by all citizens. Benjamin Franklin was thinking along these lines when he wrote that only virtuous people were capable of freedom. Democracy is a fragile form of government because it depends on a virtuous people. Sanford N. McDonnell, of McDonnell Douglas, observed, "Unless the leaders of a nation and the majority of its people believe in and practice certain basic values, that nation cannot survive as a free republic, because when you don't have things like trust and integrity and kindness and obedience and basic virtues, then you very soon create a vacuum into which laws and regulation and red tape come in. And those are all instruments of bondage, not freedom."

This has enormous implications for many other forms of human activity, including business, as several top corporate leaders explain. As Robert McClements, former president and CEO of Sun Company, pointed out, "Our system provides us with the freedom to make our own decisions."[1]

"The fact that you have the freedom to be in a capitalistic society, then you have the responsibility to maintain it for perpetuity. And, to perpetuate it means that it has to be successful. So, therefore, it has to be good. So you have a responsibility to be a good person in a capitalistic society," explains Lewis W. Lehr of 3M.

Willard C. Butcher, of Chase Manhattan, states clearly the importance of ethical decision making in a free society. "We need to reassert, throughout society, the importance and urgency of making decisions in an ethical way. Ethical decision making isn't an option. It's an obligation: in business, in education, in government, in our daily lives."[2]

THE POWER OF CHOICE

That we, as humans, are capable of accepting responsibility for our actions and regulating our own behaviors, largely through enlightenment and moral reasoning, is evidenced by the development of our social order and the establishment and functioning of our democratic societies. That experiment continues today; we are being tested continually in all dimensions of our lives. But the idea of self-determination has not always been so readily accepted by intellectuals, nor has it been valued by those despots who have wanted to subjugate others for their own purposes.

The sharp difference in the opinions of Thomas Hobbes (1588–1679) and John Locke (1632–1704) on this issue mark contrasting perspectives of man's capacity for enlightenment and self-rule.

Hobbes disliked the violence and disorder he observed during the civil war of the 1640s and during the unstable conditions of the English republic in the 1650s. He abhorred violence and strife. Hobbes sided with the king against Parliament. His argument for absolutism required it to produce real peace, individual security, and rule of law. He wrote in 1651 (*Leviathan*) that men have no capacity for self-government; that man is naturally quarrelsome and turbulent; and that life is solitary, poor, nasty, brutish, and short. Yet unlike the determinist, whose point of view will be examined later, Hobbes believed that absolute power originated in a free and rational agreement by which people accepted it.

Locke wrote in 1690 (*Two Treatises of Government*) that man can learn from experience and can be educated to an enlightened way of life. Man, he believed, has a moral sense. His ideas favored belief in self-government, and some phrases of the Declaration of Independence resound with his very thoughts and ideas. Absolutism was justified philosophically by Hobbes; constitutionalism by Locke.

The thoughtful observer will question whether people can gain this enlightenment and moral sense. Here a debate has raged for centuries and continues on today; the conclusions reached by each of us on this issue will have profound influences on our individual lives and have a pervasive effect on the direction society follows. One scientific view of man is that he is a product of a history of life events that condition him to behave as he does. His behavior is caused, and these causes can be traced to conditioning experiences in his life. Many of the adherents to this view discount to a considerable extent the effects of genetic makeup and totally downplay the concept of free will and self-determination. According to this viewpoint, what is needed to produce certain behaviors or to extinguish others is a complex arrangement of rewards and punishments. Rewards can produce desirable behaviors; punishments can extinguish undesirable ones. This is a process known as operant conditioning. Behaviors that are rewarded by reinforcement are strengthened and continue, while those that are not rewarded, or are punished, are extinguished. The scheme does not concern itself with what people believe or what their attitudes are, or with any deep undercurrents within their psychological makeup; in fact, the belief of those who espouse this system is that attitudes are a product of behavior and not the other way around.

Behavior modification has shown itself to be a powerful and effective method for altering both behaviors and attitudes. Perhaps the most striking example we can recognize in our time is in the area of civil rights. The Supreme Court ruling in 1954, in Brown *v.* Board of Education, held that the doctrine of "separate but equal" was unconstitutional. Segregation was ruled unlawful; there was to be equal access to jobs, housing, education, opportunities, public facilities, an so on. Court cases, new laws, demonstrations, and protests followed. There was violence and bloodshed and bitterness. Up until then, the prevailing thought among most in the white community was, "It will take more time for attitudes to change so that blacks and whites can live together as equals. All we need to do is educate people to change their thinking. It will take time." The movement for equality that raged in the late 1950s and 1960s, broke with this thinking sharply. The proponents of civil rights argued, "If attitudes haven't changed for the last 200 or more years, what's to cause us to think they will change in the next 200 years?" Indeed, up until that time attitudes had not changed. But the change in laws and their enforcement turned all of that around. Anti-equality behaviors were punished. Inside of 20 years, attitudes were changed. The change in behaviors, for a variety of reasons, changed people's attitudes. The philosopher William James enlightens us as to what is taking place here; he observed that habits are not a product of attitudes, but that attitudes are a product of habits.

On a much smaller scale, in industry, concepts of behavior modification have delivered remarkable improvements in performance. Compensation schemes, where pay is tied to performance, are one example. Behavior modification has shown itself to be extremely effective in improving worker safety. Historically, American industry has approached safety by first trying to educate employees in safe work methods and to change their attitudes to want to behave safely. This method has shown itself to be only marginally successful; there were always present more rewards for behaving in unsafe ways than in safe ways. Ear-protective devices are hot or uncomfortable, so they are removed. Goggles easily become fogged and are annoying, so they are taken off. Helmets are a nuisance when climbing on and around equipment, so they are not always worn. It is quicker to reach across a moving line to unjam a blockage that to shut down the machinery. When workers can get their work done more quickly and easily by ignoring safety procedures, the procedures will often be ignored. It was only after the system of rewards and penalties was changed that safety behavior changed. Attitudes had little to do with the way people behaved; the determining factors were the rewards and punishments.

It is undeniable that behavior can be managed through conditioning. However, there is considerable danger in carrying this to the extreme. It invites us to accept the proposition that our behavior is merely a product of conditioning and that what we think we choose to do because we like it, is really determined by what we have already been conditioned to like in the first place. In essence, this suggests that there actually is no such thing as self-determination, that we are not *free* to choose. According to this way of looking at things, what we perceive as our free will is merely a causal link in a chain of external events and conditions over which we exercise no control. That we have been conditioned to like particular things, causes us to want those things. So whatever it is we think we choose to do is really what we have been conditioned to believe is desirable. Therefore, some conclude, if these beliefs are true, we, as a society, ought to set up a system of rewards and penalties to create the conditions we want to see exist.

Moreover, by this reasoning, undesirable or antisocial behaviors ought *not* to be seen as moral laxness but merely as the products of an error or shortcoming in the conditioning process. Thus there really isn't such a thing as a wicked person; there are merely persons conditioned to behave in undesirable ways. Stated simply, people who behave badly are merely improperly conditioned. If I do things that harm others or inflict damage upon the environment, or if I am selfish, or sneaky, small-minded, or whatever else, it really isn't my fault, because I am a product of my conditioning and of what I have been conditioned to like or want. I need not feel guilty or responsible for my behavior. Moral reasoning is meaningless in this system, because the system is based on the proposition that we are merely creatures who respond to stimuli so as to reach the rewards we have been conditioned to like and avoid the penalties we have learned to perceive as painful.

If all this were true, we would be confounded with many unpleasant realities. If a person believes his behavior is fully a product of his conditioning, thereby allowing him to escape from any sense of moral responsibility, he abdicates, at the same time, the slightest measure of any sense of self-control; his life is not for him to live, he just "goes along for the ride." Psychologically, we know that people who feel a loss of control over their selves suffer deeply troubled lives. If the determinists' theory were true, a person could feel completely free to do anything he pleased and would be impervious to any sense of blame for his actions; his upbringing and environment would be to blame. But the same thing would have to be true for admirable actions, for those, too, if the theory is consistent, must also be merely the outcomes of his conditioning. By the deterministic theory, questions such as, "How should one lead one's life?" and "Was that a good thing or a bad thing to do?" and "Should I continue or not continue to act in particular ways?", are meaningless. So, too, would any concepts of right and wrong. These concerns would be replaced by such questions as, "Was the behavior functional or dysfunctional to the attainment of some end result?" If behavior were purely a product of conditioning, then people would not need to struggle with their selves. Who and what they are, would really be outside of their own control. Even if they were to try to place particular experiences or people in their own paths, hoping that these new experiences would condition them to different behaviors, what they chose would still not be a freely made choice. They would already have been conditioned to *want* to condition themselves to become a particular sort of person.

In advancing the proposition that there is no such thing as self-determination, that free will and freedom of choice do not exist, the proponents of determinism are tripped up by their own argument. They ask us to choose to accept it. The planners themselves would not be free to choose; their plans would be predetermined. What they think as being a "better world" is laden with qualities that, according to their own logic, they really haven't chosen but have been conditioned to desire. Moreover, if scientists were not honest and were not controlled themselves by concepts of right and wrong in their pursuit of truth, how could we trust their findings? If a scientist is not totally honest in his observations and in testing hypotheses and accepting or rejecting possible explanations, he fails to advance science as we know it. The determinists, who seek a world of properly conditioned people who supposedly have no free wills, must rely on conscience and the choosing of honesty over dishonesty for the very science upon which their theory is based.

If determinism were a reality, it would be very difficult to explain the advancements and progress of human civilization. How could social and economic and scientific progress be explained if man were not free to choose? If he were not free to choose, there would have to be a natural order to our universe at work that would be perfecting and elevating the human condition. And how could we explain the ways in which we are able to look at and address flaws in ourselves and in our world if we were not free to think and choose?

We know from our own lives that, as humans, we can say no to our appetites. We are capable not only of asking ourselves, "'Can I do that?" but also "Should I do that?" and no possible affirmative answer to the first question could justify neglecting a negative answer to the second. Man achieves a genuine measure of dignity when he allows his conscience—which raises questions such as, "Ought I get it?" and "Should I be that way?"—to control his choices and actions.

It is abundantly clear that ideas hold the potential to change the human creature. But until he chooses to accept those ideas, they will have little impact on his life. Moreover, it is only through a careful examination of his own actions and beliefs that a man is able to discern what he might choose to change. If, indeed, people did not have consciences, to trouble them with sometimes embarrassing and shaming questions, and if they were not free to choose to change themselves, it would be extremely difficult to explain the abrupt turns in behavior that we frequently observe in ourselves and others. Is there a child, or a husband, or a wife who hasn't experienced a sudden change in family living when one member explodes with "new marching orders"? "No more afternoon television. You kids are going to have your homework done *before* dinner." "This kitchen will be kept clean from here on. There won't be any dirty dishes left in the sink for days on end." "The dog will be fed before we sit down to the dinner table; and his water dish will be changed, too." "We're not going to sit around the house in our pajamas on Sunday mornings anymore. We're going to start going to church, as a family."

When a man takes control of his life, he starts taking himself seriously. He achieves a certain measure of dignity when he struggles with making himself into a person he can live with rightly and find satisfaction in being. And he becomes much more tolerable for others to live with when he accepts responsibility for his actions and is genuinely sorry for reprehensible behavior, when he says, "I regret it and want to do better in the future." High admiration is reserved for such a person.

While it is true that some amount of behavior is a product of conditioning and that much of what one likes and hence chooses is also a product of his experience, he nonetheless has a capacity to determine who he will become and what he will do, himself, freely through his own choices. The person who is sincerely concerned with his own character and its betterment is a person to be prized. Each person has this power. To the extent to which he lives according to Aristotle's position—that it is truly absurd for a man to attribute his actions to external things—he stands a chance of taking control and shaping his life in useful ways.

It has been argued by many that by the age of six to ten years a person's values and concepts of right and wrong are pretty well formed and that to try to teach adults how to face moral issues or improve their ethical reasoning and ability to choose right from wrong is largely a waste of time. Were this true, we would be enslaved in our adult lives to the thinking and maturity of a small child and forced to endure the consequences of whatever comes without the benefit of later-life experiences. This would certainly be a pitiful lot for humans to face. There is probably not a religion in the world that speaks only to young children; all of them appeal to the minds and hearts of thinking and sensitive adults, who fundamentally believe they are free to choose and who accept the responsibility for their choices. When we observe people struggling with difficult choices and watch lives change through their strong-willed determination, how impossible it is to think that humans are merely a product of their conditioning. The whole of education rests on the belief that people can learn new ideas and skills at any age and that their behavior can be changed. To think that a person can change all this but not his moral reasoning is truly absurd.

CHOOSING WISELY

The world is filled with many seemingly attractive choices that glitter brightly but are morally unsound. It can be tempting to view many of these opportunities as acceptable. The attraction these opportunities can hold for a person may be so strong, and the chances of ever being found out may appear so small, that one could easily convince himself that it is perfectly all right to follow his impulses rather than what his better judgment recommends. Whatever others might be doing or whatever appears attractive at the time, he might reason, is permissible and therefore does not demand sober inspection because it seems to be the accepted standard. The thoughtful person recognizes that, as humans, we are always choosing in everything we do. The person who yields to irresistibly attractive options or merely follows the standards set by others unthinkingly abdicates his freedom of choice. Charles Lazarus, founder of Toys "R" Us, told me he explains to MBA students something he feels is terribly important for them to remember. "My story," says Lazarus, "is, you're all going to be a success. Every single one . . . of you . . . is going to be a success. . . . Somewhere pretty quickly you're going to have an opportunity. You're going to have an opportunity to make a lot of money, maybe very quickly. What you choose is up to you. Somewhere a little further along the line there will come an opportunity not quite 100 percent, but it looks awfully good. You'll be tempted somewhere to take a shortcut, to do something that is not right and with a likelihood of being caught small, very small. It will be the biggest mistake you'll ever make. It will limit you forever. It will haunt you forever. Don't look around and say, 'Well that's somebody else. That's not me.' That *is* you. It will limit you."

Consider a problem scenario Robert Wilhelm, of Capwell-Emporium Stores in San Francisco, worried over. "Here's one of our buyers; she's a young girl, 24 or 25 years old. She is sent to market in New York City. She has anywhere from $100,000 to $400,000 in her budget to spend for the season. She goes into the showroom and is confronted with these "sharks" who'll try to wine and dine her, try to give her tickets to expensive shows." The point is, how she handles that situation is a choice, her choice. She will, if she thinks adequately, make it freely. How she decides will have an impact for the rest of her life. It would be easy to look at the corruption, the distasteful business practices, and the reprehensible characters of the business world and think, "If I am going to be part of that and succeed I'll have to behave that way too. But I'm not really like that. It's just the lousy system. I'll play the game by these standards, but that really isn't me." Those who follow this path soon become the person that their actions shape them into.

What should claim our special attention here is that the power to choose frees each human being to be the kind of person he chooses to be. And his decisions, in turn, shape him into the person he ultimately becomes. Happily, when we examine the world we learn that there are many who are choosing wisely, as Robert S. McNamara describes. "I've been talking [privately] . . . the last three weeks, to several executives of international [firms], and they've been operating in [foreign environments], and several of them told me that their companies just haven't paid a dime [in bribes] in these different environments. . . . And they also recognize that they lose business at times, particularly to Japanese as a case in point. But I think you have to make up your mind what you are going to do or not."

It can be easy for a person to lose sight of his freedom to choose. Habit patterns tend to bind people into particular ways of performing many tasks without much thought. It is also easy to forgo the opportunity to choose when one is not directly involved with a particular issue or is busy with other matters. Roy A. Anderson, of Lockheed, recalls such a situation in connection with an overseas payments problem his company once had. "I had nothing to do with it, but I had been told about the possibility that we might have to do that in Japan, of all places. And I didn't really react to it very much because I was not involved in it. But after this thing broke, [the illegal payments to get business in Japan was exposed] I thought back later on that; I had an intimation that that was going to happen or could happen. And I've often asked myself, should I have really grabbed ahold of that thing and gone to the board and stopped the thing. But, at the time, it didn't register very hard for the simple reason that it was pretty well recognized in the industry that that's the way business was done overseas. But when you look back on it, you should have called a halt even though you didn't know what was going on, but that the possibility was there."

In facing decisions squarely and thoughtfully, we are struck with the realization that the act of choosing is made difficult because there are ethical dimensions to every choice. And when we examine our options thoroughly and carefully, we always find there is some unethical aspect contained in each one. All men of depth and insight know that we live in an imperfect world, not a utopian one. There are no morally perfect choices. The big decisions, particularly, which must be made, contain ethical flaws of some significance no matter which alternative is selected. One soon realizes that this oftentimes involves dilemmas in which there is good and bad, advantage and cost, associated with each choice. Consider the following situation.

Stauffer Chemical had an agricultural plant in Mexico that had been forced to shut down because of a broken pump. No replacement pumps of that type, for the pressures involved, were available within the country; one would have to be brought in from the outside. The plant was important to that area; it employed about five hundred people. Mexico needed the product, and the plant was its only source. Until the breakdown was corrected, plant employees would be without work. Normally, this particular pump could be delivered in about two days. The plant would be down for only a short while and then back in operation; nobody would be laid off, and the product would be available without delay for commerce in that country. But unfortunately, the replacement parts were stopped at the border. To get across the border and past customs agents there were two routes. One was the paperwork route, which would take between six weeks and four months. The other was by paying the border customs agents an improper, by U.S. laws, fee of roughly $500, after which the pump and accompanying parts would be on the way to the plant in a couple of minutes. What should one do? The plant could be closed for several months if all the laws were obeyed. If the payment were made and found out, the press would carry some very damaging and unfavorable stories.

Particularly bothersome and yet quite common in management are situations which present no attractive options. David T. Kimball, of General Signal, encountered a disturbing situation early in his career when he was running a small company of about five hundred people. It dealt mostly in military-type products. There was one very large contract, for which they had competed aggressively, and they thought that they should win it. The evaluation had gone favorably, but the procurement person for the company that was about to place the order with Kimball's firm wanted a thousand-dollar stereo, and Kimball said, "We're not going to do that." The salesman on the account told him, "Well, we're going to lose the contract if we don't," and Kimball's thoughts were, "if it was going to take a payoff to get the contract then he just didn't want it." But he knew that as a result of that loss of contract his company was going to lay off about 60 or 70 people.

Another troubling type of decision is one in which what some believe to be right or desirable is a odds with what buyers show they prefer by what they choose. Robert L. Barney, of Wendy's, describes a perplexing dilemma that pits the concern about healthful foods against what customers actually want. "It's sort of a dilemma as to give . . . the consumer what he wants or what's best for him. And he's the one that actually decides. He decides whether he wants them [french fries] cooked that way [in animal fat] or to have them cooked in vegetable oil which doesn't have cholesterol. . . . If you use vegetable oil to cook your french fries in, they don't taste as good. Therefore . . . customers go someplace where they can get them cooked in animal fat. They don't know why. They don't care why. They don't care about cholesterol. They just want french fries that taste good. . . . You have to satisfy the customer. You're out of business if you don't satisfy him. . . . We can advertise on national television Wendy's light-side, nutritional meals and salad bar, and everybody thinks, 'eat light at Wendy's.' You get all these heavy people, nutritional people, weight-conscious people, and they all come into Wendy's. And along come a lot of other people. And they get up to the front counter, and they were thinking salad, light, and all those kinds of things, and they will say, 'I'll have a double hamburger with everything on it and an order of french fries and a frosty and a bowl of chili.'"

Richard J. Flamson, III, of Security Pacific, describes the situation in which decisions have to be made for larger considerations, even though the organization may be harmed in the short run, as follows: "Let's say we have a case where somebody in one of the subsidiary companies is maneuvering the books a little bit. Now it's an out and out case of you're going to get rid of them quickly if they've been falsifying the profits so that they can get a bonus . . . and they really aren't earning the money they say they are earning. But, then, what do you do in the case where it's just the opposite? Where they are earning so much money that they are storing a little away, like a squirrel with nuts, to take care of any bad things that come along. And they are doing that without the knowledge of the accounting hierarchy through the company. They're certainly not doing that for any self-enrichment. And you say, 'Well, you can't be cooking the books of one of our subsidiary companies, and so they have to go.' And yet they may be the most experienced individual in that particular line that we have, and we just can't go out in the market and hire another one to take his place, and so we're going to have a breakdown in customer service, we're going to have a breakdown in profitable opportunities. We're going through all this, and there was no self-enrichment involved, and the guy thought he was doing the right thing for the company. And he has to be terminated. There's an ethical situation, I suppose, where the ethics totally outweigh the practicalities. I would submit to you that in a smaller company the guy might get a bonus for that. But in a company this size, particularly the kind of company we are, a financial company where your products are money, you can't allow that kind of thing."

Some of the most difficult decisions business leaders are faced with are plant closings and work-force reductions. Here sharp conflicts of values are at stake, and there are no easy or painless solutions. The rescue of the Chrysler Corporation saw company survival necessitate mass layoffs. Chrysler Motor's chairman, Gerald Greenwald, explains how he experienced this great difficulty. "I felt like we were in a lifeboat in the early '80s, and there were fifteen of us, and the lifeboat was going to sink unless there were only ten of us. And there were one or two of us who had to make the choice of which five were going to get thrown out. If I've got a motivation to keep this company [profitable and healthy] that's one of them. I don't *ever* want to live through that again. We had to lay off 20,000. We had to close 20 plants in 20 communities, and, that was *very* painful personally. I know that, to those who were affected, for me to say it was painful, they'd look at me and say, 'Painful to you. What the hell are you talking about?' It was just painful and I don't ever want ever to live through that in my life."

In situations like this no other alternative exists. Sooner or later the economic realities force it one way or another, as Donald Lennox, of Navistar, points out. "You feel badly about that. You know everything [you have been told] about the negative impact is factual. . . . it will raise the unemployment rate. Many people depend on it. Local vendors who primarily serviced the plant for non-productive supplies and other services . . . would be wiped out. . . . It's going to happen. But you say, 'Okay we won't do that,' and you won't cause it today, there is a 99 percent chance it's going to happen three or four months, or six months later [and] the whole thing will go down then."

One's torment with perplexing difficulties eventually leads to the search for decision rules or some form of infallible guidance. These efforts usually take one to develop elaborate systems of rules. The overreliance on rules, when choosing, carries two confounding outcomes. First, the list of rules must become extraordinarily long and complex to handle all the special circumstances and unique situations. Anytime there are two rules, a third rule is necessary to handle cases where the first two conflict. For example, should I be truthful and tell the complete truth which might hurt someone's feelings, or should I fail to be honest and not cause pain to another human? To resolve the conflict between honesty and kindness, a third rule is needed. Once that rule is established, with all the exceptions and conditions spelled out, still more rules are needed to resolve other conflicts. Life can easily become, using this approach to resolving ethical questions, a matter of negotiating a tangle of rules and their exceptions.

Second, many people will find great satisfaction with how well they understand and follow the rules; those who are good at it begin to take on an air of superiority and a sense of moral righteousness, because they abide more closely to the rules than others do. They can be so engrossed with being perfect at obeying the rules that they neglect the injustices around them and fail to do much of anything that is productive or beneficial. There ought to be more to life than perfecting our ability to slip through a maze of regulations and adhere to a legalistic system of dos and don'ts. Man needs something larger to win his allegiance and to allow him to live a truly worthwhile existence. The attempt to live a blameless, error-free life so that he can feel secure in his own goodness is an inviting way to get through these perplexing situations. But following this path may in fact be quite unethical, because the desire to be blameless and perhaps feel self-righteous assumes the upper hand in the decision maker's thinking at the expense of all other considerations. A pursuit for self-perfection can blur a person's vision in many other worthy matters.

Trying to live responsibly in an imperfect world presents genuine difficulties to the conscientious person. As he struggles with difficult choices he becomes perplexed. What is the answer? What is fair? And then there are those who will judge his choices. It can be inviting to outsiders, viewing a situation, to stand in judgment of what a business person chooses. With a narrow or single-minded perspective, one is likely to disagree with choices made and simply conclude that the decision maker, himself, is unethical. But wisdom brings emancipation from these arbitrary forms of judgment.

Aristotle cautioned us against expecting to find infallible guidance in making ethical choices when he observed that ethics is not an exact science and that we can seek only that degree of exactness which the subject matter in each case allows. William L. Weiss, of Ameritech, says, "Good ethics, like good management, is finding the best way to handle a situation. And therein lies the difficulty of ethics. Like business itself, it is not a soft and simple discipline. Nor is it a matter of drawing out cut-and-dried answers from some mystical repository. Ethics is the art of balancing multiple claims and responsibilities honestly, fairly, and as objectively as possible. There isn't any hard principle that will apply neatly to every situation except, maybe, to 'do good and avoid evil.' But that doesn't tell you how. And often you find situations where there are no 'good' choices, and you have to do your best to find the lesser of the two 'evils'."

Clarity of thought forces us to recognize the reality of having to choose between imperfect alternatives. To languish in this predicament, paralyzed by not knowing what to do because no choice is flawless, is understandably human. But it is not courageous. It is tempting to do nothing, but to refuse to decide is, itself, a decision. Thinking clearly and considering all aspects as honestly and carefully as one knows how, that is, approaching difficult choices rationally, does not guarantee success. But irrationality through hasty, facile, or parochial thinking invites failure. A mark of maturity and wisdom is the willingness to face the tough choices we confront with calmness and to compare the available alternatives, seeing both the desirable and the undesirable aspects within each; it is to face squarely the many imperfect trade-offs the world offers, and not to fail to choose any one at all because no perfect choices exist. "That is really what management is all about," says John Bryan Jr., of Sara Lee. "That's why you can't get a machine to manage a business, why you've got to have judgment to manage a business. Someone has got to determine these trade-offs between the long-term [and] short-term of business.

Trade-offs between constituencies of a business, be they the managers or the customers or the shareholders or the institution of the company."

Experience and thoughtful reflection allow one to outgrow the assumption that problems can be formed in simple terms of good and bad and that he can hold at arm's length the many ethical choices he must make as he lives and participates in the matters of the world. Participation carries the price of facing reality and acting as best one knows how. The trick is to free oneself from self deception and to struggle honestly with the options available.

DEVICES OF SELF DECEIT

The importance of total honesty with oneself while situations are thought through and possible choices are examined cannot be overstated. The future of mankind is inextricably tied to the seriousness and honesty of people in comparing the options available before them. Their freedom to choose rationally remains intact only to the extent that this freedom is taken seriously and exercised carefully and to the extent that there is honesty of thought through removal of the blinders of self-deceit. The freedom to choose wisely demands recognition and removal of the many ways in which people deceive themselves. There are excuses aplenty that can choke off one's ethical reasoning and will to abide by high moral ideals. Several of the most commonly found excuses for an unethical action follow:

1. A *victim of necessity* pleads that he had to do it; that there were no other options at the time. In truth and perhaps through laziness, he did not even try to imagine other possible choices.

2. The person explains that it was *an innocent error* and, owing to his ignorance, he really did not realize what he was doing. He will claim also that he had no idea that the undesirable consequences would follow from his actions. Humans can think and choose; they are responsible for knowing what they do.

3. "I'll make an *exception* here," the person tells himself. Just this once I'll ignore the rules, I'll bend the truth, or I'll violate standards and agreements. It won't hurt to do it this *one* time only. By making one exception, a person is tempted to make a second exception, and then another, and so forth. Undesirable habits are easily formed. Each action has an impact on ourselves and others.

4. It's the *established pattern*, so it really isn't illegal or immoral. "That is the practice in this industry, or in that country where we do business," one might be tempted to rationalize. The implication is that he is thereby excused from adhering to what moral reasoning would conclude is right or wrong.

5.   *Self preservation* is natural. The thought is, "We can do anything if it is necessary to preserve our existence." In reality this person places himself ahead and above the glue that bonds society's stability—the concern for mankind. In essence this person is saying, "I am more important than the civilization of which I am but a tiny part."

6.   We were *minding our own business* and therefore we were not looking for what others around us might be doing. Or we didn't recognize other needs or other people's rights or needs; we were so "tuned in" to what we were doing we didn't see the opportunity. This argues that if I don't see what is happening around myself, then I have a good excuse for my negligence or wrongdoing.

7.   We had to do it in order to *protect our self-interests.* "It was in the best interests of the company; therefore we were expected to do it. In fact, we probably ought to be rewarded for doing what's best for the business." This person would argue, "one must do whatever it takes to survive." This is the "ends justify the means" argument.

8.   We *won't be found out.* No one will ever know. "It will be our little secret. Swear to it!" The driving motive is how to gain something for oneself by any underhanded trick, so long as one can escape detection.

9.   *This is unselfish* "We're doing it for our customers; we will make a lot of money, also, but really, it's for our customers." Or, "It's to keep our employees working; we'll do anything to get a contract to keep good people employed. And of course if we benefit, well, so what?"

10. It's a way of *getting something for little or no effort.* "We'll take the easy way here," the thinking goes. The idea here is to get what one desires with the least effort. It frequently involves ignoring ethical standards and bending the rules.

11. *I have no faith that doing the right thing is really the best thing* to do in the long run. Roy Anderson, of Lockheed, attests to the fact that the ethical way is the right way, overall. "When we, in this company, discuss competitive areas, competitive problems, for example, we get our lawyers in and we really discuss what's the governing principle here in terms of not only the particular business case involved, but also if it's got a little bit of a problem with respect to an ethical problem. And just what are the ethical problems? And you always come out with the right answer to that."

4

The Duty to Think

The most striking feature of many of the great people from the past whom we honor now, men such as Galileo, Socrates, Darwin, Luther, and Freud, is that they broke from the established beliefs and patterns of thought of their times and introduced radical new ideas. They are revered today not because they were esteemed by their contemporaries; in fact, many were not, and not because they were the most able in their respective fields—others more gifted surely followed. They earned their places in history because their thinking gave us added vision and greater understanding of ourselves, our world, and beyond.

The common strand that runs through each of these lives is willingness to think with integrity. To the best of their abilities they separated their minds from blinding dogmas that would have otherwise prevented free inquiry and intellectual integrity. With total honesty they observed, speculated, questioned, tested, recorded, and reported what they found and thought to be the truth. Their names are recorded in human history because they were ground breakers in their fields, not because they were the best. Human progress advances only when people think and acknowledge honestly what is and what is not, what works and what does not work, what has value and what is worthless, what is right and what is wrong and what is the truth and what is not the truth—and in each case it is logically supported with reasoning as to *why*.

SUCCESS DEMANDS THINKING

History of American business is lavish with illustrations of the truth that those people who achieved great success and left a lasting mark did so largely because of their ability to think clearly. Some recognized needs and opportunities, like Ole Evinrude, who thought there must be an easier way of propelling small boats over water as he rowed across a lake on a

hot summer afternoon, and Lane Bryant, who achieved success by fitting
large and hard-to-fit women with flattering clothing. Some solved problems, like Harvey Firestone, who devised a way, using wire, to keep tires
from slipping off their wheels, and Elisha Otis, who designed the world's
first safety hoist, which, by using a wagon spring, prevented the load
from crashing to the ground in the event of a cable break. Some saw
ways to tap new markets, like J. Walter Thompson, whose advertising
business was one of the first to recognize the importance of the wife in
buying decisions, and A. P. Giannini, whose Bank of Italy (it later became the Bank of America) served the "little guy" when other banks
would not make loans to immigrants. Others, devised new methods for
selling merchandise, like William Coleman, who earned the trust of leery
customers by "renting" them his petroleum-fueled lantern with a guarantee
that if it did not work they need not pay, and Frank Winfield Woolworth,
who placed merchandise on tables in his Lancaster, Pennsylvania, store so
customers could inspect it for themselves before purchasing. Some realized the importance of ethical business practices, like Cyrus H. K. Curtis,
who flatly refused to place fraudulent or questionable advertising in his
Ladies Home Journal, and Barney Kroger and James Cash Penney, who
personally tested merchandise sold in their stores so that customers would
be assured full value for their money. In almost all of these cases and
many hundreds more, success came to those who broke with unquestioned tradition, who invented new or improved products, who devised
superior business approaches, or who found superior ways of solving
problems or serving needs.

   Willis Haviland Carrier, the father of air conditioning, is an excellent
example of a person who added much to the world because he was an intellectually honest and tireless thinker. He became the founder of a new
industry because he did not hesitate to move into uncharted areas. He
pushed across new frontiers in science and engineering to pioneer a new
era and elevate the comfort level for millions. Carrier was special for several reasons. "First, he was one hundred percent honest, intellectually.
Second, he possessed great knowledge supplemented by a wonderful intuitive sense. Third, he always went directly to the heart of a problem—
often with an unconventional approach. Fourth, he had an uncanny fac-
ulty for selecting a project that promised the fulfillment of a human need
and was, therefore, commercially attractive. He sensed demand and then
developed something to meet it."[1]

   At the root of these examples of business success are people who la-
bored and exercised their intelligence. To be sure, the fully awakened
mind applied to its fullest is a powerful ally in our daily struggles.
Shallow and sloppy thinking, as experience shows, inevitably invites
ruin. Although the careful and deliberate exercise of our intelligence will
not always produce material or business success—luck has its say in these
matters too—careful, honest thinking, itself, is usually the source of great
satisfaction. Blaise Pascal added greatly to the value of thinking when he
observed, "Man is obviously made for thinking. Therein lies all his dig-

nity and his merit; and his whole duty is to think as he ought."[2] One fact stands clear: man dignifies his existence through rational thinking.

FINDING THE TIME TO THINK

In our busy lives, many demands present themselves, each one pressing us for our time; from every direction it seems another request beckons for our attention, for our touch, for our care. And each one seems to take longer than we thought it would. An eye-opening demonstration on this topic was performed once with a large group of working women, most of whom were also mothers of small children. They were asked how many hours each week they spent performing various, common chores and activities, such as working at their jobs, driving children here or there, shopping and running errands, talking to their husbands, preparing meals, and doing household chores. An estimate of the time spent, in hours, was recorded on a large blackboard beside each of the activities listed. The audience was shocked when these times were tallied: the total was 50 hours greater than the 168 hours in a week. Obviously the estimates made were erroneous, but the point shown by the demonstration was not trivial: people's lives are filled with many demands, and there seems to be insufficient time in a week to accommodate all of them adequately. A question we can ask is, Whose demands for our time shall we choose to honor?" Many people find it extremely difficult to say no to demands made on their time. Nonetheless, it is necessary to say no to some good demands in order to say yes to the best demands.

A hurried life may be exciting, but it is not necessarily a fruitful one. It is also exhausting. We cannot rely on luck and happenstance alone to produce the conditions and circumstances necessary for a happy and successful existence. Time is needed for reflection and for planning and soul searching. Clearly we need time to do, but we also need to find and use time to think—otherwise the thinking will not occur, and its benefits will never result.

Robert L. Barney, of Wendy's, expresses how he approaches the battle of making time for thinking. "I know in my own position I do an awful lot of thinking. I don't necessarily do it all here [at the office] either. I do it wherever I am, just trying to figure out what we're doing wrong and what we need to correct it, or what opportunities are out there, things that we ought to be looking for to do down the road and you have to plan out. It's easy for me. For example, I can keep myself busy on the telephone, involved in community activities. I do some of that. But I have to limit the amount of time I spend on the telephone spent involved in the community. And there are a lot of busy things that you can do. You can just keep yourself busy from morning to night. . . . If you deal with things as they come, you'll never know what the top five priority items [are] that you should be doing. You'll never get to those because you're doing all this busy stuff. And you've got to, sometimes, just stop."

AN HONEST LOOK AT OURSELVES AND
OUR SURROUNDINGS

The process of perfecting one's self or an organization begins with an accurate assessment—an honest look at who and what one is. The unexamined life practically never counts for much; it certainly is not worth living. It is foolish to neglect to examine one's character regularly. Laziness, vanity, and the desire to feel superior to others can, unfortunately, trip one up; they are sources of great mischief. They are apt to offer one an illusion, and falsely color what really exists. Self-examination will not be effective, it will not be accurate, and it probably will not lead to corrective action if it occurs haphazardly or infrequently. It ought to be an ongoing process. The more one does it, the more truthful and penetrating the findings become, and the stronger will be the desire to work seriously at making improvements.

It is instructive and inspiring that others are willing to share how they approach this difficult process themselves. The practical person is likely to profit from and follow their examples. Sanford N. McDonnell, of McDonnell Douglas, relates an incident that can serve as such a standard for those willing to face themselves courageously and inspect their own lives. "I've been very active in the Boy Scouts," says McDonnell. "I was impressed with the tremendous impact the code of ethics, represented by the Scouts' oath and laws, was making on the young people when I was active [in scouting] with my son. That's the primary mission of scouting, to instill those values into young people by actual training and examples. After telling all the young kids to live up to the code, one day I asked [myself], 'What am I doing to live up to it?' Upon self-examination I found that I was falling far short in many areas. Then I got to thinking, 'We expect our employees to be ethical, but what does that really mean? Do we have a code of ethics at McDonnell Douglas?' But we didn't. So I assembled a small task force of top people. I said, 'Here's the Boy Scouts of America Oath and Laws, and I want our code of ethics to look like that. I want you to cover every point in there.' And after quite a few iterations we finally came up with [the McDonnell Douglas Code of Ethics]. The more I got into it, whereas I thought we had a very ethical organization, there were a lot of areas that needed to be improved. The more we got into it, the more people realized we were serious about it. The more things came out from underneath the table and were reported up, by letters or otherwise, that needed to be looked into."

An honest examination of organizational practices can locate trouble spots and questionable methods of doing business that otherwise might never receive correction until they are exposed by someone outside the organization and prove to be sources of great embarrassment. William S. Anderson, of NCR, tells of an occasion when an honest look inward prompted a change for the better. "NCR did a study and fortunately we found very little [unethical dealings]. There were some cases that we found where payments were made to consultants to facilitate an order. We asked ourselves, 'Now, was the consultant really necessary? Was he really consulting?' Or was it because the buyer said, 'You have to employ this consultant and divide up the money' and things like that. . . . We use it as a good reason to impress upon our overseas managers that this was a dumb way to do business, that if the product you were selling was not really worth buying, you don't deserve the order anyway. That kind of business comes back to haunt you."

An unexpected, but not unimportant, benefit of self-examination and corrective effort is a feeling of relief. It comes from knowing that questionable practices have been stopped and that decent and ethical stands are being followed. In one very large U.S. corporation doing business abroad, a committee of the board uncovered instances in which payments were made that, although they were not in violation of local law or local custom, were in violation of the way top management felt business should be done in the United States. The problem was dealt with in an extremely open and above-board manner. They found no one who had broken any U.S. law in the process, so nobody lost a job because of the investigation. When it was all over, one of the managers involved said, "You know, I'm relieved to have this come up, because frankly, I didn't know what to do. My competitors were doing it, and therefore I got drawn into it. I don't like it. I'd like to stop it. And now it's all come out into the open and I can stop it." In this situation what was wrong was made right and what was out of control was put under control. Lives that were troubled through questionable practices were relieved by the removal of the unsettling burden of guilt.

INFORMATION FOR SELF-EXAMINATION

The depth and fidelity of a person's introspection are limited to the amount and accuracy of the information he has about himself or his organization. There are several obstacles to the success of this process. First, people are apt not to search very hard or deeply, feeling that they already know about themselves. Second, there is the fear that one might actually uncover a disturbing, unpleasant truth about oneself. Third, it is understandably human to have a favorable image of one's virtues and falsely underestimate one's shortcomings. Fourth, each person is inclined to conceal the unfavorable aspects of his true nature from his own view. And what he does know about himself that is not to his liking, he conceals from others. Fifth, because no one is always one way or other, our minds allow us to flatter ourselves by permitting us to think that the few instances in which we have taken virtuous actions are an ingrained pattern in our behavior, and we ignore all actions that form a different story. Sixth, we are apt to consider what we know to be grievous shortcomings and unforgivable indiscretions, however frequent, as aberrations and therefore to excuse them as being merely temporary lapses or unavoidable slip-ups.

Self-love can easily take the upper hand over a person's better judgment and trick him into thinking his faults go unnoticed. Excessive love of self produces arrogance and blindness. Whereas a person may be aware of a fault, he can easily convince himself it will go unnoticed. This is why advice and admonitions from others are so painful. They show, in no uncertain terms, that what one thought was kept hidden has been in full view all along. Because unfavorable and unflattering remarks are often ignored or rejected out of hand, and because sour feelings are quite likely to develop toward their bearer, one is rarely permitted the luxury of a full accounting of what others think about or see in him. And although it is hard to bear the painful sting of admonitions, it would be wise to ask one-self the question, "Can I bear the pain my shortcomings will surely pro-duce for me throughout the course of my lifetime?" He who is forever blind to his faults, or deceived by his arrogance into believing that his shortcomings escape the notice of others, runs the danger of being perma-nently stuck with these shortcomings. It takes a secure person to listen to and entertain uncomplimentary perceptions others have formed of him, and it requires remarkable character to actively invite and search out such information and not become unduly affected by its irritations or to harbor ill feelings toward its source.

The founder of Motorola, Paul Galvin, is reported to have developed this capacity. In the course of running his business, Galvin managed to convince his associates that he did not consider himself infallible. They soon learned that they could go to him and say, "Paul, your decision yes-terday was wrong." If the new facts they supplied stood the test of his scrutiny, he would accept their analysis. Some recall his words, "Tell the fellows we're changing. My decision yesterday was wrong." He pur-sued good, clear thinking and did not stand on his position or office, be-cause he was not too arrogant or proud to back down or accept other ideas. Results were what he was after. Galvin often said, "Follow the right decisions regardless of when, or how, or by whom these decisions were arrived at."[3] Here was a man who was particularly impatient with those who could not admit their own mistakes.

Humans are in a predicament: How can they obtain reliable infor-mation about themselves? How can they tolerate the unpleasant sting of the truth? How do they develop a resolve to act positively to correct those matters in need of remedy? Everyone needs to find revealing information about himself and to discern which bits of it are to be trusted for their ac-curacy. Friends are often quite tender and, hence, unwilling to provide painful information. They are afraid to offend, and also, having much the same likes and dispositions as we do, they are apt to be much like us and likely to not notice our faults. In truth they may tend to perceive in us more virtues than shortcomings.

An adversary, however, is much more likely to serve as a faithful monitor. Propelled by dislike, he is sure to ferret out our slightest slip-ups and defects, and to make these known in such large and alarming ways that even we cannot miss them. A person's willingness to give due consideration to distasteful challenges is, indeed, a real measure of his character. Nathan S. Ancell, of Ethan Allen, had enormous respect for a man by the name of Bill Morrissey, the plant manager of a small furniture factory his company had acquired early in its history. As Ancell explains: "In spite of the fact that I hired him and he reported to me, . . . he, in the course of the next six months, wrote me, in longhand, four- five- and six-page letters questioning everything that I was doing and telling me that he was nervous about the fact that [he was worried], 'were we going to take advantage of that factory and take advantage of the people?' And he challenged me strong[ly]. I've got the letters in my vault, yet. He challenged me and questioned me. He didn't know me that well. He didn't know whether my motives were make-believe or whether they were genuine and honest. He challenged me like no employee would ever challenge a boss. He had guts. And he wasn't afraid. . . . And by challenging me honestly and straightforwardly, he made my respect for him grow by leaps and bounds. I'm a tough guy in business and a lot of people may not love me because I'm very demanding and I'm very tough. . . . But I have got a lot of respect and I learned that from Bill Morrissey."

Within each organization there are many hundreds or even many thousands of minds and pairs of eyes, capable of finding and identifying all kinds of shortcomings and opportunities for improvement. Effective organizations are led by people who realize this and develop methods for bringing useful information and creative ideas into the open. Douglas D. Danforth, of Westinghouse, explains a company policy aimed at encouraging employees to come forward with what they think ought to be looked into by higher-ups. "[For] an employee who believes something is going on that should not go on, either defective material or misuse of corporate funds, we have an established vehicle for that individual, not as a tattletale, but he has immunity to come forth and tell us about it."

AT&T has a system that attempts to catch faulty thinking at the very beginning and before major decisions are made that might go sour or be perceived as bad; it has something called the Office of the Chairman, which is made up of the chairman, the president, and the three vice chairmen. Also sitting in that group is the senior vice president of public relations. The reason the senior vice president of public relations is involved is that AT&T wants the person whose job it is to be the conscience of the corporation to be more sensitive to the outside environment than anybody else there. They want that person to be a part of every decision that is under consideration. AT&T wants to catch the faulty thinking at the very inception, and this has been a tradition in the Bell system for many years.

Monsanto has an inside group with the job of raising tough questions and monitoring the company's actions—a social responsibility committee of the board. This committee reviews the major items of Monsanto's behavior, including such things as hazards policy, safety practices, and equal opportunity results—how the firm is doing on hiring and promoting minorities and women.

The world seems always to have an abundant supply of critics, who gladly observe and remark on every bit of human activity they can find. Setting themselves up as adversaries, they can prove quite useful by helping us out with harsh and difficult criticism. They are rarely totally right; they err, too. But they do cause their targets much consternation, as well as giving them the opportunity to think about what they are doing and the many possible implications their behavior holds. Richard L. Gelb, of Bristol-Myers Squibb, points out the benefits of an ongoing dialogue held with critics of his firm. Certain religious groups and others around the world feel that the infant formula companies, Bristol-Myers Squibb being one of them, are destroying infants by taking them off the mother's breast and putting them on to the bottle. Gelb says, "We have now, literally, for 15 years engaged in some serious dialogue with these groups, which has led to significant changes on our part in terms of some of our marketing practices. We've accepted the fact certain countries, less developed countries specifically, that perhaps the practices we were following were inappropriate [and] were changed. I think these groups have come to respect Bristol-Myers Squibb now, and every time they are out there talking about the problem, Bristol-Myers Squibb is held up as a model company that has provided leadership. And that even though, in certain areas we don't agree. . . . they still believe in us. In other words, where we have honest differences they accept those."

In the United States, formula makers believe the bottle is perfectly appropriate if the mother wants to feed her infant that way, for whatever the reasons are. The critics do not agree with that. They do not think companies should give free infant formula to the hospital so that when the infant is discharged it can go home with a supply of infant formula. The formula companies, however, do not believe that that is how the breast-feeding or bottle-feeding decision is made. They do not believe that mothers think, "A, ha! We got a free can of infant formula, so I'll feed my child on the bottle." Most mothers realize that one free can of formula will last for only about three or four days. For the export market, however, there is no question that some manufacturers, both in the United States and abroad, saw their mission as one of selling product, and not necessarily as being good for children and mothers. The American companies sat down with their critics and were able to go back to the foreign countries and have some success.

Unsolicited complaints provide a rich source of material for self-examination. Letters, both anonymous and signed, are frequently sent to business leaders by well meaning individuals who have legitimate concerns. The prudent person in business will not trivialize these signals. Successful leaders do not ignore or take these notices lightly. Cigna's chairman and CEO, Robert D. Kilpatrick, for instance, personally follows up on any complaint he gets. Each complainer will receive a personal telephone call or letter from him. To Kilpatrick, complaining letters are good indicators of the need to look over particular parts of the firm.

Olin Corporation's chairman, John Henske, believes that it's wise to pay serious attention to anonymous letters, and not to dismiss them lightly or too quickly if upon checking on their accuracy the early indications are that no problem exists. "I've gradually learned over the years [that] to ignore one of those letters is a serious mistake," says Henske. "The normal pattern is, you investigate or have your auditors or somebody investigate, and it always comes back at first 'no problem.' And you wait three to six months and you find that it was a problem. So I've gradually learned that when the first signal comes back, 'there is no problem,' to have someone go back and double-check it. I find most of those letters are written by people who are genuinely concerned about the company and aren't trying to get somebody in trouble. They're really trying to help the company. And they're serious about it and to take them any other way is a mistake."

Certainly, an important concern is whether there really is something of substance behind an anonymous letter and what the magnitude of the problem really is. One gauge of a problem's magnitude is the number of people complaining. It's also terribly important to have a good look at *who* is doing the complaining. Gerald B. Mitchell, of Dana Corporation, sees it this way: "If we have a facility with 250 people and I get a letter from it, that's kind of interesting. I get a letter and I respond to it. I get a second letter, I get a little warning bell. You get ten letters, you have a problem. It doesn't matter if they're talking about the lunchroom or pot-holes in the road or that a foreman punched somebody or that you've got sexual exploitation going on in the plant. It's always the volume. The volume tells you that something isn't right, because very rarely do you have one little instance that causes problems. If we have a plant in North Carolina, the woman writes and tells you that she's being abused by the foreman or by a supervisor. That could be anything. She could be mad at the supervisor. They could have been living together. Anything could have happened. You don't really know. That's just one letter. You get eight letters, you have a problem, and you have a serious problem. You better get down to North Carolina and get it fixed up really quickly. . . . It's just like a thermometer. When the volume of letters goes up, you've got a problem. If somebody writes and tells you that there are drugs being done in one area of the plant, that's serious. You better think about what you want to do about it, depending upon what they say. You get six letters, you have a drug problem. You have fifteen letters, you have a fire burning. You have to do something. So the letters are very important to me personally."

Not all the whistle blowers are sincere. Some, as Delbert Staley, of NYNEX, observes, have other matters on their minds. "Unfortunately, it turns out that an awful lot of the whistle-blowers are disgruntled employees. They're people who have either been demoted or passed by, and they have various reasons why they want to stir up trouble. Every now and then you run into one where there is something behind what they have to say. One of the first things you find out is that if an individual signs the letter they probably feel fairly strongly about it."

The paths through which information travels in an organization's hierarchy can easily become clogged. When this occurs, those at the top are guaranteed a good measure of ignorance of what is going on. The trick, as astute leaders know, is to create a climate in which people are not fearful of coming forward and in which they have confidence that their views are welcomed and will be seriously considered and sincerely appreciated. John Henske, of the Olin Corporation, tries to get this message to employees. He says, "What you try to say to people . . . is if you blow the whistle on factual matters . . . you will not be punished; just the opposite. You'll be rewarded in some fashion." Even if people are sometimes mistaken, it is probably better to have a flow of information containing some mistaken beliefs than not to have a flow at all. Henske uses an approach he finds useful: "If the person is guessing that there's something wrong and reports it as factual, that would be a mistake. The person who thinks there's something wrong and comes forward and says, 'I think there's something wrong but I don't have any facts', won't be punished for it." Few skills earn a leader a favorable image more quickly than that of empathetic listening. Robert Barney, of Wendy's, saw this quality in that firm's founder, David Thomas. "He was always a good listener. He was always asking people questions. I watched him in action talking to some people that he had a lot of respect for and he would ask them different things."

NOT TAKING ONESELF TOO SERIOUSLY

Most of life's tumbles are not caused by getting tripped up over external things, but by stumbling over one's own ego. "All of us in life, whether you're a teacher, or a businessman, or a priest, or anything else, should worry about whether our egos have gotten out of control. I think more problems result from an imbalance of the ego than a lot of other things. . . . It can destroy companies and families and individuals," says Michael W. Wright of Super Valu Stores. A sense of importance, fed and nurtured by flattery of self, is a source of great mischief. It deadens one's feelings toward others and toward pursuit of the truth. It declares "false" to the slightest criticisms one may receive. It stops dead the processes of self-improvement.

Out-of-control egos can transform ordinarily nice people into painful fatheads and insufferable snobs, whom no one can stand to be around or work alongside. Jack D. Sparks, of Whirlpool, cautions people, "Always be yourself. Don't try to be something you're not, because people are going to spot you if you start to pretend to be something you're not." It should not be surprising that most people reach high places in industry in part because they avoid this "shortcoming."

To no small degree, those who are successful at running large organizations are able to do so because they have mastered control of themselves. As Mike Wright, of Super Valu Stores, explains, "As you get higher in [the] organization, you worry about whether people are really telling you the truth. I think you can change by being at the top, and you won't know it, and other people won't be telling you. They are scared to. So you've always got to keep saying, 'What am I doing to be a jerk around here?'"

Each person has the capacity to constantly learn and improve his character. The best way to do that is to keep looking for areas for improvement. J. E. (Jim) Casey, the founder of UPS, advised, "Don't over-rate yourself. Lean a little the other way—be constructively dissatisfied—and you'll go farther."[4] No doubt a good bit of one's success results from unusual abilities, hard work, and an attractive personality. But many people who have succeeded keep their egos in check by telling themselves that luck—being the right person in the right place at the right time—helped, too. Richard J. Flamson III, of Security Pacific, expressed the idea this way: "I firmly believe that being successful in a corporation is over 50 percent luck, being in the right place at the right time. It has nothing to do with [being] the smartest guy in the building and in this company it has nothing to do with ownership because nobody owns as much as 5 percent of the stock, so it's not going to have to do with family pressures or things of that sort. It's luck and desire."

Another way successful leaders maintain control over their egos is to see that the organization's success, and ultimately their own success, depends upon many people. Jim Casey, of UPS, tells us, "You cannot be successful entirely through your own efforts. All of us, if we are to accomplish anything worthwhile, will do it largely through the help and cooperation of other people who work with us. We must help others to help us."[5]

Donald E. Petersen, of Ford, points out that the business news media and stories in business magazines tend to portray a misconception—the leader doing everything and calling all the shots. "Among the many things that are unfortunate in reporting and writing about business and business activity," says Petersen, "is the tendency to highly personalize the achievements of the chief executive. I do not leap tall buildings! I do not go home in one bound, eighteen miles! I do not dream up, design, develop, manufacture, assemble, sell a product heroically, all by myself! It is a team process that has been going on for quite some considerable time."

EXAMINING THE EVIDENCE WITH INTEGRITY: QUALITY THINKING

In the course of living, each person is called upon to make choices, to decide what he can do and decide what he ought to do. This requires thinking. He is therefore challenged to uncover what is and what is not, to discover what is true and what is false. Each person is challenged to think—to think carefully and critically. In doing this we cannot escape the importance of getting all evidence and all the attitudes, and perceptions, and feelings surrounding the situation at hand. These must be placed in full view for us and other persons to digest, to contemplate, to speculate upon, to debate over, and to use as the basis for arriving at an informed judgment.

In so doing it is necessary to attempt, as best we can, to eliminate our tendency to avoid careful examination of situations and ourselves. As honestly as possible, it is important to guard against the subtle and unseen influence of prejudices and partialities. The only hope of consistently reaching solid decisions and advancing our causes intelligently is through the open examination of evidence and possible choices, using the principles of logic. The ideal—quality thinking—is approached by perpetual questioning and by eliminating false preconceptions that can easily affect judgment before evidence is given an unbiased examination.

The climate in which an organization's members work at arriving at decisions—that is, do their thinking—has a profound impact on the quality of those decisions. The intentions of the "Sloan meetings" at General Motors serve as a good example of a climate that is supportive of open debate and free inquiry. The words of Alfred P. Sloan to the GM board of directors capture the flavor of this climate. "Gentlemen," said Sloan, "I take it we are all in complete agreement on the decision here. Then I propose we postpone further discussion of this matter until our next meeting to give ourselves time to develop disagreement and perhaps gain some understanding of what the decision is all about."[6] An important idea behind these meetings, as Sloan explained, was this: "It is the right as well as the duty of every managerial employee to criticize a central management decision which he considers mistaken or ill-advised."[7] Criticism was not only *not* penalized but was encouraged, as a sign of initiative and an active interest in the business. It was supposed to be taken seriously and given honest consideration.

Timm F. Crull, of Carnation, explains how the man who started that company's sales organization wanted its meetings to be run. In the company's sales meetings, issues were discussed in such a manner that good thinking would occur to everyone's benefit. As Crull recalls, "One of the great attributes he had was that he had the ability to instill in the people under his direction that we were equals and that we should not be subservient to a title, that if we were right we should respect our opinions and express them and that we would not be criticized. And when we went into a meeting we always knew that. We were told and taught to tell what we thought and not worry about the consequences of being judged, by being far out this way or not knowing what's going on. We were given the opportunity to really express our opinions. And we now are instilling that throughout the company as guys that worked under him have come up into the leadership of the company. One of the first things we do when we go to any meeting or any session is tell them to forget who we are, that this is an open discussion, an open meeting, and that everyone is to speak their piece. At the end of that meeting we'll make decisions on what we're gong to do, and then we all go shoulder to shoulder to accomplish the objective. But in the meantime, it's all our responsibilities to ourselves and to our company and to our employees to say what we think we should do. I think a real strength of this company is that the people are not afraid that they are going to be prejudged or judged on what they say."

Knowing what we do about human nature and the imperfection of humans it may be tempting to advance various seemingly valid arguments as to why the ideals expressed here might never be fully realized. But we stand to do ourselves a great disservice, if we sell short man's capacity to engage in free-flowing debates. The fact is, many managers and employees in well-run organizations engage in honest expressions of opinion. And they do so freely and in basically unrestrained and polite ways. Arthur Ochs Sulzburger, of the *New York Times*, shares an example of an issue debated at that organization. "The most current debate going on in our shop is one where we called upon all political candidates to open up all of their files. And some people around here say that that was not an ethical thing to have asked; that it is not proper to ask a man, to force him to authorize the FBI to give you the raw data in his file. I think, personally, that we've gone too far. I think that if a man runs for the Presidency of the United States, he has to be expected to have everything, just about everything. But I think there is a line. I'm not quite sure where the ethical line is. I don't think that's fair to ask you if you are running to open the raw files all the way in your history—every unproven accusation. Some idiot calls up and it pops into your file and there it sits—completely raw data. I think that's totally unfair. Those are the kinds of issues we debate a lot of the time. We tend to debate a lot of these things quite publicly. A newspaper is like a sieve. There is really no such thing as keeping a secret at the *New York Times*. . . . We've debated and at last came down on a conclusion on whether or not we should take condom advertising. We traditionally have never taken it. About two to three months ago we decided that we might take it under certain circumstances, not when it relates to birth control but when it relates to health. . . . This is one which was really kicked around for a long period of time. And whether or not our readers are the kinds of people who need this kind of information."

At Arthur Andersen, as Duane R. Kullberg explains, open debate is expected from all professionals. "Internally we will carry on tremendous debates about whether or not this position is right or wrong. . . . Internal debates are okay; in fact, they're expected."

Helpful to the climate of honesty and openness is a willingness to look at mistakes, admit to them, and work to keep them from occurring in the future. Here the leader can do things that have quite an impact in creating this willingness. Douglas Danforth, of Westinghouse, explains the value of openness. "I do that with the board of directors. When I make a mistake, I tell them I made a mistake. They love it. And they are more supportive of me than if I tried to hide it. I clearly think it's a much better policy. And you sleep better! You really do."

The way to face every experience is to see it as a lesson. As thinking beings, humans have the powerful capacity to make every experience one from which they can learn something, not merely as an isolated experience but as part of a learning process in which they are engaged as long as they live. Robert Kilpatrick explains a system they find beneficial at Cigna: "Sometimes I find we erred, most often unintentionally, but we do err. [We have a] kind of process here I think is part of our tradition when we are doing a postmortem on most anything. I have a requirement. I want to see, What lessons did we learn? It can be something that went wrong, or it can be something that went very well. I can't tolerate someone who will try to cover up a mistake. If someone has admitted to a mistake and made an admission that he's going to do something better, I don't criticize beyond that point. I don't probe beyond that point." The end of the matter is this. We stand to enrich our minds and our lives by regularly asking ourselves this question: What have I learned from my mistakes?

Candor and iron-tough honesty in examining events and expressing thoughts enable discussion to be deep and productive. Politeness ought surely be observed, as discussants explore for realities and search for fruitful insights. Ideas that conflict with long-held beliefs are unsettling, and their expression can seem offensive. But to overlook these ideas or to sweep them aside to spare another's feelings is unethical because it means refusing to give one's best efforts in the pursuit of truth. Richard E. Heckert, of Du Pont, tells us, "There are lots of situations where we have to be pretty brutal with each other when we're facing up to reality." Ted J. Saenger, of Pacific Bell, adds more to this point: "You can't have quality thinking if you have sloppy thinking. You can't have quality thinking if you . . . lack pretty good candor. . . . If you're willing to accept sloppy, surface kinds of thinking, then you're willing to accept some greater inaccuracies as you go forward, and that's unethical."

It is important, obviously, to discuss and examine issues and ideas carefully and thoroughly. But sooner or later a judgment is called for. Once the thinking is done, a decision must be made. There are times when all the evidence points in one direction and yet the answer sheer logic presents just does not feel right. We ought to recognize the value of what our instincts can offer. Using *only* one's feelings and instincts without careful, deliberate thinking is foolish. But it can also be very silly to neglect our intuitive side. Paul F. Oreffice, of Dow Chemical, recollects a situation that illustrates this point. At the time of the incident, Oreffice was president of one of Dow's operating divisions. He received a telephone call from the president of another division within the Dow organization. "I wasn't his supervisor or anything. He just wanted to talk to somebody else. He said, 'Paul, this is occurring in one of our countries. Here are the things they want us to do in order to be able to get all this business. You know, on paper, it's not even unethical, but it doesn't pass my personal smell test. It could be justified on paper. I just need to talk to somebody. Am I exaggerating? Some of my people say I'm exaggerating. It doesn't smell right to me.' He described the thing to me, and I said, 'Bob, it doesn't smell right to me either.' He said, 'Thank you. I just needed to talk to somebody.' He turned the whole thing down."

KEEPING MINDS ALIVE

The "machinery" necessary to perform first-rate thinking is a first-rate mind. Such an instrument needs to be cultivated, perfected, and kept in tune through constant use and challenging exercises. It can grow weak and flaccid through disuse; it will atrophy if kept from regular exercise. We are reminded by Samuel Johnson that curiosity is a characteristic of a vigorous intellect. We are curious to the extent that we are willing to face squarely what we do not know and struggle to learn something in order to fill that void. It is easy to understand how an unhealthy ego can get in the way of this admission of ignorance.

Not surprisingly, those who are the most successful have a tendency to work at the learning process—they are curious. Douglas Danforth, of Westinghouse, suggests that all people, particularly young men and women early in their careers, work at being curious. "Have a curiosity about what's around you," advises Danforth. "In the business world, if you start out in engineering, have a curiosity about marketing, about manufacturing, about finance. Don't let yourself stay just within your own envelope or your own discipline. Because people are very willing to share their knowledge and experience, the most flattering thing you can do is to ask, 'Tell me a little about what you do in marketing. I don't understand anything about it. Would you mind having lunch with me, or if I stopped by after work, would you chat with me? Could I make a trip when you call on a customer? I've never sold anything.' I really believe that helped me, because I did have a curiosity. I started in manufacturing. I was curious about the marketing side and finance. I've had a great interest in finance. It's incredible what you can learn just by demonstrating a bit of curiosity." At the core of curiosity is humility. Socrates expressed his humility toward learning when he said, "I neither know nor think that I know."[8] The important lesson to be grasped here is this: It is humility that allows one to escape the bonds which prevent him from admitting his own ignorance thereby freeing him to open his mind to learning.

It is tragic when a person dies mentally while he still lives. We are challenged to avoid this tragedy by keeping ourselves mentally active and our minds alive and growing. We are all vulnerable to rigidity and narrowness of thought and action, mental deterioration, and eventual stagnation. Even the best of us can permit ourselves to become obsolete. Unwanted and unnoticed forces are at work daily, pushing us in this direction—unthinking habit, fear of failure, doing just enough to survive, the procrastination, exclusive reliance on old solutions and methods, avoidance of opportunities and new endeavors because they seem too complex or difficult, unchanging routine void of new experience, and the attitude, "I already know enough to get by." Hearts and minds not exposed to novelty will die prematurely. Through self-renewal—a process of regeneration to keep our minds alive and growing—we can avoid this mental decline and death. There are many ways—new experiences, new hobbies, travel, new friends and acquaintances, continuing education, an so on. The aim should always be in view and pursued deliberately and conscientiously: to avoid mental and emotional death through ongoing learning and new experiences. This will enable us to live richer, fuller, more productive, and more satisfying lives.[9]

II
TO ASPIRE NOBLY

5

Living a Big Life

The chief tragedy in most lives is not dying, but making small what clearly could be made large. People all too frequently fill their minds with trifling matters, neglect opportunities, pursue insignificant purposes, and please themselves most with things of little importance or merit. In many small and uncaring ways, many people allow their lives to trickle by and count for very little. Many people spend their time doing things of minimal consequence; they never truly live for anything worthwhile at all. Many people don't live big lives; they live little lives.[1]

REGARDING ONESELF HIGHLY

What a man thinks of himself is reflected in what he does to himself and what he does for others. A salesman is passed over for a promotion he thought he should get, and that evening he stops at a tavern on his way home from work and drinks himself into a silly stupor to ease his disappointment. The office manager has had a grueling and frustrating month, with an overload of work, nagging and demanding superiors, and a surly and irresponsible staff. At her wit's end, she hurries off with her monthly paycheck and enjoys her Friday evening buying herself "rewards" at the nicest shops and stores in town. At 35 years of age, the superstar of the organization, the one spotted by top management a dozen years earlier as an up and comer and given every opportunity and "plum," has just been made vice president, with a salary and perquisites befitting the position. A few days later this person trades in a current-model, American-built automobile to buy a $90,000 European luxury sedan as a sign of having arrived. Unable to face the ups and downs that life presents by relying on their inner resources, people daily treat themselves in much the same way as they deal with small children. They ply themselves with rewards to recognize life's triumphs or pamper themselves to ease its pains.

Life becomes ruined or rich, depending upon what it is that one chooses to pursue. There are objects that glisten and substances or sensations that anesthetize the senses. Many a man has made himself blind to the grandeur and depths of what life's experiences offer. The escapist misses much of life's meaning and merely exists, unable to face alone what goes on within himself, tricked by the illusion that he is being spared emotional bumps and bruises. And all along, he languishes in an abyss of meaningless sensations.

It can be inviting to focus one's main concerns in life on little things—the shallow and the frivolous. It is a mark of real character to be dissatisfied with these and, instead, to be consumed with weightier matters—being alive to things of genuine merit. Those who prize life, live it; and this means to experience it in its fullness, learning the hard-to-learn lessons that oftentimes come through painful experiences. Those who take themselves and life reverently, struggle with the many difficult tasks of worthwhile living: trying to perfect their minds and character, trying to find the right ways to live, trying to understand their own significance and what their lives could be, and trying always to put the best things ahead of good things. A society characterized by widespread substance abuse, poor health habits, cheap popular diversions devoid of depth of meaning or beauty, and overreliance on material objects to ease pain or to signal success, is one made up of people who have very low opinions of themselves. A society that exhibits a reliance on situational ethics (where actions are evaluated within a situational context rather than by application of moral principles) as a way, *not* of thinking, but to justify doing anything its members please to do, is composed of people who really do not believe they are capable of struggling competently with difficult choices.

The person who is concerned with his own worth, who recognizes the importance of using wisely the privilege of living, and who therefore has lofty expectations for his life's outcome, is hard to satisfy. It is useful to our discussion here to recognize the difference between conceit and self-esteem. The conceited person thinks of himself as being wonderful and superior to others, but his thoughts do not prompt him to act any differently or any more nobly than the next person. The person with high self-esteem, however, demands a great deal more from himself and from life's possibilities than what the common standard asks.

Self-esteem causes a person to honor himself as a human by demanding the very best from life's possibilities; this is a quality of character not to be disparaged or regarded lightly. Shakespeare helps us think along these lines when he wrote, "Self-love, my liege, is not so vile a sin as self-neglecting."[2] Through being alive to the low, to the little things that appear bright to naive eyes and alluring to facile minds and musical to untrained ears and insistent to wills with little resolve, a person neglects himself. The person who esteems himself little, prefers just to get by; he is easily pleased. This person is dead to what is high, and because of that, his life remains unnecessarily small. The root of the difficulty lies in the failure to find and put the very best things first, ahead of the good.

USEFUL MODELS AND PATTERNS

Ask most college students which actor is married to the hottest rock star at the time, or what is occurring in the story line of a popular soap opera, or how to wear the latest fad in clothing, and they will be able to tell you in more detail than you would expect. But ask those same students how and why Socrates met his death or how one can show that the earth really does revolve around the sun, or ask them to explain current problems and issues of national importance, or ask them practically any question about great literature or art or music, and they stare blankly at you, dumbfounded. Through listening to what most people discuss, anywhere, one cannot escape the conclusion that most of the things they fill their minds with and worry over are little things; their thinking is narrow, shallow, and largely self-centered. Lottery winners on television commercials aimed at getting others to purchase tickets are shown spending their winnings on luxuries that cannot possibly improve their knowledge, their understanding of themselves, or their character.

In their lifetimes, most people never truly experience greatness. Only a very small percentage of the population ever hears or is moved by a great idea. Most people never read a great work of literature. Few ever enjoy, let alone have an elementary understanding of, great art or classical music. Daily, we hear poor speech, wretched grammar, and statements full of ignorance and bigotry spewing from the mouths of common people. Millions of lives that could be changed are never touched or altered by the works and thoughts of the greats—the geniuses and the initiators of movements who have altered the world and made it better because of what they thought, stood for, and did. By putting just a little thought to it, we can easily see that the ordinary person, exposed to a steady barrage of only cheap forms of diversion and entertainment—shows with flimsy story lines and gutter language—has little hope of being raised above mediocrity. Instead of elevating, these pursuits anesthetize. Instead of ennobling, they degrade. And instead of inspiring one to loftier heights, they create despair and cynicism. For less than the price of a dozen albums of current, top-selling hit songs, which will not be listened to five or six years from now, one could purchase a good sampling of inexpensive recordings of the world's most loved symphonies. For less than the cost of a current motion picture show, one can purchase two or three nicely printed copies of great pieces of literature. There are many good things to be experienced and enjoyed; and among the enjoyable are to be found the great, which can enrich any life immeasurably.

The average person in this country has access to vast amounts of knowledge and culture. Through recordings and the written word, anyone can have contact with great people from the past and present. Think of it! With just a little effort one can have contact with the genius of people like Bach, Mozart, Beethoven, Plato, Tolstoy, Shakespeare, Joyce, and Shaw. Through the written word one can choose companions from among the greatest people in history and the greatest minds that have enriched our civilization—companions who can serve as models and give the average person a higher standard for his own life. Through the written word, today's reader can know more about the lives and work of many great people than their contemporaries knew about them. The person who reads selectively can be stirred by the bravery of many of the greatest generals or moved to loftier heights by the acts of kindness, courage, or decency of those who led good lives. Through reading, anyone can fill his mind with an understanding of the wonders of the natural world and how it works. He can learn the sciences and learn about those who have advanced the sciences. And he can learn important lessons from the successes and failures of those who preceded him. All of this and more is available for anyone to have and make a part of his own life. Yet few among us seem to even know that these possibilities exist, and fewer still are moved to do much of anything about it. Indeed, many lives are negligently allowed to dwell on little things, and many minds are filled with matters of little consequence. These folks are never moved to the magnitude of what their lives could be, and they are never likely to become so moved unless they have great models that become important parts of their lives.

In any field one can find greatness to serve as a model to be inspired by and to learn from. These examples or models are not easily spotted, particularly when one is not familiar with greatness because he has rarely been exposed to it. In the popular media, something to which many minds are attracted, great ideas and works of substance and merit are indeed sparse. The emphasis there seems to dwell on the superficial, the sensational, the eye-catching stories and scandals, and not on what expands and uplifts the mind.

It's worth considering what most captures the business person's attention and activates his dominant desires. Wealth, power, profits, and prestige are all familiar concerns, but do they constitute the greatness that occupies the heart of the big life? Advancing and acquiring are far different from building and achieving. Quite often the greatness that does exist in the world of commerce and industry remains hidden beneath the exterior trappings people confuse with success. It is the building of factories and distribution centers; it is the organization of highly effective corporate bodies; it is the discovery, development, and commercial introduction of useful products and services; it is the competent and humane treatment of employees; it is the countless struggles to produce worthwhile and lasting economic benefits. And the exciting truth is that there is no end to the possibilities and what might be accomplished.

REJECTING MEDIOCRITY

The person who seeks greatness and works hard to stand for greatness, often must stand apart from the majority. The ordinary often reject greatness. Mediocrity always feels uneasy in the presence of excellence, because by its mere presence excellence is a standing attack on mediocrity, showing it for what it really is—something small and insignificant. To many people mediocrity is inviting; it is easy and cheap. It seems to calls out to people, saying, "You do not want to be different and stand alone. Come, be like all of us. Fit in and be accepted. Why risk ridicule and failure? Do what we have always done before now and follow the old, sure ways we have always used and nobody will notice you. You will be safe here with us. It is easy."

Mediocrity is a great leveler; it raises up the below average and sinks the above average. It can help to improve the stragglers, but it kills off any hope of major strides forward in human progress. Deliberate mediocrity is a form of destruction to those who might otherwise dare to seek excellence. Mediocrity destroys what could be and what people could become.

In theater the concept of tragedy involves situations in which persons are destroyed by their own character flaws. What a person shapes himself into, his character, is in no small way a consequence of what he has made himself alive to. Mediocrity is the source of a significant flaw: it settles for the second rate. And the tragedy resulting from a second-rate standard is a life that has never fully been awakened to greatness and never experiences the richness and magnitude a big life enjoys.

Mediocrity is easily justified by those who are willing to settle for it, and invariably the justification for mediocre actions boils down to the familiar line, "Everybody else is doing it." And when everybody else is doing it, mediocrity is usually afoot with its mischief, holding people down to living insignificant lives. Everybody may be padding his expense account, or short-changing customers with less than the best products and services, or failing to tell the whole story to regulators and inspectors and customers, or using scare and high-pressure sales techniques to get customers to buy things they do not really need or want. Everybody may be living by these easy standards—everybody but the determined soul who rejects mediocrity to pursue excellence.

This is the person who does not accept the legal standard as the ideal. His standards are higher. In all that he does, he never allows the norm that mediocrity sets to have an influence on his standards and behavior. J. C. Penney wrote, "I believe much tension and dissatisfaction in the world of business arises out of too many people trying to get material gain without giving their best. For example, the clerk who fools his customer, palming off on him some service or article of second-rate value, is, first of all, fooling himself. Second-rate standards never make a first-rate person. The individual who doesn't give what the finer honesty demands—his best—may and, in a measure, sometimes does, succeed; but the success not only falls short of what might be but will be of a kind which collapses under pressure."[3]

When Charles S. Sanford, Jr., became chairman and CEO of Bankers Trust of New York, he explained at a meeting a distinction he saw between being excellent and being a winner. To him, being excellent had certain connotations. Being a winner didn't necessarily carry the same kind of ethical standards that one thinks about as excellent. He stated that one can win by lots of different ways, but if one is the best, and by that, meaning "the best" as measured against the highest ethical standards as well as other standards, then one has achieved excellence.

THE TRAGEDY OF THE UNSEIZED MOMENT

Big lives are characterized by action, by doing the right things when opportunities present themselves. Timidity and humility are markedly different from one another. The humble person realizes how puny he is and places himself at the service of others and of great ideals. But the humble person is not necessarily fearful to act. Timidity, on the other hand, holds one back from doing. The words of kindness or encouragement are never spoken, the reprimand is never issued, the flawed decision or policy is allowed to be implemented, the errors in the report go by unchecked, the inspections are never completed as they should be, the problems are never corrected. These are the omissions caused by timidity. What could be is never caused to be because one is too timid to act when one could act. As a result, the grandeur of life is never realized. The unseized moment passes on and the timid person remains, to merely exist, living a little life. Life is full of opportunities—moments which call out for bold and daring action. Mediocrity and timidity can choke off all that is best and deepest in us until our noble impulses retreat; great opportunities are allowed to pass by, our finer motives go unexpressed. By allowing timidity to prevail, the rich possibilities available are nipped, and the full flower of the big life remains unopened, its full fruit unborn. This is why the big life starts with really living—doing—when the moments of opportunity call for action.

A LOVE FOR THE DIFFICULT

Few people will quarrel with the proposition that success in any field requires honest, hard work. Nothing of any great consequence has ever been accomplished easily and without considerable sacrifice. We are all aware of that. But it can also be difficult to accept the fact that hard work does not guarantee success; it just gives it a good chance to take root. It is not uncommon to find people whining about the fact that their business has failed, or their pet project has gone sour, or a hoped for sale was never made even though they worked extremely hard expecting an agreeable outcome. The mature person recognizes the risks in life. It is unrealistic to expect success or a satisfying outcome to any endeavor we undertake just because we try hard. Work alone is not the only difficulty that one who seeks a big life must be willing to endure. There are also the difficulties of poor timing, bad luck, and superior competition, which can keep even the hardest workers from attaining success.

Practically everyone, if pressed on the issue, will admit that hard work is necessary for success. Yet relatively few folks are known as always willing to give their best efforts in all that they undertake and for extended periods of time. At least three reasons for this unwillingness are immediately observable. First, it is easy to be misled, to some extent, by something we have enjoyed as a blessing: the search for a better way. Although this effort has in fact led to finding better ways and will lead people to discoverstill better ones in the years ahead, it has also put into man's thoughts the belief that no matter what one does, "there must be an easier way of doing it." Whatever it might be that one is doing, he is apt to convince himself that there must be a shortcut, an easier solution, or an effortless and painless path. So there is the tendency to search to find it. Sometimes an easier and better way does exist. Its discovery is a happy occasion. But there might not always be a less difficult path, and when there is none and an easy way of circumventing difficult work cannot be found, the inclination to give up entirely can take control and lead to the easy road, acceptance of the second rate.

Second, when a person is misled by the belief that satisfaction comes from having, he is very apt to love only the fruits of his labors and not his labors themselves. The person who does not deeply enjoy what he does is hard pressed to stick with it during the difficult periods.

Third, the belief that one can get what he wants immediately, whatever it might be, is so appealing that one may not be inclined to question it carefully. To many the thought of having to work several years to get what they truly want is unthinkable. The abundance we enjoy today, in this country, makes it possible to secure loans, make purchases, and begin enjoying at once practically anything we can reasonably imagine. Thus the idea of having to wait many years to achieve a desired result can be difficult for many people to accept. As an illustration, we want to be able to read a book rapidly, to digest its complex ideas and appreciate the beauty of its style all in one or two sittings. Many people fail to appreciate the fact that anything which can be read rapidly is not worth reading. If the subject has any degree of depth it will cause us to think, and thinking of any real merit requires time.

In maturity we know that one's best efforts to perform the difficult never come easily or quickly. A person may have to discipline himself for many years just to develop the skills necessary to perform a complex function or activity. Yet often we hear it said, or perhaps have said ourselves, "I'd never be able to do that, I don't have the patience." The seeds of mediocrity are indeed abundant.

Worthwhile accomplishments demand discipline, hard work, and willingness to give one's best efforts for extended periods. Examination of the lives of practically all the "giants" in every field, from music and the arts to business and the sciences, reveals the importance of discipline and hard work. Great accomplishments are not so much a product of genius but of deliberate and abiding persistence. If one is ever to accomplish something of real significance, it is necessary to develop a taste for the difficult. Love of the difficult is learned through doing the difficult. And through that, one's understanding and values change to recognize what has lasting merit and what does not.

The paths of least resistance, the easy way out and the shortcut, generally produce very little of substance. These are not attempted when one learns to love the difficult. But how can this be reached? There are so many distractions. By taking oneself seriously and through undertaking increasingly difficult endeavors, it is possible to develop the capacity for hard work, for self-discipline, and for making a habit of always giving one's best. The trick lies in paying attention to the excitement found in doing and in developing one's taste for the pleasures found in that activity. It is a good idea to forget about how soon one will be able to enjoy the prizes at the end. This ideal is reached when the challenge of the difficult is genuinely enjoyed. This enjoyment permits one's efforts to be so directed that he can persist with the drudgery often required. Surely the difficult exacts a tremendous toll. A person may tally the cost of the difficult and find it neither cheap nor easy. But before he concludes that he cannot afford the effort and rejects the challenge altogether as too costly, he would be wise to ask himself if he can afford the consequences of not paying the price.

THE COURAGE TO BE AN INDIVIDUAL AND RISK FAILURE

Fear of failure and fear of rejection by others are yet two more results of the poison of excessive self-concern. The higher standard that excellence demands from an individual, to lift him over mediocrity, invariably requires him to adventure into areas unknown and untried. Imagination, courage, and self-confidence are needed. A little thought enables us to realize that the free-enterprise economic system has been abundantly productive, because it has encouraged people to try new methods, to introduce new products, to open up new markets, and to start risk-laden ventures and enterprises. The hope of success, the profit motive, the spirit of adventure, and the desire for self-expression have all enticed the risk takers to act boldly. In the pursuit of excellence and the quest for a higher standard, failure surely abounds, but the courageous refuse to be deterred. And it is courageous people who tend to be the ones leading big lives. A big life, it should be mentioned, is not one of only gigantic successes; many have failures in them too. A big life can risk failure and can live through failures unshaken and ready to try again. The big life is lived for great things, and because of that, it can withstand failures.

THE BIGNESS IN LIVES

Careless thought can lead to the belief that only famous people, those whose names appear in history books or in the popular media, have enjoyed living big lives. Truth compels us to say that fame has very little to do with bigness. In many instances the spotlight of attention is shunned by people living big lives, because those doing big things do them for their real value and not to capture self-serving acclaim.

The ability to live a big life, one that places the best ahead of the good, is not beyond the reach of the ordinary person. We are glad to know that there are many opportunities available to anyone to live such a life. The more one looks outward rather than inward—toward challenges and adventures instead of toward ease and comfort—the more the vision needed to find these opportunities is enhanced. Bigness is usually found when people choose to live by what mankind honors most and holds as its highest virtues—truth, decency, kindness, courage, loyalty, courtesy—instead of merely doing what seems most expedient in order to get something for themselves. It is found whenever they choose the things they can be proud of, the things that last.

Bigness is also found when people spend their time on useful activities and do not waste it on trifling matters. Each person, as we know, has only so much time to spend. And each has relatively few talents. A useful question that each person can address is this: How can my limited time and my few talents best be spent? Smallness in lives arises when time and talents are unwisely spent on the trivial. Bigness in lives is revealed when the person spends all his talents and all his time on what is most worthwhile. This is to say, we see bigness in lives that participate in the world, building, mending, redirecting, adding, and improving the human condition, and are not squandered on the insignificant.

Happenstance alone does not determine the extent to which a life is made rich with enjoyment. The sincere and frequent expression of gratitude, an essential element of a big life, elevates the human experience in at least two ways. It honors and thereby encourages what is good and what provides genuine and lasting satisfaction. And it heightens and enlarges one's capacity to appreciate and enjoy the finest things. Ungrateful hearts, which are frozen and thereby made impenetrable to good, permit smallness to take root. But gratitude makes possible a big life because it magnifies the good and enables the grateful person to enjoy good things in big ways.

As one traces to its source to find the secret of the big life, he is led back to man's heart, where he finds, dominating there, the desire for usefulness. Few lives are fully mastered by negative qualities—cruelty, meanness, destructiveness. And too, those generous servants of mankind, whose hearts are ruled by principle and love, are less abundant than we would all prefer. But between these extremes are to be found many decent persons who have slipped into uselessness. Unknowingly, unthinkingly, and unintentionally they have gone the way of least resistance. It is worth our while to awaken our concern to this matter, for it is indeed a peril of the first rank.

Within every one of the most thrilling stories in the human experience is found usefulness: the driving need to pursue a cause, to mend an ill, to uplift the weak and broken, to add abundance and knowledge to the world—to contribute to the progress and enrichment of mankind. The inspiring accounts of tireless souls who have wrestled with their plight and who have struggled to overcome hardship and handicap show this: these people have triumphed because they directed their best energies toward the service of some useful aim. Every life, if it is to count for something, must be useful, for without this lodestar to guide him man, wanders hopelessly into ruin. Bigness is found in lives that are directed toward the useful. In such lives the desire for usefulness is not a transient element which only appears at moments of convenience or scrutiny. If a person is to amount to anything, usefulness must be a permanent element of his character, and it must rein supreme in his motivations.

6

Standards to Shape Lives and Organizations

In a society that prizes freedom, such as ours, it is helpful to remind one-self what that freedom really means and involves. A raw notion of freedom may lead some to think it means they should be left alone to do just as they please and live their lives as they choose, without restraints. But upon some reflection, most would recognize the fallacy in this concept and arrive at the realization that absolute freedom is impossible. Absolute freedom, left unchecked, inevitably would lead to absolute chaos. To have order and to protect the rights of others, there must always be restraints on each individual's freedoms. The peace and happiness of all concerned require limitations on freedom—the freedom of the individual and the freedom of collective individuals, or the state, must necessarily be placed under some restraints. These ideas are elementary to any student of civics. But the relationship between restraints and freedom goes much deeper than this.

FREEDOM THROUGH DISCIPLINE

Today's view of freedom tends to perceive restraints merely as infringements that place limits on one's actions. The Puritan ideal of the controlled and ordered life, with restraints on self-indulgence and other excesses, has been out of vogue for many generations, and the quality of life it created has been unfairly and inaccurately portrayed. Yet by making some large decisions, Puritans freed themselves from many other problems and from many pestering little decisions.

As one begins to think about the relationship between freedom and restraints, it becomes evident that while restraints may limit some freedoms, they at the same time make other freedoms possible. In fact, an important truth is that freedom is impossible apart from restraint. For example, the desire to run a first-class restaurant makes demands on a person that preclude the freedom to serve chili, french fries, and hot-dogs.

The freedom to be a highly respected public accounting firm is achieved by paying the price of being faithful to the standards of that profession and having all of the firm's employees live up to a high measure of personal honesty and ethical conduct. The simple truth is this: The curtailment of some freedoms creates other freedoms.

By examining freedom from this angle it is easy to see that one's freedom *to* do certain things exists only to the extent that one is free *from* other things. A person's freedom to become an admired leader is made possible only to the extent that that person is free *from* caving in to unsavory actions, which although they might return immediate results, would strike a blow at decency and honorable business dealings and hence ruin his standing in the eyes of others. The biggest force that visits people to intrude upon their *freedom to* is their own pressing whims and fancies—their appetites.

Man's chief battle is with himself. To achieve the *freedom to do* what he truly wants to do and to become what his best talents and potentialities permit, a person needs to discipline himself. In a great many cases this begins with a disciplined approach to living that enables him to say no and thus become *free from* the tyranny of his ruinous appetites. Freedom is far from saying yes to whatever may entice us at a given moment. Even the most able may cancel the hope of ever reaching those goals within reach of his abilities and worthy of what intelligent people would feel proud to honor and aspire toward. Many a life rich in possibilities has failed to blossom fully, because it was impoverished in the realm of discipline. The trick lies in saying yes to, and thereby becoming mastered by, the right urges—a challenge met best by first freeing one's self from what leads away from the worthwhile. It starts when we say no to debilitating impulses in order to be free to answer ennobling ones. Scarcely more than superficial observation is needed to see that unbridled appetites and whims cut away the possibility of living an ordered life and place a person into a state of bondage from unwanted controlling forces. The man who cannot restrain his appetites is far from free, but under their awful bondage.

The feat any person must achieve in order to escape this self-bondage is to make one great decision: to give his loyalty to the authentic standards and principles that dignify life. And he must discipline himself to pursue these standards without compromise. J. C. Penney, in writing on this idea, explained why the disciplined are free. "People who put themselves under the discipline of great principles and conscientious practices," he wrote, "go far in liberating themselves from the pitfalls of haphazard or inferior standards. They do not have to stop so often to patch up the road, so to speak, but can proceed straight ahead on a wide way. Lack of discipline can be very costly in wasted time and effort."[1] This is to say that the recognized standards of morality and virtue that society honors are such because they have passed tests of experience in billions of lives and have demonstrated themselves as reliable guides for reaching human fulfillment.

Those who adhere to these standards are not so much restrained as they are made free; they are freed from the ill-habits and terrible troubles neglect of these standards brings. By making large decisions, a person can free himself from both the pestering of his many little whims and appetites and the problem of having to decide anew, every day, every little question, which would make an ordered and productive life impossible. Viewed from this perspective it becomes evident that those who are the most disciplined are really the most free.

Disciplined lives are generally admired; they do not escape the notice of others. "Those that are successful," comments Joseph L. Jones, of Armstrong World Industries, "have managed to discipline themselves over a lifetime, and those that can't give up that extra drink or whatever seem to fail. . . . I think that if [people] lead a disciplined life and they, indeed, do follow the tenets of good taste in their action, I think they are admired by others. Even some of those who can't discipline themselves will still admire that in someone else and therefore, I think that these people emerge as leaders."

That a cultivated, high standard of values is crucial to one's success in organizations, is widely recognized among business leaders. "The quality of the personal values that you exhibit," says John H. Bryan, Jr., of Sara Lee, "is far and away the most important determinant of your success. In my business, I watch the success and failure of hundreds of people: those who get promoted, those who don't. Clearly, it is the character possessed by a person that is the most distinguishing trait which makes for success."

STABILITY FROM STANDARDS

Many observers of the business scene have read of or are immediately familiar with a pathetic scenario that is played out over and over. Someone in the business world, someone perhaps in a known organization and otherwise enjoying a successful career, is disgraced, convicted of a white-collar crime. It's a scandal. The person will lose his job. His family is disgraced. There is an embarrassed company, lawsuits for damages, and a prison term for the wrongdoer. For this person the pressures were too great. The temptation for quick riches was too strong, and the level of personal ambition was too high. It was simply too much for the person to bear.

A tree, like a human life, combines two elements. As we look at its base we first notice a solid trunk that shoots skyward. As we lift our eyes, our gaze includes its branches, which reach upward and outward. And from these grow shoots and leaves exposed to the elements nature hurls its way. Many a tree, under pressure from the forces that blow, has been known to come crashing to the ground. The destruction is caused not from the strength of what can be seen but from the insufficiency of what cannot. And so it is with each human life. Each needs a strong foundation to hold it solidly upright, unaffected by the external pressures and temptations that cause the less resolute to eventually crash. Disciplined lives, rooted in stabilizing standards and guided through the labyrinth of complicating circumstances by clear thinking, have a good chance of standing tall in the winds that uproot the weak and the confused. To that end, many people have devoted their efforts to developing systems of standards for individual and organizational conduct and elaborate guides to enable themselves and others to make better choices.

PRINCIPLES, RULES, AND CODES OF CONDUCT

Practically all major corporate bodies have rules, principles or codes of ethics. Although some firms have recently adopted or updated their policies relating to ethical conduct, these efforts are not new for the majority of the country's largest and best known organizations.

It is difficult to classify or categorize the myriad of ethical guides and codes of conduct. Each firm has its own unique approach. By and large, however, these codes and guides are published in the form of a folder or pamphlet and distributed to all members of the organization. A firm may have several types of statements. These documents represent many hours of serious effort by many capable people, and they are not lightly regarded. The codes of conduct, sets of rules, and ethics statements found in industry today can be categorized as follows:

1. Professional and trade association codes and standards;

2. General statements of principles, values, or ethical standards;

3. Statements of intentions to serve or to be responsible to various constituents;

4. Detailed guidelines for business conduct; or

5. Answers to commonly encountered questions employees face in situations having ethical dimensions.

PROFESSIONAL AND TRADE ASSOCIATION CODES AND STANDARDS

What might be surprising to today's readers is that codes of ethics are nothing new. Edgar L. Heermance compiled and published, in 1924, a handbook of codes of ethics. It listed the codes of about a hundred professional and trade associations that had been adopted between 1900 and 1924.

NATIONAL SCHOOL SUPPLY ASSOCIATION
Code of Ethics
Adopted 1920

The members of the National School Supply Association, ever mindful of their slogan: "Service to the School Children of America," pledge their best efforts:

1. To recognize in the American school child "the seed corn of the nation," and to keep the welfare of the child first and foremost in the conduct of our business.

2. To produce and sell the highest quality of school merchandise, believing this to be a fundamental demand of education in a Republic in which the education of all citizens is of paramount importance.

3. To so conduct every business transaction that school authorities will recognize and appreciate the superior service rendered schools by the members of this Association.

4. To accept the principle that the school buyer is guided by the same motives as the seller, urging that all disputes be submitted to the Appeals and Grievances Committee of the Association for the final satisfaction of the customer.

5. To welcome fair competition as an assurance of the largest opportunity for service to school authorities, making service and the adaptability of goods rather than price the basis of preference.

6. To train salesmen to be more than mere bid-fillers or order-takers, and to recognize the vital principle of truth and personal service to the teachers and pupils who will use the goods.

7. To carry stocks of merchandise sufficient to give prompt and satisfactory service so that at no time in the year a pupil shall be hampered in educational progress through lack of materials or equipment.

8. To base all selling prices on the cost of production and selling, allowing only a legitimate profit as related to the investment in the business.

9. To be constantly on the alert to find better merchandise and better methods so as to keep the American schools at all times fully abreast of the progress in all fundamentals of education.

10. To follow sound ethical principles in the conduct of our business, and to put every transaction on the very highest plane of business honor.

Code of Business Practices

1. Do unto others as you would have them do unto you.

2. Do not make false or disparaging statements respecting competitor's products, his business, financial credit, etc.

3. Do not harass competitors by fake requests for estimates on bills of goods, for catalogs, etc.

4. Do not sell goods at or below cost, as "leaders," coupled with statements misleading the public into the belief that they were sold at a profit by reason of the seller's superior facilities.

5. Do not use the samples or reputation of one manufacturer for the purpose of getting an order and fill it with similar goods made by another manufacturer.

6. Regardless of reported actions of competitors the facts should be ascertained before acting upon reports or inferences that would cast suspicion upon a fellow member.

7. Make no deductions, rebates or discounts which would camouflage the contents or amount of a contract unless plainly stated on the face of the bid and invoice when shipment is made.

8. Any member of this Association convicted of a violation of school laws of the territory in which he operates is automatically expelled from membership in the Association.

9. Any member of the Association who influences the cancellation of a contract already taken in good faith by another member of the Association and who profits by the cancellation, shall be subject to an investigation on the part of the Appeals and Grievances Committee if the party injured so desires, and findings of the Appeals and Grievances Committee shall be final.

10. The members of this Association are responsible for the merchandising methods for all acts or activities on the part of their salesmen in the field.

11. To discourage advertising of an unfair, misleading or demoralizing nature.

12. To aid every legitimate effort to elevate the standing of the school supply business in the eyes of buyers and sellers, to uphold the prestige of the National School Supply Association, and to make prompt report to the Business director of any established violation of this Code of Business Practices and any subsequent additions thereto,

whether by a member of the Association or by another, thus to make good our slogan: "Service to the School Children of America."

PUBLIC UTILITIES ADVERTISING ASSOCIATION
Standards of Practice
Adopted December 18, 1923

Realizing our obligation and responsibility to the public, to the seller of advertising service, the advertising agent and our own organization, we, as public utility advertisers, pledge ourselves as follows:

1. To consider the interests of the public foremost, and particularly that portion thereof which we serve;

2. To claim no more, but if anything, a little less, in our advertising, than we can deliver;

3. To refrain from statements in our advertising, which, through actual misrepresentation, through ambiguity or through incompleteness, are likely to be misleading to the public, or unjust to competitors;

4. To use every possible means, not only in our own individual advertising, but by association and co-operation, to increase the public's confidence in advertised statements;

5. To refrain from attacking competitors in our advertising;

6. To refrain from imposing upon the seller of advertising service unjust, unreasonable and unnecessarily irksome requirements;

7. To furnish to publishers, when requested, technical information which will help them keep reading pages and advertising columns free from mis-statements;

8. To refrain from and discourage deceptive or coercive methods in securing free advertising, and to do everything possible to aid the publisher to keep his columns free and independent;

9. To require standards for ourselves equal to those we set for others;

10. To stand unequivocally for "Truth in Advertising."

GENERAL STATEMENTS OF PRINCIPLES, VALUES, OR ETHICAL STANDARDS

These are broadly stated platitudes. They are usually less than one page in length. The contemporary samples shown below are typical.

ARMSTRONG WORLD INDUSTRIES, INC.

Principles

1. To respect the dignity and inherent rights of the individual human being in all dealings with people.

2. To maintain high moral and ethical standards and to reflect honesty, integrity, reliability and forthrightness in all relationships.

3. To reflect the tenets of good taste and common courtesy in all attitudes, words and deeds.
4. To serve fairly and in proper balance the interests of all groups associated with the business—customers, stockholders, employees, suppliers, community neighbors, government and the general public.

McDONNELL DOUGLAS
Code of Ethics

Integrity and ethics exist in the individual or they do not exist at all. They must be upheld by individuals or they are not upheld at all. In order for integrity and ethics to be characteristics of McDonnell Douglas, we who make up the Corporation must strive to be:

1. Honest and trustworthy in all our relationships;
2. Reliable in carrying out assignments and responsibilities;
3. Truthful and accurate in what we say and write;
4. Cooperative and constructive in all work undertaken;
5. Fair and considerate in our treatment of fellow employees, customers, and all other persons;
6. Law abiding in all our activities;
7. Committed to accomplishing all tasks in a superior way;
8. Economical in utilizing company resources; and
9. Dedicated in service to our company and to improvement of the quality of life in the world in which we live.

Integrity and high standards of ethics require hard work, courage, and difficult choices. Consultation among employees, top management, and the Board of Directors will sometimes be necessary to determine a proper course of action. Integrity and ethics may sometimes require us to forgo business opportunities. In the long run, however, we will be better served by doing what is right rather than what is expedient.

SHOPSMITH, INC.
Corporate Philosophy

1. Treat other people with the utmost respect and courtesy.

2. Maintain company-wide dedication to the optimum of customer service and satisfaction.

3. Maintain the highest possible moral standards within the organization and in all our relations with the outside world.

4. Undertake only those endeavors we can accomplish in a competent and professional manner.

5. Maintain total corporate commitment to growth.

JAMES RIVER CORPORATION
Fundamental Values/Beliefs

Ethics Highest standards of integrity, ethics, and fairness must override in all transactions and relationships.

Finding a Better Way The most important corporate management priority is sustaining a system of values or corporate culture that reflects a company-wide commitment to: exploring uniquely cost effective approaches to problems and opportunities; a willingness to experiment and to take calculated risks; developing and implementing winning strategies; and excellence in individual performance.

Value to Customer Sustaining superior financial performance in a manufacturing company requires that the primary thrust of the entire organization be directed toward providing superior value to its customers.

Involvement Maximum productivity and job satisfaction for all employees can be realized by providing opportunities to participate in decision making, by offering opportunities to assume responsibility commensurate with ability, by providing visible recognition for group and individual achievement, and by creating an atmosphere of openness and trust.
Ownership Employees should be provided an opportunity to share in the financial success of the Company through stock ownership and profit sharing.

Jobs First The Corporation can make the most effective social contribution by creating and maintaining secure, safe and productive jobs.

Profit Orientation A strong and pervasive profit orientation and understanding should be maintained and reinforced.

Independence Corporate independence, consistent with shareholders' interest, provides the best means to sustain these values/beliefs.

STATEMENTS OF INTENTIONS TO SERVE AND BE RESPONSIBLE TO VARIOUS CONSTITUENTS

These statements indicate clearly the fact that corporations exist to benefit not just one interest group. In fact, in many of the documents found in this category, the idea is expressed that the corporation exists at the pleasure of society and that its success is largely determined by the degree to which it meets the expectations of its several constituents. The examples below show what a few companies see as their constituents.

SECURITY PACIFIC CORPORATION
Fulfilling Six Commitments.

-To customer
-To employee
-Of employee to Security Pacific
-Of employee to employee
-To communities
-To stockholder

MONSANTO

Objectives and Policy Guidelines
-Customer Objective
-Employee Relations Objective
-Social Responsibility Objective
-Shareowner Objective

PROCTER & GAMBLE

P & G's Beliefs about Responsibility
-To Consumers
-To Customers and Suppliers
-To Employees
-To Shareholders
-To Society

DETAILED GUIDELINES FOR BUSINESS CONDUCT

Guidelines for business conduct are generally published in the form of booklets between 15 and 50 pages in length. They go into rather specific detail regarding what is and what is not permitted by law and by company policy. The content of a company's business conduct guidelines or code of ethics depends, of course, to a large measure on the nature of its business and the sorts of issues, questions, and temptations company personnel face. The general areas covered include such things as the protection of company assets, including proprietary information; how business will be conducted, including what practices are fair or unfair and legal or illegal; what employees may or may not do on their own time insofar as political activity and outside business interests are concerned; and general points of law the employees may run up against as they discharge their duties and responsibilities.

ALCOA
Policy Guidelines for Business Conduct

-Proper Standards of Conduct in Business Transactions
-Freedom from Conflicting Interests
-Complying with Antitrust Laws
-Purchasing
-Product Safety and Reliability
-Equal Employment Opportunity
-Accident and Injury Prevention
-Industrial Hygiene Protection
-Environmental Protection
-Public Affairs

FMC
Code of Ethics

-Responsibilities
-Conflict of Interest
-Relationships with Customers, Suppliers and
    Contractors
-Antitrust
-International Business
-Protecting FMC Assets
-Intangible Assets
-Information Gathering for Business Intelligence
-Accuracy of Company Records
-Employee Relationships
-Product Quality and Safety
-Employee Safety
-Substance and Alcohol Abuse

-Environmental Protection
-Government and Public Affairs
-The Ethics Oversight and Violation Reporting
-Compliance and Discipline
-Management Responsibility
-Additional Requirements Mandated by
      •Government Contracts
      •Commitment Statement
      •Truthful Reporting of Information
      •Gifts and Entertainment; Illegal Practices, Payments, Bribes
        and Gratuities
      •Former Government Employees
      •Protection of FMC and Government Property:
        Cost Consciousness

FIRESTONE
Guidelines for Business Conduct

Conflicts of Interest
   •Speculation in the company securities and use of inside
    information
   •Personal financial interest
   •Outside employment and activities
   •Disclosure is always the key
Competitive Practices
Dealings with Suppliers and Customers
   •Reciprocity
   •Kickbacks and rebates
   •Receipt of gifts, gratuities and entertainment
   •Dealings with customers and potential customers
Dealings with Public Officials
Political Activities and Contributions
Government Inquiries
The Handling of Confidential or Proprietary Information
Integrity of Records and Financial Reports
Use of Agents and Non-Employees
Other Personnel Policies

HILTON HOTEL CORPORATION
Code of Conduct

Legal and Ethical Practices/General
Conflicts of Interest
Gifts
Disclosure of Private Information
Using Private Information or Company Position for

Private Gain
Political Contributions
Annual Questionnaires
Discipline

ANSWERS TO ETHICAL QUESTIONS

Answers to commonly encountered questions employees face in situations having a large ethical dimension may be printed in the form of questions and answers. For example, McDonnell Douglas published a 32-page manual of questions and answers covering topics such as how to record, allocate, and charge costs on government contracts, how to avoid conflicts of interest; maintain product quality; and handle customer, subcontractor, and supplier relationships. It tells employees where to go and who to contact if they have any questions, doubts, or concerns. And they are advised, "If you would not feel comfortable talking with any of these people [in the normal channels and chain of command], you should get in touch with the Ombudsman or other designated official in your component, or if you feel it necessary, with the Corporate Ombudsman." Hilton Hotels Corporation, as another example, publishes a form letter for employees to use in order to refuse or return gifts, which are, of course, prohibited by company policy.

The Boeing Company publishes a 20-page pamphlet entitled "Business Conduct Guidelines," which summarizes corporate policies, (regarding such matters as conflict of interest; acceptance of business courtesies; and use of company time, materials, equipment, and proprietary information) and answers common questions employees have in these areas and the corporate policy answer to them. Examples are:

Question: It is the holiday season and I have just received at home a 10-pound box of prime steaks from a supplier with a card that says "Merry Christmas." May I keep the steaks?

Answer: No. Return the steaks to the donor or send them to the corporate vice president of industrial relations for donation to a food bank. A polite thank you letter and explanation of Company policy on accepting business courtesies of appreciable value would be appropriate.

Question: I have just received a copy of a competitor's proposal in the mail from an unknown source. What do I do with it?

Answer: Immediately contact your supervisor and the senior manager in charge of the company's proposal efforts and turn the proposal over to them to decide what to do with it. You may also need to seek advice from your operating company ethics coordinator to determine what steps should be taken. Proper intelligence gathering is a legitimate marketing strategy, but use of apparently proprietary information received from unknown sources is never an approved activity.

Question: I have access to a company truck which is not currently being used, and want to use it to move my furniture to a new apartment. I plan to pay for the gas I use. Is this in violation of Company policy?

Answer: Yes, it is a violation of Company policy. Use of Company property for personal reasons is clearly a violation of Company policy.

Question: I am active in my local school district and volunteer my time and effort to improve the quality of education for the residents of my district. An important levy is on the ballot and I am actively campaigning for its passage. May I use Company reproduction equipment to make copies of information in support of the issue so that my neighbors will be informed?

Answer: It is Company policy to encourage its employees to participate in the political process and to be active in the community. However, the use of Company reproduction equipment for this purpose would be a violation of Company policy unless approved by the corporate office of public affairs and the management of the Company.

Boeing's brochure also contains "Questions to Ask Yourself" for its employees to raise in their minds when deciding what to do. For instance, in the area of acceptance of business courtesies, employees are encouraged to ask themselves:

Will my fellow employees wonder if my business decisions were influenced by the acceptance of a business courtesy?

Will other vendors, suppliers or customers feel an obligation to provide similar business courtesies to me in order to obtain Company business?

Am I trying to justify accepting a business courtesy by arguing, "Everybody else does it," "I deserve a break today," "No one will ever find out?

ETHICAL GUIDES FOR MAKING DECISIONS

Moral philosophers have struggled with the challenge of finding standards and methods for making ethical decisions. Much has been written on these matters, which attests to the importance people have placed on the need to act ethically. Entire volumes have been devoted to categorizing, summarizing, and explaining each of the many ethical decision-making theories. Some guides for ethical decision making, like the Golden Rule and Kant's categorical imperative, are fairly straight-forward and within the grasp of the ordinary person to understand and follow.

But much more elaborate schemes have also been proposed; these are quite difficult to understand and apply. One of the major snags we run into as we try to find a *perfect* guide for ethical decision making is that it becomes complex and beyond the grasp and practical use of the ordinary person. The emphasis of many of these complex systems tends to be more on making the most ethical choice than it is on improving the person who makes the decision. These ethical decision-making guides appeal more to a person's mind and his reasoning ability than they do to his heart. Whenever a person is motivated merely to make himself flawless, his self-serving urges can crowd out finer impulses and his quest for the betterment of the human condition can easily become lost or ignored.

The principles, standards, decision-making guidelines, and codes of conduct found in industry as well as other places are generally sound, logically speaking. They can be useful in saving people from making serious mistakes and for protecting the rights and interests of everyone concerned. But unless a person sees to it that he *is* the kind of person within, whose heart and feelings embrace the ideals that ethical standards and decisions attempt to advance, very little of significance will be realized.

In considering the merits of any decision-making guide, it is important to be concerned with its impact on both the decisions made and the decision makers themselves. The kinds of decisions a person makes are really a product of the kind of person he is—what he lives for. The beauty of the Golden Rule is that it is not just a mechanical decision making guide but a natural expression of human love for other people. Kant's categorical imperative is a natural outgrowth of the idea and feeling that no one is above the laws of decency and right and wrong and therefore one should never make an exception to these standards for his own convenience.

IMPROVING THE SELF

A great adventure that each person is capable of making successful is the one of building himself into the person he might become. That humans have the ability to change and improve themselves is truly remarkable. It separates us from all other creatures as the only one that can consciously be a part of the process of shaping itself. This can be a grand and noble undertaking. And through the process, the shaper himself is truly more human, for he is exercising his wonderful powers of choice and self-direction. What nature starts, the human creature can complete. The discussion here may well begin with this optimistic yet challenging proposition: If one worked as hard perfecting himself as he did on succeeding at his career, he would truly become a wonderful person.

At the root of the process of perfecting oneself is honesty and self-control. These are essential in forming the habits that mold and define each person. Anyone who has read Benjamin Franklin's autobiography will recall the moral code of 13 virtues he set and worked to cultivate. It is revealing of today's standards to compare Franklin's ideals with the qualities that popular self-help books now claim to be important. Franklin's ideals were temperance, silence, order, resolution, frugality, industry, sincerity, justice, moderation, cleanliness, tranquillity, chastity, and humility. Clearly these are poles apart from current-day buzz words and expressions like "one-upsmanship," "looking out for number one" and "assertiveness," which have captured considerable public following.

Dr. Franklin knew that the trick in making these virtues a part of his character was to acquire the habit of displaying each. Hence he had a little book with a page for each virtue and columns arranged for the days of the week. He would give himself marks for success or failure in living up to each virtue, a remarkable example of self-discipline through the watchful control of one's own behavior.

In more recent times, in his book, *Be My Guest*, Conrad N. Hilton described ten ingredients that he believed lead to successful living. In his essay "There is an Art to Living," Hilton raised the question, "What is this thing—success?" and then explained his ten ingredients; these being:

1. Find your own particular talent.
2. Be big: Think big. Act big. Dream big.
3. Be honest.
4. Live with enthusiasm.
5. Don't let your possessions possess you.
6. Don't worry about your problems.
7. Don't cling to the past.
8. Look up to people when you can—down to no one.
9. Assume your full share of responsibility for the world in which you live.
10. Pray consistently and confidently.

The influence that habits have on forming a person's character ought not to be overlooked or underestimated. Benjamin Franklin was strongly of this opinion; his approach to perfecting himself centered largely on the formation of habits. He was in good company in his thinking: Aristotle held a similar view. In his *Nicomachean Ethics*, Aristotle emphasized the connection between consistent moral actions—that is, habits—and the kind of person who is capable of taking these actions because of his settled and efficacious disposition toward acting morally. It was Aristotle's belief that a person habituated to desiring and acting well, seldom has to reflect at great length about the possible choices that are available to him; the evil or wrong ones have already been dismissed. He does not act mechanically and without thought; the thinking has already been done. By reaching a high level of moral excellence through his good habits, it was Aristotle's view that a man could move through life making many decisions having ethical dimensions spontaneously and without undue effort. It was his belief that a key to making good choices consistently is a permanent commitment to living rightly.

Ethical actions are most likely to spring from a character thus constituted—one that is firm and stable. Reuben Mark, of Colgate-Palmolive, a stickler for paying attention to minute details, believes that even the so-called little things are really big things if there are ethical overtones. For instance, he pays for all personal telephone calls made from his office. In Mark's words, "It becomes more and more important that you not deviate from the pattern yourself." This is because good habits become self-reinforcing. In reality we may be more of a product of the many little things we do than of the few big ones we tend to remember most.

A man's reputation is largely a product of what he has put into the minds and eyes of others by his actions. And that is more a product of many little things than of just a few unusual or irregular ones. An important point worthy of our attention here is this: People usually are not overly aware of the little things they do in their lives on a regular basis— their habits. Yet habits add up to create the kind of person one is. R. Gordon McGovern, of Campbell Soup, says, "It's the accumulation of the small things over time that add up to [one's] reputation, . . . that is, something that is constructed by small increments over time."

Some habits, and therefore parts of a person's character, are developed early on in life. The value of good parents and their active role in the parenting process is crucial to stable and intelligent youth. In the case of John D. Rockefeller, "his parents taught him to keep strict account of all money which passed through his hands, and to make regular donations to the church and the poor from his meager boyhood earnings. It was the combination of habits and attitudes instilled by early training with the opportunity afforded by the old system when it was possible for an individual to accumulate such wealth which led to his success."[2]

But the process does not stop there because intelligent adults realize the need to continually work at the process of self-improvement. Sanford N. McDonnell, of McDonnell Douglas, believes that people can change, if they really want to, no matter how old they are. "I can tell you that since I started this [company ethics training] program," says McDonnell, "I feel I am more ethical than when I started it. I started it because, basically, I thought it was just a good idea. But the more I got into it the more I could see where I could do things [differently]. My thinking [and] my behavior [were] uplifted by conscientiously getting in and asking, 'What does this all mean and how does it apply and what do we mean by ethics?' "

THE EVILS OF PERFECTIONISM

As individuals work to perfect their lives and perform useful service in the world, the perils of perfectionism ought to be recognized. We know from experience that people will not live perfect lives, but they are capable of living extremely useful lives. We can see the sense and value of working toward perfection, but we can see also the need to be realistic in our standards. A little thought allows us to realize that not only is it unrealistic to believe we can achieve perfection in our lives, but also it is unwise to give all of our best efforts toward perfecting ourselves.

A more sensible aim is to live a useful life—one that is productive and counts for something large. Although the pursuit of perfection is laudable, there is danger in allowing this pursuit to go unchecked. To the perfectionist nothing is ever quite good enough; anything less than flawlessness is intolerable. Many conscientious people work toward perfection but are fortunate enough to have a healthy amount of realism and will accept something less than flawlessness in their tasks. But perfectionists never seem to know when to call a halt to their efforts, no matter what it is they are working on. Always unsatisfied with what has been achieved, they continue on with their efforts, devoting additional time, worry, energy, and resources to creating the state of perfection they so eagerly desire. If their object is to work to perfect themselves, they run the risk of becoming self-obsessed and critical to the point of self destruction. If they lack optimism they may fail even to try, or they may give up trying early on, saying that the entire endeavor is a lost cause.

Among the many evils of perfectionism stand two inviting temptations: (1) to lower one's standards and (2) to become hopelessly embroiled in rigid, legalistic adherence to a body of rules. Without a good measure of humility, that is, when the ego is so fragile it cannot tolerate blame and a sense of imperfection, perfectionism is quite likely to occur, and a lessening of ideals or a legalistic rule-mentality are likely to take hold of a person's loyalties. There are lofty ideals to work toward, and a person can work toward these wholeheartedly so long as his humility permits him to take a full accounting of his many imperfections.

The flawless life, when it is reached by adhering to lowered standards or to legalistic systems of rules, is never so grand as the one full of bold, though imperfect, struggle to reach the larger ideals the rules are really aimed at advancing in the first place. The virtue of humility is much more than a nice-sounding ideal; it is a necessary element if one is to continually *reach for* the highest goals. Humility enables one to weather the acknowledgment of mistakes and shortcomings without being blown off the course toward great and useful ends.

The perfectionist stands a good likelihood of leading a miserable and unproductive life. Perfectionism frequently causes scarce resources—time, talent, energy, and the like—to be spent unwisely and toward polishing things which are already good enough and quite useful. For this reason alone perfectionism is really wasteful; it uses scarce resources where they are really not most needed. Moreover, our experiences show us that the joy and sense of fulfillment that an ordinary, healthy individual derives from a worthwhile enterprise is never experienced by the perfectionist, because the perfectionist is unable to find satisfaction in what is flawed and he is adept at spotting flaws—even in what is useful and uplifting.

The ultimate waste from perfectionism is a wasted life. Like the unhappy skeptic and the ill-tempered cynic, the perfectionist, in the extreme, is unable to produce or enjoy much of anything because he is fully consumed lamenting over the flaws and minor weaknesses he finds, and because he is never fully able to devote his energies and talents toward useful ends in an economical and productive fashion.

7

Serving a Worthwhile Cause

When the human animal sets out to attain a sense of worth and achieve success, the avenues chosen usually lead to neither. People are frequently tripped up by the mistaken notion that success and self-worth can be realized directly through acquiring possessions, or by living a spotless life, or both. Experience shows us that a sure way to fail ever to achieve a sense of significance is to attempt to grasp directly what most people perceive success to be: wealth, power, prestige and a flawless reputation. By following along these paths, the individual really focuses his attention inwardly and tries to serve his self; but as has already been shown, the self has a ravenous appetite that constantly soars to demand more—more possessions, more perfection.

Trying to please an uncontrollable appetite gives more pain than joy. Self-centeredness always assumes the upper hand in these cases, and through it humans enslave themselves, becoming trapped in a state of self-bondage. A. P. Giannini, founder of what today is the Bank of America, summed it up well when he said, "I don't what to be rich. No man actually ever owns a fortune—it owns him."[1] Conrad Hilton saw this too; he advised people, "Don't let your possessions possess you. . . . They are nice to have, to enjoy, to share. But if you find even one that you can't live without—hasten to give it away. Your very freedom depends on it."[2]

THE ESCAPE FROM BONDAGE

We are all familiar with at least a few people who have escaped the self-bondage (already discussed) and have achieved meaning, and hence happiness, in their lives by devoting their attention and energies outwardly and not upon themselves. They have achieved meaning by finding some worthy cause that captured their full loyalty and serving it faithfully. They are known by their friends and acquaintances as being above the pettiness that occupies the minds of the majority of people. And they are genuinely unconcerned with and unaffected by the vestments of success. This idea has been enormously helpful in steering people toward living useful and productive lives. It was expressed vividly by Cecil Rhodes as he thought back over his own lifetime. "I fear that I did not work at Oxford as much, or get as much good out of the University, as I should have done," remarked Rhodes. "But I did read some Greek, and especially some Aristotle, and one sentence of his has influenced me more than almost anything else. It is one in which he says that the greatest happiness in life is to be derived from the conscious pursuit of a great purpose."[3]

Life is not lost by dying; it is lost by not caring. It is lost when one spends it thoughtlessly in thousands of small, uncaring, or self-serving ways. Great lives are lived through the pursuit of great ideals and worthy causes. We are indebted to D. Elton Trueblood for pointing out, "Man is so made that he cannot find genuine satisfaction unless his life is transcendent in at least two ways: (1) It must transcend his ego in that he cares more for a cause than for his own existence, and (2) it must transcend his own brief time in that he builds for a time when he is gone and thereby denies mortality."[4] Man escapes self-bondage when he is loyal to and fully absorbed in a cause. Human lives are dignified through serving, not through being served. "Through experience," wrote J. C. Penney, "I learned that to be free, one must follow; to gain success, one must serve. . . . I think the tests and adventure come with putting money second and opportunities for the future first."[5] This is the conclusion of the matter: Man does not find satisfaction in what belongs to him but through what his life belongs to.

THE DISCIPLINE OF LOYALTY

Legend has it that when General Washington's mother was asked what she had done to teach her son to be a great leader, her reply was, "I taught him to obey." If obedience is thought to be just a desirable quality, this anecdote will be dismissed as a cute story with a nice-sounding message. But what claims our special attention is its profoundly important insight into the art of leadership and the value of loyalty. It is a gain in clarity to realize that obedience may include the discipline element in loyalty. It is the tendency to comply, or fulfill, or conform in action, to some principle, command, or authority. Obedience makes loyalty mean something.

Through observing great leaders we are struck by the inordinate amount of loyalty they displayed toward the causes they served. We know great leaders by their unswerving and unapologetic obedience to what their cause tells them to do. Their leadership is only as strong as their ability to follow. That is, the strength of their leadership is derived from their obedience to the commands of their causes. Great leaders have very definite beliefs about what it is they are serving and rarely, if ever, are they swayed by conflicting commands from other interests and what is popular or pressing them at the moment. This is not to say that they are closed-minded in a general sense, but it is to say that their minds are clearly made up insofar as the causes they are pursuing. A large measure of what makes them attractive to followers and adds to their ability to lead others, comes from their loyalty to the cause they have committed themselves to serve.

One has little difficulty recognizing that without self-control, or obedience, there can be no loyalty. The loyal person serves a cause that he looks to for guidance; his cause tells him what to do. He does not follow his *own* impulses. His actions are directed from outside his self by his cause.

A very different type of person—one who also appears to be directed by influences outside himself—is the one who is influenced first by one cause or call, then another, and later on by others still. Obviously, such a person, if in a position of leadership, will confuse and eventually lose followers. But there is more to it than that. This person really has not made up his mind. He is still in doubt and truly unable to be loyal to anything. Most significantly, the reason why this person changes so often is that his real intentions are focused on serving himself. And because they are so focused, he is unwilling to pay the price or endure the consequences that loyalty to a cause may demand. Stated bluntly, he is self-absorbed; he loves himself more than anything else.

A person is loyal when he has a cause, when he willingly and thoroughly devotes himself to that cause, and when he expresses his devotion in some sustained and practical way. Loyalty is not a "sometime thing." And it is not merely a state of mind; it requires action. Clearly, without loyalty there is no escape from self-bondage.

A WORTHY MASTER

It would indeed be tragic if the world of business held no worthy causes for men and women to serve. The creation and distribution of goods and services elevates the quality of life. To view the creation of wealth as an evil suggests that lives spent in the miseries of hunger and privation are better than those spent living with plenty. Surely humans were not created to suffer a miserable existence. There appears no sound reason why business people should feel ashamed that they are primarily concerned with adding to the level of material abundance and the security and comfort it provides. John J. Nevin, of Firestone, points out the importance of the wealth-creating functions of business. "I don't apologize for being a businessman. . . . The fact is that most of the good things that happen in this world can only happen because somebody else is also generating wealth. So generating wealth is a sine qua non. There is no way you have educational communities in this country, there is no way you have hospitals, there is no way you have homes for the aged, there is no way you have the social programs that deal with poverty and all, unless you're also generating wealth. . . . Go to Viet Nam and you'll understand that. You [will ask], why are they tolerating this poverty? And you can't find anything in the country that you could use to alleviate it." "What's the use of having big ideas," Cecil Rhodes is reported to have said to Charles G. Gordon as a justification for striving after wealth on the diamond fields, "unless you have money with which to carry them out?"[6]

However, if the purpose of a business is only "to create the highest possible value for investors through long-term profit on investors' capital," as one large firm describes its primary responsibility, that business runs two important risks. The first is that this purpose won't be big enough or worthy enough to win the loyalty of sensitive, thinking people. As J. Henry Smith, former chairman and CEO of Equitable Life, said in an interview printed some years ago in *Nation's Business,* "Instead of feeling loyalty to just an institution people are tending to feel a sense of loyalty to the whole human race. I believe there is the increasing sense that if your company is doing the wrong thing by the human race, you ought to try to change what it is doing, . . . and this is a very good development."[7]

The second risk of running a business in which the only thing that matters is the bottom-line profit, is that the people in such an organization will very likely be led to do absolutely awful things to employees, to customers and consumers, to the environment, to the communities in which they operate, and to the nation. Enlightened and broad-minded leaders will want their employees not to follow without questioning when they perceive conflicts between what their firm is doing and what their own principles and causes demand. "I think," said Robert A. Schoellhorn, of Abbott Laboratories, "loyalty means being steadfast in following the principles of honesty and integrity. Loyalty does not mean blind obedience. I would consider someone disloyal to me who did not express a contrasting point of view that he or she held strongly and that was important." So while business is capable of winning the loyalties of well-meaning people, it is only able to do so and to contribute positively to the betterment of the world by serving some worthy purpose that is larger than its own self-interests.

A JOB, A CAREER, A CALLING

Much of the excitement and satisfaction people find in living is derived through working, and the nature and amount of fulfillment they experience depends on how they approach their work. Seen as a job, one might find enjoyment in the pay and benefits and working conditions, in the social atmosphere, in the sense of pride gained through a prestigious assignment or title or accomplishment, and in the satisfaction of using the knowledge and skills and expanding talents that one has.

Seen as a career, a person can find satisfaction in each job along his career path and also find fulfillment through ascending in the organization's hierarchy. One gains a sense of accomplishment by advancing on the rungs of a career ladder and from doing well in any particular trade or profession. But the nature of these sensations of satisfaction is largely self-centered. For those whose goal is limited to having a successful career, the focus is on self. "What will I get out of it?" seems to be the person's major concern. A new district sales manager tells friends about the move he is about to make to a different part of the country, the increased level of importance he will have in the organization's hierarchy, about the larger office complex he'll be in, about the increased sales promotion budget he'll have to work with, and on and on. His focus is on the enjoyment he expects to come to himself.

This perspective is pathetic, because it is unnecessarily limiting when one considers the possibilities that could dominate the newly promoted sales manager's mind and capture his best efforts—improvements in his organization's performance, greater customer service and satisfaction. The perspective that looks outward at a great cause to serve, instead of inward and at being served, is surely more uplifting and promises far more lasting satisfaction.

When work is seen as a calling, the possibilities for useful service and adventure and for deep and lasting satisfaction are beyond imagination. This is possible for any ordinary life. The view of one's world from a larger perspective, seeing its benefits as contributing to a larger good, can transform an ordinary life into an extraordinary adventure. Dickinson C. Ross, of Johnson & Higgins of California, describes the kind of change that can come into a person's life when a person shifts his attention and actions toward these lines. Ross recalls a man who started in the insurance business in Pasadena prior to World War I. "His mission as he got started in the insurance business, because he believed in this mission, was to provide an estate for every individual he could work with. He found that there was only one product at that time which could provide an instant estate for people, and that was life insurance. So he was a missionary, really. He made a wonderful living and that was his feeling." Many years later, this man told Ross that it wasn't the product that made the difference. It was the God-given privilege he had, to be able to respect his fellow man and look for a way to be helpful to him. He said all of that came together and was really the pattern of his success. As long as the focus of one's commitment is constantly upon the cause being served, the job or career becomes a calling, and one's work is no longer seen as just an economic exchange of pay for performance. When this occurs, the individual transcends his self. He enters into an exciting cause and thereby dignifies his existence.

In each of hundreds of offices of AT&T managers and executives across the country stands a small bronze statue of Angus Macdonald. These represent "The Spirit of Service" for AT&T. Angus A. Macdonald was a member of a telephone plant crew that worked out of Boston. In the blizzard of 1888, when the lines going across the countryside were getting caked with ice and looked as if they might go down, Macdonald and his coworkers kept telephone service alive. On the night the blizzard struck Macdonald, along with others from his crew, put on snowshoes. "Out into the drifts they fought their way, their faces set against the bitter winds, carrying coils of wire, clearing snow from the cross-arms, finding the breaks and mending them. Their fingers numbed with cold, they worked for hours—and the New York–Boston line did not fail. On their line, which followed the right-of-way of a railroad, some 25 people were marooned about a mile out of West Boylston, in a stalled Boston–Northampton passenger train. In addition to their duties in patrolling the line, the telephone men undertook the task of carrying provisions to these sufferers until railway traffic was again able to move."[8]

Another variation of the theme of service to a cause is provided by the picture of Henry Ford drawn in a John Hancock Life Insurance Company advertisement. "Young Henry Ford saw something quite different in the shadows of the shop that night. He saw his little automobile speeding a doctor to a remote farmhouse to save a life. He saw a million miles of roads opening up for all Americans the glories of their big country, . . . making the man from Maine a neighbor of the man from California. He saw people riding to work, to market, to school, to church freed at last from the old tyranny of distance. And he saw new jobs, better incomes, more free time for everybody. . . . Such was the vision of young Henry Ford in the little shop on Bagley Avenue. . . . Like every enterprise we look upon as basic, . . . the auto industry has earned its success by contributing something deep and lasting to the welfare of all Americans."[9]

In more recent years, William B. Walton, Sr., cofounder of Holiday Inns, describes how the company he served as president saw its purpose. "We saw ourselves—all of us, from the chairman of the board to cleaning people—as a company of people. We were in a crusade to bring to the American traveling public a highway haven, a home away from home to rest and refresh them."[10]

The spirit of personal commitment to great causes is alive in many parts of today's business world, and the sense of its value and importance can spread. In describing his organization, Robert E. Mercer, of Goodyear Tire & Rubber, says of Goodyear; "Here's a corporation that's providing freedom and mobility to people in this country and around the world."

Bernard M. Fauber, of Kmart, in articulating what he sees as the purpose of that organization, says, "I want Kmart to be thought of as the best place to shop, retailwise. When I say best, not just price but to get something for your price, to be treated well, and to shop in pleasant surroundings."

Ted J. Saenger, of Pacific Bell, sees the role his organization plays in the economy of the country as follows: "We're part of the infrastructure. If we don't do our job right, a lot of people can't do their thing right. And so quality telecommunications and allowing business and social interaction and movement of information that takes place over our network . . . like the highway system . . . is pretty important."

Robert A. Schoellhorn captures the chief purpose of Abbott Laboratories. "I hope and expect that we will be seen as revolutionizing health care delivery through new and improved technology and by persuading society that it does not have to ration care to answer the question of who gets the benefits of our expanding medical capabilities."

Nathan S. Ancell, of Ethan Allen Furniture, connects what his firm produces with a larger purpose. Interior home furnishings, in his belief, are for a grander purpose. "When I differentiated what this company is and does from what other furniture manufacturers and lamp manufacturers and textile manufacturers do—I've always said that one of the great differences between our company and other companies in the industry is that we have a soul. We have a corporate soul. . . . We care. . . . We care about your home . . . a good environment will help your home and family environment."

Gerald Greenwald, when he was with Chrysler Motors, saw that company's purpose as being more than mere survival or profitability. "I think we at Chrysler have a special responsibility today. The American people did give us a helping hand. I think our responsibility begins with building the best quality, best value cars and trucks for the American public that any company worldwide can. And, in the process, be a role model for what a hard-hitting, competitive company can do at a time when we are questioning our capabilities as Americans and American industry."

CORPORATE COMMITMENTS TO GREAT CAUSES

American business can take pride in the sincere interest some of its largest and best managed organizations have taken in establishing worthy purposes. These purposes are spelled out in formal statements.

The product of many hours of careful thought coming from many minds, such a statement can provide a powerful point of focus for an entire corporate body. Once they are stated, printed, and distributed for all to see and then thought of by all as receiving honest, strong support from all levels, especially the top, these statements can encourage employees and promote high levels of loyalty to worthwhile aims.

LEAVING SOMETHING OF VALUE

A cause well served is evidence of a life well lived. Through service the human creature dignifies his existence. Significance is achieved when one leaves the human condition a little better than he found it. To be sure, each life is capable of this sort of endeavor. Although it is only dimly seen by many, a freedom which each person has is to soberly reflect on the possible opportunities available to himself and wisely select the ones that are truly worth living for.

It is indeed a great tragedy when one realizes after it is too late that he gave most of his living efforts to what really matters least and gave least to what matters most.   At a talk he delivered to business-school students at Harvard University, Richard J. Mahoney, of Monsanto, expressed the idea this way: "If you go finally to meet your Maker and you're giving an accounting of yourself and you say, 'Well, what I did was I got my company's return on a share of equity from 12 percent to 20,' that sounds a little thin to me as a qualification. If you don't . . . do all the things you ought to be doing, then you've squandered your life."

Values that guide us

AVON PRODUCTS INC.

Avon is a caring company that helps people around the world to feel better about themselves.

We do this by...

PROVIDING CONSUMERS with superior products and services. The welfare and satisfaction of our consumers come first, above all other considerations.

EARNING THE TRUST of our shareholders, the owners of the company, through the achievement of consistent, above-average growth in the value of their investment in the company.

ENCOURAGING EMPLOYEES to develop their full potential. We provide an environment in which they can grow, treat them with dignity and fairness, and reward them for creativity, productivity and risk-taking.

ENHANCING THE QUALITY of life in the communities we serve, by sharing our time, our talents and our resources.

The Bristol-Myers Squibb Pledge

To those who use our products...
We affirm Bristol-Myers Squibb's commitment to the highest standards
of excellence, safety and reliability in everything we make. We pledge
to offer products of the highest quality and to work diligently to keep
improving them.

To our employees and those who may join us...
We pledge personal respect, fair compensation and equal treatment.
We acknowledge our obligation to provide able and humane leadership
throughout the organization, within a clean and safe working
environment.
To all who qualify for advancement, we will make every effort to
provide opportunity.

To our suppliers and customers...
We pledge an open door, courteous, efficient and ethical dealing, and
appreciation of their right to a fair profit.

To our shareholders...
We pledge a company-wide dedication to continued profitable growth,
sustained by strong finances, a high level of research and development,
and facilities second to none.

To the communities where we have plants and offices...
We pledge conscientious citizenship, a helping hand for worthwhile
causes, and constructive action in support of civic and environmental
progress.

To the countries where we do business...
We pledge ourselves to be a good citizen and to show full consideration
for the rights of others while reserving the right to stand up for our own.

Above all, to the world we live in...
We pledge Bristol-Myers Squibb to policies and practices which fully
embody the responsibility, integrity and decency required of free
enterprise if it is to merit and maintain the confidence of our society.

OUR PRINCIPLES

We are a company committed to quality and excellence in everything we do.

Our first responsibility is to the people who buy and use our products and services. We are dedicated to providing them with superior quality and value.

Our wholesale and retail customers provide the link to our consumers. We are dedicated to giving these customers outstanding service by providing products they need when they need them. Our customers are expected to make a fair profit on our products.

We believe in our commitment to employees who are, each of them, individuals with dignity and merit. It is our employees—individually and together—who make us strong. It is our constant goal to provide fair compensation as well as orderly and safe working conditions. Employees are encouraged to express their views and opinions—and management is encouraged to listen and respond.

We place special value on innovation...the results of which will be our common reward.

We are dedicated to equal opportunity for employment, development and advancement for those qualified.

We must provide competent management with integrity whose actions are just and ethical.

Our suppliers contribute significantly to the quality and value that goes into our products and services. We must be selective in choosing outstanding suppliers—and treat them with respect, courtesy and fairness.

We believe in being good neighbors. We are dedicated to making our communities better and supporting causes consistent with their importance to the good of the community. We must strive to protect the environment and natural resources around us.

Our final responsibility is to our shareholders. Pioneering new technologies, creating new products and penetrating new markets are activities which require investment of resources; thus, both our present and our future products and services must be sufficiently profitable to generate funds to insure growth while providing reasonable returns to our shareholders.

Campbell Soup Company

8

The Paradox of Profit

Intelligent and sensitive men and women will rightfully question whether what they do rests on high moral ground. Seeing others in the grip of poverty, they will wonder whether they should enjoy wealth. They may question whether profits are morally justified. It is appropriate, therefore, to carefully examine profit, the profit motive, and the right to acquire property, which we enjoy in this country.

It is surprising to find existing in free societies considerable popular confusion about profits and the profit system. Casual observation shows that the profit system suffers many ignorant attacks from those who are antibusiness and that it is unintelligently defended by those who support free enterprise. Moreover, much of the news reporting done on profits and corporate earnings performance is less oriented to informing the public than it is to arousing its interest and passion.

It is fair to say that the critics of capitalism, in general, and business, in particular, suggest that profit is a dirty word. What proponents of private enterprise see as legitimate, healthy, and robust profits, these critics label as "obscene," arguing that profit equates with greed and that profits unnecessarily arise at the expense of others. These arguments rest on the proposition that acquisition and use of property are basically evil and corrupting actions, that a person is debased by the pursuit of profit and the accumulation of wealth. This perception of business and the profit motive is aptly captured by the claims made by one unsuccessful Presidential aspirant in a speech given before his party's 1988 national convention. His rhetoric contained charges that major corporations are "ripping off consumers" and that the American public is "gouged by corporate greed."

Defenders of the profit system, basically those who like it, are generally hard pressed to muster a credible, logical defense for what they hold dear. Their usual rejoinders to those who attack the profit system are, "If you don't like it, why don't you go live somewhere else?" or "Capitalist countries are richer than collectivist economies."

THE NATURE AND FUNCTION OF PROFIT

Misconceptions about the nature and meaning of profit and about wealth and the right to own property are widespread.[1] A few general observations are in order, therefore, to provide perspective and clarification of the subject. The fundamental task of management in all economies is to create value. In capitalistic economies this is equated with the earning of profits, but even in noncapitalistic economies the creation of value is a sine qua non if material advancement is to occur. Management is successful when the resultant output exceeds the value of the sum of the individual inputs—money, materials, equipment, labor. Even nonprofit organizations such as schools, libraries, social-service agencies, hospitals, museums, and the like must be profitable in this sense in order to justify their existence. That is, they must provide greater value to society, however measured, than the sum of the value of the various inputs. If they do not, they are a net drain on that society. Thus the necessity of profit, correctly seen as the creation of added value, is not unique to capitalism nor to private enterprise.

The results of healthy (profitable) economic activity are to lift people out of poverty and improve their level of health and material well-being. Clearly, the likelihood of finding human misery is far greater in a world of privation than a world of plenty. To think that poverty ennobles humans or that material wealth corrupts them from a moral perspective is unfounded. As far as we know, a credible argument, backed with substantive evidence, has never been made that would convince any fair-minded person that greed is unique to people of capitalistic economies and caused principally by profit-motivated behavior.

In capitalistic, democratic nations the primary task of business is to provide quality goods and services, wanted by people, at competitive prices and to do so efficiently and thus earn profits over an extended period of time. Profits are a reward to the investors who risked their money in the business venture. If that venture is effective—producing the wanted goods efficiently—then profits generally follow. If not, losses will ensue. Profit making in free-enterprise economies follows risk taking; the former always demands the latter.

All business investments and ventures, of course, do not pay off. All are not profitable. Business is full of risks, and it is not uncommon for business ventures to go sour, where losses, not profits, result. Profit, as an accounting concept, is what remains after all expenses, including taxes, have been paid; it is the difference between revenues and costs, and it does not always turn out to be positive. The last to be paid are the investors who earn the profits. All others, including employees, suppliers of raw materials and services, creditors, landlords, and tax collectors, are paid first.

Profit is really a reward for the risks investors assume. In modern, free-enterprise economies there is generally a direct relationship between risk and possible reward. It is important to recognize that most technological and economic advances occur through the process of trial and error. No one knows for sure, beforehand, whether some new technology or product will actually work successfully or find acceptance in the marketplace, and thereby produce healthy profits. In a very real sense business is a "crap shoot." It needs bold risk takers, who should put in time and effort to do their homework and discover the most logical and most likely ways to be successful and then devise plans and methods aimed at reducing their level of risk. But complete certainty never exists, and sooner or later one of thousands of lucky, or shrewd, investors hits a jackpot while others, following different paths, profit modestly or not at all. Interestingly, capitalistic economies far outstrip other economic systems when it comes to advancing technology and its application. Hoped-for profit serves as a great inducement to speculate and take risks. And when someone is successful and is thus rewarded with profits, society benefits through the progress made and the taxes collected on those profits. It might also be pointed out that the government, which taxes the investor on the profits earned, does not risk a penny of its own money.

The desire to be profitable spurs businesses to generate wealth efficiently. Profits, when returned to the owners of invested capital, are taxed, and thus society benefits. The remaining profits can be reinvested in existing or new businesses. Money invested in a business is spent on such things as research and development, technological improvements, the expansion and updating of production and distribution processes, employee training and development, and additions to the property, plant and equipment used to produce. Investments, such as these improve (1) the quality of products produced, (2) the productive efficiency of the business, (3) the quality of working conditions, and (4) the productivity of labor, making it possible and justifiable for people to earn higher pay. When business earns profits, wealth is created in that economic system. These profits, in turn, are invested back into the ongoing enterprise or used to fund new businesses. Without profit there could be no investment, and these socially desirable results would not occur.

Popular among many is the belief that profit is something that arises only at the expense of others—when laborers are cheated out of a fair wage and customers are tricked into buying shoddy goods that they don't really want or need. Clearly, history shows that labor has at times been ill treated and ill paid and that consumers have been cheated and shortchanged. To argue that these deplorable practices are necessary to generate profits neglects the way most businesses operate today.

The perception that everyone must lie or cheat in order to earn a profit and succeed in business is inconsistent with experience and is entirely contrary to what most successful business leaders today believe. Typical of their opinions on this matter is the one voiced by Andrew C. Sigler, of Champion International, who says this perception is erroneous. "You can't be a profitable company with those dishonest kinds of people. You sell to your customers every day. If you are one of those types of people you won't be in business very long." Profits are made through producing quality goods that people are willing to buy. A business is profitable because it can produce something of value, in an efficient manner, that is wanted by others. And the firm that does that, stands a better chance of succeeding than the firm that attempts to profit by underhanded schemes.

The perception that the large companies in this country earn enormous profits on each dollar of sales, that is, that they are gouging customers, is unfounded when the facts are examined. In 1986 the net profit earned on each dollar of revenue of the 1,000 largest U.S. companies was 4.7¢; in 1987 that figure was 4.9¢; in 1988 it jumped to 5.9¢ and in 1989 it was 5.2¢. Historically, profit margins have been about 5¢. When one considers the fact that many state sales taxes are 5¢ or 6¢ on the dollar, a clearer understanding of the magnitude of profits is obtained. The table below shows the profits earned by 50 widely recognized U.S. firms on each dollar of revenue.

Profits Earned on Each Dollar of Sales
of 50 U.S. Companies in 1989

Aetna Life & Casualty	3.3¢	Goodyear Tire & Rubber	1.7¢
Alcoa	8.7¢	Hewlett-Packard	6.6¢
American Express	4.6¢	IBM	6.0¢
Anheuser-Busch	8.1¢	Johnson & Johnson	11.1¢
AT&T	7.5¢	Kellogg	9.1¢
Bethlehem Steel	4.7¢	Kmart	1.1¢
Boeing	3.3¢	Lockheed	0.1¢
Bristol-Myers Squibb	8.1¢	Marriott	2.4¢
Campbell Soup	0.6¢	Maytag	4.3¢
Caterpillar	4.5¢	McDonalds	12.0¢
CBS	10.0¢	Mobil	3.2¢
Chevron	0.9¢	Motorola	5.2¢
Chrysler	0.9¢	New York Times	3.9¢
Coca Cola	13.3¢	Pacific Gas & Electric	10.5¢
Colgate-Palmolive	5.6¢	J. C. Penney	5.0¢
Delta Airlines	5.5¢	Philip Morris	6.6¢
Walt Disney	15.1¢	Procter & Gamble	6.2¢
Dow Chemical	14.1¢	Quaker Oats	3.5¢
Du Pont	7.0¢	Reebok International	9.6¢
Eastman Kodak	2.9¢	Scott Paper	7.4¢
Exxon	3.4¢	Wal Mart Stores	4.2¢
Ford	4.0¢	Westinghouse	7.2¢
General Electric	7.3¢	Weyerhaeuser	3.4¢
General Mills	5.8¢	Whirlpool	3.0¢
General Motors	3.3¢	Xerox	4.0¢

Profit is generally measured in terms of money. But this can be somewhat misleading, because money alone does not account for the many other forms of profit: the intangible benefits of progress, growth, enjoyment, material comfort, and increased possibilities for human betterment, to mention just a few. Samuel Gompers, one of the founders and the first president of the AFL, identified dramatically the importance of corporate profits when he said, "The worst thing a company can do to its employees is to fail to make a profit."

One can easily be deceived by ill-explained news reports of corporate earnings. Such reports tend to sensationalize profits by reporting percentage increases from one year to the next or by reporting only the dollar amounts. Instead of informing the public, these accounts tend to mislead the ordinary person, causing him to conclude that business is greedily gouging customers every time they make a purchase and that profits are, if not a necessary evil, just plain morally wrong. The fact that General Motors, for instance, earned over $3.5 billion profit in 1987 may sound sensational. But it means relatively little unless we consider other factors, such as the rate of inflation, total sales, the level of risk the investors incurred, the amount of stockholders' equity, and the total assets employed.

Profit, in the business sense, is an accounting concept and is best understood when it is presented as a rate, not an amount; this would be expressed as a percentage, computed by dividing the dollar amount of profit by the dollar amount of investment. A high rate of profit, expressed as the rate of return, indicates a high rate of productivity of the money invested to produce that profit. It is in the economy's interest to create wealth efficiently for economic growth. And profitability, when expressed as a rate of return, is a measure of this efficiency. Seen in this light, the ordinary person can understand why profit benefits the entire economy.

One type of statistic used by the news media is exceedingly misleading. It is the percentage change in profits from one year to the next. The fact that a company's earnings rose 80 percent or 125 percent from one year to the next sounds sensational to many naive minds and leads to all sorts of erroneous impressions. If a company's earnings last year were $100 million and this year were $185 million, the news media would report that the company's profits rose by 85% in one year. This is accurate and truthful, but it does not always tell the entire story. That $185 million profit may really be only a 12 percent return on equity and a 6 percent return on total assets. Or the $100 million in profits from the year earlier may have been a very poor business performance. Interestingly, it should be pointed out that national news stories usually report only huge increases in year-to-year or quarter to quarter earnings of firms in industries that are in disfavor with the public at the time, such as oil companies were during the Persian Gulf crisis in 1990, when there was a sharp increase in gasoline prices. The careful observer will realize that similarly large *drops* in profits are not reported on the evening news in the same fashion.

PROPERTY RIGHTS

The right to own property is a significant feature of modern, industrialized countries. The founding fathers of this nation, educated men of devout religious convictions and strong moral concerns, believed firmly in the idea of private ownership of property and saw it as a basic human right to be protected by law. If people were not permitted to own property, it is difficult to image how they could take care of themselves freely and provide for their own material security in freedom. And without property rights guaranteed by law, it would be impossible to police society to prevent the strong from taking property from the weak for their own use. Survival of the fittest may make sense in the animal world, but its processes are abhorrent when practiced by human beings.

As thinking creatures who are aware of their selves, humans who exercise control over their own lives and who are responsible for themselves as adults enjoy a far greater sense of dignity and psychological well-being than those who do not. And the right to own and exercise decisions over the use of property is an important dimension of that individual liberty.

Failure to earn profits sooner or later results in the demise of an enterprise. As Robert E. Mercer, of Goodyear Tire & Rubber, puts it, "Profits are like breathing. If you can't breathe you can forget everything else that you're doing because you're not going to be around much longer." If you don't make a profit, you can't live.

"A profitable, growing business," Reginald H. Jones, of General Electric, explains, "provides new employment opportunities, new products and services, and new capital for a healthy, expanding economy. Moreover, it provides the material resources by which the nation can support other important noneconomic services, such as education, churches, the arts, the national security, and even government."[2]

Without property ownership, it should be mentioned, there could be no charity; it is impossible for a man to be charitable if he holds title to nothing that can be given to others. If it weren't for the profits earned by companies in photography, woolen mills, and publishing, for example, the Eastman, Julliard, and Curtis schools of music would not exist. Robert McClements, of Sun Oil, points out that the generosity of Americans to flood and famine victims in other parts of the world is possible because of the healthy, market-based economic system in the United States which creates profits. In his words, "We are a generous people and we gave. . . . We gave not because we *had* to give, but because *we had it to give*, and we had it because our economic system works."[3]

LONG-TERM CONSIDERATIONS

When William Spoor was named CEO of Pillsbury in 1972, he assumed the reins of a company that was moving in various directions with its products and was languishing in flat sales and sagging profit levels. With the aim of improving Pillsbury's competitiveness and profit performance, Spoor moved quickly to implement a new strategy that gave the company greater focus on specific markets. He set financial targets. The idea was to focus on food-related markets; Pillsbury sold off its non-foods business units. Business ventures or product lines that could not return adequate levels of profit were also sold. The buying and selling off of businesses is an everyday occurrence; it is a reality in the world of commerce.

To some people, these actions, like the one's described about Pillsbury, may seem to indicate firms pursue selfish courses of action merely for the benefit of their greedy stockholders. But this is not a fully accurate perception of what is taking place. There is something to be said of the ethical demand to be responsible, and this means profitable. William L. Weiss, of Ameritech, observes, "Running a business on a sound basis is an ethical imperative. Keeping a healthy business can only be done if it stays at some reasonable profit level. . . . Our economy will not tolerate anything else."

A sensible commitment to profitability encourages competitiveness and the effective and efficient use of scarce resources. If a business cannot be profitable over an extended period with a particular product in a market, it ought to get out of that venture, because through losing money it is not creating wealth and it is not improving the standard of living. Instead, it is causing a net drain on the economy. Michael D. Wright, of Super Valu Stores, explains, "Some people in society . . . somehow want to equate . . . profit motive with some kind of evil intent. . . . It seems cruel and you say it's the weeding out of the weak and . . . the strong survive. But that weeding out process, in itself, makes for a more productive, efficient society which benefits everybody."

One fallacy, against which everyone ought to be guarded, is the idea that profits tell the whole story about a firm's performance. Obviously they are a record of what has already occurred, but they may not provide an accurate picture of things to come—of future performance. R. Gordon McGovern, of Campbell Soup, says, "I don't think that profit, per se, measures the whole structure."

Wise managers are rightfully concerned about the future and about whether their organizations are poised to perform effectively in the years ahead. Philip E. Lippincott, of Scott Paper, explains, "The numbers [profits] are indicative of, 'are you doing a lot of other things right?' They don't tell you a lot about the qualitative goodness of your business, nor do they tell you a great deal about the foundation that you're putting in place to sustain that entity in time."

Profits, then, are a *post* measurement and as such tell very little about the quality of the nonmonetary or good things the company is doing or about the quality of the investments being made in research, personnel, production and marketing capabilities, and relationships and reputations, to name a few of the footings which the future of an organization is built upon. Michael D. Rose, of Holiday Inns, believes this is how one sustains consistent profitability. "Profits," he says, "tend to be very short-sighted and you have to invest in things and invest in people. If we were only worried about today's profit we could run this business a lot leaner than we do now; and I think we run it pretty lean. But you really have to invest in people."

The idea these business leaders bring out is that it is not the job of the manager to maximize profits each year but to *optimize* them, so as to assure long-term consistency in profits over decades. Richard Madden, of Potlatch, the forest products company, sees this as meaning, "To earn a growing profit at a reasonable rate of return for . . . shareholders over time." Says Madden, "You may be able to maximize the profit today by stopping planting trees. And we could. Millions and millions of dollars go into tree planting. . . . We could maximize [profits]. But what we say is the growing profit, reasonable rate of return, that total optimization of the total return over time to shareholders, is obtained by good people, good financial support, and a keen sense of social responsibility to all the publics with whom we deal. . . . This means not only the shareholder. It means the customer, it means the supplier, it means the communities in which we operate." Michael Rose, of Holiday Inns, advocates the long-term perspective, too. "I'm sensitive of our responsibility to preserve a business enterprise that will be healthy and profitable twenty, thirty, fifty years from now and not just the next quarter."

This long-term approach is not easy to understand nor to maintain; there are many unknowns in the future and many pressures and temptations in the present. It is particularly troublesome to pursue in publicly held companies, which can be easy prey for takeover artists. Levi Strauss, being a privately held company, avoided the threat of a takeover and hence the pressure for immediate profitability. As Walter A. Haas, Jr., says, "There wasn't the pressure on [us] for quarterly profits. And I had a goal in life and that was to try to help our neighbors." But Safeway, being a publicly held company, was not so fortunate and, as Peter A. Magowan explains, was under tremendous pressure to maximize profits in the short term to try to avoid a threatened buyout. These pressures can easily be detrimental to the foundations necessary for long-term profit consistency and stability and to the various constituents who have an interest in the company's survival.

"Once the takeover speculation starts," explains Magowan, "the new shareholders that come in are only for the short term. They want to get Safeway sold out to somebody who wants to pay a high price, and then [they want to] bail out of the stock as soon as that transaction is completed. They don't have any loyalty to the company. So that's the kind of thing that can affect management on the short term. The banks look at the short term. The credit ratings, Standard and Poor's, and Moody's, they're looking at corporate America on the short term, trying to determine its creditworthiness each quarter. And a management that is only interested on the long term . . . and would ignore all these short-term pressures, could really run into trouble. They could get taken over. They could have their rating depressed. All the stock analysts that are following your stock, they want high quarterly earnings. On the other hand, you've got the employees; they want job security on the long term. You've got your customers; they want to be taken care of on the long term. And certainly the younger management that wants to feel it's going to have a greater role to play in a larger and more successful company; they are interested in long term. We are faced constantly, running a business, deciding what do we do long term, short term. The two best examples in our business are being competitive on the price and being willing to stand up to the union and take a strike if we have to. If you're only interested in the short term, we could maximize profit in this company by raising prices. We would lose business eventually, but in the short term we would make a lot of profit, where we would sign contracts that we know we can't afford, to avoid the cost of the strike. . . . If we get our labor cost into a noncompetitive mode we're in real trouble long-term. So management will say, 'We've got to be competitive in price, even though it costs us in the short term.' And we will stand up to the unions to the point of taking the strike if necessary, which will be very costly to the short term. And remodeling stores, that's the third leg of it. Remodeling stores is costly on the short term but it pays off on the long term."

PRESSURES AND DANGERS

The pressure placed on companies for profits can become too strong and cause hard-driving, shrewd-minded competitive competence to give way to short-sighted and underhanded schemes. It is possible to press too hard for profits. When this occurs, cautious judgment can become an early casualty. A vivid illustration of this occurred with Beech-Nut Nutrition Corp., the second largest baby food manufacturer and a subsidiary of the Nestlé Corp.

Over the years Beech-Nut had been stripped of its profitable divisions, chewing gum for one, and reduced to a single product, baby food, which had almost never earned a profit. An investment group purchased the baby food division from Squibb Corporation in 1973, almost entirely with borrowed money, and ran it on a shoestring. With a 15 percent market share, they could not match the marketing outlays of Gerber Products Co., which held a 70 percent share of the market. Losses mounted, and within five years Beech-Nut owed millions to suppliers. Of the company's sales, 30 percent were from products containing apple concentrate. The company was holding on to life with savings from cheap concentrate. In 1979 Nestlé purchased the company for $35 million. Nestlé invested an additional $60 million into the operation, hiked the marketing efforts, and increased sales. But losses continued and the pressure to reduce costs persisted.

With pressures such as these, Beech-Nut, it was revealed some nine years later, began a deal that was too good to be true. It entered into an agreement in 1977 to buy apple concentrate from Interjuice Trading Corp., a wholesaler whose prices were 20 percent below the market. Research and development chemists at Beech-Nut were suspicious. Although there were no tests at the time to prove their suspicions, they surmised that the Interjuice products were extensively adulterated, if not totally synthetic. But when Beech-Nut's director of research and development wrote a memo in 1981 to company superiors saying that he suspected the apple concentrate that the company was buying to make juice and other products was a blend of synthetic ingredients, a "100% fraudulent chemical cocktail," his superiors took no action.

Six years later, Beech-Nut pleaded guilty to 215 felony counts, admitting to willful violations of food and drug laws by selling adulterated apple products between 1981 and 1983. The company was fined $2 million, and a year later two top executives were sent to prison.

A BROADER PERSPECTIVE

As it has been pointed out, profit is extremely important. In fact, it is necessary if the life of a business is to be sustained. But profit alone is not nearly a large enough purpose to hold the enthusiasm and loyalties of employees, nor is it broad enough to cause attention to be placed on the other vital elements needed for a business to continue to perform effectively. This perspective is held by many high-level corporate leaders from a diversity of industries. Can an organization operate successfully solely for the quest of profits? In other words, does it exist just to make profits? "I don't think so," says Robert E. Fomon, of E. F. Hutton; and Charles W. Parry, Alcoa agrees saying, "The answer is no. That is just silly."

Profits are only one, although important, element; an organization needs to stand for more. "It's hard for me even to think about what we do that's purely for profit," said David E. Collins, when he was with Johnson & Johnson, "because that concept at Johnson & Johnson is so outmoded." Profits are one effective way to measure past performance, but they don't *drive* the enterprise. Philip Lippincott, of Scott Paper observes, "I think it's a great way to keep score, but I don't think it's the principle motivation." John H. Bryan, Jr., of Sara Lee, sees profits as a benchmark for the vitality of a business but not as an explanation of why it exists. Profits, according to Bryan, are "Not the reason for the existence of a business." This is not to say the profits are unimportant or can be neglected. Delbert C. Staley of NYNEX puts it this way: "I don't think you can drive it [the business] purely on a profit basis. . . . that doesn't say you *don't* have to be profitable."

A broader perspective is needed. Rather than focusing attention on "What's in it for me?" successful leadership concentrates on "How can I create real value for my customers?" To emphasize only profits could mislead managers into not creating value for customers and not building and investing for the future. The "profits only" or "profits are Number One" approach denies the difficult task business leaders must face in balancing the interests of the many constituents their enterprise serves. Richard E. Heckert, of Du Pont, identifies several of the important constituents he believes a business must satisfy. "I work for the shareholders. I work for the employees. I work for the customers. If I don't make a good profit, I'm not doing a very good job for the owners and for the employees. If I make too much profit, my customers worry. And it's a constant balancing act trying to deliver as much value as possible to the consumer and satisfy as well as you can the needs and demands of owners and employees." In Pennsylvania the law permits managers to look at the balanced interests of all constituent groups. Firms in that state are protected from a stockholder who would say, "You must take care of me first."

To ignore customers' interests is to invite disaster; successful managements, indeed, see their role as, in large part, working for the customer. Delbert Staley, of NYNEX, provides an excellent example of one of the ways a company does this: "We have a unit . . . that is selling our services, selling long distance service, selling usage, selling networks. We have another unit selling equipment, which shows them [customers] how to cut on their telephone usage, to cut back to the minimum. Are they in conflict with each other? I don't think so. If you try to sell people more than they need, for profit purposes only, eventually you're going to lose them as a customer. Some guy is going to come along and sell these [customers] on the fact that you are selling them things they don't need."

The broader, longer-ranged, balanced view demands discipline and the will to say no, to easy paths, to selfish desires, and to any of the constituencies that want a larger share than is prudent for the long-term best interests of all. "The balanced view," notes Joseph L. Jones, of Armstrong World Industries, "is the best policy for a company to satisfy all of these people, to take care of them all. If you ignore your employees, you're absolutely dead. And yet, if you pay them too, much you become noncompetitive and you can't compete. And they have no jobs."

VALUES DRIVE AN ORGANIZATION: THE PEOPLE-SERVICE-PROFIT LESSON

In any human undertaking, the first step, once the desired result is clearly in mind, is to decide upon the methods to be followed. But once this is done, attention should be placed almost exclusively on the means and making them work, and the ends being pursued should largely be forgotten. All great purposes and endeavors of any significance are fraught with subtle traps and delaying setbacks, which will easily discourage and interrupt the steady efforts of the impatient and less persistent—those who are too quick to give up following otherwise good paths because they don't appear to be working at the time, or working rapidly enough. It requires keen intellect and pains taking preparation to identify or devise methods that will work to bring about a sought-after end. And it requires greater skill and delicacy in carrying forth endeavors to know enough to persevere through difficulties and continue following plans, and not succumb to the temptation to abandon them for other courses that might appear more expedient at the moment.

Eagerness to reach one's goals, the compulsion to complete the unfinished task, is a mark of achievers. But unbridled ambition can assume the upper hand and wash away the persistence needed to stick with a well devised scheme that is momentarily slowed by snags and short-lived obstructions. Thus computer or telecommunications salespersons, for instance, eager to have a good year and earn a place in the million-dollar sales club, may abandon the plan of working closely with customers through helping them plan for the futures of their businesses and deciding which computer or telecommunications products and systems are going to be most useful to those businesses. Instead the salespersons may replace that approach with a hard-sell tactic, to get them to purchase any hardware they might be tempted to buy because it looks attractive or because it might help to solve current, but not necessarily long-range, problems. Labor relations representatives of a company may strike a bargain with union leaders to settle quickly a strike or dispute, even though by doing this they force the company out of being competitive because the agreement is unwise and uneconomical.

The profit paradox is also a vivid example of this phenomenon. It can be stated in a variety of ways, but the United Parcel Service founder, Jim Casey, said it about as clearly and directly as possible nearly 50 years ago. "Are we working for money alone?" Casey asked. "If so, there is no surer way not to get it."[4] Profit, like happiness, is the by-product of purposeful living. To get it, forget it!

An extraordinary man once coached college athletes at a state university on the West Coast. He was quiet, deliberate, unassuming—an ordinary-looking man. Yet he approached his task in ways radically different from other coaches. He never tried to get his players "up" for a game emotionally. He would tell his players before games, "When it's over, I want your head up. And there's only one way your head can be up, that's for you to know, not me, that you gave the best effort of which you're capable " He was as much concerned with his players' character as he was with their ability, because he wanted players who didn't care who got the credit for good playing. He emphasized constant improvement and steady performance and often said, "The mark of a true champion is to always perform near your level of competency." Coach John Wooden retired after 40 years of coaching, leaving a record unparalleled in American collegiate athletics. During the 27 years he coached basketball at UCLA, his teams never had a losing season. In his last 12 years there, they won 10 national championships, 7 of those in succession. His teams of those years hold the longest winning streak record in any major sport—88 games, spanning four seasons. But the amazing fact is, *he never talked about winning.* "I honestly, deeply believe," he said, "that in not stressing winning as such, we won more than we would have if I'd stressed outscoring opponents."[5]

That this powerful idea has not escaped many of the nation's most successful business leaders is not surprising. If one opens the Brunswick Corporation's annual report, the very first thing to be seen is the firm's values. The second thing presented is the numbers, the financial performance. The company's chairman and CEO, Jack F. Reichert, says, "I do that intentionally because I don't believe that numbers drive values but I believe that values drive numbers. . . . The three values that drive our company: (1) We will either be the highest quality producer in every market that we serve, or we will exit that market. We will either be the best or we won't be in that business. (2) That the only reason we are in business and have retained shareholder earnings is to serve customers and to serve customers, hopefully, at a profit to ourselves. And (3) that the most important resource we have in the company is people: their personal dignity, pride in what they do, and trust that they have in management."

At Federal Express, the succinct and comprehensive people-service-profit (P-S-P) concept governs every activity. Each Federal Express manager is expected to follow scrupulously this successful formula: Take care of our people; they, in turn, will deliver the impeccable service demanded by our customers, who will reward us with the profitability necessary to secure our future. People-Service-Profit, these three words are the very foundation of Federal Express. The order is important. The first leads to the second, and both of these lead to the third.

Nathan Ancell, of Ethan Allen Furniture, explains a similar philosophy he has used for years to guide that growing company. "We'd have a board meeting at the end of the year, and I would report to our little board the summary of what happened during the year. The first thing I said was, 'Do we have better people in our company? Do we have better people on December 31st than we did January 1st?' Secondly, 'Do we have a better image with the public from what little products we have?' Thirdly, 'Do we have better productive facilities than we had in the beginning of the year?' And fourth, 'Do we have a workforce that is, from a moral and ethical standpoint, more stimulated and motivated than we had in the beginning of the year?' And fifth, and I emphasize that I put this fifth and we've put it fifth every year since then, 'Did we make enough money to do the things that we had to do?' The point of that being that we did not put money first. You ask a businessman why he's in business, and 99 percent of them will say, 'To make money.' We never said that to ourselves. We said that making money is the *result* of performance. It's not the *cause* of performance. . . . we never had any real 'downs.' When the industry had a 'down' of 15 or 18 percent, we had a 'down' of maybe 4 or 5 percent. But we always came out okay at the end of the year and increased our productivity, facilities, people, management. I must say we really never had any serious 'downs.' "

At DeLuxe Check Printers the commitment is, "To serve our customers as the best supplier of financial documents and related products and services." Eugene R. Olson says, "Most people who run companies say, 'the shareholders are Number One,' and I have a hard time with that because I really feel that if you treat your employees right, then your customers will be treated right, and if your customers are treated right, it will follow to the shareholders. Shareholders are certainly important. We never forget them, and we want to make sure that they are treated right. And if you take a look at our stock record, and our dividend record they will show you that they have been treated right. But if you only worry about them first and put them as a top priority, you might start to be short term in your thinking and start to cut corners on some costs, try to improve profits in places where you shouldn't, and that would be the wrong way to go."

Gen. Robert Wood Johnson, son of the founder of Johnson & Johnson, wrote a credo for his company which has continued to evolve over the years. One early version appeared in *Or Forfeit Freedom,* a book the general wrote in 1946. It very clearly set up a sequence.

Our Credo

We believe our first responsibility is to the doctors, nurses and patients, to mothers and fathers and all others who use our products and services. In meeting their needs everything we do must be of high quality. We must constantly strive to reduce our costs in order to maintain reasonable prices. Customers' orders must be serviced promptly and accurately. Our suppliers and distributors must have an opportunity to make a fair profit.

We are responsible to our employees, the men and women who work with us throughout the world. Everyone must be considered as an individual. We must respect their dignity and recognize their merit. They must have a sense of security in their jobs. Compensation must be fair and adequate, and working conditions clean, orderly and safe. Employees must feel free to make suggestions and complaints. There must be equal opportunity for employment, development and advancement for those qualified. We must provide competent management, and their actions must be just and ethical.

We are responsible to the communities in which we live and work and to the world community as well. We must be good citizens--support good works and charities and bear our fair share of taxes. We must encourage civic improvements and better health and education. We must maintain in good order the property we are privileged to use, protecting the environment and natural resources.

Our final responsibility is to our stockholders. Business must make a sound profit. We must experiment with new ideas. Research must be carried on, innovative programs developed and mistakes paid for. New equipment must be purchased, new facilities provided and new products launched. Reserves must be created to provide for adverse times. When we operate according to these principles, the stockholders should realize a fair return.

Johnson & Johnson

Reprinted with permission of Johnson & Johnson.

The overriding aim of the Hilton Hotel Corporation, as Barron Hilton sees it, "Is to be recognized as the world's best first-class commercial hotel organization. To constantly strive to improve, allowing us to prosper as a business for the benefit of our shareholders, our guests, and our employees." And how is this done? "We put people first, product, and then profit, because we believe unless you have the people in the jobs doing their jobs properly and unless you've got the product that follows, there's no reason to talk about profits because if you haven't got the people and the product, you aren't going to have the profits," says Hilton.

Hilton's Corporate Mission

To be recognized as the world's best first-class, commercial hotel organization, to constantly strive to improve, allowing us to prosper as a business for the benefitof our shareholders, our guests, and our employees.

Fundamental to the success of our mission are these values:

PEOPLE Our most important asset. Involvement, teamwork, and commitment are the values that govern their work.

PRODUCT Our programs, services, and facilities. They must be designed and operated with superior quality, to satisfy the needs and desires of our guests.

PROFIT The ultimate measure of our success—the gauge for how well and how efficiently we serve our guests. Profits are required for us to survive and grow.

With these values come certain guiding principles:

QUALITY COMES FIRST The quality of our product and service creates guest satisfaction, our No.1 priority.

VALUE Our guests deserve quality products at a fair price. This is how to build business.

CONTINUOUS IMPROVEMENT Never standing on past accomplishments, but always striving—through innovation—to improve our product and service, to increase our efficiency, and profitability.

TEAMWORK A tradition at Hilton that gets things done...now!

INTEGRITY We will never compromise our code of conduct —we will be socially responsible—we are committed to Hilton's high standards of fairness and integrity.

A striking illustration of the power of placing primary attention and emphasis on employees and customers first and profits next is found in the recent past of the Ford Motor Company. Now the most profitable automaker worldwide, Ford did not always enjoy that enviable position. Faced with stiff competition at home and from abroad in the late 1970s, Ford had, like GM and Chrysler, suffered declines in market share and drops in earnings due principally to sales of foreign imports. The only hope of finding a way out of the malaise was to build better cars. This meant using advanced technology and eliminating product defects—a most formidable challenge.

Profound changes in Ford's product line and quality could come only through a more dedicated work force that felt pride in being part of the competitive struggle. It became readily apparent to Ford management that if employees on the assembly lines really didn't care about their work, no amount of inspection and control from without could possibly force quality up to the levels to which the worldwide competitive struggle had driven it. Quality had to be "Job One," and the employees had to care about it if Ford were to make that a reality. A radically different atmosphere had to pervade the entire organization from top to bottom. Management at Ford struggled for well over a year fashioning guiding principles and values.

After many months of thoughtful discussion three basic values: people, products, profits were deliberately listed in that order. Why are people first? Chairman and CEO, Donald E. Petersen, says, "Because people are our most important asset. Everything that we are and can accomplish can only be done by people. So they're really the beginning of everything."

MISSION

Ford Motor Company is a worldwide leader in automotive and automotive-related products and services as well as in newer industries such as aerospace, communications, and financial services. Our mission is to improve continually our products and services to meet our customers' needs, allowing us to prosper as a business and to provide a reasonable return for our stockholders, the owners of our business.

VALUES

How we accomplish our mission is as important as the mission itself. Fundamental to success for the Company are these basic values:
People — Our people are the source of our strength. They provide our corporate intelligence and determine our reputation and vitality. Involvement and teamwork are our core human values.

Products — Out products are the end result of our efforts, and they should be the best in serving customers worldwide. As our products are viewed, so are we viewed.

Profits — Profits are the ultimate measure of how efficiently we provide customers with the best products for their needs. Profits are required to survive and grow.

GUIDING PRINCIPLES

Quality comes first — To achieve customer satisfaction, the quality of our products and services must be our number one priority.

Customers are the focus of everything we do — Our work must be done with our customers in mind, providing better products and services than our competition.

Continuous improvement is essential to our success — We must strive for excellence in everything we do: in our products, in their safety and value - and in our services, our human relations, our competitiveness, and our profitability.

Employee involvement is our way of life — We are a team. We must treat each other with trust and respect.

Dealers and suppliers are our partners — The Company must maintain mutually beneficial relationships with dealers, suppliers, and our other business associates.

Integrity is never compromised — The conduct of our Company worldwide must be pursued in a manner that is socially responsible and commands respect for its integrity and for its positive contributions to society. Our doors are open to men and women alike without discrimination and without regard to ethnic origin or personal belief.

One plight from which man appears unable to escape is that of having to rediscover old truths. Henry Ford himself, founder of the giant automobile enterprise that bears his name, had boldly lived by the creed that any business that first thought of earning a fixed dividend was bound to fail. Either profits would come from doing a job well, he believed, or they would not come at all. Henry Ford ably captured the essence of the profit paradox, under examination here, over a half-century earlier when he remarked, "A business absolutely devoted to service will have only one worry about profits. They will be embarrassingly large."[6]

9

Setting and Living up to High Ethical Standards

Clearly, unethical and unspeakable activities have occurred and do occur in business. And some seem to result in material gain—at least in the short term. However, the popular belief that people engaged in business are corrupt *out of necessity* and that business survival and prosperity can occur *only* through wrongdoing appears untenable. There are too many instances to the contrary. Although deplorable behavior is not essential to success, our special attention is called to this realization: it does not follow that highly ethical standards arise in business naturally. The astute, high-minded person will therefore seek to find ways to acquire and maintain highly ethical standards for himself and his organization.

Experience shows that the individuals and organizations that have succeeded at this have deliberately sought ethical conduct as a rare prize and, once achieving it, have actively nurtured and protected it. In some organizations the traditions fashioned by their founders have formed the basis of cultures rooted in praiseworthy principles and standards.

Ethical standards of conduct are propagated from one person to others most effectively through example in everyday actions. This calls to light the importance of careful attention to the little details and otherwise unconscious habits that form the larger patterns by which persons and organizations are recognized. Those who are most successful at maintaining high ethical standards know from experience that both appearance and substance need to be made right. Image, too, is important. Decisions and actions must not only be good, but they must look good and smell good as well.

TONES FROM THE TOP

Today's enlightened corporate leaders regularly and actively take steps to establish and support highly ethical tones for themselves and their organizations. They know that there are always temptations to be found in business—especially where people can use unfair or illegal tactics to gain advantages for themselves and their organizations. The pressures of competition can be tremendous, as can the desire to make good in a job and win recognition, a bonus, or a promotion. A sensitive leader is aware of human frailties and the danger spots where, in the face of the attractive traps which abound, ordinarily good people may weaken.

A strong and unambiguous message from the top is one way by which a tone for ethical conduct can be set. Once, for example, Raytheon was bidding to win contracts in third-world countries, and some of its managers were sorely tempted, in dealing with agents, to compete on the going terms. Sensitive to the situation, company chairman and CEO, Thomas L. Phillips, gave a summary of Raytheon's official posture at a strategy-setting meeting, saying, "We don't want any *dirty* money at Raytheon of any description. And if you ever get into a situation where you ever have to give or get *dirty* money in order to win some business, the only proper thing to do is not to win that business; it is to bow out completely. And when you come back and tell your boss that's the reason you had to get out, that will be perfectly acceptable with Raytheon. . . . It's very important, when it's a hard decision in making a choice between signing a very profitable contract and looking like a hero because of it or doing the right thing, doing the *right* thing will take preference in this company." There, he said it. In clear and unambiguous terms: unethical tactics are not acceptable, and being beaten by competitors who take unfair advantage will not be criticized.

In many firms, time is spent to inform all employees as to what is and what is not acceptable behavior. This can be a source of relief to good people, who would prefer never to have to wonder how to behave in tempting situations. It helps them tremendously to have a concrete picture of what will and what will not be tolerated. Like many other large American firms, Armstrong World Industries has operations in other parts of the world. Shortly after the head of its Japanese company, a Japanese man, was named to that position, he was brought to Armstrong's home office in Lancaster, Pennsylvania, to meet with the company chairman, Joseph L. Jones, who explained to him, "I really can't tell you what to do in Japan, what price to put on the goods you're selling, where to sell it, how to promote it, or indeed, what products you should import for sale. I don't know the Japanese market. I can't give you those details. We've chosen you because we think you have business ability. We've chosen you because we think you're honest. We have chosen you because we think you're diligent and hardworking and that you want to make our company successful in Japan. Let me give you the principles and objectives that I want you to hold up in front of yourself every time you make a decision. And if you make them in keeping with these principles, I feel confident that you'll make the right decisions for our company." Jones signed the printed copy of the Armstrong principles (see Chapter 6), making a ceremony out of it, and gave it to him.

Six months later, when Jones visited the Japanese operation in Japan, he found that the Armstrong principles had been translated into Japanese. A copy was on the wall of this manager's office. The head of the Japanese operation had ordered additional copies and called all of his eight people in to have a signing ceremony for them when Jones was there. To these people, the principles of conduct not only meant something but were genuinely honored.

A clearly understood reality of organizational behavior is the powerful influence that the person at the top has in setting the moral tone. Once set, it is most difficult to elevate it, but it can be damaged rapidly. One CEO summarized this important lesson: "You have to set a whole moral tone in running the company. If you've got a boss who people know is going to skate the fine line or look for the deal that isn't quite correct but he'll take it because it's good for business, that permeates the whole organization. He sets that tone. If he sets a clear tone, and makes it black or white in as many cases as it can possibly be, if not all cases, then everybody in the organization will know that. If there's somebody who comes along who doesn't like that standard, he's either going to get caught and fired or he's going to leave."

Conducting business on legitimate terms only always puts matters on a solid basis. By saying to employees, as Jack F. Reichert, of Brunswick Corporation, did, "We are not going to make money any way but the right way," and as another CEO of a major electronics firm told his employees, "We're not going to get business in a way that's either illegal or improper," at least two messages go out: not only is highly ethical behavior expected, but also the company does not need or want all of the business it can get. Most highly successful leaders are of the opinion that there is plenty of legitimate business available through honorable dealings. Moreover, they believe that if there is to be any bending done to get business, it will be done by others coming *up* to high standards set by well intending firms and not the other way around. In defending the Foreign Corrupt Practices Act, which makes most facilitating payments illegal, the head of a large electronics company stated, "It's a good thing to have an Act like that. Sure, we lose business to some of our competitors in other countries, but so be it. I don't want that business anyway."

The unspoken message here includes the idea that the organization will focus its attention, and hence compete only on the basis of things that are of real and economic value to customers, and that honest value and service will be exchanged for honest money. When good minds are focused upon competing on real grounds instead of bribes and the like, improvements in products and processes are made, efficiency is bettered, and real value is added. Society benefits through increases in real wealth as well. The thoughtful observer will, with a little reflection, realize that dishonest forms of competition do not add to economic growth and development nearly as much as honest competition adds. And, these underhanded forms of competing aren't nearly as interesting and challenging as are the honest ones.

BUILDING A GOOD COMPANY REPUTATION

A highly regarded, ethical reputation is a prized accomplishment. It cannot be purchased or created through public relations stunts and manipulations. Instead, it is built in thousands of big and little ways; it is grown and polished through years of the dedicated pursuit of high ethical standards. And there are benefits. The firm or person with such a prize is nearly always beyond reproach. A firm that lives by high ideals attracts good people. Its reputation seems to speak out in subtle ways, saying, "If you aren't decent and honorable we won't have anything to do with you." Irving I. Stone, of American Greetings, characterizes his company's posture with regard to questionable practices bluntly: "If there's anything that's not ethical, not right, we won't touch it." Temptations which would otherwise present themselves tend to stay away, so strong is the message.

At the offices of the Goodyear Tire & Rubber Company, placards can be found with a slogan that has been around that company a long time—"Protect Our Good Name." Goodyear's Robert E. Mercer says, "Yes, Goodyear is profit oriented. But there are caveats on making money. You have to make it the right way. You don't make money by shortening the product line, or the service, or running around the law."

Elisha Gray, II, Whirlpool's first CEO, laid down a corporate philosophy that is still, today, found in the company's strategic plan. His thinking was to secure and continue building a lasting business, basing it on a strong reputation for integrity and service. The philosophy Gray laid down for the Whirlpool Corporation was, "to conduct our affairs in such a manner as to be known for honest, innovative, good quality products and services, . . . fair competitive prices, . . . a healthy climate for both corporate growth and individual contribution . . . dedication to the free enterprise system, and good corporate citizenship in every community in which we do business."

The James River Corporation was founded by two men who, early in its existence, saw the need to establish certain values and beliefs to guide the growth and direction of their expanding firm. They sought an honorable identity for the growing company which they were building. The cofounder and president, Robert C. Williams, explains, "We had the luxury, setting out in this company, in seeking a new identity to establish values and beliefs as we wanted. . . . We had the freedom and flexibility to set it up the way we wanted it and we wrote those down. . . . The first and most important value and belief we wrote down back in those days was ethics. We were a competitive bunch that put the company together and we played hard to win the business game. But, like any other game, you win by playing by the rules. There is no real reward or justification in winning by any other way than by the rules."

On a much larger scale, many firms in an industry can agree to compete by a common set of standards, lest one or more be moved to take the low road to gain an advantage over the others. The need to survive can become a strong incentive to do almost anything. And when firms are in situations where they are being beaten out by competitors who engage in unlawful or unethical actions to gain an advantage, they are tempted to follow suit in order just to stay alive. Without a common set of standards, firms in a hotly competitive environment can easily slip to the lowest common denominator in terms of conduct.

The defense contracting firms in this country have been the subject of much controversy when it comes to ethics. Little public attention has been directed at the many efforts that the largest and best known firms in that industry have made to set a standard of highly ethical conduct. The Defense Industry Initiatives is a case in point, as Sanford McDonnell, of McDonnell Douglas, explains. "We in the aerospace industry have formed a grouping called the Defense Industry Initiatives, in which 40 companies have agreed to develop codes of ethics and training programs and self-policing programs to ensure they are being adhered to. [And we have] meetings where we interchange data on how to do that and an annual reporting by an independent body on how well each company is complying."

ENFORCING STANDARDS

Experienced business leaders emphasize that it isn't enough merely to have high standards and a system of communicating them and to train people as to what the standards are and what they mean. Principles must be practiced; they need to be lived. And when they are not adhered to, swift and firm corrective actions must be taken, or else they will mean absolutely nothing. The level and tone of meeting and enforcing standards is more important than the mere existence and communication of the standards themselves. Courage is a welcome companion to those who find themselves in tough situations, where doing the right thing from an ethical perspective conflicts with the expediencies of easy profit and competitive advantage. The pursuit of justice through insistence on conforming one's life to standards, and not the reverse, is a mark of character. Neglect deadens the power of standards to influence. The leader who does not deliver on promises to adhere to them is bound to lose credibility, just as the leader without any compassion will surely lose followers.

A certain level of tenderness and compassion for the frailties of others is desirable, and a cold, "by the rules" approach has its limitations. Balance is critical; the trick is to tread the fine line. For most people in today's world, who have a tendency to accept any value or standard as being as good as any other one in order to feel they are open minded, enforcement of standards is particularly difficult. This situation therefore requires one to temper mercy with justice (not the other way around), as the experiences of Lewis W. Lehr, of 3M, suggest. "I have seen a few cases where perhaps people cheated on an expense voucher or something like that and I've been disappointed. But I think I could probably rationalize why they did it. It didn't make it right. But oftentimes you can't give [them] a second chance because it was wrong and you can't let a message like that go throughout an organization, that some person can do something illegal and still be part of the group. There are exceptions, of course, . . . the ones that kind of tug at your heart strings are when it's done very naively, that you feel a little sense of responsibility for apparently not laying down enough ground rules, or establishing [better] management guidelines, or principles."

Adherence to rules and ethical standards in an organization can be pursued both through selection and through training. It would be unrealistic to believe that all people are flawless when it comes to standards of right and wrong. And the thought that everyone can be trained to adhere to pristine levels of honesty goes against what the world has experienced to date. An effective principle of managing people involves placing them in slots where they can be useful through their strengths, and not held back because of their limitations. The idea is to match people to tasks where their strengths will be put to use. This principle can be extended: keep people away from situations where the temptations will get the better of their frailties. Some amount of training can change people, allowing them to acquire new skills and develop latent abilities. Integrity and character can be included here. But enforcement of standards has to be a part of the effort also. Selection and training are part of an effective answer, too. At Kmart, as the chairman and CEO, Bernard M. Fauber, explains, newly hired people are watched, and judged, in part, in terms of their integrity. However, once they are put into a position of trust, a serious infraction of ethical conduct is dealt with firmly. "We bring on young people from college at the entry level and then have the advantage of watching them in every move they make, everything they do, how they mix with people, their attitude toward their work, the product, the money," says Fauber. "So we are able to judge, on the spot, the degree of their integrity at a very early stage. . . . That isn't to say that someone doesn't stray as they get further up. Occasionally it happens—not very often. When they reach the point of being a store manager we have certain rules and it's made known to them, in no uncertain terms, that there is no deviation from these rules. There is no second chance. There is outright dismissal." Enforcement of standards can also take place before an infraction has occurred, through subtle signals set in motion by top management.

In an effort to enforce adherence to high standards, organizations can, and many do, audit their own actions and the patterns of decisions made. Self-policing is a powerful way of encouraging compliance to high standards. At Lockheed, for instance, special "inside" company auditors review accounts where there could be a shading of interpretation to make certain that charges to government contracts do not contain even a hint of nonallowable costs, such as entertainment, which the company writes off. The worry that companies like Lockheed have is that one of these nonallowable costs might creep into the list of charges made to the government. Special audit procedures are used to prevent such mistakes from happening.

A self-test also can be useful to the enforcement of standards. The UPS founder, J. E. (Jim) Casey, gave the following list of questions to think about, to help assure that his employees were not put into the position of doing something unethical, thinking that it was expected of them by their employer.

> Are we always careful not to engage in practices that would give false impressions of our company?

> Are we careful not to ask or expect people to accept conditions of work that we would be unwilling to accept if we were in their places?

> Do we ever make promises we don't intend to keep?[1]

When an infraction of ethical standards occurs there can be a tendency to want to let it go by—to ignore it with the hope the matter will soon be forgotten. This is understandable. It is very unpleasant to confront a wrongdoer and proceed with disciplinary action. The belief that an unpleasant situation can be buried or ignored, and thereby kept from the notice of others, nearly always proves to be incorrect. The many shortcomings associated with this approach emerge when one considers the many possible problems to which it can expose an organization. For one, it conveys the message that the rules of conduct are really just for appearances.

The tougher course, the direct, strict, aboveboard approach, is demanding and difficult to maintain, but it yields better results overall. The flavor of this approach is aptly captured by the words of Litton Industries' chairman, Fred O'Green: "Super diligence is given all the time to holding to high ethical standards. We want everyone to know we mean it when we say we expect ethical conduct. If there is wrongdoing, we will go right to the authorities. People caught doing wrong will be dismissed."

In business, as with any other human activity, people will from time to time go beyond the bounds of good conduct. When one of these unfortunate incidents occurs it results in an individual tragedy—loss of honor and reputation, shame and embarrassment, and reprimand or termination, or worse. Yet, at the same time, there is a brighter side: the pursuit of ethical conduct for the larger body of people is continued.

The culture of an organization is a fragile balance of norms, each one sustained by careful and deliberate adherence and support from everyone, especially those having the greatest influence. Each person would like to think that his organization's culture is such that ethical behavior is expected of everyone and that unethical behavior will not be tolerated but properly punished when uncovered. "When those things come to light," says Thomas H. Cruikshank, of Halliburton, "you crack down on them. You discipline the ones that are involved. That sometimes involves prosecution. Sometimes it includes dismissal, but I think you have to react. You have to show that the company does not tolerate that."

Strict measures are not easily and lightly taken by caring, feeling leaders. Nonetheless, logic tells us they must be taken, if the delicate and important corporate culture is to be maintained for everyone's betterment.

Many years ago, at CPC International, one of the purchasing agents accepted a present of 500 shares of stock in a company which CPC International was purchasing from. The value of the stock was about $4 a share, making the value of the gift around $2,000. This was discovered. What to do? Even though this person had 18 years of service with the company, there was no choice. He was immediately terminated.

There is always the understandably human tendency to view incidents of misconduct apart from the larger picture, as isolated, irregular events. Wisdom is reached when one comes over to the realization that the course of the whole of humankind is far more important than the direction or tragedy of a single life and that living up to standards has a profound influence on the direction that the former takes. One does well to realize that adherence to standards today perpetuates them for future generations. As an illustration of how a leader can act when wrongdoing is uncovered, once a group at Scott Paper "moved" some business between years. At the close of a year, sales were recorded in the next year's account—clearly against company policy. This infraction was picked up through the normal control systems in the business; the people that did it were not trying to hide it. As the chairman and CEO, Philip E. Lippincott, recalls, "It was something that we had to come down on fairly hard in the sense that it is not an accepted practice. . . . The people are being penalized to some extent for behavior that is inconsistent with what we believe in. And we want everybody to know that doing what's right is most important . . . to be sure that we continue to grow and perform in the right manner."

The commitment to high ethical standards, some leaders believe, should be so strong that neither cost nor convenience considerations should take precedence. Robert H. Malott, of FMC, illustrates this level of commitment. "We found that one of our division managers had shifted some income from one year to another, not taking anything into his pocket. I don't think . . . [there were] any tax problems. I don't think . . . [there were] any contract problems with the military. It was solely the fact that he did this. The group manager called and said, 'We've got so many problems we're dealing with, we've got these people coming in, we've got that, we've got this project, and so forth. I'd like to delay the investigation you've asked us to undertake for one month.' I said, 'I want this done and I want it done now. The track that I've set, that you are familiar with and signed onto last week, we're going to follow it.' You have a few examples like that, and the word gets out."

ATTENTION TO LITTLE THINGS: THEY ARE BIG THINGS

The legendary Amos Alonzo Stagg, respected and admired coach for 42 years at the University of Chicago, was revered more for his character and uncompromising honesty than for producing winning teams. Once, when Stagg's baseball team was defending its college title, a batter singled and one of Chicago's players was racing home with the winning run. Stagg shouted at him, "Get back to third base. You cut it by a yard."

"But the umpire didn't see it," the player protested. "That doesn't make any difference," roared Stagg. "Get back!" It cost the game but a character battle was won.

Establishment of a highly ethical tone in an organization requires going beyond merely stopping illegal and unethical practices; it also involves not permitting cut corners. It says no to practices and actions that, although not strictly illegal or unethical, are not honorable or not decent, or just don't seem to smell good or appear proper. Attention paid to what some may think as being little details goes a long way in setting the right standards of ethical behavior, which help keep people away from more serious difficulties later. When he was chairman and CEO at Bethlehem Steel, Donald H. Trautlein put a stop to permitting executives the use of the company plane to travel to physical examinations, taking four days to do it. To him, that did not pass the "smell test." Bethlehem Steel used to have its fairly large corporate services staff perform services in the houses of employees. Even though the employees were billed for these services at a fairly competitive rate, Trautlein also ended this practice, because, again, it just didn't look good for employees to call the company when they needed a plumber or electrician or painter for their homes. In his words, "It just set the wrong kind of standards."

When he was controller at Ford, Robert S. McNamara billed out over $2 million to corporate executives who had made use of company facilities without compensating the company for them. He billed them for misuse of the corporate resources, not so much to penalize individuals for misbehavior, as to set the standard for the expected behavior .

Many American firms believe it makes sense to establish specific guidelines on what is and what is not permissible. For example, no professional person, from the day he or she joins Arthur Andersen & Company, can own a share of stock in any client firm. This prohibition extends to the employee's spouse and any dependent children. Toys "R" Us has a similar restriction. "We don't trade anybody's stock that we deal with, ever," says Charles Lazarus. "From me on down, we do not buy stock of a company we do business with."

Employees of Motorola are not permitted to accept gifts. "At Christmastime, if somebody sends you a calendar, in this company, you'd better send it back," says the vice chairman and CEO, William J. Weisz. "We have a very tough policy on whether or not there can be any untold relationship which might question your ability to make a judgment in one fashion or another."

BENEFITS

The firm whose leadership assumes a strong commitment to lofty ideals and ethical dealings may encounter a competitive disadvantage from time to time or lose out on some profitable opportunities in the short run, but it usually comes out better off eventually. The consensus today among top-level executives from America's largest and best run companies is that it always pays to do the "right thing." However, we should be reminded that the strength of this belief will be tested when the human desire for riches and rewards takes its place in one's motivations. The person who, before deciding, calculates only the tangible benefits in every situation reveals by his actions where his heart lies. This is especially true where the ethical course is taken primarily because it is the most profitable one. Nonetheless, a knowledge of the real and worthy benefits of pursuing highly ethical standards might help to sway those who are less than altruistic from making bad choices.

Reputation

A good reputation inspires confidence in others, and it attracts the right sorts of people and business opportunities. People prefer to do business with straight shooters. Trust is essential in all human relationships, and particularly in business. Contracts may be put in writing, and then checked by attorneys, accountants, and any number of experts and professionals. Deals may be made between parties who arrive at agreements after exhaustive discussions and shake hands. But even after all the prudent safeguards and precautions have been taken, to feel comfortable with the deal one must trust the other party. Our day-to-day dealings are seldom performed with the legalistic precision in which major transactions are framed; we would not get anything accomplished if they were. So trust is an indispensable element for business, and the person who earns a large measure of it through principled dealings and a commitment to high ideals is accorded the confidence of others.

Opportunities generally flow toward the centers of confidence. David T. Kearns, of Xerox, observes, "Integrity, believing people, is a fundamental in getting ahead. If you are consistent, people understand that. That image that people build over a period of time is of extraordinarily high value. Not just to yourself. But people know that and understand it. There isn't any question in my mind about that. That is a plus, and the biggest negatives are people who are seen as shady."

Not only is integrity important to one's advancement within an organization, but it also is a primary reason why others will choose to do business with a person or organization. The situation described by Jack Peters, of J. Walter Thompson, is a good illustration of the importance a good reputation can have, especially in rocky times. "I'm very aware and protective of our reputation. It's been damaged in the past, I think. We went through a very, very rough patch a number of years ago. It didn't help us to go public. We had a situation where management started playing monopoly and bought up all kinds of different businesses. They took their eyes off the basic business we are in and forgot that we were a supplier of a service. Then, there was a time in about 1972 when our stock went down from $60 to about $4. Our clients were leaving one after another. If it were not for the personal relationships that some of us had with clients—trust—this company would have gone. They'd have come for the furniture. There would have been no more J. Walter Thompson, Inc."

A person's believability is a product of many things, including whether or not he keeps a clean record and follows through with agreements. This especially includes things that later turn out to be to his disadvantage. The often used expression "consider the source" is well known because it is true. And the more experienced and sophisticated people grow, the more they do take into account the source. It is not uncommon to be faced with conflicting stories or interpretations. Then the question is who to believe. We tend to believe the more believable source, and this is usually the most honest person—the one whose stories have been demonstrated to be the most accurate over time. Maintaining high standards and thus protecting one's reputation is essential to one's believability as Arthur Ochs Sulzburger, of the *New York Times,* recommends. "One should remember the kind of business we are in. We are constantly shining the light on what we perceive to be wrong. And therefore it is incumbent upon us to be as clean as we can conceivably be. And we try to run the company in that manner. The last thing I would want to see would be the *New York Times* indicted for having condoned a business practice that even marginally [could be] conceived to be unethical."

Business Week magazine described then vice-chairman of Walt Disney Productions, Roy E. Disney (Walt's nephew), as a person committed to high standards and watchful and protective of his company's reputation: "Business deals," wrote *Business Week,* "are guided by his strict moral standards. He'll buy nothing related to gambling, for example, to avoid besmirching the entertainment company he loves. And when . . . [Disney's personal-business manager] once made a verbal offer on ranch land he mistakenly thought Disney wanted, Disney bought it even though he could have backed out. 'Do the right thing,' he often tells . . . [the manager]."[2]

Keeping Temptations Out of Reach

A dishonorable thought in a person's mind invites its evil friends to join it. And the only way to guard oneself from the mischief that could be brought by these unwanted guests is instead to fill one's mind and heart with high ideals and busily pursue the right purposes. A summary of the matter is this. The man who succeeds in his struggle for right stands an excellent chance of escaping the crippling effects brought on by the temptations of wrongdoing. How, for instance, when running the 1984 Olympic Games in Los Angeles, did Peter V. Ueberroth keep away questionable opportunities that might have come to the surface from less than honorable sorts? "We set our standards," recalls Ueberroth. "And when you set your standards you keep those offers away."

Keeping away from one trouble tends to ward off other troubles; evils tend to travel in packs. As Frank Carlucci, the former chairman of Sears World Trading Corporation (he later served as U.S. Secretary of Defense), commented, "There are certain people you just don't want to deal with. There are certain kinds of deals we just don't want to be associated with. Indeed, there are certain countries that I would be very hesitant to go into. I would look very closely at what I'm getting into in those countries."

Paul F. Oreffice, of Dow Chemical, explains why that company has and continues to turn down business that they didn't consider ethical. "In some countries the ethics are not what they are in this country," he observes. "We more than once have said no, we will not pay somebody off and make a contribution someplace to get the right to build a plant, or something like that. . . . There were a couple of occasions on which tax people [in another country where I worked] came around and said, 'We can settle this. All you have to do is give me so much.' Well, I found out earlier you just don't do that sort of thing. Some companies did because it was the expedient way out, and the tom-tom starts beating. Once you do it for one, another 20 will come along."

Avoiding Demands for More

In many parts of the world, business is conducted on terms where bribery is just part of the process. While it may be commonplace to require under-the-table payoffs in some cultures, it does not follow that the practice is sound from a economic perspective. "A number of instances that I've been involved in where bribes were asked for, I took the position, no, we're not going to do it no matter whether it's a great economic opportunity or not. Our company is just not going to do this," says John Swearingen, of Continental Illinois and former CEO of Amoco.

In his poem "Dane Geld," Kipling reminds us that bribes once paid don't save us from troubles but instead invite more, that you might pay Dane geld, but you never get rid of the Dane. And Kipling concludes that poem with the only sensible policy and the reason for it.

> We never pay anyone Dane geld,
> No matter how trifling the cost;
> For the end of that game is oppression and shame,
> And, the nation that plays it is lost!

Former NCR chairman and CEO, William Anderson, recounts an incident which demonstrates the value of a reputation for honesty that occurred early in his career with that company. He had just been made manager of NCR's operations in Hong Kong in 1946. The head office of Asian operation was in Shanghai.

Shortly after arriving in Hong Kong his two salesmen—two Chinese who had been in the company prior to World War II—came to him and said, "Of course, you know, we have to have in our contracts a cushion to give rebates because we're selling cash registers now."

And Anderson asked, "Well, what do you mean?"

They said, "Well, you know, a guy wants to buy a machine, I have to pay the cashier or I have to pay the manager 5 percent, maybe less or maybe as much as 10 percent so you should give us an allowance for bribes, if you really want to call it that."

Anderson would have none of it. "That's ridiculous," he said. "Why do we need to do that?"

Their response was, "Well, you know, this is China. In Shanghai, the head office is doing it. They're giving the salesmen allowances, entertainment allowances or whatever you want to call it. Why can't we have it?"

Anderson persisted, "No. I'm not going to give it to you. For one thing, how do I know that you're really going to be spending this money to get the order as against putting it in your own pocket? I don't want that. If you start paying off this guy," he continued, "he'll get greedier and greedier. The next order he places with you he may want more and we'll never get anymore business from this guy without paying him." And his last reason was, . . . "Okay, you pay Mr. A to get that order and you don't pay Mr. B, and Mr. C, and Mr. D in this organization. B, C and D know about us. Don't think they won't know about this. And they're not happy about it. And they're not happy about their boss. The boss, for whatever reason, maybe because he's caught. If he is stealing in this particular area, he's probably taking it from other sources as well. He may not be there long. Now you go and sell to Mr. C and Mr. C says, 'Well, I know how you got all these orders before. You got them only because you paid off my boss and I didn't like it at all. I'm an honest man or I'm a dishonest man. You never paid me. I'm going to go to your competitor who's going to take care of me better or who may be more honest than you.' So I say on all three counts we stand to lose rather than gain. So I refuse to do it."

The two salesmen said, "Oh well, you know we're going to lose business."

And Anderson responded, "Well, I don't believe it." As it turned out, NCR didn't lose any business.

Courage and Motivation to Do Right

Sometimes the mere knowledge that someone else had the backbone to do the right thing when facing beguiling opportunities can give added strength to one's own resolve, enabling him to overcome temptations. Where organization leaders set a good example and foster a climate with a high moral tone, they are setting a higher standard for those who would drift to a lower level of conduct. Standards can act as a lifeline for those who are struggling with doubts as to where to go and what to do. Thomas Phillips, of Raytheon, discovered some time later that his statement, "We don't want any *dirty* money at Raytheon of any description," had proved helpful to one individual and spared the company possible embarrassment. "I didn't know of anything specifically going on at Raytheon," recalls Phillips, "but years later I found out that one of our guys was close to getting into trouble and, hearing that speech at that time, he made the right decision at the right time and it prevented us from being in trouble."

A Sense of Stability

Adherence to high standards gives an organization's members a great sense of stability. An organization which is built on a solid foundation of ethical standards not only guides people to do the right things from a business and ethical perspective, but also provides them with an inner feeling of stability that comes from the knowledge they are ethical. Those who base their living on lofty ideals seem to be unflappable in moments of turmoil and stress. Tex Schramm, when he was associated with the Dallas Cowboys, described then head coach Tom Landry, a man reputed for his steadfastness to the highest ideals, as just such a person. The impact that this type of individual can have on an organization is tremendous. "One of the things," said Schramm, "that epitomizes the Cowboys is stability, its longevity, its solidness. Landry by his personality and by his appearance personifies stability, personifies steadfastness. He's the kind of a person . . . if we were going to war in this country, if there was any kind of trouble, there's the kind of guy I'd want to have taking care of me in some fashion. He's a very stable, solid individual. He portrays that image."

Conducting Business on a Strictly Business Basis

Short cuts, tricky schemes, payoffs and the like pull competitors away from the real task of business: to create value. When the highest standards are not followed, value is compromised and less real wealth is created than otherwise could have been. When someone is involved in less than honorable dealings and using unscrupulous methods, he never knows whether what he does has any real value. Indeed, the sad fact is that those who stoop to underhanded methods never have this concern. Thus these people ultimately lose out in a couple of ways: they never get to find a source of genuine worth in their own lives, and they are forever caught in a quagmire of dealings and relationships that are not based upon the predictable rules of right and fairness but upon the slippery surface of chicanery, where they have to live by their wits, making up rules to suit each situation as they go along, and always worried that even lower scoundrels may slip up from behind and do them in.

10

A Good Conscience

No one can know with certainty beforehand whether a particular decision will produce a desired result. The world is too complex and filled with too many unknowns for that. Business abounds with risk, and although some people have definite opinions as to what should be done in a particular situation, it is not possible to know beforehand how each competitive move will turn out. This is burdensome and presents enormous challenges to the best of minds. To avoid or at least reduce the likelihood of error, many put considerable effort into preparing for each decision. The available information is gathered, studied, digested, and discussed. The tools of analysis, logic, and rational decision making, are used wisely to reduce the likelihood of a slipup. Nonetheless, mistakes, sometimes serious ones, are made by even the finest managers and executives. Those with healthy egos weather setbacks and failures in judgment and move forward to try again. Their pride may be bruised in the process, but they will not feel a sense of shame. They may feel they have erred, but their consciences will not trouble them.

Just as there are tools for making business decisions rationally, so, too, are there time-tested guides for making decisions ethically. And when people approach their lives and their work in this manner, taking care that their decisions are ethical, they can feel certain that even though a mistake may occur, resulting in some damage to their pride, they need not add to this burden a troubled conscience.

PERFORMING AT ONE'S BEST: THE VALUE OF A GOOD CONSCIENCE

Benjamin Franklin, who was quite concerned with health, pointed out that the person who desires to have pleasant dreams should preserve, above all things, a good conscience. Such a state of mind, said Franklin, renders one immune from the vexations of guilt and the censures of others. Perhaps the greatest benefit to be derived from being honest in one's dealings is a clear conscience; without one, happiness cannot be attained. One can make honest errors and still have a positive sense of self-worth. But this is placed in jeopardy when there is dishonesty. James R. Eiszner, of CPC International, expresses an emotion that is sometimes only dimly felt, but that quickens our awareness of the difference between feeling wrong in making an honest mistake and feeling shame in doing something reprehensible. "It's one thing to be wrong, and we're all wrong. But if I did something that I felt was criminal or coercive or improper or just plain lousy, I would not sleep very well." There are just too many important things to worry about in living a productive life; it is senseless to add to these worries the pain of a troubled conscience.

From a larger perspective, namely that of an organization, doing the right things, which are the things people can feel good about, is an important element in a productive and dedicated, not to mention better emotionally balanced, work force. Perceptive executives know this and work hard to build the kind of organizational climate and standards of conduct that will achieve it. Why? It's the right thing to do, and it is also good business. As Joseph L. Jones of Armstrong World Industries puts it, "You start with the fundamental concept that good always overcomes evil. . . . You're successful . . . because you continually try to do the right thing. You don't do things that are wrong and create the army of enemies who you've wronged who would like to do you in. . . . If you do things right and you treat people right, you treat your customers right, they come back. They buy more goods from you. Your people can agree with what you're doing instead of going home at night and feeling that they're doing things that are not in keeping with their conscience. They go home and they feel good about it. So they want to work harder to do it. It simply works. It's in the best interest of the business to do these things. . . . I have never been asked all the time that I have been with the company to do anything that was not in keeping with my moral standards. Therefore I can put my whole energy into it and make it work. Now if you ask me to do something that I don't agree with, . . . that I fundamentally feel bad about, . . . at best I'm going to try to avoid doing it, and at worst, I'm not going to do it." We can all benefit by reminding ourselves that in the long term people do not perform at their best unless they are able to work with a clear conscience. Most people have a pretty good sense of right and wrong and are not wholeheartedly committed to things they do not fully believe in.

That a good conscience is a worthwhile aim gets little argument. The task at hand then becomes to find ways to pursue a good conscience intelligently and wholeheartedly. Fortunately, we are not without trustworthy guides to help us achieve this worthy prize. These guides are: honesty, openness, forthright dealings, integrity, reason, and a sincere concern for others.

THE MOST SENSIBLE POLICY: HONESTY

As a boy, J. C. Penney worked in a grocery store; for a short time he thought he might like to be a grocer. But an incident that grew into a lesson in integrity cut short that aspiration. At the evening meal his family members were encouraged to recount happenings of the day that were of interest. One night young Jim told of something he had observed at the store that led him to characterize the grocer as "foxy." It was an unfortunate choice of words. "The grocer stocked two grades of coffee. One, a well-known brand of package coffee, sold for fifteen cents to twenty cents a pound. A mocha-java blend sold for forty cents. . . . [Penney] noticed that the grocer poured quite an amount of the package grade into the mocha-java cannister, and sold the result at forty cents."[1] His father was not amused and had him think long and hard about the grocer palming off inferior coffee as being the best and about his calling the grocer "foxy" for it. The next day, following his father's instructions, young J. C. Penney collected the pay that was due him and quit. Jobs at that time and where he lived were not plentiful, but in his family, honesty came first.

The essence of honesty is being straightforward—the overriding intent is to get the truth out, free of distortion. Its aim is to not deceive or mislead in any fashion. Practically everybody recognizes honesty when he sees it. We seem to be able to detect it instinctively. However, the legalistic orientation, to which many these days have been drawn, and the inclination toward situational ethics—a popular and convenient standard that says, "There are no standards or absolutes. What's right and wrong all depends on the circumstances"—can easily seduce anyone's eyes and heart to wander from the spirit of this great ideal, from honesty. Quite frequently honesty can frustrate one's ambitions and interfere with one's methods of reaching them. We are aware of at least a few persons who have shown themselves capable of unspeakable acts, so strongly were they drawn to do what honesty would have prevented.

A person may "speak around" what he really means because he has a hidden agenda. This person may know what he is getting at, but others do not. People with a hidden agenda keep their intentions and motivations hidden from the full view of others. They craftily try to set up a series of events or decisions to get what they ultimately want, while all along they are pretending to be saying or trying to get something else. They want others to think there are other things going on than what they really have in mind. The point is that a person who tells it like it is, and who is not afraid to speak out against what he believes is wrong, or who plainly voices his disagreements, is the one who is seen as having integrity.

The person who keeps his thoughts to himself, or who is not quite leveling with others, or never lets others know what he is honestly thinking, is seen quite differently. In recalling his West Point experience, Stanley C. Pace, of General Dynamics, tells of the importance of owning up to direct questions and not skirting behind clever words in the attempt to deceive. The idea is to address the problem and not make frivolous excuses. The discipline learned at West Point, recalls Pace was, "You address the issue, you address the question, you respond to the question, you respond to the problem. I think you have people, the culture is such that they're able to dodge and weave and not face up to the hard facts. I think you need to face up to the problem and discuss it." Devious behavior can be very destructive to an organization and, if once found out, is ruinous to the standing in the eyes of others of the person responsible for it.

Honesty is not legalistic. We are all aware of situations where the words spoken or written are technically correct or accurate but are in fact misleading. While he was chairman and CEO of Singer, the late Joseph B. Flavin worked at making sure the words used in press releases were not only correct but also *not* misleading. At that company a small group of managers and executives would go over public announcements before they were issued. They would ask, "How would the Street think of that?" And someone might say, "They'll think this . . . " If the group suspected that the public might be led to think something which wasn't true, another wording would be prepared. The group had an overriding intention in issuing statements: to inform without misleading the public.

Honesty removes the great burden of worry that always accompanies a trail of deceit. Richard E. Heckert, of Du Pont, recalls a plant manager at that company who recommended, "Tell the truth. You can remember what you said." This Heckert found to be sound advice. Later, he expanded on this ideal by observing, "When you're honest you never have to worry about wondering what you said to somebody and then contradicting yourself, because you can always remember what really was true."

A pattern of honesty in an organization accumulates through many small actions, to form a strong message that goes out in many directions to reach many people—particularly to those who transact business with that company. The merchandise count policy at Toys "R" Us provides an excellent illustration of this idea. In the early days of Toys "R" Us, manufacturers would send to warehouses bicycles in carload lots. They were shipped "load and count," which meant the receiver had to accept the shippers' "load and count". The railroad insisted on it, because they did not check the box cars that were filled in the factory. They weighed the railroad car empty, and then they would weigh it filled. Theoretically, the cartons inside should equal the weight. When Toys "R" Us would get a carload of bicycles from a manufacturer like Murray [Ohio Mfg. Co.], who would send carload after carload, they would check it carefully and then report whether the manufacturer was over three bicycles or was short five bicycles. As Charles Lazarus recalls, "When we first did that years and years ago, they'd say, 'That just can't be,' and they would show us a diagram of how they loaded it. 'I'm sorry, that's what we got. And that's what we're going to pay for.' Over a number of years in arguing that, . . . our count is absolutely accepted. We can be over. We can be short. Whatever we say we are, they accept it. . . . When you have a relationship with a manufacturer that starts on that basis and when you negotiate to do something, they know that you're basically honest."

Dishonest claims are discovered eventually; deception is usually short lived. An early crusader in making print advertising believable was Cyrus H. K. Curtis, publisher of the *Ladies Home Journal*.[2] Every piece of advertising copy offered was carefully analyzed, and all questionable claims were eliminated promptly. Outside chemists were hired to analyze doubtful products, and those found harmful or incapable of delivering on what they promised to do were excluded from the magazine. By Curtis's code, claims had to be true. The Curtis Publishing Company built believability into its advertising pages, and readers of their magazines, sensing the publisher's intention to protect them, displayed their loyalty through renewals. This is not merely good from an ethical perspective; it is a sound business practice as well. Jack Peters, of J. Walter Thompson, argued forcefully that misleading advertising is really a disservice to a product and the client. "The market place reacts strongly to that stuff," said Peters. "Consumers are really smart. . . . I have learned that you really cannot mislead the people. . . . Their ability to see through the misclaims is so strong."

SHINING A LIGHT ON THE TRUTH

"Tell them the truth," said Paul Galvin, the founder of Motorola, who insisted on honesty and fair play with the company's distributors, "first because it's right and second they'll find out anyway. If they don't find it out from us, we'll be the ones to suffer."[3] The truth always comes into view; therefore, it makes good sense to expose it, the sooner and more completely, the better. It was A. P. Giannini's credo that, "the truth will always serve the people best and that people will best serve themselves when they are told the truth."[4] It is one thing to have a problem or an unpleasant incident or a situation that is embarrassing or troublesome. Acts to try to conceal these matters are incapable of negating their existence; they only add another ugly chapter to the unpleasant story, which grows more complex and more sordid with deceitful attempts to keep them from others. One can easily be misled into believing that inquisitive minds and snooping eyes will not find out the hidden secrets. But they do. They always do. History is lavish in examples of men who miscalculated that they would not.

Shining a light on the truth is more sensible than trying to keep it hidden. David T. Kearns, of Xerox, in considering many situations, says, "Our experience has been, every time you're better off to get it [the truth] out because it's best for the company. I also think it's right. From an overall relationship perspective you are better off. If you are up-front with things, you can deal with them much better."

Like other industrial giants, Westinghouse spends millions of dollars each year cleaning up toxic wastes that they did not know were harmful and had toxicity, twenty years ago when they were using them. If company employees find something wrong, they are encouraged to call in the environmental protection people immediately because it's in everyone's interest to do so. And this has happened. "We do tell [the environmental authorities]," says Douglas D. Danforth of Westinghouse. "We get their support. And jointly we can work out a solution . . . Negative events in our society come out sooner or later. Even if they did not, it's much better to be up-front than it is to hide something."

As a superb example of honesty and forthrightness, when he headed Zenith Corporation, John J. Nevin chose to deal with a television failure openly and immediately. The failure was a major problem for Zenith, and it was costing considerable amounts of money to fix the sets. The senior engineering executive walked into Nevin's office one day, closed the door, and said, "John, this failure is much more serious than we thought. There's reason to believe that we might have a radiation problem." He explained the problem to Nevin.

Twenty-four hours later, John Nevin was on a plane to Washington. He and the senior engineering executives met with people from the U.S. Bureau of Radiological Health. The men from Zenith told them what they had discovered in their latest tests. Zenith had long had a good reputation as a reli-able television manufacturer, and its leaders knew that nothing would strike terror in a mother more than the suggestion that the television her child was sitting in front of was a radiation hazard. The regulatory bodies in Washington, D.C., have a procedure that, by law, they must follow to establish that a manufacturer is not in conformity with the radiation standards. And if the regulatory agency reaches the conclusion that radiation standards are not being met, the manufacturer has an opportunity to protest. If the protest fails, there is a formal investigation of whether there's a health hazard. These steps take time, and both the regulators and the Zenith executives knew it. They agreed that morning that they were going to waive all these procedures. Zenith just agreed: Here is the test that will be set up, beginning immediately, to determine whether there is any hazard. In this case the Zenith people were dealing with scientists who said they wanted to be involved in the testing program.

The regulatory agency issued a press release that said, "Zenith has found certain of its receivers . . . to be not in conformity with radiation standards. The Bureau is now beginning an investigation to determine if there were any possible adverse health effects." Within three months enough testing had been done to enable the Bureau to issue a bulletin saying that the worst impact on the consumer would be the equivalent of the radiation dosage equal to what one gets with a dental X-ray. The company moved quickly to eliminate further health hazards.

Speaking honestly and acting in a forthright manner does not always work to the benefit of those who are so open and aboveboard; in fact, it may work to their detriment. The political climate at a particular period of time or in a particular geographic location may prompt retribution against a company in spite of the fact that its leaders are sincerely trying to do the right thing once an honest error has been uncovered. A situation that the Olin Corporation once faced provides an illustration.

Olin has a coring plant at Niagara Falls that uses a mercury cell process. Since the early '70s that facility has been under very strict regulations about how much mercury can be allowed to escape into the watershed. It's a very small amount of mercury. The physical volume that they're allowed to discharge in a day would be about the size of a dime. Olin has its own environmental people monitor the process. A number of years ago one of these people (an Olin employee) visited the Niagara Falls plant. Looking over the records of graph samples, the analysis of graph samples, and the reduction of that data into daily reports, she was troubled because she was unable to follow the mathematics. From the data available, and using her own mathematical methods, she concluded that the graph samples were indicating that the plant was discharging more than the final report said was being discharged. This she brought to the plant manager's attention and to her boss at corporate headquarters. Thereupon, the corporate scientists calculated what the graph samples indicated and confirmed the finding of the environmental staff specialist.

The plant had been independently monitored by the regulating agencies within the federal government and the state government. Environmental people from these bodies had taken their own graph samples and done their own calculations. And neither of these regulatory agencies had ever concluded that the Olin plant was violating laws or failing to report properly. This had been going on for about five years. But now, with the evidence brought to light by their own people, it was discovered that some misreporting had occurred unintentionally. The state was happy. The federal government was happy. Nobody was complaining. The question therefore arose at Olin as to what to do? Should they just change their practice from there on, or what? The easiest thing to do would be for Olin to change its practice from then on and report correctly. Management talked about that and concluded it really wasn't the right thing to do. What they did instead was to recalculate everything from those five years and refile every report. Olin went to the federal government and the state government and the county and the city and told them what the proper numbers were and what had happened. They believed that the full disclosure was the right thing to do because it made the records accurate.

In response the federal government decided to bring criminal action against Olin. The company fought it in the courts and eventually won the case. Their argument with the Justice Department was, it is best to encourage people to come forward if they later discover they have made a mistake. The Internal Revenue Service will slap interest penalties on people for failing to report income tax information properly, but they do not put criminal charges on them for tax evasion if they have come forward voluntarily. In the words of the company chairman, John Henske, "What you really want is for people to come forward and say, 'Look, we've been doing something that we should not have been doing,' and getting it out in the open and building from there. But why bring criminal charges against us when we did it voluntarily? All you'll do is set an example saying, 'Wait until you get caught. Don't report.' "

Observers are unwelcome visitors when people are secretly ashamed of what they are doing. In fact, the wrongdoers may conclude that the observers are the source of the troubles that ultimately evolve out of their misdeeds. Openness discourages wrongdoing because it invites witnesses in to inspect what goes on. Firestone's John Nevin explains a company practice of openness that produces this effect. "We may pay a middleman a big sales commission to move some tires in some Middle Eastern country. That's part of the cost of doing business. The minute you find out or have any reason to even suspect that that money is going to a government official, you don't take the sale. You may go so far as to get a written guarantee from this guy that it is going to be used for that purpose. We'll frequently go to the point where we'll tell the guy, 'We're going to pay you this commission, but we're going to publicize it. We're going to report that that's the commission that we paid.' Now if he's involved in some shady deal, why, he's going to back off very quickly."

The truth can dissipate doubts and suspicions and false accusations. Some years ago Caterpillar was accused by one of its competitors of dumping in the French and Spanish markets, because of the company's pricing strategy. The French equivalent of the IRS in the United States investigated the charge. The French auditors came to George A. Schaefer, who was running Caterpillar's operations there at the time, and said, "We can ask for your invoices to your French dealer and your invoices for your product manufactured here to the Spanish dealer, but we can't ask for their invoices to their customers or your invoices to your selling agent in Geneva. But," they said, "if we could get the invoices all the way down the chain, then we could have the whole story. We can't legally ask for that." Schaefer told the auditors, "You can have anything you want. I will give you a serial number of any machine that's been manufactured here which we have sold to our merchandising company in Geneva, which in turn has sold it to our dealers in France or Spain, and then if you want I'll give you the invoice from the dealer to the customer." The French officials said, "You can't get that kind of control from your dealer." Schaefer said, "They'll respond if we request it, because we review the dealer's transactions. We want to be sure that everything is going as it should be." The French officials were amazed. Schaefer did exactly that, clearing up the matter in a straightforward fashion.

CREDiBILITY

Trust makes possible one's ability to influence—to lead—and those whom we do trust generally are highly regarded for both their competence and their credibility; each quality leads to the establishment of trust. Credibility is no fringe on the outer garments of a man's personality, but a solid part of his character's core; it is built up slowly, over time, the product of well-formed habits. Credibility is rooted in the felt urgency to get the truth out to others—to employees, to shareholders, to buyers and suppliers, to government officials, and to the general public—in an open and above-board way. But there is more to credibility than mere truthfulness. At the heart of it is openness, a quality we have little difficulty in spotting in others, for it reveals itself in practically everything they say or do. What is most worth realizing about openness is that it builds one's credibility and hence fosters the acceptance of the truth one speaks. If someone wants to lead, he must give due weight to building his character with the sturdy materials of openness and credibility that form the basis of trust. When a person becomes totally open with himself, he looks deeply into his own motives and assesses honestly his own actions. Without openness he could never effectively monitor himself or work to build consistency between his words and his actions.

A leader needs to be whole; he can not separate his life from his business life. John W. Fisher, of Ball Corporation, sees effective leaders as having this quality of consistency. "You can't say one thing during the day then, on off hours, do it unethically. You've got to be sincere. A hypocrite is the worst kind of leader you can have in corporate America. It catches up with him. One thing I think I've learned: . . . you can get away with things for a while. Soon you are going to be caught one way or another. The world is built that way. I think this is a principle a lot of people overlook."

Sincerity and honesty can spread, from heads of organizations to others in and throughout those organizations. And when it does, people feel more secure in what they do and have more confidence in their leaders and the worth of their own work. Joseph B. Flavin, of Singer, said, about communicating with employees, "I think that's the best morale builder there is. Talk. Don't hide. No matter how bad things were, we were there, good and bad."

During the time of a major reduction in operations at Bethlehem Steel, the chairman and CEO, Donald H. Trautlein, found it important to be available to all employees. "I'd get a threatening phone call or two at home; they weren't very often and I never had an unlisted number. I never stopped going to the grocery store. . . . I just wasn't going to hide or make myself unavailable to people who might want to come up and talk about the problem."

Gerald B. Mitchell of Dana Corporation says, "If there is anything in a facility that you can't talk about, you have an ethics problem." This captures the spirit of openness, upon which credibility and trust are built. Openness requires the lawful sharing of all public information. The idea top level leaders say is important is to be up-front with news, good or bad. Richard A. Clarke, of Pacific Gas & Electric, says, "We are consistent about revealing news, good or bad. . . . We've learned that by getting out front with news, whether it's good or bad, you can, to a much greater extent, manage it so that it doesn't have the impact it would have if we just sat on bad news and it came out through other ways and other means." Advises Stanley Pace, of General Dynamics, "Assume an open house.

Assume an open visibility. Assume open access. I'm willing to talk about it, any aspect of anything that we're doing and trying to do."

FORTHRIGHT DEALINGS

When one considers those with whom he most prefers to do business, he is invariably led to the conclusion that they are those persons and organizations known for their straightforward manner and honesty. This is to say, they are forthright. Here is found a useful guide not only for doing the right things, but also for achieving a clean conscience. As a guide, the business person can ask himself, "Am I able and inclined to be forthright?" One's inclination to be forthright is only as strong as he is honest and fair.

Approaching the task of making a reality out of his mail order business idea, Richard W. Sears devised the unique policy of "send no money." The problem, as he saw it, was not a matter of his needing to trust his customers but of them to trust him. By his send no money policy, Sears sent goods for inspection without charge. Customers could examine the merchandise at the railway station and then return payment to Sears if they decided to accept what was shipped. His catalog copy had to be deadly honest and totally accurate; otherwise, customers would not continue to buy. He and other pioneers of the mail order trade, such as W. Atlee Burpee, who succeeded by sticking absolutely to the truth and shipping only high-quality, reliable products, realized that their businesses could be built only on policies of absolute honesty and square dealings. They believed, and this turned out to be true, that customers would respond favorably to such treatment.

Forthright dealing also involves treating others fairly. This can encompass many things. Certainly it includes not gouging customers; it also means treating everyone in an evenhanded fashion. The Timken Company was started in St. Louis in 1898 as the Timken Roller Bearing and Axle Company. It built both roller bearings and complete axles with the roller bearings in them. Originally the axles were for carriages, but with the automobile industry emerging, the company was moved to Canton, Ohio, in 1902. By 1910, the Timken management perceived that markets for the tapered bearings transcended those for the axles, and therefore they concluded that if they wanted to sell bearings to other axle builders, they'd better get out of the axle business.

So, that year the company was split in two. One part of it became the Timken Roller Bearing Company, which is still in Canton, Ohio, and which made tapered roller bearings. And the other part, the axle portion, was moved to Detroit as the Timken-Detroit Axle Company. This was later merged with Rockwell interests to become Rockwell Standard and then Rockwell International. But before the merger of Rockwell and Timken-Detroit Axle, the Timken Roller Bearing Company was selling tapered roller bearings both to Rockwell and to Timken-Detroit, which was competing with Rockwell. Willard Rockwell said that he felt that Timken

Roller Bearing was giving preferential prices to Timken-Detroit. But, according to William R. Timken, Jr., now chairman of the board at the Timken Company, Mr. Timken assured Rockwell, "No, we have a one price system. We treat all customers equally fair because that's the way we want to do business as a company."

Rockwell never believed him until the two companies were merged. When that occurred, the first thing Rockwell did was to rush and get the books to see what prices Timken-Detroit had been buying bearings at. And he found that they were exactly the same prices as he had been paying and that Mr. Timken had been completely truthful all along.

RELIABLE GUIDES

In seeking ways to achieve a good conscience, it is useful to look for the paths others have found to work successfully. There are many attractive options available, yet only a few trusted, time-tested guides prove to be reliable. These guides, the ones that work so well, have important distinguishing characteristics. First, they are direct and fairly simple for the average person to understand, accept, and apply on a day-to-day basis. Second, they require the user to habituate himself not to be selfish and self-centered. They cause his attention to focus on the feelings, interests, and welfare of others. Third, they insist on openness, whereby matters and issues can be examined freely and honestly and where the light of public view can drive away what, if allowed to remain alive by hiding, would produce disgrace.

There have been, as there will continue to be, many fine and quite sophisticated philosophical theories, models, or techniques for making ethical decisions. Entire volumes have been written by brilliant scholars on each, and others have written still more to explain to the world what the original thinker meant. But to the ordinary person these are of little use; they are just too complicated and time consuming to apply. Moreover, they fail to speak to people at a basic level such that the philosophy can really change their lives. As simple as it is, Rotary International's Four-way test—1. Is it the truth? 2. Is it fair to all concerned? 3. Will it build goodwill and better friendships? 4. Will it be beneficial to all concerned?—can do far more good in guiding people in making decisions than intellectually sophisticated, complex philosophies that may be deeper and more complete but are also too sterile and forbidding for the ordinary person to use on a daily basis.

Trust Your Feelings

If something just does not feel right, then it probably isn't right. People tend to make the little decisions with their hearts and the big ones with their heads, but they would probably be better off approaching life the other way around. The former president and chairman of the board of the Emporium Stores in the San Francisco Bay Area, Fred Hirschler, would tell his people, "If you feel uncomfortable about a decision then don't do it. Wait a while. See if there is another way of accomplishing it."

Human emotions are remarkably reliable guides; the bad and wrong just plain "stink," and cause internal discomfort. A person may rationalize all he wants to. He may use all sorts of excuses to perfume a harmful action, but the bad odor of those actions still remains. It's just covered over with an excuse. When he was CEO of Bethlehem Steel, Donald Trautlein presided over the distasteful but unavoidable necessity of down-sizing that giant steel producer to save it from extinction. Cuts and cost-reduction measures had to be taken. The compensation level for top executives was no exception even though it was significantly below what companies of similar size were paying. It was certainly below what it would have been were the firm profitable. Trautlein and his staff looked at every corporate service and eliminated them all. The fleet of four airplanes was eliminated, for example, as were the executives' medical examinations and so forth. "We looked at every service and everything that somebody could say, 'Look at what these fellows [top executive] are doing while they are laying the people off.' And we felt that if we could not pass the 'smell test,' . . . we ought to discontinue it, and we did," said Trautlein.

Put it into Public View

If you would not be proud for others to see you do it, then don't. Walter A. Haas, Jr., of Levi Strauss, said of the apparel business, "It's kind of a dog-eat-dog business. It's a tough business. And there are a lot of practices carried out by various competitors that we just refuse to follow. . . . We don't do anything we can't set up in front of a television camera and say, 'This is how we did it.' "

Thomas Laco, of Procter & Gamble, says, "Procter & Gamble Company will not ask you to do anything you can't discuss with your family at breakfast." And Gerald Mitchell of Dana offers this advice: "We at the company don't have huge bylaws on ethics. We just say that if you can't sit down and talk to your family about it at dinner, don't do it. If you are not comfortable talking to your family, don't do it. We don't care who's asking you to do it or who's telling you to do it. That's always the best bottom-line judgment. You understand the laws. You understand the regulations. We want you to abide by the laws and abide by the regulations. But above all, abide by what you feel comfortable discussing with your families and your in-laws and your children particularly. That works for us."

A variation of this "openness to public view" is what many firms informally call the *New York Times* Test. George A. Roberts, of Teledyne, explains: "The *New York Times* test says merely that we want you to understand that tomorrow morning the *New York Times* will have your decision on the front page in full detail. And if you will pass that test with your name associated with it, go ahead and make the decision. That's fine."

Consider the Other Person

In the scramble to succeed and move ahead, it is deceptively easy to lose a sense of compassion for the other person; the emphasis on one's own success and standing can easily block it. This is why, at least in part, the Golden Rule is so useful, not only for making decisions that do not injure others, but also for living a worthy and useful life. David T. Kimball, of General Signal, while listening to an after-dinner talk when he first got out of college, was greatly impressed by a speaker's message about earning the respect of the people below in the organization and not worrying so much about the admiration of the people above. He boiled it down to two words, "Look Below," and wrote them on a 3 x 5 card, which he kept on his desk for the next fifteen years. The idea here is that no matter how brilliant an analysis or a plan is, if the actions called for aren't tolerable to others, especially to those who may not have much say in the matter but must carry them out, it probably isn't a good path to follow. It likely will not even be supported by those who are expected to make it happen.

Elisha Gray II, Whirlpool's first CEO, like many other business leaders before and after him, found the Golden Rule served him exceptionally well. "In the course of making any business decision," stated Gray, "I find it useful to ask myself, 'How would I feel if I were at the other end of this deal?' On numerous occasions I did not like the answer I got, . . . and that was generally enough to change my course of action." Says Roy A. Anderson, of Lockheed, "[It] is a fundamental principle that you don't try to take advantage of somebody even though you have the opportunity to, because you would not want a person to take the same advantage of you."

Many years ago the head of a successful company was questioned about his firm's directors' meetings. In describing the ways in which that group approached the problems and issues being faced, he said, "We never have a directors' meeting but what there stands at one end of the conference table a vacant chair. And never do any of us make a decision or cast a vote but what we first think of the Man of long ago were He sitting there, and say to ourselves, 'What would He have done?' I don't know . . . just what such things have meant to us. We are not religious, but somehow or other we always seem to be going ahead." If the head of that company did not "know . . . just what such things have meant," his interviewer did. "So far as I know," he wrote, "that firm has never had a strike, labor trouble, financial trouble, or any of those business disturbing things."[5]

III

TO ADVENTURE DARINGLY

11

The Virtue of Boldness

A large measure of the quality of life, both material and social, is made possible through commercial activity; that is, by business. Intelligence, imagination, and keen practical judgment are called upon in their finest forms to fashion the commercial applications of technology into methods of production and, ultimately, finished products. Remarkable care and insight are called upon to create imaginative ways of marketing goods and services and to combine the elements of productive enterprise—people, materials, money, equipment—in a well organized and efficient manner so as to earn healthy profits. The challenges here are formidable and the risks can be numerous. But the fruits of success are equally great and offer adequate rewards for those who, through having good ideas, diligence, and some amount of good luck, can persevere to reach them. One's role and work in business, no matter what the field or level, can be made either an exciting and captivating adventure or just a dullish ride. Those whose aim it is to better the human condition through their contributions to commerce and commercial enterprise, generally travel the former path. Those who seek only security and safety for themselves tend to travel the latter one.

In all fields of human endeavor the journey one takes is made exciting and all consuming when approached with fervor and with a long-abiding commitment to a cause. In business this commitment can be seen in many activities, from introducing new products or processes to devising creative methods of advertising, and from working to elevate awareness of and commitments to environmental issues to developing a better system of accounting for costs and expenses. Opportunities to contribute in ways that make a positive difference always exist, no matter what one's role or level is and no matter how large or small the scope of one's responsibilities are. But if the path of improving matters is attempted, this aim will not be reached successfully if one does not have strong convictions about one's work. Intelligence and ability are inadequate, alone, to meet the challenge of making major improvements of any significance. This calls for the important character trait of willingness to commit oneself to a cause and working for it boldly and unhesitatingly.

RELATIVISM: THE CLOSING OF ONE'S MIND

The world is filled with many inviting and oftentimes conflicting standards of conduct and purposes which can present to anyone a great amount of confusion as to what to do and how to live. People living in the present age are understandably hesitant to choose how they will live; many prefer to remain tentative, believing that they will decide these matters at a later date. But in many lives a commitment to a position is never made. The refusal to decide arises out of fear of being laughed at, or fear of failure through being wrong, or fear of offending others by espousing a contrary or controversial view or standard.

A popular belief with which we now live is openness—the acceptance of others and all standards and beliefs. This ideal, many believe, calls each of us to be open minded and therefore tolerant. Clearly tolerance is a necessary dimension of a pluralistic, democratic society. However, we need to be made aware of the dangers into which an inadequately formed concept of tolerance can lead people. Many among us mistakenly confuse tolerance with a refusal to hold definite beliefs about much of anything. This primitive conception of tolerance embraces a line of reasoning that goes something like this: (1) There really is no certainty as to which standard of conduct or point of view is correct or best. (2) It is supremely important to accept all others and to be accepted by others— one must not offend another person in any way. "If we believe our way or standard is best," the adherents to this concept of tolerance reason, "then we might offend someone else." (3) Therefore, we must take the view that any standard or point of view is as good as any other. It's all relative. "Who are we to say," these people would argue, "who or what is right or wrong? All positions are equally valid." This is relativism. Today it is seen as a virtue, because it is thought to be a reflection of one's tolerance.

Socrates rejected what many people today regard as a virtue: the abiding acceptance of all beliefs and standards as being equally good or correct. He reasoned instead that there *is* a real and objective right, wholly independent of our opinion and wishes, which it is our whole duty to try to discover. The struggle to find the real and objective right will never be completed; one might inch toward it, but we know it will not be reached completely. But the person who refuses to engage in this quest, through either blindly accepting whatever is fed him or through remaining tentative and open to everything and believing that all points of view are equally good, never struggles with life's questions; he never really thinks deeply about these weighty matters. The person who accepts everything as equally good or correct may consider himself tolerant and open-minded, but the sad fact is that he really never thinks at all. What he considers to be tolerance is really closedmindedness. He never opens his mind to struggle with the difficult questions having to do with, "How ought one to live?"

Just because one firmly believes that a particular standard or ideal or point of view is best or true, and just because he argues strongly for his beliefs, it does not follow that he is intolerant of others and their views. It does not mean that he cannot and will not coexist in a civil manner with others who hold dissimilar views. It does mean, however, that he disagrees with these other views—tolerating and agreeing are not the same thing. Tolerance does not require that people accept *every* position as equally right or as good as any other position. Nor does it require one not to believe that others' views are faulty or wrong and that one's own is the most correct. This misconception of tolerance tends to prevent people from exercising their thinking about life's deepest questions and from committing themselves to a position, and as a result it yields them a closed, not a searching, mind. We ought to be made aware of this: there is no real and lasting safety in refusing to decide or in refusing to take a stand—there is just more confusion. Without a point of certitude, man has no perspective from which to view his own experiences and their correctness and he is left without any reference for deciding how he should live and act. The so-called open-mindedness that relativism advocates, frustrates the search for a certitude.

A tendency into which anyone can easily slip is to sit back and not voice his thoughts and concerns and not take a stand, attempting to avoid ridicule for being wrong or for being labeled as intolerant. But the good life is not lived in this fashion; he who lives the good life takes a stand after careful and prolonged deliberation, at the same time he is committed to living up to particular standards and pursuing definite causes or purposes without hesitation. This necessitates daring to be different and boldly committing to a position despite what may be popular, pleasing to others, or expedient.

The stand that Dow Chemical took with one of its products is a good example; the chairman & CEO, Paul F. Oreffice, explains the situation. "We had a product, an agricultural chemical, 245T, relatively small, not very important to us. EPA, one day, on what we considered some real trumped up charges, banned this product. We had a simple way out: forget it. It was a minor product; . . . we really had in the laboratory something better. We knew it was going to be obsolete in a couple or three years. The proper economic decision was to say, 'Good-bye, we will not do anything about it.' But then we said, that we had 20 years of science behind this product. It is a good, safe product. If we let them ban this one on some trumped up charges, what happens when the next one comes along? So, we decided to fight it and had a fight for several years that cost us not just money but goodwill, frankly, with regulatory agencies. And as we fought it, we kept saying, 'economically this makes no sense.' But we were standing on an important principle, that scientific evidence should be respected."

There are repeated calls for U.S. companies to sever all ties with South Africa—to get out. Many U.S. firms have done just that, for a wide array of reasons. But these are not the only views, and although it is not popular or acceptable to those who call for divestment, many U.S. companies believe that their presence in South Africa is the right thing for various reasons, and profit is not among the more important ones. Firestone Tire & Rubber Company has a 25 percent interest in Firestone South Africa Pty. Firestone is a subscriber to the Sullivan Principles and is a member of the U.S. Corporate Council on South Africa, a group of chief executives of companies with businesses in South Africa. That group has called for an end to apartheid and for a way to change the system. For several years Firestone has dedicated approximately 25 percent of its dividend income and trademark fees from Firestone South Africa to support educational and training programs that are responsive to the needs of blacks there.

At one time when calls were being made for U.S. firms to divest their holdings in South Africa, Firestone took a write-off of $105 million to close a plant in Albany, Georgia, and to do some restructuring in a troubled smokestack industry. Its total investment in South Africa at that time was $4.8 million; if that sum had been written off along with the larger amount, no one would have been too concerned, it was so small compared to the other write-off. But this option was not followed, largely because Firestone's leaders did not think it was the right course of action. Firestone's chairman and CEO, John J. Nevin, explains: "I can't believe that the problems of that country are going to be resolved by withdrawal of American investment and the withdrawal of all the pushes in the economic community. . . . If the South [in the United States] had remained the rural South in the postwar years that it was in the war and prewar years, we wouldn't have seen the dramatic change in race relations in the South that we saw as the South industrialized. It's one thing in a farm community to say, 'All black people will live here and they'll all work on this kind of a job on the farm.' You can't do that in a plant where there is interaction day after day. . . . We're running two tire plants in South Africa. We are absolutely desperate for skilled people. The South African blacks that we get, we've got to reeducate in language and in mathematics. And, with Control Data, we're doing [that]."

Firestone is involved with bringing black South Africans to the United States for university education, on the promise that they'll go back to their country after they quit or finish their education here. Firestone also has an educational foundation. And it has a vocational training school, which was set up in conjunction with Ford and a couple of other U.S. companies, to provide skill training for blacks in South Africa.

According to Nevin, "My view at the moment is that society doesn't realize that it doesn't have enough white people to staff plants for the modern world. . . . Amongst the senior industrialists, that awareness is very deep. I've been in South Africa and sat down with senior South African businessmen, and they will say things to you that are very blunt, like, 'The day when this country is going to make so much money on diamonds and gold that it can screw up everything else is over. We've got to enter the industrialized world, and we're not going to enter the industrialized world unless we've got skilled labor. You're not going to get the skilled labor from the whites. They're already working at the prime jobs.' The other part of it is the market. When you say, 'Have I got an economic interest? Is there an economic advantage to it?' You bet your life there is. The growth in the markets in South Africa is totally dependent on the development of a black middle class. If you're never going to sell automobiles and tires and air conditioners and television sets to anybody but the white population, the opportunity in that market is very limited. So the two go together."

RISK THAT NECESSITATES BOLDNESS

In the 1950s, in this country, Ford was the first to introduce certain safety features in its automobiles: the collapsible wheel, door locks, padded visor and instrument panel, and seat belts. Under Robert S. McNamara's leadership, Ford employees looked to find where they could gather information on how to reduce fatalities. Their search led them to the Cornell Aeronautical Laboratories, which had been hired by the U.S. Army Air Corps in World War II. The aeronautical research unit found that more lives were being lost not from airplanes but from automobiles. And after the war this research effort continued with the state police in North Carolina. Based upon their findings, Ford introduced several safety features. However, that decision was strongly opposed by others in the industry and some within the Ford organization, who argued (1) that safety doesn't sell automobiles and (2) that it is a societal problem and should be dealt with by society or government. McNamara differed with this approach. He moved boldly to do what he believed should be done.

In the affairs of life it is advisable to approach situations and decisions thoughtfully, exercising careful analysis and good judgment. But there always comes a point at which a great leap of faith is required. The decider himself, if he is ultimately going to make his venture a success, must believe that what he is about to do will actually work. One never fully knows beforehand whether a decision or contemplated action will prove successful; certainty eludes us all. The only way to know for sure is to try, to test, to boldly move on and implement the decision or idea.

Science itself is based upon the process of experimentation. We know it as trial and error. It is the way by which the truth can be verified and progress is made. The timid, the ones who are overly cautious and consumed with worry about security and with the fear of failure, the hesitant, the unduly conservative are all incapable of this step. Who could know whether safety in automobiles would be welcomed favorably by consumers? Marketing studies and other types of before-the-fact analyses help to cancel out some of the unknowns of life, but eventually the bold step of actually trying must be taken.

A rarely recognized virtue is boldness, the willingness to wager that a decision or an idea or a point of view will work. Boldness is a virtue not only because this willingness advances knowledge and civilization but also because it brings forth a large measure of the hard work and effort required to make an endeavor a success.

Daring ventures that carry people into the unknown are doomed by tentativeness because it holds back one's full energies of commitment. Unhesitating boldness can surmount difficulties and setbacks, overcoming them to make a wager a success. Anything less than total confidence that the scheme will work tends to destroy its chances from the very start and permits skepticism and doubt and the ensuing worry to siphon off the energy needed to carry the venture to a successful completion. Anyone can unthinkingly squander his energies on hesitation and worry, when he could otherwise be directing his strongest efforts to make a hoped-for improvement work.

Fear of failure is the nemesis of boldness. It holds people back from gallantly spending their lives on what could be worthwhile and exciting, albeit not risk-free, ventures. A clock has value only because it runs. Life, as Robert Louis Stevenson reminds us, ought to be dashingly used and cheerfully hazarded. Only in being *spent* does life have value, and hence meaning. The timid who risk nothing sell their lives cheaply. Little is made different in the world because of them; more good is done by those who live boldly.

Of course, in any business enterprise the possibility of failure ought not to be neglected or miscalculated. A realistic assessment of failure encourages cautiousness and deliberate care in implementing any course of action. Analysis and clear and careful thinking are required here. But cautiousness can become so large that it squelches any amount of risk taking. This is why it is reasonable to allow for some level of mistakes, so as not to cause fear of failure to destroy boldness. William D. Smithburg, of Quaker Oats, expresses the idea under examination here with this thought: "Mistakes are not sins. Mistakes are a common result of a series of risks. Therefore you're always going to make mistakes; nobody bats 100 percent. But . . . the fear of failure or mistake should not be a prevalent motivation. It should be the desire to achieve and to grow and to make profits . . . and to accept a certain degree of failure."

RISKING THAT THE MEANS FOLLOWED WILL PRODUCE THE ENDS DESIRED

When one thinks of risks in business his thoughts are most apt to dwell on the gambles taken in launching new products, or venturing into different markets, or introducing new technologies. However, when we think about it we can easily recognize that there are many other risks as well. And although the negative consequences of these are not usually as severe as the aforementioned risks, failure, nonetheless, does have a price. Not all of the means used by people in business are risk free; they do not always work, and they do not always produce immediate results. Their occasional failure to procure results or achieve desired aims quickly will oftentimes discourage less resolute persons from staying the course and persisting with the belief that the means they chose will eventually bring the hoped for results.

The desire to get what one wants today, and the wish to move through life experiencing only victories and never suffering failures, can easily cause a person to abandon his methods. They may cause him to change a way of behaving or treating others even though his experience may tell him that that way is best. The resolute person will wager that high standards of ethical conduct and highly principled methods of human relations will eventually work for the best, even if they only seem to be causing trouble at the moment. Mammy Yokum in Al Capp's *Li'l Abner* said it well: "Good always triumphs over evil 'cause it's nicer." What is meant by "risking" in this context is sticking with a belief even though the wrong may seem so overwhelmingly strong.

James R. Eiszner of CPC International illustrates this idea this way: "I was in charge of a development team that was responsible for the development of some new products, and the team was extremely successful. But my immediate supervisor did an enormously good job of accepting all the credit for the work. My staff all knew it had been me that led the effort and did the work and not the boss. 'How can you let him do that to you?', they asked. 'He's playing politics with it.' And I kept saying, 'Let's do our job. The politics will take care of itself. I don't need to worry about politics. If my efforts continue, I will be appropriately rewarded. And if they aren't, I'll find another way to do something about it.' I have become chairman of one of the top 100 companies in this country, and he never came close to making it."

Realism and practicality demand an honest assessment of each situations and a frank admission of what works and what does not. Soviet President Gorbachev is attempting this: he sees the only hope for his country in adoption of a market economy and greater political freedom. Foolproof, infallible methods do not exist in the world as we know it; each method has its limitations. In some circumstances, no single method or combination of means will easily produce the results we desire. Whenever a method does not seem to work right away there is a strong incentive to abandon what were earlier believed to be sound and sensible means.

A tragedy is present whenever an individual, so eager to reach his goals, is unable and unwilling to stick with a sound and sensible approach because it is slow to produce what he wants. The immature, who are frequently deluded that they can have whatever they want and have it immediately, are often left without any source of certitude, because they are incapable of staying with a steady course of action and relying on basically sound methods. To live above the confusion that the overly eager create for themselves, a bold person commits to a standard and holds to it, even though it doesn't always procure immediate results.

Much of the richness of living comes from sticking with one's beliefs, whether in business practices, in treating people, or in standards of ethical conduct. The long-range view offers a far better look at reality than the short-range perspective. The long-range view allows one to operate more on principle than on expediency. Robert Wilhelm, of the Emporium Stores, provides one of countless examples of this idea. "We tried to stop anyone from making a decision that was short range and not good for the long run, such as how to price goods. If you continually put your goods on sale, the mark-downs can eat you up."

The constant emphasis on results and single-minded concern for bottom-line performance can easily force people to abandon basic principles that work for the best overall, so hungry are they to achieve immediate success in one particular area or in one specific instance. This is one reason why management-by-objectives (MBO) efforts can harm an organization, as was pointed out in Chapter 8. It makes good sense, therefore, to appraise performance partly on the means to the ends followed, and to reward people partly for that, rather than to judge them only on bottom-line results. It is thought, for instance, that customer service is an important determinant of the eventual profitability of a public utility such as a telephone company. Therefore, it makes good sense for utilities to evaluate employees to some degree for their service to the public, and not solely on the basis of short-term profitability. This also suggests why the People-Service-Profit concept works so well; it encourages employees to focus attention on the means that best produce profits overall. Safeway, for example, assesses the performance of store managers in terms of four factors that are known to generate profits: price, service, quality (particularly of perishables—meat and produce) and breadth of selection.

RISK-TAKING IN BUSINESS

The entrepreneur is about to launch his new enterprise. His product is believed to be well made, and it promises to find strong customer acceptance. The basic organization is in place to finance, produce, and market the new product. Marketing surveys have been conducted. Prototypes have been made and tested. The investors and the creditors have gone over the business plan many times. Will it be successful? Nobody can predict for certain. It takes a gamble, a trial, a great leap of faith that the venture will be a success. Were the owner to know all the problems, frustrations, setbacks and difficulties beforehand, he might never begin. If he is bold these worrisome difficulties are not the focus of his attention. Once the venture is begun, the enterprise may struggle, and problems may arise. Disaster may lurk around any corner as financial obligations fall due. Once underway, however, there is no turning back; and without faith it will work, it is impossible to withstand the troubles which will surely follow. The virtue of boldness is not simply in taking a risk, and it most certainly is not in wild, uninformed gambling on poorly conceived schemes. Rather, it is in the optimism to venture forth gallantly and make the enterprise or scheme work successfully. It is the abiding commitment to face whatever may come, no matter how terrible or tragic the problems may be.

At the root of boldness is faith, the belief in one's self and beyond and the expectation that an agreeable outcome will eventually prevail. Without faith life is limp and ill-directed. If a challenge can be met, experience and skill are enough; but if it can not, then only faith can muster the resolve and the wherewithall to accomplish it. The late Joseph B. Flavin, of Singer, had this sort of enthusiasm. "The question I've been asked . . . a thousand times is 'Why did you come to Singer in 1975, when it was looking like that?' And the reason was, I spent about three months looking at the company. They were kind enough to give me all the data, and I concluded I could do it—I could fix it." We need to understand this: there are people aplenty who can do the ordinary—the possible. They can be hired for an ordinary wage. But the real rewards are for those who perform the extraordinary—the impossible.

If they wish, those who lead a successful enterprise can start playing it safe and stop pursuing improvement and growth. The need for security and stability can easily lure people in these directions. This is not altogether without sense or benefits, but it can also lead to complacency. Boldness is the antithesis of resting on one's past accomplishments. The importance of staying technologically strong and in a position of world leadership has been made strikingly clear to many American firms which have slipped badly from dominant, competitive positions they once held in world markets. Paul F. Oreffice, of Dow Chemical, observes, "I think we had a period of time in this country in which we got lazy, mentally lazy a little bit. We were the biggest industrial country in the world, and so [we thought] everything was fine."

The pressure for near-term profit is one very big cause behind the lack of commitment to finance long-term technological improvement. It discourages managements from undertaking risk-laden new ventures. The corporate raiding "game" played by takeover specialists adds to this process. Industrial builders, on the other hand, are bold risk takers and commit their organizations to daring ventures that do not always pay out immediately. As John E. Swearingen, of Continental Illinois and formerly of Amoco explains, "Any oil company can cut out . . . exploration . . . and . . . can show an immediate increase in profits which may be as much as 35 to 40 percent of . . . earnings. But unless you continue to carry out [exploration] you are going to liquidate the company."

Boldness can be seen in firms that move forward into new technologies. To do this they may have to get into new areas where growth is expected to occur after established products and lines begin to die out. It also involves moving forward into new technologies to enhance the capabilities of existing product lines. There is no escape from it: boldness involves risk taking. Henry Ford II insisted, for example, that the Ford Motor Company move into electronics, so as to have the technological base he saw it would need in the years ahead. As Ford's chairman, Donald E. Petersen, recalls, "It was clearly critically important that, meaning long-term, we were going to be just better off getting . . . better control over all the function processes of our product through the use of electronics, and to get on with it, rather than waiting until we could prove to ourselves through a set of numbers that it was all going to pay out and there'd be the plus-profit. For a long time it just showed up on our books as a huge cost with, therefore, a huge loss of profit."

BUILDING SOMETHING WORTHWHILE

Business has a unique obligation to society to create worthwhile products and services and to perform this function efficiently. It has an obligation to be productive and advance the material standards of society; it also has an obligation, as does every other citizen, to help advance social justice. Certainty never exists. The strength of the belief of those at the highest levels of leadership that a particular standard of conduct or approach to an end is correct is particularly important. Timm F. Crull, of Carnation, points out about CEOs, in symbolic terms, "they really plant the seeds which grow into trees in the next decade or so." The kinds of people brought into an organization and the way they are treated, the standards of product quality and customer relations and ethics, and the levels of technological sophistication may not show immediate results, but they are reflected in the reputation and eventual success of the company.

A useful perspective for business leaders to take is to regard themselves as what David T. Kimball, of General Signal, calls "custodians of the future." The emphasis, by this way of thinking, is upon building for the future, and not upon quarterly financial measures of performance. In Kimball's words, "If you make your decisions on that, over the long haul you're going to come out okay. And the organization will come out okay. Never mind you can't optimize it for . . . the bottom line. You can't say, 'Well, I'm to take every step and we're just going to optimize the bottom line for this particular event.' And you've got to say, 'that's a foundation on which I am willing to build my career, on which I am willing to tie the organization to.' And you'll have your successes and failures, but over the long run success will be there."

It is also helpful to consider not oneself, but the future leaders and participants of the business and its customers and suppliers and stockholders. Richard J. Mahoney, of Monsanto, points this out as one of the many good reasons he believes it is unwise to opt for what is labeled the quick-stock-fix approach. "We have invested substantial assets toward the future, and we must make the future happen as quickly as possible. We will, however, continue to make moves that provide a durable result. The quick-stock-fix scenario has a siren song appeal: liquidate everything in sight, decimate research, buy in shares, . . . fire everybody . . . then the earnings per share go up, stock goes up, and your options are worth a fortune. I've got a lot of options, a lot of stock options. . . . I could have made everybody in that room there millionaires and myself a multimillionaire by doing it. I could run this stock up in no time. There's nothing to it. It's very easy. I'm doing this [the long-run course] for the next guy. This isn't for me."

The structure of ownership of American corporations makes it quite difficult to boldly adhere to the means which are genuinely believed to be best for long-term growth and stability. Short-term profit performance pressures, like those coming from institutional investors, discourage many firms from trying to add something of lasting value. Institutional investors have no loyalty to the firm whatsoever; if they can increase the value of their funds by a couple of percent by dumping their shares, they'll do it.

This is not to say that the short-term perspective is unimportant. No company has the luxury of operating just for the long term; companies need healthy profits now to be able to pay current obligations and have a flow of funds available for further investment. A firm must perform well today so it can live tomorrow. Delbert C. Staley, of NYNEX, captures some of the flavor of this idea. "The first and foremost thing, in my thinking, is that unless I have a strong, vibrant company, I'm not doing any good for anyone. When people question why I'm cutting back on jobs or cutting costs or squeezing the organization, that's generally the answer I give them." A delicate balance of short-term and long-term interests is required. But an overemphasis on current stock price and current growth rates and dividend levels for short-term stock owners can be detrimental to the survival of a company and to the stability and long-term health of a nation's economic structure.

The argument that only the stockholders' interests should be considered in making decisions ought to be called into question. If stockholders are only interested in short-term gains, it is unlikely that they will perceive the need for an organization they invest in to do anything to advance the interests of other constituents, such as the employees, the suppliers, and the communities where that business has operations. Efforts at social justice, such as increasing opportunities for the disadvantaged, which are costly in the short run but produce greater benefits eventually, will not be made.

It is not in the best interests of all shareholders to buy today and sell tomorrow, taking the profits and going on to continue the process and thus pressuring one firm after another to take a short-run perspective. If too many firms are operated in this fashion, it could easily cause devastation to the entire economy. What matter to long-term shareholders are continuity of technical programs, continuity of a good employee base, and the continuity of good supplies and customer relationships. When the threat of a takeover forces a firm to get rid of technical development, shrink its workforce dramatically, and kick customers and suppliers just to get extra dollars merely to improve short-term profits and thereby satisfy investors with short-term horizons, then sound business practices are thrown aside.

The belief that the worth of a firm can only be measured by its market value defies logic. This method of valuation can easily neglect the quality of the building processes underway to sustain an enterprise in the future. And this method clearly ignores efforts at social justice, community betterment, and the adherence to ethical standards. John Swearingen, of Continental Illinois, says, "There is nothing I've ever seen that could prove to me that the stock ought to move up five points in one day. It isn't worth that much more today than it was yesterday."

There is a certain amount of what may be thought of as safety in pursuing only those ventures and programs that can definitely guarantee a bottom-line benefit. Although a disregard for bottom-line considerations is foolish, an obsession with the bottom line can be equally harmful. Many things done within and by a business organization have to be done on the strength of the belief they are right and capable of making the organization a good entity which contributes positively to the world, beyond the narrow scope of profit. Men and women must willingly wager that the schemes, programs, and policies they implement are not only economically prudent but also that they will lead to worthy ends even though the income statement will not reflect it immediately.

Among the commonest downfalls of man stands indifference. Its most extreme form is found in the desire to remain unbothered by external matters. One tragedy of indifference is that it deadens one's desire to give effort to what can make a difference. Such lives are lived for what is easy and, because of that, they are sold very cheap; they are lived but they add practically nothing to human progress. A more common form of indifference can be seen in the inclination to play it safe, to take the tried and true paths. Many a life has limped along, unstirred with much enthusiasm, just getting by. Those afflicted with indifference miss much of the richness living offers. They prefer to play it safe instead of trying to carve out new possibilities. Safe may be prudent if one aims only to hold onto what is. How often we see lives spent simply trying to enjoy through consuming or by fitting in or by taking the safe and easy paths. But safe can never be admired. Neither can rashness be esteemed. Cowards may try to protect, but fools are erratic and they wrecklessly throw away their talents and efforts on what is ill conceived—the ludicrous.

A third model offers an ideal. It is the careful, the deliberate, the concerned—all sparked into animation by boldness. All great ventures hold great uncertainties, and, as a consequence, demand great faith and the willingness to wager that the undertaking will work. It is not enough merely to believe in what one does. It is necessary to go forward and prove it by staking one's self on it and by making the dream a reality.

Efforts made in management development and training, safety newsletters, "no questions asked" exchange policies, detailed quality inspection procedures, extra time given to corporate communication and employee dialogue with the firm's leaders, and equal opportunity policies are just a few of the many things done by business people, and done well and enthusiastically, because people believe they are important. Even though proof does not exist that these efforts will produce bottom-line benefits they are done well and enthusiastically on the strength of the belief that they should be done.

12

Integrity: Wholeness of Standards and Actions

Often admired and always respected, the person with integrity faces many of the same difficulties and opportunities others do, but somehow negotiates his way through life's bends and snags on a higher plane and above the confusion that engulfs those of less solid character. Where others stumble or fall because of character flaws, this person is able to stride forward freely.

There is wholeness in what the person with integrity says and does. There is consistency between his actions and what he purports to honor. He pursues his aims along the high road and is uninterrupted and undiminished by temptations for quick or easy personal gain. He seems undisturbed by the opinions others hold or express about him and what he honors. His upright conduct is made possible through steadfast adherence to unbending principles and standards, and his character is marked by an undaunted quest for important ends far larger than his own needs, comfort, and interests.

What he did in the past is consistent with who he is now and what he can be expected to be in the future. And because of his steady approach to life along these paths, others recognize him as being incorruptible and worthy of their confidence and respect. "Integrity" and "integer" have the same Latin origin—*integritas*, meaning whole, complete. The person with integrity is undivided. His standards and actions are sound, and they are one. This person is consistent in what he says and does.

THE NATURE OF INTEGRITY

The human creature hungers for many things: for the physiological necessities that sustain and perpetuate life, for security and a sense of well-being, for the acceptance and approval of others, for self-esteem, and for self-expression. Much of human behavior is aimed at satisfying these appetites, and each appetite, when pursued within certain bounds, helps advance the human condition.

The pursuit of life's necessities gives rise to improvements in agriculture, manufacturing, and commerce. The pursuit of security and safety gives rise to improvements in planning. The pursuit of social relationships gives rise to the formation of families and communities and the regulation of behavior within these social complexes. The pursuits of self-esteem and self-fulfillment give rise to self-development and creative expression.

Each person has modest appetites that serve him, in a sense, by making him more human as he looks after his own welfare and the welfare of others, thus elevating the quality of living. But these appetites expand if they are fed purely for their own sake. Anytime a person desires something inordinately, it can become an absorbing passion, making him its servant, thereby destroying his likeable qualities. The man who can be trusted is the one who can say 'no' to his overexpanding appetites and who knows right from wrong.

We all know of those who have allowed their pursuit for material possessions or food to swell uncontrollably into greed or gluttony, or allowed the pursuit of sexual relations to lead them away from marriage with a lifelong companion and turn into unbridled lust. Overconcern for the approbation of others can turn into a never-ending obsession for praise. Pursuit of a healthy sense of self-worth can go too far and turn into conceit. And the pursuit of self-realization can grow beyond a useful level and turn into an empty pleasure when it is pursued solely for the benefit of one's self. Whenever someone turns his attention primarily to the task of satisfying one of his appetites for its own sake, that task can quickly turn into an obsession destroying his character and also destroying the possibility of ever satisfying the appetite itself. Like an addiction, the obsession becomes the source of more pain than joy. The Romans had a proverb: "Money is like sea water; the more a man drinks it the thirstier he becomes."

When an appetite swells to become an addiction, the person will do anything to feed it, so helpless is he under its domination. The sure footing of reliable standards and worthy aims pursued on a high plane is thereby lost, and his character is diminished if not destroyed. Whenever the satisfaction of one's needs becomes preeminent in one's concerns, the issues of right and wrong are relegated a subordinate level of importance and ethical conduct is at risk.

Integrity requires that we be impervious to the persistent, nagging demands of our appetites for "still more" and to an overconcern about praise and blame coming from others. The belief that just a little bit more of whatever it is a man wants will satisfy his appetites, plus his actions aimed at putting his cravings to rest, invite compulsiveness to take root. The person with integrity is able to ignore the clamoring cries for more from his appetites that promise to bring happiness and pleasure if they are met.

Two essential elements enable a person to escape the cries for "more" coming from within. First, one needs a purpose or cause to follow that he honors more than anything else, including his own comfort and well being. By following such a cause, outside of the self, the individual becomes able to transcend the cries for "more" coming from his appetites within and is thereby able to neglect his pestering whims. Second, he needs to be loyal to his cause. He must obey its demands.

Popular among many is the belief that one can acquire wealth and approval and recognition first, and then go on to develop the qualities of honesty and dependability. That is to say, after appetites are satisfied, one can work to achieve integrity. This fallacy has disastrously affected many lives, and history is strewn with the wrecks of men who have gambled that it would work. Appetites when fed for their own sake rarely loosen their hold on men's minds but swell larger as they are fed.

THE OPINIONS OF OTHERS

As social creatures, humans have a strong need to feel loved, needed, and respected and to enjoy a close and lasting bond with others. It is widely believed that these social needs will be met to the extent that one shapes his behavior so as to be pleasing to others. To a large extent this works, so it isn't surprising that people are deeply concerned with their own standing in the eyes of others and that much of what they do is intended to gain them approval.

Great benefit arises from this. The desire to have a good reputation and to escape criticism serves as a strong deterrent to unwanted behavior. Social forces of this nature maintain civilization to a far greater extent, and surely more effectively, than laws and the policing actions necessary when laws are violated. The need to maintain a good reputation has far more influence on behavior than the fear of punishment. But the need for approval can also become an obsession and destroy both peace of mind and genuine character.

The desire for popularity puts people on the trail of pursuing praise instead of what may be praiseworthy. Here one is on shaky ground; what may be popular today may not be tomorrow, and what may meet with acclaim from one group may bring censure from another.

Integrity rests on neglecting the changing and conflicting opinions of others and faithfully following what one believes to be standards that are worthy of his obedience. Writing to his sister, Benjamin Franklin expressed this same idea. "One's true happiness depends more upon one's own judgment of one's own self, or a consciousness of rectitude in action and intention, and the approbation of those few who judge impartially, than upon the applause of the unthinking, undiscerning multitude, who are apt to cry 'Hosanna' today, and tomorrow, 'crucify him.' "[1]

We are left with the sobering conclusion that self-satisfaction of the highest kind has its basis in virtuous and self-approving conduct. A useful question people can consider before taking any action that will guide them toward integrity is not, "Will it be praised?" but "Ought it be praised?" And no amount of favorable responses to the former can justify an action that receives a negative answer to the latter.

Integrity is largely a matter of doing what one believes to be right as his conscience so guides him. The ideal is to be unconcerned with winning the praises of others and impervious to their criticism. The greatness of Abraham Lincoln is revealed by his steadfast adherence to what he believed to be right and good for the nation, despite the bitter attacks against him in the press. When asked why he did not try to defend his actions, Lincoln said that history would be a far better judge of him than contemporary critics and that if he were to respond to every attack it would not be possible for him to attend to the things that really required his attention.

Conscientious people often ask, "How well am I doing on this project?" And it is indeed important that each member of an organization work toward a level of performance that will please higher-ups. After all, people are being paid to perform in the ways their leaders deem appropriate. But beyond the normal concern for solid performance in keeping with their superiors' wishes and expectations there is a point at which a person can become obsessed with pleasing everyone. Frequently this overconcern is tied to something more than just winning the superior's approval; it is motivated by the hope of moving up in the organization. In these situations the concern is not to perform well primarily to help the organization succeed, but to perform well enough to win attention and praise in order to achieve a promotion or an advancement.

Concern for one's own advancement need not be condemned, but self-serving efforts to look good and win something for oneself can easily lead one to try "anything" just to succeed and move ahead. Whenever a person's concern focuses primarily on moving ahead in an organization, it is possible for his integrity to be pushed aside and his actions to become unreliable and treacherous. Douglas D. Danforth, of Westinghouse, warns, "Don't necessarily worry about the third job up. Because if you do every job as best you can and you give it your all, you're going to be recognized, and you're going to succeed, and you're going to go up forward to the limit of your God-given and developed ability."

The willingness of millions of eager men and women to work hard to succeed sustains the vitality of the nation's economic performance. But eagerness to succeed can extend beyond healthy hard work and efforts aimed at excellent performance. We see this with people who resort to the "game" of power and politics. Popular articles and books on this subject suggest ways their readers can move ahead and get what they want.

The idea behind the power game, as it is frequently referred to by these writers, is to gain some advantage for one's self, through any number of innocent looking means. However, these prescriptions unleash enormous opportunities for compromising one's integrity. For by following the advice given on how to acquire and use power for one's own advantage, it is tempting to overlook the difference between a course of action that is right and a course that is merely expedient and self-serving.

Playing the power game and worrying over how to gain and use power for one's purposes involves manipulating situations to one's advantage.

One peril that is always associated with gaining and exercising power is collapse of character. This is because in the process of gaining the power needed to do something, one is apt to become engrossed with gaining more power for its own sake. History holds many examples of self-serving people who have become obsessed with power and as a result have destroyed their characters and eventually themselves. Gerald Greenwald, of Chrysler, advises against the power and politics mystique and the advice offered by writers of popular self-help books. He urges dedicated hard work as the only sensible approach to getting ahead. "I've listened to others describe corporate politics. And I have to say I've seen very little of it. I won't say I haven't seen any. . . . Personally, . . . if I want to get ahead, the way for me to get ahead is to do my job so well that my boss gets promoted."

HAVING ONE'S OWN STANDARDS

One keeps his needs from turning into obsessions by ignoring the expanding demands for "more" coming from within. This includes remaining unconcerned with winning praise from others. Self-control alone is insufficient in these matters. Having definite standards and worthwhile aims and the tenacity to choose what is right above all other considerations are also necessary. Clarity of purpose and honesty in thinking are other important dimensions which lead to integrity in a person's character. It is difficult to imagine someone standing up and battling for causes or standards for extended periods of time who is deficient in these areas. One's resolve in defending or advancing causes or standards is made possible by genuinely believing in them. And the depth of a person's belief is enhanced by the amount of careful thought he has given it.

Standards, if they are to count for anything, must be personal. Frequently, the adherence to one's standards will be tested to the point where there is a cost associated with holding to them. The beliefs of Neil Harlan, of McKesson Corporation, serve as an illustration here. "I'm not willing to be chairman and chief executive officer of a corporation that ignores the problems in the communities in which it lives. And, we don't. . . . As long as I'm chief executive officer of this company, we are going to do these things [support causes in the community]. Then the stockholders can make up their minds whether they want a chief executive officer who's going to do those things. And if they don't, well, they can get another one."

Organizations, too, can be found that abide by standards their leaders believe to be right and follow honorable paths even though these paths will not necessarily lead to some material advantage. These include anything from equal employment opportunities to quality products.

Just as with an individual, a company may have to bear a terrific price in order to live up to a standard. Douglas Danforth, of

Westinghouse, describes one situation that illustrates this idea. "We are in the engineered materials business. I know of cases where we have produced and shipped a batch of material that probably would have functioned. The customer probably would never have found it. But we recalled it and reproduced it because we felt in the long run we were going to be better off and our integrity would not be questioned in any way."

In other cases, sales are lost or at least placed in jeopardy because a company would have to lower its standards to get the business. For instance R. R. Donnelly, the biggest printing company in America, will not print *Playboy* or *Penthouse* or any magazine or material that they believe is not in good taste. And Blockbuster Video will not include X-rated movies in its stores for rental. Any number of business leaders have refused to entertain customers in ways these leaders did not consider proper, despite the fact that refusal might result in loss of sales their companies could otherwise have made.

DOING WHAT ONE BELIEVES IS RIGHT

In contemplating an action, many among us are prone to ask, "What's in it for me?" There is a tendency in our time to calculate every action with the belief that the intelligent way to live is to maximize what one can get for oneself. The thrust of economic theory and management decision-making tools and techniques embraces this viewpoint. Illegal, harmful, or evil actions, of course, are not to be seriously considered; they are ruled out. But a serious shortcoming to this way of thinking is that it places adherence to standards and pursuit of worthy ends in a subordinate position to that of grasping whatever benefits may be had. Integrity demands thinking on an entirely different plane.

Merely avoiding illegal or improper actions may meet the law, but those who are known for their integrity live to reach higher standards. The notion that the good life is achieved by logically calculating every action so as to maximize what one can gain is one of the popular superstitions of our age. The reasonably perceptive person will quickly outgrow this concept of how to live; he will see that it may achieve some gains but does not deliver integrity. Socrates stated that, "A man who is good for anything ought not to calculate the chance of living or dying; he ought only to consider whether in doing anything he is doing right or wrong— acting the part of a good man or of a bad."[2]

What is "right" from a business standpoint, the textbooks claim, is whatever maximizes profits or the shareholders' wealth; the correct decision, their authors tell us, is the one that produces the greatest return. Were this philosophy to be followed all of the time, integrity in business would be unheard of. There are many business leaders who are guided by a higher standard of conduct than cold calculation of the bottom line. Integrity can only be attained when people struggle with the question, "Am I doing right or wrong?" instead of, "What will I gain by doing things one way or another?" It should not be surprising, therefore, to observe that in practically every situation where integrity manifests itself, we find people struggling with one question only: "What's the right thing to do?" and then having the resolve to do that, as the following examples illustrate.

The Bank Check Order

In the days before checks were personalized, banks would buy them in large quantities—maybe a half a year's supply at one time—with the bank's name printed on them. A newly hired salesman for Deluxe Check Printers, eager to do well, took an order from a West Coast bank—5 million checks! Elated with his huge sales order, this young salesman telephoned company president, George McSweeny, to tell of his windfall. Stunned by the news, Mr. McSweeny asked, "Five million checks? What is the size of the bank?" The salesman told him. "Well, that will be more checks than they'll need for several years. You go back and tell him that's more checks than he'll need," said McSweeny. "He should cut that order way back to less than a million. And give him the reasons why—they could spoil or be damaged or the bank's routing number could be changed." This was done. The bank's president was flabbergasted but thankful for the honesty and fair treatment he received.

The Tylenol Disaster

In 1982, authorities concluded that Johnson & Johnson's Tylenol, manufactured by their McNeil Laboratories unit, was linked to several deaths in the Chicago area. Some person or persons, had laced Tylenol capsules with cyanide. Johnson & Johnson got the report on a Thursday morning. The McNeil management acted immediately, recalling first one lot and then a second without lengthy discussion.

When more information about the poisonings became known a decision to remove *all* capsules from the market was made at Johnson & Johnson headquarters in New Brunswick the following Tuesday. That decision, which cost $80 million after taxes in loss of profits, was made by the chairman of the board, James Burke, with a consensus of senior management. However, the initial decisions were made by the people from McNeil, without checking through the hierarchy. Their immediate concern was for the public.

What's most revealing about this situation is that neither top management at McNeil, in Fort Washington, Pennsylvania, nor senior Johnson & Johnson executives, in New Brunswick, New Jersey, knew what the economics of their decisions were going to be when they issued the recall notices. In fact, they didn't total the costs until much later, because, in their thinking, that had nothing to do with the decision. Their most urgent concerns were for the public welfare.

The Mexico Earthquake

Historically, Carnation has been an international company. Anywhere in the United States or abroad where Carnation participates, that company has a policy of jumping in immediately when disaster strikes to help people by providing food products and money. In the case of the 1985 Mexico City earthquake, Carnation chairman, Timm F. Crull, notes, "We immediately donated, not thinking about our brand . . . or helping the image of the company. It's not even important. It's our responsibility to help our communities that we do business in. And we will immediately donate money or products or whatever is necessary without hesitation, and we have people who are doing that in almost every operation or unit of our company."

A Moral Obligation

Doing the "right thing" is not something one does if it is convenient or because it returns benefits. It is done because someone believes it should be done—because he believes higher concerns call for it. Levi Strauss & Company, with its genuine commitment to human dignity and fairness, works to make every work environment one of equal opportunity. Once Levi Strauss & Company bought out a plant in Blackstone, Virginia, that was all white. Shortly thereafter Levi's plant's manager, Paul Glasgow, came to top management and said, "I think the time is right to integrate the plant."

Their response was, "Good. We're with you."

He then went to the leaders in that small Southern town, to make his intentions known. Glasgow learned that they wanted to divide the plant into "black" and "white" sections. Levi's management said, "No, we're not going to do that."

The town's leaders then asked for a dividing line to be painted so as to keep blacks on one side and whites on the other. And, again the company refused.

Next, separate drinking fountains and toilet facilities were requested. And again Levi said, "no" to that proposal. The people at Blackstone didn't like Levi's stand; it violated their long-standing customs. An attempt was next made to pressure Levi; the local employment service stopped sending applicants to the plant for available jobs.

Paul Glasgow asked headquarters in San Francisco, "What will we do?" And, Walter Haas, Jr., who was chairman and CEO at the time, said, "Close the plant."

The plant never was closed; it is still operating. And it is operating there on Levi's terms of equal opportunity. Because of this courageous stand, the employment practices in the whole community were altered.

13

Putting What's Right, First

One measure of the depth of a person's character is the way that person is alive to what is, in fact, real but perhaps not quite so obvious—to the abstract ideals and values that define civilization and are the requisites for human progress, as opposed to the tinsel-like, tangible objects that glitter brightly. When we consider the enormous effort the vast majority of people give to acquiring objects that are believed to be sources of happiness and comfort, we realize what their uppermost concerns are. Yet the triviality of these pursuits is rarely called into question, despite the fact that possessions, that are thought to be priceless, once acquired, soon seem to tarnish and then are quickly ignored or forgotten, as something else that glitters even more brightly captures their interest and attention. Many lives are lived according to a value system that places pre-eminent worth on objects that can be bought and sold, as opposed to qualities and ideals that ennoble mankind. These lives are absorbed in a shallow world where the only reality is that which can be touched or seen. They are unstirred by the deep concerns of life.

We are all familiar with remarks like "Let's stick with just the facts," and "Keep to only what can be proven." There is a conception of reality that includes only that which can be observed and measured physically, in terms of distance, mass, and time. This holds that reality is revealed only by what physical evidence provides and as such is limited to certain, select sense experiences. The ethical, the purely intellectual, and the spiritual are all discarded. After all, those who adhere to this construct of reality reason, these other matters are unscientific.

This supposedly rational perspective appears valid, and therefore it goes largely unquestioned and unchallenged. But when we examine this thinking with any rigor, its flaws become apparent. We find that this conception of reality arbitrarily eliminates whole areas of human experience merely by a definition of its proponent's own making. Challenged to explain why they adhere to this conception, all that the adherents to this way of viewing the world can say is that they prefer to define reality in the terms they choose to define it in. They arrogantly decide in advance which kind of evidence they will inspect and they rule out every other kind. To prejudge, as these people do, is actually disloyal to science, which by its nature is humble and open to all phenomena.

THE REALITY OF INTANGIBLES

What is real? If you cannot measure it, some would say, it does not exist. Those who hold this view tell us we ought to live in their world of reality by concerning ourselves just with those things which we know to be real—what we can see and touch and measure. There are tangibles, which these people perceive as being real and there are intangibles, which they believe are not. Their reality includes what is tangible and little else.

What is more real, one might ask, than a concrete building or an iron bridge? They are, after all bodies of substance. Nevertheless, a nuclear bomb can obliterate what is generally regarded as real and permanent. What we perceive as real can be vaporized with atomic devices, and now with lasers. Many scientific theories that were once accepted as reality have been overturned and replaced by newer ones. And some beliefs once thought to be real from a rational perspective have later been proven incorrect.

These thoughts throw open a door to the liberating idea that reality includes much more than the mere arrangement of atoms in some configuration, which we now realize can be completely changed, and scientific truths supported by evidences that can be overturned with additional information and a new perspective. If our conception of reality shifts from only that which can be seen and measured to include that which makes a lasting imprint on or produces a difference in the world, we are thereby permitted to embark upon a radically different way of living.

By this concept of reality, the unseen is just as real as the observable. A work of literature or art or music or poetry can touch lives and move hearts to feel and appreciate revelations and beauty. The splendor of a seascape, or a sunset, or a majestic mountain may be more real in our experience than the physical forms themselves; reality may lie in an entirely different realm, unbounded by form or physical substance. The fortune a person acquires today will likely be gone within a few decades or less, but the lives that fortune touches may be changed for the better or the worse, and thus leave a lasting imprint on the course of civilization. The profit a company earns shows up on an income statement at year's end and may be reinvested in other ventures during the years following, but the ways in which the employees who produced the products that generated that profit were treated, and the level of honesty that was met in selling those products to customers, are apt to be remembered far longer and influence the lives of people far more than the profits themselves. A person may have many fine possessions today and may live a full and exciting life. But within the span of less than a century—hardly a wink in terms of time—all that remains is a memory of that person's character and reputation and the aftermath of what he did, both good and bad.

If our concept of reality shifts from only what can be seen to include what makes a lasting difference in the world, our approach to business in particular and to life in general is likely to be altered dramatically. Things that were thought to be fuzzy and insubstantial—like cruelty, meanness, and selfishness or honesty, decency, and kindness—can now take on added meaning. The undeniable truth is that these things do last, and they do possess potent, permanent influences on minds and hearts and on the course of humankind.

From our own experiences we can see that a good bit of the trouble and confusion that many people face and struggle against is caused because they fail to truly live in this sort of reality, concerning themselves instead with what merely exists in the conventional sense and what glitters in the present. It is indeed odd that people are influenced most by what they cannot see, yet that they concern themselves most, as evidenced by their everyday actions, with what they can see and touch.

In the same sense, what we tend to mistake for knowledge—tangible content, facts, data, theories, information—may in fact be of little value as compared to the unseen thinking processes and values—clear thinking, integrity, insight, compassion. Everyone will, at one time or other, encounter circumstances where his command of factual information is inadequate to the challenges presented and he will have to face people and situations with whatever reasoning skills he has mastered and with whatever integrity and character he has developed. At that point, he will be struck with the understanding that what is most real are those abilities once counted as intangibles. Benjamin Franklin held this important insight in his thoughts when he wrote, "It is certainly of more consequence to a man, that he has learnt to govern his passions in spite of temptations, to be just in his dealings, to be temperate in his pleasures, to support himself with fortune under his misfortunes, to behave with prudence in all his affairs, and every circumstance of life; I say, it is of much more real advantage to him to be thus qualified, than to be a master of all the arts and sciences in the world beside."[1]

In bettering society, in building a business, in raising a family, and in all other human pursuits, people are apt to concentrate their efforts on what they perceive to be the reality of their many tasks: the tangibles—highways and hospitals, cash flows and warehouses, pay checks and dishwashers. But the quality of a nation, a business, a family is built upon the intangibles—values and forces, although unseen, that determine whether there is stability, cohesion, vitality, longevity. Surely bills must be paid, and youngsters need food to grow; but they also need attention and care and work and responsibilities to keep from growing badly. The unseen, the intangibles, are indeed quite real.

At some time or other each person makes a choice. Which should capture his primary concern, the tangibles or the intangibles? One's concept of reality is bound to determine whether those aspects whose impact is potent and enduring—the intangibles—will have any influence on his thinking and actions. And certainly it is a test of one's character when circumstances place before him a choice between opting for tangible gains or foregoing them, or perhaps giving up something of measurable worth altogether in order to maintain a standard or adhere to some ideal.

We would be wise to remind ourselves that tangibles can be gained and lost and gained back again. They are renewable. But many of the intangibles are not so easily regained once they are lost. A person's reputation, for example, once lost is very difficult to rebuild to a favorable and exemplary level. Each human act is recorded, and its impact is irretrievably imparted into the future as these familiar lines from the *Rubaiyat of Omar Khayyam* remind us:

> The moving finger writes; and having writ,
> Moves on: nor all your Piety nor Wit
> Shall lure it back to cancel half a line
> Nor all your Tears wash out a Word of it.

Fantastic as the idea can seem, when subjected to analysis we can see the sense in treating the unseen as reality and giving primary attention and importance to the many intangibles, which affect people for the better or the worse, instead of to what conventional wisdom holds as real. Those who can comprehend this sobering insight stand to live far differently from those who cannot.

FAIR PLAY IN THE COMPETITIVE STRUGGLE

The emphasis on winning that permeates practically every aspect of our society can easily turn one's concern from pursuing purposes in an upright fashion to doing anything just to succeed. We may be sure that competitors are not cozy bedfellows, but that does not mean they must do battle using underhanded methods. There are more reasons for honorable forms of competition than merely the realization that a certain level of etiquette makes life more tolerable. Without fair play and honorable competitive methods, the struggle could degenerate into a dog-eat-dog, jungle environment, where treachery and strength count for more than decency and quality performance. This level of conduct would certainly befoul the system and create a condition where nobody could prosper. Competitors in an economic system have an obligation to keep the battlefield clean so that real progress occurs and effective competitors prosper. All customers thereby gain. Surely there is no advantage to an economy—tangible or intangible—where reprehensible moves are the main forms of competition.

A question many business people face at one time or other is, What should one do when a competitor stoops to dishonest or unethical schemes? Salesmen at Levi's once told their manager that the competitors were knocking them and their product—telling retailers that their product was inferior. What, they asked, were they to do about it? The answer came back: Levi's salespeople will not do anything with respect to their competitors. They will not knock their competitors' products in retaliation. Instead they were instructed just to show Levi's products and point out their quality. Men can rise above wrongdoing; they need not return ill deeds with more of the same. It never pays to kick a skunk.

Ethical forms of competition work. Leaders of the best and most competitive firms insist on them from all employees. John H. McConnell, the chairman and CEO of Worthington Industries, says, "Even though I don't like competitors—I've always told our people they take bread off your table if you give them a chance—we never bad-mouth them in public or to a customer. . . . We'll do anything to get business, . . . anything that's not illegal or unethical. We'll do it through quality and service and that type of thing." Abbott Laboratories is committed to a similarly high standard says the chairman and CEO, Robert A. Schoellhorn, who says, "Fair play needs to stay a part of our economic system." "At Abbott Labs," says Schoellhorn, ". . . we do not criticize our competitors or their products. There have been, and continue to be, opportunities for us to generate publicity or participate in a debate or jump on a bandwagon when someone is in trouble. But we simply will not do that as a matter of policy. When it comes to publicity, I feel very strongly that issues concerning products should be debated in a calm, informed, and objective environment, not through managed hyperbole in the press."

There are all sorts of illegal and unethical ways of gaining an advantage over competitors. Perhaps the most common one is by under the table payments—bribes to get business. It has been shown earlier that there are hidden and undesirable consequences, other than the possibility of getting caught, for those who pay bribes. Perhaps the most damaging consequence is that it does not encourage a firm to strive to become the best it could possibly be and thus to provide the best value for the dollar customers spend. Bribery causes sales decisions not to be made on the basis of value. Without honest competition for improved performance, firms can easily become lax and uncompetitive, in which case they may be forced to rely entirely on payoffs to sustain their sales. But certainly this is short lived; it ultimately affects the profit level as a cost factor and without investment in performance improvement the firm soon becomes uncompetitive.

A clear and unambiguous commitment to ethical dealings can set the stage for business operations on a higher plane and reduce the likelihood that temptations to unethical behavior will be seriously considered. Robert C. Williams, of the James River Corporation, describes an extremely tempting situation his company once faced, in which a product was rejected because of management's commitment to only the highest ethical standards. "Right in the beginning of the company we were working on developing filter papers for the automobile industry, and this was a very important product upgrade to get our company turned around from a losing operation to a profitable one. And we were told by one of the buyers that we were dealing with that, some extra would be required under the table to get our approval finalized in this company. Our response was, No-thank you. If that is what's required we'd figure out some other way to sell our products. That was a very difficult decision—to turn down good business—but on the other hand it was not difficult as far as ethical considerations were concerned."

Sound business involves competing on the basis of product quality, service, and price—elements of value. It therefore demands fair dealings. If products and services do not provide value in and of themselves, then buyers are shortchanging themselves or their customers and sellers are placing their long-term future in jeopardy because they have to rely on something extra, such as a bribe, to remain competitive. There is a host of other ways of making a sale that, although not illegal technically, are questionable from both ethical and sound business perspectives.

Philip E. Lippincott, of Scott Paper, identifies his company's posture regarding competition—how Scott Paper will compete. "Most of our salespeople would say that we are losing a lot of business because we are unwilling to compete in the marketplace as aggressively as some of our competition. And they would point out that some of our competitors are willing to offer bigger allowances to more important customers, or other things that we said we were not going to do. We'd like our products and certain services to stand on their own. All of them don't. But where they don't, then the pressure ought to be on us in finding more creative ways to sell it, rather than taking what would be an easier route."

Much could be written on fair-play or sportsman-like competition. The essential ingredient of fair play is refraining from taking unfair advantage of competitors. In the world of business, as in other arenas of competition, all opponents are not equally gifted. Some are larger, or more experienced, or quicker to act, and so on. Some firms may enjoy the advantage of owning vast resources acquired at low prices, or have a more advanced technological base, or have built up a larger market share, to mention just a few advantages. But they have gained these advantages fairly. They did not get them through underhanded methods.

It is heartening to find instances where corporate leaders insist on a high standard of fair play in their organizations, for it indicates that fair-minded competition is viewed as being more important than immediate, tangible gains. It shows a strong commitment to placing the interests of society and the economic system ahead of the possible profits a firm might earn; and, it clearly puts what's right into first place. Lockheed's chairman and CEO, Roy A. Anderson, provides an excellent illustration of what this can mean. That firm was bidding on an overseas job, a major contract worth millions of dollars. When Anderson learned that Lockheed employees, through a business consultant, had gotten hold of a competitor's original proposal he immediately called the division involved. Was this true?, he asked them. "Do you have a copy of it?" Yes, they did. The chairman asked, "Do you think that it's fair for you to be making a proposal?" Lockheed withdrew from the bidding. Upon explaining to the prospective buyer—a foreign government—why they withdrew,

Lockheed's people were met with the reaction, "Well what difference does that make?"

THE ADHERENCE TO BELIEFS AND STANDARDS AT A COST

It is easy to profess a lofty ideal. And one might live up to it a good bit of the time when its adherence is not made difficult by other competing wants. But the severest test of character comes when circumstances force a choice: adhere to an ideal or standard at a cost, or not? If a person is not willing to bear the cost of living up to what he professes to believe it becomes patently obvious what he does honor. For example, Cyrus Curtis, a century ago, could have brought in handsome sums of easy income to his publishing company just by selling the general list of magazine subscribers. But he chose not to. He didn't think it was right. In 1901 his editor of the *Ladies Home Journal*, Edward W. Bok, extended the prohibition, and with Curtis's approval issued a policy forbidding the giving or selling of reader correspondence for anyone's reading, particularly to advertisers. Moreover, no advertising matter of any kind was permitted to be included in a department editor's replies to readers; neither were the magazine's writers and editors to mention their own books or pamphlets. Curtis and Bok believed that their subscribers and readers should not be thought of merely as sales targets.

By its own actions we can conclude that the investment community looks upon publicly held corporations merely as bodies that earn streams of income for their shareholders. As a consequence there is tremendous pressure from this constituency for managers and executives to "make the numbers." After all, that is how they are evaluated. In this climate the prevailing attitude is that every sales dollar counts; if one firm doesn't make a sale, a competing one will. Costs must be watched closely. "Don't be wasteful," employees are instructed. And if a segment of a business is not performing adequately it is swiftly sold, despite the agony caused to individuals and communities. Yet despite these strong pressures, we can find firms today that are led by people who are willing to make the tough choices forced upon them and come down on the side of what they profess to hold in esteem. Sometimes this is done even though it diminishes profits. Richard D. Wood, of Eli Lilly, for instance, explains that Lilly does not make a profit on each drug it manufactures. Some drugs are losers financially. Certain drugs are made and sold because the company feels its primary obligation to society is to provide medicines for people.

The pressure for profitability and growth is intense; healthy competition is one result of these forces. But healthy competition and fair competition need not be thrown aside just to succeed. Strong and effective leaders are able to achieve both. Edmund T. Pratt, Jr., of Pfizer, explains how he approaches this challenge. "There is pressure to maintain that growth record. I almost never speak to our people without ending up saying that anything we do at the cost of compromising our integrity is not worth it. As far as I'm concerned, I want them to know that that's the *worst* possible thing that could happen to us. I'd rather have us have a bad year or a number of bad years rather than to achieve the kind of results we want by some kind of compromise of our integrity." This is not an unusual a stance in industry. John Hoyt Stookey of National Distillers (now Quantum Chemical), echoes this sentiment, "One of the things that . . . we mean by ethical behavior is that we will forego profit in order to adhere to a standard of conduct. I believe that's a message a CEO needs to convey loud and clear to an organization and I find myself doing that."

Under Jack F. Reichert's leadership, for example, Brunswick Corporation gave up an order worth in excess of $2.5 million. That company had been given the necessary permission by the State Department to sell 500 very large outboard engines to Iran. But the State Department later came back to Brunswick and asked, "Will you please send back that contract? Those outboard engines are being used to transport troops across the marshes in Iran. We can't force you to do it, but we'd like to have you do it if you would." Reichert's response was, "If that's what the State Department and the Department of Defense want us to do, that's what we do. We are an American-based company with American ethics."

The contract subsequently went to Yamaha in Japan, and Yamaha filled the order. The issue in this case was not one of whether Iran would ever get the large outboard engines; there would always be someone willing to supply them with what they wanted. The State Department knew that, and so did the Department of Defense. The decision by Brunswick really didn't keep Iran from getting the engines; they just wouldn't be getting them from an American company which had decided to put patriotism ahead of its own bottom line.

The voluntary act of complying with what a nation's leaders ask citizens to do for the good of the country is very patriotic; it stems from the belief that as citizens their first obligation is to preserve and protect their land, their freedoms, and their form of government. Walter A. Haas, Jr., then head of Levi Strauss, put a lid on price increases when President Nixon asked all of industry to be conservative in its pricing policy on a long-term basis. This was well before the price controls of the early 1970s. Other firms in the garment industry chose not to hold down their prices, and Levi, because of this decision, did not earn the profits it could have otherwise.

KEEPING COMMITMENTS

People will generally keep commitments when it's convenient or when they are legally obliged. But a person's real faithfulness to others and to what he believes is right is revealed in situations where there is nothing to force him to honor whatever actual or implied agreement exists. Will he choose to be bound by what he believes to be right, or will he opt for whatever immediate gain may be had?

In the days of fake cures and dubious medical products there also flourished a wide array of other schemes, some advertised in mail order papers, designed to part customers with their money. One that the Post Office Department later ruled was "using the mails to defraud" was the "Work at Home" scheme. A company offered a simple-to-use device called the Home Knitter, which sold for $5. Users could purchase yarn from the same firm and turn out socks, sweaters, mittens, and the like, which the firm, in turn, promised to buy back. To many farmer's wives this looked like a good way to earn pin money.

One of these firms persuaded Richard W. Sears to order 10,000 dozen wool socks; to him it looked like a good buy. When the Home Knitter Company received the Sears order, they added a line to their mail order advertising the unit: "Sears, Roebuck & Company have ordered 10,000 dozen of our socks." Sears, Roebuck & Company soon thereafter was besieged with letters from unhappy housewives who had been "taken in" by the Home Knitter scam. "The concern won't pay me—they claim my work isn't right. I can't get my $5 back as they promised," they wrote. "I saw your name mentioned and know you are reliable." Each "home knitter" who wrote, received a $5 check from Sears, Roebuck & Co., which although it had had nothing to do with the sale of the mechanical device, did not want its good name implicated with the scam.[2]

The Appliance Buyers Credit Corporation was a separate corporation created by Whirlpool to do financing for distributors and dealers. Bad debts overcame this concern in 1963, and its creditors stood to lose $20 million. Whirlpool could have walked away from the creditors. It had no legal requirement to bail them out. Some of Whirlpool's directors wondered if their stockholders would sue the company for assuming liability that was not legally necessary. Whirlpool's board voted to stand behind the debts piled up by the credit corporation, which resulted in an after-tax loss of $10 million that year.

The concept of "buyer beware" seems now to be replaced by "seller take care." Some firms assume responsibility for product failure or damage far beyond warranty periods even though their products are not used as accompanying instructions direct. Westinghouse, for instance, has stood behind its products on a number of occasions long after a warranty period has expired, as Douglas Danforth explains, "When we have a turbine generator out in the field—I think a turbine generator is warranted for 18 months performance—where we have found a problem with the metallurgy of the turbine blade, we have moved in and fixed that at no cost to the customer. It costs millions of dollars."

LOYALTY TO CUSTOMERS AND SUPPLIERS

J. E. (Jim) Casey, founder and former chairman of United Parcel Service, once observed, "I sometimes think it unfortunate that so many kinds of business transactions must be measured in terms of money. For in each transaction involving money our selfish motives are apt to take possession of us and tempt us to act in ways detrimental to someone else."[3] Indeed, it is part of the competitive economic system to base business decisions on performance, costs, profits, and so forth. And there are many benefits to be gained from approaching decisions from a purely economic perspective. It is fair and impartial, and it spurs forward economic growth, efficiency, and ultimately prosperity; it is a cornerstone of a healthy economy. Yet at the same time, if pursued in an extreme fashion and without regard to other considerations, it can be damaging to individuals and damaging to the long-term well-being of an economic system. For instance, decisions to sever long-standing business relationships and to form new ones in order to save a few cents here or there may not always bring benefits to all concerned. New trading partners may not prove to be as reliable and cooperative as established ones.

A longer-term perspective requires a broader view of a business relationship—seeing the relationship in terms other than just today's costs and margins and profits. Robert Wilhelm, of Emporium Stores in the San Francisco Bay Area, insisted on fairness to the major manufacturers his firm purchased from. "Before a buyer could drop a major manufacturer, it had to be cleared with the buyer's boss. We felt an obligation to be loyal to manufacturers we had been buying from for years. We didn't think it was right to cut them out for our short-run gain."

Some amount of give and take—for example, the extension of various forms of credit to help out trading partners—adds enormously to the betterment of the business world and immeasurably to the humane side of it. This is something that is often unseen by outsiders and neglected by those who would do practically anything to shave a nickel in costs. Character is revealed when a person or a firm forgoes a little profit today to help out someone else who is suffering from a downturn or a disaster. In the longer scheme of things, everyone wins by this approach.

Once flooding occurred along the Ohio River. Irving I. Stone, of American Greetings, relates how that firm responded. "We sent out a letter to everybody in that area telling our customers, saying that if your merchandise were flooded out—damaged—let us know and we'll get you an extra order at no charge. We got many back into business right away; we sent through orders to get them back into stock."

A community perspective leads to actions of help and support, while an individualistic perspective leads to actions aimed at bettering one's own lot in the short-run. A solid understanding and appreciation of what were presented as the intangibles earlier enables one to comprehend the community perspective; this is the belief that although one is out to succeed, an extra measure of success gained at the expense of the welfare of others is intolerable. Donald D. Lennox encountered this attitude among the companies his firm did business with as he set out to accomplish the nearly impossible task of turning around the ailing International Harvester Company (now Navistar) into a profitable concern.

Some of the larger companies, like Dana Corporation, were extended to about $45 million. Lennox explains how leaders from other companies helped. "They put their jobs on the line in many instances. . . . There was . . . quick cooperation from, I would say, our lenders. While they were demanding, which they should be to fulfill their responsibilities, at the same time [they] did not come in like a band of vultures and say, 'Well, we looked at the assets there and we believe they could be sold for more than they owe us. There's some profit ahead, so let's close them down.' They . . . went the extra mile to work something out. . . . Generally speaking, there was an ethical atmosphere."

LOYALTY TO EMPLOYEES

Where employees are perceived by management as just another element of production, as just an expense that should produce an output, their treatment is nearly always shameful. Economically correct decisions—those that advance one's gain to the maximum—are not always defensible from a humane perspective, which includes the intangibles of compassion, understanding, and willingness to lend a helping hand when needed. When these two interests, economic and human, come into conflict, as they often do in a dynamic, competitive economy, the decision maker is ultimately thrown back on himself. That is, in deciding what to do in such situations, he makes a statement of what he senses his purpose in life really is. Is he here for himself, primarily, or is he here to contribute to the betterment of humankind?

There are no simple or easy answers in these situations. For example, a plant closing that does away with several hundred jobs can be a tragedy for the employees who are thrown out of work and for their families. And yet a year or two later many will be employed in better and more rewarding and satisfying jobs and they may even say that the plant closing was the best thing that ever happened to them. Others will experience the opposite in their lives and be miserable.

To a large degree American industry is working to do what is economically sound and prudent and also what is humane and compassionate. Loyalty to employees does have a place in business. Courageous leaders—people with great compassion, who try to follow the Golden Rule, and try to do what is right in making tough decisions—are willing to sacrifice some of the economic gains that could be had in order to assure the well-being of employees who have served faithfully.

To those who have been trained in the discipline of just meeting the numbers, those who can see only the tangibles, this balanced and broader and more humane perspective is difficult to grasp. James R. Eiszner, of CPC International, cites an example of this type of thinking when his company brought back to the United States, employees who had served abroad. "When they go over there and become outmoded, which happens, or fail, which happens, we bring them back and we try the very hardest we can to find a position which is suitable for them within the

U.S. operation. We had a group of people all come back at one time who were housed in one section of the company. And it was known by the other, aggressive employees as the "elephant graveyard," because they— these paper performance youngsters, the business school trained guys, who say, 'I'll do my job. You, pay me well.'—couldn't understand why we were carrying these people on the payroll after they came back. And, of course, the answer was these people have given us twenty or thirty years of very, very dedicated, loyal service, doing the very best they could and in most cases satisfactorily, although diminishing in satisfaction as the years went by. And we brought them back and we just tried like the dickens to make sure they were treated fairly and given every opportunity to blend back into the American scene. We were not always successful. We were several times. . . . I guess three out of the four adjusted and found decent jobs here and the fourth we finally let go after three years. I think that's an obligation we have as a corporation, and I don't think a raider would share that obligation. . . . You try to get a guy to give up his American career to serve this company overseas. That's a rare "beastie" and we owe him."

An unpleasant reality of business is the necessity of having to sell off certain segments that no longer fit in with changed strategies or can no longer be managed productively and profitably. Those who are unable or unwilling to face up to these tough situations and management decisions should not be in positions that require it. But another part of that same reality is the people dimension; and those who are incapable or unwilling to deal with this reality can cause harm to employees unnecessarily.

When a reduction of employees is necessary, voluntary retirement programs are very much a part of the corporate scene today as a way to induce people to leave and, in return, take with them attractive compensation packages. But the sale of segments of a business presents an entirely different kind of concern. How can one know whether the buyer of the business, or segment of a business, will treat the employees associated with it fairly and reasonably? While some may sincerely question whether this ought to be a legitimate concern of the companies that sell, those who have a strong sense of loyalty to employees believe otherwise.

There are cases where a management's loyalty to its employees has led it to be unwilling to accept the highest offer received because it would jeopardize the employees' job security and benefits of employees. Bankers Trust of New York is a case in point. Once, that organization put a part of its business on the market. Several prospective bids were received, and negotiations were entered into with the most promising one. As part of the negotiations, Bankers Trust stipulated that it was not just selling an asset but a business complete with loyal employees. Bankers Trust expected the purchaser to provide for the economic security of the employees in comparable terms. The employees, after all, entered their employment with Bankers Trust, and through their service they had earned certain pension benefits.

The first proposal back from a prospective buyer was examined by Bankers Trust and found to be lacking in this dimension. The prospective buyer acknowledged the void and agreed to write down, as part of the agreement, what the terms would be. Its next proposal contained what Bankers Trust saw as "sketchy" terms. They started to spell out what they felt their employees should have to treat them equitably. To that, the prospective buyer said, "We may have to offer you less for this business." Bankers Trust replied, "Fine. This deal is negotiable."

The next proposal from the prospective buyer was similarly vague about employee pension benefits. At that point Bankers Trust broke off the negotiations, because they felt that this buyer never did plan to treat employees fairly and provide them with the level of benefits as they had had while employed at Bankers Trust. In total it cost Bankers Trust between $4 and 5 million in unrealized gain to hold to their standard on fair treatment of employees.

In commenting on his firm's stance, Vice Chairman Philip M. Hampton said, "It was an attempt by the organization to put at least the profit maximization behind the welfare of the set of people [who] had been long-time, loyal employees who were being restructured into a different world. And, it really was a concern for the people and not the profit that did it. And we justified it to [the] people who were very hard minded, bottom liners as, 'We are making a strategic change and the strategic change doesn't necessarily have to be done at the opportunistic edge.' . . . it was sold to the board that way. And they bought [accepted] it."

At Olin Corporation, Chairman John M. Henske says, "In selling off . . . businesses, one of the criteria that we set as our goals was to put the companies in hands where those people would be better off than they were in our hands and to try to protect as many of the jobs, rather than shutting a business down. We have had instances where we would have been financially ahead to shut the business down and write it off and pay the people severance pay, than to sell the business under the terms we did. . . . One we sold for what amounted to two-thirds of the inventory value."

ACTING ETHICALLY AND RESPONSIBLY

As a young man, J. C. Penney had developed an entrepreneurial flare; at 17 he took to raising watermelons. The summer crop was bountiful and the prices to be gotten were quite good: a nickel for for an average melon, a dime for the largest and best ones. He hired a horse and wagon to peddle his melons from house to house.

One Saturday morning an idea came to him. It was the big day of the county fair. He drove the wagon as near to the main entrance as he could get and was soon busy selling melons. It didn't last long. Feeling a hand on his shoulder, he heard his fathers words, "Better go home, Son. Go on—Now!"

Hurt with embarrassment, he went home. His father followed and found him in front of the house slumped on the wagon's seat.

Did he know why he was asked to go home? "No sir."

Did it mean anything to him that the fair was supported by concessions? Again, "no." His father went on and explained that everyone inside the fairgrounds had paid a fee.

"But I wasn't selling inside the grounds," young Jim argued.

"That's just it," his father told him. "Without paying anything toward the support of the fair, you were taking advantage of those who did. Everyone is entitled to earn a living, you and everyone else, but never by taking advantage of others."[4]

It was an important lesson in character, and young Jim was soon off and selling his melons in the proper way.

Not taking advantage of situations or other people when it is possible and easy to do so and not necessarily illegal is a good indication that ethics and a sense of fairness and responsibility are afoot. At one time or other, practically everyone will encounter a situation in which he could easily get away with doing something unethical and thereby gain some material advantage. In some of these cases others might see it but are unable to speak out against or do anything to stop it. In other cases no one would ever know. In many instances the only force that stands between a person's wants and some reprehensible deed is that person's concept of right and wrong and his resolve to act ethically.

The Tylenol situation that Johnson & Johnson faced has been cited as an example of a firm acting ethically—being responsible and highly concerned with the well-being of the public. An even better illustration of putting what is thought to be right from an ethical perspective ahead of profits involves Zomax, a Johnson & Johnson product. In this situation, and even though the FDA did not want Johnson & Johnson to do it, the company voluntarily pulled Zomax off the shelves in order to protect consumers. True to their credo, it was Johnson & Johnson's belief that its first responsibility was to the doctors and patients who rely on their products.

Zomax was a prescription analgesic (a powerful painkiller), which McNeil Laboratories, a Johnson & Johnson company, brought to the market in the late 1970s. It was nonnarcotic but as potent as morphine. It had the potential of replacing all of the narcotic analgesics, which although used widely, have a terrible addiction problem associated with them. Zomax had the potential of substantially replacing those, both in institutional and household settings. It held enormous promise.

In 1982 Johnson & Johnson began to get reports of allergic reactions to Zomax. In January 1983 they got the first report of a death from the use of the drug—an allergic reaction, called anaphylactic shock, resulting in heart stoppage. Throughout this period, Johnson & Johnson was working with the FDA, trying to figure out what the reasons were. In February four more deaths were reported, making five deaths in total.

Top management held an emergency meeting in order to get to the bottom of these tragedies. (Prescription drugs are very potent. This is why they require a physician's prescription. Because of their potency a few deaths may occur in the millions of instances where these drugs are used.) The evidence suggested that the deaths in these situations were associated with using the product intermittently, as opposed to using it chronically. Zomax was used without difficulty by arthritis sufferers on a chronic basis (taken regularly). However, the deaths had occurred in instances when people had used the drug intermittently. This fact presented Johnson & Johnson with the problem of what to do about the millions of bottles of Zomax in medicine chests, literally around the world.

Because the evidence suggested that it was intermittent use that raised the potential for this allergic reaction, and because Johnson & Johnson knew that people would use it intermittently, the question became: What to do? Top management considered the possibility of communicating to physicians worldwide. That could be done. But there was no way they could effectively communicate to consumers worldwide. They chose, therefore, to withdraw the product. David E. Collins, when vice chairman of Johnson & Johnson, explained: "The FDA did not want us to withdraw this product. . . . The point is that the decision to pull that product back, which was a decision not mandated by the FDA, not even asked by the FDA, was a decision which we took because you couldn't protect the consumer any other way."

TASTE, DECORUM, AND HUMAN DIGNITY

While there exists a wide diversity of views about what constitutes good taste and bad taste, some business leaders are not to be lulled into believing that anything and everything ought to be condoned and that there really cannot be a high standard for people to strive for. Some businesses do hold to high standards in taste and decorum. These standards are of their own choosing, despite what others may think is permissible. At the same time, they do not force their standards on others. They simply think it important enough to make it a concern in their own lives and in deciding how they choose to do business. At the basis of these beliefs and efforts to elevate the human condition lies a certain measure of respect or reverence for human life.

As we are all aware, there is a big difference between people who act properly because they seek approbation and those who think thoroughly about the reasons for tasteful conduct and live accordingly. The former are generally seeking something for themselves; the latter aim at elevating the human experience, which they believe begins with an honest reverence for human life and a deep sense of self-respect. Clearly, a person can take himself too seriously and, by holding too strictly to inordinately high standards and cultivating a thin skin, become offended at the slightest provocation. The self-centered prude makes an issue of what ordinary people shrug off and choose to ignore and quickly forget. Such behavior should be seen for what it is—a veiled attempt to call attention to one's perceived flawlessness.

Each person somehow arrives at a conclusion as to what he believes to be acceptable insofar as taste and decency and decorum are concerned.

It is rare to find complete agreement on these matters—*de gustibus non disputandum est*, which is really a kind of joke. But, indeed, taste is subject to standards and judgment; some businesses have made known the standards they intend to live by, partly because of what their leadership believes to be right or wrong and partly because of a genuine desire to elevate the quality of life in the communities in which they operate. To this end, Thrifty Corporation has discontinued selling "mature magazines" in its stores. So has Southland Corporation in its 7-Eleven stores and the Kroger Company in its drugstores. The use of sex in advertising is something Levis will not do. And Armstrong World Industries will not advertise its products on television programs that have excessive sex or violence.

At Hallmark upper management gets involved in passing judgment on what the cards convey; they have a taste committee to review such matters. And, as Chairman Donald H. Hall reports, "The acceptable level of people's taste in terms of sexuality or whatever has changed dramatically. We have a tremendous governor on what we do here, in that we occasionally run into a product that has been passed and approved that a person down in the manufacturing department may say, 'I don't want to work on that product,' which is kind of refreshing."

Although taste standards are honored because of deeply held convictions, they often prove to be a positive influence on business success. Major League baseball provides an excellent illustration of this. To make baseball not just the American pastime but the American Family Pastime, it was important to create an atmosphere and environment where the entire family could enjoy the sport. To that end, when he was commissioner of Major League Baseball, Peter V. Ueberroth and team owners set about to make ballparks suitable for the entire family. "It [the ballpark] is not a place to go and get drunk and pick fights and raise hell and throw beer on people," said Ueberroth. "It's a place to go and enjoy a sport which is America's pastime. . . . We felt it was essential that we cleaned up ballparks. We are not neoprohibitionists. We are not in favor of the banning of alcohol, but we thought we could set some new standards of responsible behavior and effective alcohol management. And we put those into play, including many things: cutting off beer at the seventh inning, reducing the [maximum] container size from 54 oz. to no more than 24 oz. in each stadium of baseball. Whenever we have incidents we go a lot further than that—to no alcohol sections, [or] we'd go to only low-alcohol-content beer. In many stadiums we've gone to no hawking of beer or alcoholic beverages, so that somebody has to get up out of his seat, go up during or in-between innings and get them [beers]. And you can't buy six. You can only buy two. . . . So we've tried to stop people from just getting out of control in the ballpark feeling we have some responsibility that when they leave the ballpark, not to have them stumble out and get in a car and be in that dangerous environment. . . . The results have been good, because from flat attendance in baseball, we now have dramatic upsurge of attendance throughout all of the cities."

THE PROTECTION OF LIVING BY WHAT'S RIGHT

Every human life is visited by troubles and setbacks. Each of us is forced to endure the emotional pain that accompanies disappointments, problems, and the stream of other difficulties living presents. Part of our character is shaped by how we respond—how we live to endure and overcome the painful and unpleasant periods in our existence. Another part of our character, perhaps a greater part, as well as a large measure of our life's experience, is determined by the troubles and difficulties we unthinkingly create for ourselves and thus permit to be added to our many other burdens.

Many of the difficulties we struggle against, and hence much of the pain we ultimately experience, is of our own making. What otherwise might have been avoided has been created by our own deeds to confound us and bring us added misery. A liberating idea worth understanding is this: By always doing what is right—by following the established rules that mankind has, through centuries of trial and error, come to honor—we can escape much harm and pain. To do what one knows he ought not to do is rightly labeled, dumb. And, to justify these actions through rationalization is deceitful. To believe that one can get away with acting wrongly, even though he might succeed at it for a while, is foolish. For it is, in reality, an ill-calculated attempt to mock the lessons of human experience and escape the consequences. A reliable fortress we can all take refuge inside is always doing what is right. Although it cannot shield us from the disasters not of our own making that pervade our world, it will provide us safety from those that are—when we act in ways against which the lessons of human history advise.

14

Living Positively

The root of success for practically all undertakings lies within the control of the individual; it is himself. The commitment he holds to while carrying out a pursuit, the level of enthusiasm he gives in the course of a venture, his ability to persevere in an endeavor in spite of setbacks along the way, and his steadfastness of purpose and refusal to retreat in the face of a formidable challenge or to be diverted by petty concerns while in quest of something worthwhile, are all insignia of positive living. The greatness and wonder of the human creature is seen in his spirit. In the face of adversity, in the midst of disaster, and with bleak prospects for an agreeable outcome, the human spirit has shown itself able, somehow, to rise to the challenges at hand, buoyed by a faith that the venture will succeed, that an answer will be found, that mending and rebuilding can restore, that a brighter future exists, and that life tomorrow holds rich and rewarding promises.

The greatness of the human spirit is found in its will to do, to succeed by being brave, ambitious, determined, resourceful. No matter how rough the road, how pessimistic the forecast, or how distracting the incessant stream of daily troubles may be, life goes on. It must. And in the course of living, each person, consciously or otherwise, comes to terms with, and decides how he will approach, others, his work, his triumphs and setbacks, the world itself: as one who says yes to his circumstances and lives with enthusiasm or as one who says no and suffers a miserable existence as a complainer and a bitter critic of all that goes on.

The encouraging reality is that there have been enough of the former—the builders and lifters—to have kept the march of human progress moving. There are plenty of uplifting stories of brave souls who have wrestled with fate to inspire the rest of us. And the good news for all of us is that everyone is free to choose whether he wants to be one of those souls, whose positive living adds to the betterment both of civilization and of his own experience as part of it.

The measure of a person's true worth is not how good he has been but what good he has done. A flawless life counts for very little if it has failed to contribute. The good life is not achieved so much by being perfect as it is by producing something worthwhile. Positive living sways man from turning away from the world, enabling him to live better in it; and it excites his endeavors to mend it.

The tasks ahead are large, and human abilities to meet them often seem inadequate. Why hold such grand dreams? Why keep trying? Why believe success is possible? To the negative, to the doomsayer, to the cynic, and to the spiritless, empty people who find it easier to say no to life, there is no hope. These people foresee only defeat and sorrow. Their lives are limp and battered, twisted, stunted. But there are others who are not so quick to concede, so easy to defeat, or so lacking in courage to stay with it. These are the ones who say yes to life with all its problems and setbacks and defeats and hardships—and its possibilities. Their enthusiasm and devotion make anything seem possible. To them the prize is just within reach.

The hope people hold onto, their faith in themselves and beyond, is not something some have and some do not have because nature molded them in one fashion or other. It's there because they *choose* to put it there. It's there because they value it and want it there. And it stays there, deep within themselves, because they live it every day, totally and unhesitatingly. And because they do so, it is nurtured and enriched and enlarged.

Some of this optimism may reach out and enter into other lives. It can be infectious, especially if one allows it to be. And indeed, any man of wit and substance will let it be. This will not guarantee anyone success or even an easy road, but it does make success more likely. And it seems to make the difficult road a little easier. For there is at least one common bond among all contributors and all successful persons: enthusiastic belief in what they do. They live with enthusiasm. They reject idleness and daydreaming, and they are not prone to childish fantasy, but their dreams and intentions are not small either—they are grand. They seek to do great things, and they are buoyed and sustained in their quests by equally great levels of enthusiasm. They produce positively because they choose to live positively.

Any human undertaking requires a structure, a plan of action. Purposes are far more likely to be accomplished economically and successfully if they are pursued by following logical action steps—when the work is carried out according to a well formed plan. Plans are products of the mind; they are logical. But it is also helpful not to forget the other structure, which should be constructed alongside this logical plan. It, like the plan, ought to be completely formed within the builder before the physical building process begins. This is the emotional dimension—the hopes, the expectations, the strength to persevere in spite of setbacks and tragedies, the willingness to put up with the necessary but tiring attention to the many unpleasant details, the eagerness to carry out a venture, the expectations for successful completion, the willingness and resolve to pick up and begin again if failure occurs, and the mental energy and readiness to continue as long as it takes, even if failure reappears again and again.

Just as one forms plans in his mind to guide his hands as they physically build, he also ought to give his best efforts to forming the right sorts of convictions and level of enthusiasm and belief about the worth of his effort to carry him through or over the rough spots as he pursues his dreams. This is the complement to logical planning: positive living—the building up of one's hope and faith and enthusiasm and bigmindedness that will move his outward efforts forward daringly and triumphantly. And, like the plan, it too is a product of the self. If positive living is a product of one's self, and if it really can make a difference in each life, then we have a guide as to how to approach our undertakings: before we start with the building process itself, we ought first to build up ourselves and our spirit to build.

REALITY ACCEPTANCE

If by a decree all men were to be made equal in wealth, if each were to have the same sum of money and each held title to equivalent plots of ground and equal shares of all other property and objects of tangible worth, that wealth would not long remain evenly divided. For although they may be made equal under the law, men are patently unequal in temperament and ability. And there is no human force that can make it otherwise. The resourceful, the imaginative, the industrious would soon build what they began with into something of greater worth. Those with discipline and intelligence would apply themselves and their talents to whatever it is they are best suited and work to achieve worthwhile aims.

We need to think clearly about what inequality in human abilities implies. We could wonder how a person might do well with the talents and possessions he has. One does not grow wealthy through disappointment and sorrow over what he doesn't have or what he cannot do. One can only achieve by investing his resources and applying wisely the talents he does have. Nothing can ever make people equal in ability, but each man can make something of his abilities. The first step on that road is to understand one's own particular aptitudes and inclinations. There are many forces and traps that lead people astray from understanding their abilities and a resolve to put them to effective use.

Clarity is served when we recognize that big dreams and daydreams are not the same thing. The former may be grand and just a little beyond one's reach today, but maybe not tomorrow; the latter are sheer nonsense, only utter fantasy. A great difficulty faced by many youngsters and young adults is learning about themselves and discovering their own particular interests and aptitudes. How often we hear little boys proudly announce their intention to play major league baseball and little girls candidly express their expectation to become the next popular music superstar. The realization that one was not meant to become a doctor or an accountant because his or her particular passions and talents do not lie along those particular lines can be bitterly disappointing to the individual as well as to others close to that person. Many people fail and as a consequence are understandably disappointed and cynical because their dreams were not oriented in the same direction their abilities could have taken them. Part of this is attributable to the influence from others whom they have tried to please. Instead of allowing their own thoughts and feelings to guide them, these, now bitter, failures listened to what others wanted for themselves instead of what their own heart and mind were quietly saying all along. We see, too, many a life directed toward the popularly held measures of success—a high paying job, a prestigious title or profession, a mark of status. How often we find people trapped in careers that they absolutely hate because they simply need the income or want recognition. Each person, each company, each community, each organization, will have abilities and limitations and opportunities unique to it. An important question each ought to face is, "Where can these talent and resources be applied most effectively?"

At one point or other some calamity or setback befalls every life. The person's abilities may be diminished; his sight, his alertness, his strength and stamina, all these things, may be lessened or wiped away. And yet we know of a few whose reservoir of inner strength remains intact and swells to make up for the loss. How can we explain the will to continue on found in men like Robert Louis Stevenson who, although bedridden and nearly going blind and confined to a darkened room, wrote some of the greatest works of literature? What is there in a man like Beethoven who, while deaf, wrote the most moving compositions music has known? We may be limited in our scientific understanding and thereby bounded in our appreciation of the technical particulars and the scientific genius of Thomas Edison. But all men, learned and simple, are unbounded in admiration for his will to shrug off his partial deafness and turn it from a frailty into an advantage for quiet concentration on the purposes he considered important. This is positive living: turning thoughts away from what we do not have and concentrating what little ability we do have on important issues.

In many lives we see useless reactions to the realization of both weaknesses and setbacks: first discouragement, and then despair, and finally resignation. This is the course of the negative person. But an alternative course offers a brighter ending. Positive thinking dwells not on the "can't be done's" but on the "can be done's." Strong and vibrant imaginative powers and the ability to visualize possibilities are at the heart of this aspect of positive thinking.

By dwelling upon one's own ills or shortcomings, one actually becomes more ill and less able to perform. But by directing one's thoughts outward, to matters outside of the self, the possibilities can be perceived and thinking can be spurred on by a desire to visualize the "can do's" and "can be's." Dwelling on one's limitations too often focuses attention on what cannot be done, bringing about cynicism and depression. Overconcern with one's loss is, in the end, wasteful. It only causes too much worry to be placed on the loss and what is no longer possible because of it.

Despair and resignation are a type of death. They seethe and fester inside a self-pitying individual, who spends his remaining days agonizing over his shortcomings, his "could have been" hopes, and his disappointments. He may not be able to do much about his shortcomings, but he does have the freedom to choose whether to dwell on them.

When examined from a positive perspective, shortcomings may be seen as helpful signals that suggest to people, "Don't try this, look somewhere else and try another venture." Like trail markers, they often tell the adventurer where to go by telling him where *not* to go. But the search will be fruitless if the adventurer's imagination and insight, his ability to visualize possibilities, is not rich and strong. Barring dumb luck, which can show itself to be our best ally in times of trouble by plopping before us the obvious answer or dropping us into circumstances that carry us away from problems, the only way to a good ending is to rely on one's own imagination. And because dumb luck visits erratically and cannot be counted upon when wanted, most people are forced to learn to depend upon themselves.

ENRICHING AND USING ONE'S IMAGINATION

A healthy imagination is not a gift. It is not something a few are born with and many are not. And it does not develop naturally in each person. Certainly there are genetic and environmental influences that, by their nature and occurrence, are different for each person. There might never be equalities in ability and potential, but this does not mean a person's mental abilities and imaginative powers cannot be developed. Just because nature did not endow a person, richly with them, it does not follow that he cannot improve and perfect them considerably. Truth compels us to say that he can if he thinks he can, and he will if he applies himself to the task. Each human has these freedoms: to choose and to improve through self-development.

With the felt urgency to develop imaginative and visualizing skills comes the belief that these abilities can be acquired in their full flower rapidly and easily through completing courses, workshops, and exercises in creativity. To a limited extent these methods can be helpful, but they do not move one very far or keep him moving for very long in this direction. A study of the history of science and the development of technology reveals that imagination, in the words of Edison, "is 99 percent perspiration and 1 percent inspiration." The trick is to apply oneself productively—to work and not to worry. Everything comes to the person who works while he is waiting for a happy ending.

The best way to develop one's imagination is to busy oneself with a specific task and work hard at it. Scientific breakthroughs and advancements are not simply the product of keen insight; the vast bulk of them are the result of hard work on real problems, of painstaking and backbreaking toil, of countless hours of trial-and-error drudgery. The great break-throughs in science, or any other field for that matter, are not so much a testimony to the value of insight and imagination—some mysterious hidden power only a few lucky people are gifted with—as we may be led to think. They are, in reality, more of a testimony to the importance of hard work, of getting on with the task of doing, and of untold hours of painstaking care. Even ordinary ideas, in ordinary lives, in ordinary circumstances can be made great and turned into real value through hard work.

Hard work is not an ordinary occurrence, but it is not a mystery to the ordinary person either, whereas creative thinking and imagination tend to be. A great novel, a great invention, or a great business venture are not great because they were formed that way in someone's mind, fully and completely. The formation of the idea probably took hard work and probably was recast many times as the actual work was pursued. The point is that these ideas were not created great, but they were *made* great. They were made great by great amounts of effort, by hard work.

Whenever intelligent people labor hard and seriously to solve one problem, they will generally see opportunities to make improvements or solve other problems elsewhere. The team of employees that sets about to find a faster way of performing a piece of work will usually also come up with a better way of performing that work. Anytime intelligent thinking is applied to one problem, it will usually find and solve several other closely associated problems.

There is a widespread tendency to sit back and wait for the perfect answer to come to mind, for some grand idea to pop into one's thoughts, complete and in its entirety. This misconception of how successful, creative, and productive people operate is perhaps fueled by laziness or procrastination. If one worried less about not having a great idea to carry him forward and instead busied himself with working at ordinary ideas, he would very likely be surprised at the results he would achieve. Even in ordinary circumstances, there are extraordinary possibilities. Unlimited possibilities, oftentimes hidden, lie waiting for people even though they have many limitations. It isn't their limitations that are the tragedy; it is the limitations to the effort they are willing to exert, effort that if expended would unlock the possibilities and make it possible to achieve great things. Even the dullest jobs, if attacked with sincerity and zeal, can turn out to be exciting and lead to significant results and genuine fulfillment.

THE REALITY OF THE PRESENT

We are all familiar with people who appear hesitant and unsure about the future; they have doubts and suspicions and fears about what lies ahead. These fears can be heightened by worry about one's own well-being and worry over what one now has and how he might hold on to it. Minds filled with these trepidations cause people to want to retreat to the past. Those who live this dream are heard saying, "If only things were this way or that way, if only I had this or that, if only I could be this or do that, if only, if only, if only, . . . I'd be happy." A mistaken belief is that happiness is found in having just what one wants.

Unable to imagine, because they are unwilling to forget themselves and work in the present to reach something worthwhile, many minds dwell in a dream about the past. These thoughts create nothing for their holder but a cloud of complaints and discouragement, which travels about in search of other negative persons so it can rain misery and despair on them too. And what's more, these other negative people actually welcome it. But positive people will not stand under these clouds; they are far too busy embracing whatever lies ahead.

What's striking about the positive person is his ability to see the future as a field of possibilities: as a vast opportunity to contribute something worthwhile, as an unfinished painting to be made beautiful, as a mine of undug riches, as a town of new friends to be met, as a land of great opportunity and adventure. Positive living involves the realization that the fullness and richness of living is not an end but a process, an adventure, and that the good life is not achieved by having but by doing and living boldly. The man who strips himself of positive convictions about the future stops living altogether.

Common to positive people is the attitude that the past is done. It's over and behind. They choose to pin their hopes only to the future. In their minds it's their choice whether that future will be positive or negative depending upon whether they say yes or no to life. Edwin Markham captured this attitude of optimism nicely in "The Look Ahead":

> I am done with the years that were: I'm quits;
> I am done with the dead and old.
> They are mines worked out: I delved in their pits;
> I have saved their grain of gold.
>
> Now I turn to the future for wine and bread;
> I have bidden the past adieu.
> I laugh and lift hand to the years ahead;
> "Come on: I am ready for you!"

Openness to change is another characteristic of the positive person. It's also a good indication of a person's suitability as a manager. In business there is no substitute for positive people. By its very nature the free-enterprise, market-driven economy causes business to be the institution most responsive to change. No other institution—education, church, government—has shown itself to be as responsive to change as business. The free-enterprise market system forces it. The reality of business is this: Change or die. And business people are too concerned with results to let outdated ideologies get in the way of success. If they do not change, someone else will, and will thereby replace them. Business is change oriented. Managers are, in fact, professional agents of change. This is why success as a manager is very often tied to one's ability to create and implement change.

ENTHUSIASM

A popular misconception equates enthusiasm with the peppy exuberance characteristic of cheerleaders. There is far more to it than superficial effusiveness. Sustained actions aimed at an ultimate goal are more indicative of enthusiasm than are shallow-minded glibness, smiles, laughs, and handshakes. The exterior expressions are nice, but there is a major difference between form and substance. Substance involves hard work. In describing enthusiastic, positive thinking, Michael W. Wright, of Super Valu Stores, says, "That doesn't mean you always run around saying everything [is] wonderful and rosy, but you accept the fact that when you have a problem you learn how to correct it." Positive living involves positive actions, and one's enthusiasm is not shown by smiles and happy talk but by active attention to the tasks that need it.

Negative thinking chokes off productive efforts; it contributes nothing useful to the cause at hand. It is a form of resignation to the circumstances and problems that appear overpowering and insurmountable. One sad feature about negative thinking is that not only can it overpower and cripple mentally those who use it but it can also be spread to others who are not fully convinced of the value of their own work or who are easily discouraged by setbacks, infecting their thinking and actions as well.

In describing his father, Conrad Hilton, Barron Hilton notes the importance of positive thinking: "He was a positive thinker throughout his lifetime. He felt that if a person had positive thoughts about accomplishments, and not negative thoughts, that positive results would follow. But if you took a pessimist and he only thought negative things in his mind, then negative results would be effected. . . . That philosophy of, 'Be big, Think big, Act big, and Dream big,' I really think was one of the cornerstones of his own personal success."

Enthusiasm results from having something to look forward to: a cause to serve, a purpose to achieve, a part to play in a campaign, a deep-seated belief in the worth of an endeavor, a feeling that a venture will be successful, and an active role in helping make some great dream a reality. These conditions are, to a large extent, controlled by the way people are managed.

Enthusiasm can be created in a group of people. Good managers know this, and they work hard at making it a top-level priority. They work at it especially hard when difficulty prevails. Robert Wilhelm, of the Emporium Stores, observes, "Selling requires enthusiasm, not just when things are good but especially when times are bad. When the economy got "off" and times were poor, managers were told, 'Now is the time you should get out on the selling floor and talk to your people. Talk to your buyers. Smile if it kills you. You need to be a positive influence. Tell them things aren't that bad. They will get better. Selling is nothing but enthusiasm. Don't forget to talk to the person who is having a good sales day. Tell that person, You did good today.' "

"Enthusiasm brings with it a certain amount of aggressiveness and the willingness to give an extra amount of effort," Kmart chairman and CEO, Bernard M. Fauber, notes. "You absolutely must be willing to give that extra effort to be successful. . . . You can survive, but in order to stand out there and be a little better than the other individual or corporation, . . . it's generally, if you trace it back, a little extra effort, that you give that extra enthusiasm, the extra time, a little more than the other person is willing to give."

LIVING FOR WHAT IS IMPORTANT

There are many things a person can do that can have absolutely no meaningful, positive impact on his own or the world's condition; there are just a few things that can. There are many things which we cannot control, there are few that we can. Positive living requires knowing these differences and acting accordingly.

Knowing that his own life is counting for something worthwhile, that it is making a difference, that valued results are being effected because of him that otherwise would not, gives a person not only a sense of self-worth but a feeling of self-control. And this knowledge, the realization that one can and does control meaningful events, is key to living positively. Without it there is no justification for one to believe in his purposes, in his freedom and ability to choose and to act, or in himself as having any genuine merit.

There are things people can change and things they cannot change. Yet even though this reality is generally acknowledged, many lives are spent battling the uncontrollables or complaining about them, instead of making small gains where change and improvements are possible—on the controllables. And not surprisingly, the feeling of self-control, and hence an important source of self-worth, comes from busying oneself with the latter.

Successful and happy people channel their energies in meaningful and productive ways. They use whatever limited energy they possess to secure every possible positive and meaningful result they can. They know that they cannot do everything and that, in fact, they are really quite limited in what they can do. But the point is that they are not worried or slowed by these thoughts. Instead they are enthusiastic about what they can do. Worrying and complaining, to be sure, add nothing to an individual's life or to the improvement of a situation; they only cheat a person out of adding a positive touch and earning the satisfaction that could be gained from it. So, too, it is with back stabbing and political maneuvers—actions that can go on in organizations.

Frank W. Considine, of National Can, recalls an incident that occurred when he was being pushed ahead in the organization perhaps a little faster than he now thinks he should have been. Out of jealousy because of his rapid movement in the organization, one of his contemporaries developed a dislike for him. Considine chose not to respond in kind. "Because it was politics and I was being pushed a little faster than I should have been, I can remember at the time saying to myself, 'Well, I'm going to do the right thing. I'm not going to let it bother me.' It did bother me. But I'm not going to change my method of operation. This fellow, after about two years, found out that he was wrong and we became very, very close friends. . . . He would have loved to get me out of that company. So you do the right thing and it will always work out for you. Sometimes it gets a little rough, but it works out."

The rumormonger, the tattletale, and the gossip are so overwhelmed by the things they cannot control and the insignificant negative ones that they can, that they tend to neglect what matters. In the end they add only pain to others' lives and fill their own lives with the same. Unwilling to channel their efforts toward useful purposes, they cheat themselves out of being the people they could become, were they positive instead of negative. And because of this they forego their chances to produce useful results.

Richard J. Flamson III, encourages employees at Security Pacific to rise above pettiness regardless who happens to be right or wrong in a squabble. "We want our people to be courteous and we want them to try to put themselves in the customer's place. And we want them to understand that because we have 2.5 million customers in California, we're going to run across those customers in an antagonized environment from time to time, just because of the size and the number of contacts that are made. And the customers are going to be wrong many, many, many times, and we're going to be wrong, hopefully not as many times. But they [employees] need to develop the attitude that they've got to get that over and behind them and go forward and be aggressive, yet courteous to our customers."

It is deceptively easy to become consumed in little things. Success in a venture is gladly accepted by the one who undertakes it, but failure and losses are not so easily faced. If failures and losses can be put behind quickly, future endeavors can proceed unimpaired and undiminished. It is sad when a person paralyzes himself by sulking from the misery he feels from a defeat, dooming himself to a failure and to having to live with the burrs of life.

Excessive fear of mistakes can paralyze. Caring for one's cause more than one's self is a way to freedom from the paralysis that fear and ensuing worry cane bring. The late Paul V. Galvin, founder and longtime head of Motorola, gave this suggestive advice: "Do not fear mistakes. Wisdom is often born of such mistakes. You will know failure. Determine now to acquire the confidence required to overcome it. Reach out."[1] Here we have yet another glimpse of positive living: reaching out for the future optimistically by first letting go of ourselves.

15

Building Solid Relationships

Business activity is as much social as it is strictly economic. The health and soundness of that activity, therefore, depends as much upon the quality of the relationships business encompasses as it does on the economic realities of profit-producing functions. It may be flatly stated that the quality of economic performance and the satisfaction people achieve through working in business are tied to the nature of the relationships formed and maintained in the course of business activities. A sobering reality is that many of these relationships are fragile, and if they are strained or neglected, will not long endure in a form that will benefit all concerned.

NEEDED: SOLID RELATIONSHIPS IN BUSINESS

Most business relationships involve forms of exchange—goods and services are exchanged for money; labor is exchanged for wages and benefits; the use of property is exchanged for rents and royalties. What's more, many of these exchanges are carried out by strangers. The parties may be many miles apart and know of one another only by hearsay information or by a general reading of each other's reputation. Reputation obviously carries considerable weight in determining whether one voluntarily chooses to enter into a business relationship with another party. Moreover, most relationships continue at the pleasure of the parties involved.

Someone who feels he has been ill-treated or thinks he is receiving an unfair bargain is likely to take steps to extricate himself from that arrangement and, if he believes there is due cause, to take legal action. The free-market system has ways of permitting parties to work out their differences, to discover cheats, and to discontinue business dealings that are unsatisfactory. But those processes are sometimes very slow, and justice can be very costly. So the high ideal of establishing and maintaining sound business relationships should be relied upon far more than the market processes and the machinery of the legal system.

No one achieves much of note when he tries to go it alone. Great business accomplishments are generally found to be the result of highly organized efforts. The dividing line between success and failure is often traceable to the cooperative spirit of the parties involved. Here it is possible to realize the special importance of the many factors that affect the climate of working relationships. Any leader worth his salt knows instinctively the value of relationships. Those that are positive are generally helpful to the accomplishment of organizational purposes. They add a dimension of enjoyment to work.

Information, no doubt, is a core element of any advanced economy. Accurate, timely, and useful data—qualitative and quantitative—are essential to managing and carrying out the work of any enterprise. Figures on the market, on costs, and on production are part of this picture. So too are attitudes, perceptions, opinions, and feelings. Timeliness and accuracy of information spell the difference between success and failure. The point here is that honesty, goodwill, the spirit of cooperation—let the list of fundamental aspects of solid relationships go on—make it possible for business people to obtain and use the accurate and timely information they need.

Specialization permits speedier breakthroughs in science and technology, and it allows for higher levels of competency to be applied to work. It carries the price of interdependency and the need for professionalism. Our ignorance of the quality of work performed by highly trained specialists places us to some degree at the mercy of the good intentions and capabilities of these professionals. These realities make plain the importance of professionalism. Because few people are able to judge competently the work of specialists, professionalism carries with it the obligation to hold a high regard for those who depend upon their work.

Whenever one's most urgent concerns are for success and advantage he may be led to act in ways that destroy many of the important relationships that enable a business or an economy to function effectively. Although individuals may advance their own causes temporarily by shady schemes, their meager gains do not offset the harm they inflict on the foundations upon which sound and lasting business dealings are based. Sadly, the illusion of success achieved through these methods can blind a person to the damage he has inflicted upon an organization or upon the entire economic system. Worse still, his mind may be deadened to the fact that even his own long-term best interests are diminished.

Serious thought leads to the realization that all benefit when everyone considers first whether an action or a decision is likely to build better relationships and hence strengthen the ability of a business or an economy to function smoothly, instead of placing primary concern on self-interest. Were people to measure the success of their transactions in terms of goodwill and stability of relationships in addition to profit and loss, every fair-dealing participant would be much better off, financially and otherwise.

It is odd, therefore, to find that in America very little attention, if any at all, is ever given to this idea in business textbooks or during the course of instruction of business students. Yet experienced and successful business people recognize the importance of solid relationships for financial success, peace of mind, and personal satisfaction. The most thoughtful participants in business regard the building and maintenance of good relationships as more than just a duty; they also see it as a necessary element for long-term survival of our civilization and its economic institutions. Emerson wrote, in his essay, "On the Conduct of Life: Wealth," that "Society is barbarous until every industrious man can get his living without dishonest customs." Economic freedom is too important to be dealt with casually and irresponsibly. Each person who plays a role in private enterprise can do so in ways that will perpetuate it for future generations. Economic activity is not separate and apart from other forms of social intercourse but very much at the core. One cannot isolate his business life from all other aspects of his life any more than he can separate his head from the rest of his body.

IDEALS OF AN ECONOMIC SYSTEM

Everyone's well-being, financial and otherwise, is tied to the level and quality of economic activity. Virtually everyone participates, as consumer or producer or both, in the economic community. And practically everyone regards the economic system as something that ought serve himself. Each person would like it to be arranged and run so that he prospers. Yet danger is present when everyone views the economy only in terms of what and how he can benefit in it. He can easily lose sight of his obligations to the capitalistic, economic system: to understand it and how it works, to maintain it and help make it work well, and to improve it where possible and when changes necessitate improvements. If people are to participate intelligently in meeting these important obligations, it is necessary that there be common ideals for them to work toward, so as to maintain and perfect the free-enterprise economic system.

Economists measure economic performance in terms of four parameters: growth, inflation, productivity, and employment. Indeed, these measures do provide an accurate index of the performance of an economy. But they fall short of indicating the *wellness* and the *goodness* of the economy—whether it will likely continue to perform well and to everyone's benefit and whether those participating in it are treated by it as humans ought to be treated. A broader view of the economy would be useful to this end, and in this broader perspective, ideals of an economic system might be set forth in order that it be made a good system.

The following ideals are generally regarded as desirable; they embrace three important concerns: (1) past economic performance, (2) the likelihood of healthy economic performance, in the future, and (3) the goodness of economic activity in terms of commonly held ideals and aspirations for human betterment.

1. Wealth and prosperity are created intelligently. The "right" things are produced, meeting as many needs and wants as possible. The economic system is effective because the most needed and valued goods and services are produced from the available resources.

2. There is efficiency in the production and distribution of goods and services. There is a minimum of waste in these processes. Output for the limited inputs is maximized.

3. The sharing of prosperity allows each member of the community to share in the fruits of production. Material goods are used and enjoyed, not stored away in closets and bins needlessly and beyond what is needed to provide security against possible hardships.

4. Each able-bodied citizen participates in producing goods or services, and each is compensated in keeping with his or her contributions. Each can be compensated generously, because each produces well. Thus there is a distribution of wealth and income whereby poverty does not exist. There is full employment. This creates a very large middle class and hence a high level of aggregate demand.

5. Advances in knowledge and technology are fully applied, and they are applied rapidly after they become known. There is full use of new methods, ideas, and advances from all fields of knowledge. These advances are put to use to improve products, to produce new ones, and to produce them more efficiently and better.

6. There is stability: price stability, wage stability, employment stability. Inflation and deflation are minimal. Shifts in employment are swift, allowing for time to educate and retrain workers.

7. Steady and robust growth occurs. The economy steadily improves in its ability to produce goods and services.

8. There is freedom of economic choice. People participate freely. They are free to choose occupations, to establish businesses, to buy and sell. They are free to choose what they do in the economy and how they do it. Everyone has a fair chance to participate. Participation is a function of ability; there are no other forms of discrimination. Success is a consequence of performance.

9. The economy is free of destructive strife, labor unrest, meanness, unfair competition, and the inhumane treatment of people. The expression of virtues—honorable and decent behavior—is rewarded. The system promotes morality and ethical behavior. Living a worthy and good life is compatible with successful participation in the system. Wrongdoing is not tolerated.

10. Lives are enriched through participation in the economy. Work is ennobling to each person's existence. Self-worth is achieved through working.

11. The power of exchange is not onesided, whereby some are at a disadvantage and can be victimized or cheated. All people are intelligent participants.

NOT TAKING ADVANTAGE OF OTHERS

When people are in a position of power and have the advantage to do pretty much what they choose to do despite the effects their actions might have on others, it is unmistakable what they honor most. Character is revealed by self-restraint, especially when one stands to gain by acting otherwise. One incident that confirms our confidence in man's ability to live by a high ideal involves Levi Strauss & Company.

In July 1872 an immigrant tailor in Reno, Jacob W. Davis, wrote to the San Francisco dry-goods house of Levi Strauss & Co. For nearly two years he had been buying duck cloth and denim from them. He added a note containing a business proposition, along with a check he was remitting to balance his account. Sending two samples of overalls he had been making for workingmen in his area—one of blue denim and one of off-white duck—Davis inquired as to whether Levi Strauss would secure and bear the expenses for a patent to be taken out in Davis's name for the copper-riveted trousers he was making, but not nearly fast enough to satisfy all the orders he was getting. In exchange, Davis would give Levi Strauss half the rights to sell the new type of trousers in all the Pacific states and territories. The balance of the United States and half the Pacific Coast he would reserve for himself.

Workingmen's pants sold, ordinarily, for $9 or $10 per dozen; Davis could get $36 per dozen for his. The partners at Levi Strauss, Jonas and Louis Strauss, decided promptly; they contacted patent attorneys who forwarded a petition within a week for Davis to sign.

By August 9 the petition was returned and an application for Davis's "improvement in fastening jeans. . . . in order to prevent the seam from starting or giving away from frequent strain or pressure" was submitted. Unfortunately, it was rejected. It took an additional 10 months and three amendments before the patent was finally granted, on May 20, 1873, assigned to Davis and Levi Strauss & Company of San Francisco.[1]

In those days an obscure tailor in far away Reno would have been unable to have stopped Levi Strauss from stealing his idea. Who would have ever known it was Davis who first had hit upon the idea of securing pockets with copper rivets? Levi Strauss could have stolen Davis's idea, but it did not. The company chose not act that way; it wasn't honest. Stealing the idea was probably never even contemplated. Nonetheless and importantly, it sets a standard of honesty for others to think about any time they are in a situation where no one might know or be able to do anything to stop an act that takes advantage of someone else.

From a purely financial perspective, price gouging—charging whatever can be gotten when circumstances permit it—may be legal and even within the parameters of what economic theory says is desirable. But as one of the cofounders of Holiday Inns, William B. Walton, Sr., says, "Whenever you are guided by the principle of charging whatever the market will bear, you are not thinking right about people."[2] It could be added: you are thinking only about yourself. Seeing themselves as a "nice" company run by "decent" people with a good image in the public eye, top management of Holiday Inns has constantly denounced and fought against price gouging by isolated local management.

Fair pricing is not only a company policy but is seen by top management as an essential part of the attitude of respect for one's neighbor, a key principle that the company was built upon. Walton notes, "If the price wasn't fair to the traveling public, including business people and families, we were stern enough about it to warn such an inn that we'd remove it from the system and take away our name and sign from the premises. We did that in some cases."[3]

By gouging customers the seller may reap short-run economic gains, but in so doing he destroys his genuine concern for them and thereby renders himself incapable of truly serving those whose purchases sustain his enterprise. Eventually the disregard for the customers shows up in other aspects the of business and may invite its collapse.

The consuming public is not the only party to be gouged or squeezed in the course of the many business transactions occurring every day; businesses can do this to one another also. If one has to depend on "squeezing" others for his success, to earn a profit, it speaks poorly of the true value of the contribution he can make as a businessperson. There are, to be sure, many ways by which one can take advantage of others in business transactions. One is in paying bills quite slowly.

Robert L. Barney, of Wendy's, commenting about his firm's posture on paying its suppliers, stated, "There are some people that believe in stretching the credit as far as they can stretch it, using the other guy's money. The little guy out there, the supplier, is the one that hurts when you do that. We don't believe in that. We believe in paying our bills on a timely basis. And we pay. We believe in our suppliers making money, being profitable. If they aren't, they aren't going to be in business long. And if you want a long-term relationship they need to make a profit or make some money out of this thing too. So you don't squeeze them to where they can't make any money or it isn't a good deal for them. It's important that your suppliers make money as well."

Relationships between business firms are strengthened by cooperation even though the short-run dollars and cents approach may dictate a far different course. Many times, for instance, steel has been received from suppliers to Worthington Industries that could have been sent back. But as the chairman and CEO, John H. McConnell, explains, "Our philosophy has always been, if we can apply that material to another job, we'll just keep it. We . . . tell the supplier, this material is not what we ordered but we're going to use it. Otherwise they would never know they sent a bad order to us. . . . If it's salvageable in any way we will use it, and they know this."

Instead of gauging the success of a transaction entirely on self-gain, a business person would be far better off taking into account the benefits to be gotten by all concerned. In this way he would be able to make his future more secure and much increase his opportunities for continued, profitable, and satisfying exchanges. By sticking to this principle, Levi Strauss built long-standing relationships that have been worth far more than what might have been realized by squeezing a few more cents out of initial agreements.

Former chairman and CEO of Levi Strauss & Company, Walter A. Haas, Jr., recalls an incident which compresses the issue fairness in business into a single point. It occurred when his father ran that company. Shortly after World War II, a man named Stafford and his son called on the elder Haas at his office in San Francisco. Stafford had a plant in Sedalia, Missouri, called the J. A. Lamy Manufacturing Company. He was looking for some contract production. The two men negotiated a contract whereby J. A. Lamy Manufacturing would produce a hundred dozen trousers a day. And when it was over and the deal was struck they sealed it with a hand shake; the relationship continues on today.

On the drive home that night Walter Haas, Jr. said, "Dad, I saw the figures and we could have gotten that production for ten cents a dozen less than you agreed to pay." The dad's reply was, "Of course, I could have probably done better than that. First of all, Son, you make a contract with somebody, both sides have to be happy with it. And they're happy with it. And because they're happy with it, I expect that one of these days we'll get the other five hundred dozen in that plant." And they did.

FAIRNESS

To anyone who has been the victim of an injustice—unfair bias, prejudice, or deception—the importance of fairness takes on special meaning. Fairness serves to weed out injustice and dishonesty; its full flower is the even-handed treatment of all concerned—an ideal no thoughtful man will lightly set aside. Few actions have more marred the reputation of a business than the neglect of fairness.

One practical result of fairness is that it places relationships on a secure footing. It makes an economic system more predictable and more productive, because competent performance becomes the chief determinant of everyone's success. Distrust and confusion reign in the competitive arena in its absence. When fairness goes, sound economic performance, intelligent thinking, and human rights and dignity go, too. When fairness goes, the rules of jungle become the only logical code: Don't be weak, kill first or be killed, do anything to survive. In this environment creative thinking and problem solving and intelligent analysis are not often spent on matters and in ways that lead to human progress and material advancements; competitors, instead, become consumed with the task of staying alive and ahead of those who are inclined to take advantage of them. The majority of efforts are thereby directed at activities that produce little or no benefit for the well-being of all concerned. Fairness, therefore, is critical to a sound economic system; an economy's ability to function productively requires it. Robert C. Williams, of the James River Corporation, notes that "Fairness must override all transactions and relationships."

Attention from the highest levels indicates the importance business leaders place on the elimination of unjust bias and the maintenance of fairness. For just as with an economy, they know that fairness is crucial to the well-being and to the smooth and successful functioning of their organizations. An executive vice president of E. F. Hutton in Europe was once discovered to have tried to influence senior management at corporate headquarters in New York so that his people would be given much larger bonuses than they were entitled to. In exchange, he demanded that his employees promise to give some of it back to him. The chairman and CEO terminated him immediately.

At Kmart, the chairman and CEO, Bernard M. Fauber, insists that buyers treat all salespeople in a straightforward and fair manner; it is important, he believes, to maintain solid relationships with suppliers, and that requires fair treatment. "My belief," says Fauber, "is that anyone who wants to see us, we should see. I have no problem with one of our buyers telling [them], 'No, I can't use your product.' But at least we must see you [suppliers] and talk to you and look you in the eye and tell you why: It isn't as good as the other product, you can't supply them in sufficient quantity, or the price is high."

The public is well aware of the scandals and news reports revealing unfair stock trading on Wall Street. What goes largely unreported is the fact that brokerage houses have, and continue to insist on, high standards of fairness by not allowing insiders to take advantage of privileged information before it is made public. Robert E. Fomon, of E. F. Hutton, recounts one such episode. "A couple of senior officers bought a stock for their own accounts with knowledge that we were going to do a public [offering] of this company, which was little known, and therefore the publicity of taking it public would have inflated the value. And they bought it in anticipation, essentially of higher price based on our taking the company public. Actually it was public, but creating a bigger name for the company. In that case, they were good employees, I did not terminate them. But what I did was, I told them that they could not sell the stock they bought. They would have to hold it for six months after the public offering, which they did. And the stock went down and they didn't make any money."

A difficulty associated with living up to the high standards that fairness demands is the perception that it frequently carries the price of bearing a loss or forgoing a possible gain. This is not always true. In fact, on many occasions quite the reverse is the case. Fairness demands that business be conducted on the merits of quality, service, performance—value given for value received. Richard E. Heckert, of Du Pont, points out that it is far better to run business strictly on business terms, instead of relying on payoffs and dishonesty to gain an advantage, "Fraud is fraud the world around," says Heckert. "Basic dishonesty simply can't be rewarded. We have never paid an important payment that is anything other than just a tip. . . . We just think in the long-run we're better off not to start down that road and I can't honestly identify lost business because of sticking to that policy. Now we may have lost some, but I'll never know about it. So be it. If I'm playing it straight, generally we get our price and we get the business, because we have the reputation for being straight shooters. And it turns out that even corrupt governments like to deal with straight shooters. They somehow have the feeling that they're getting a square deal."

BEING A GOOD CITIZEN

The enterprise that is primarily concerned with squeezing every last dollar of profit out of the areas it serves and that ignores the responsibilities of a good citizen not only can damage the quality of life in those areas but may also find itself in treacherous straits. Negative public opinion can quickly swell to form a backlash.

Citizenship involves being a good neighbor, not a nuisance, and living up to one's obligations. In free-enterprise democracies it is important that each individual works to maintain a pleasant community and a strong nation, without having to be forced to do so by legal action. If we want to have a better nation, then each citizen must become a better person. An excellent example of a fundamental of good citizenship is the story of J. C. Penney, as a boy, raising pigs in Hamilton, Missouri.

From the start Penney's pig business was very successful; he could turn a dollar and a half into twenty dollars' profit. But his father eventually came to him and said, "You cannot continue with it because it's offensive to the neighbors."[4] The incident worked its way later to influence the J. C. Penney Company policies and actions.

Many business leaders regard goodwill and positive relationships with one's neighbors as important obligations of citizenship by. Pacific Gas & Electric, for example, recognized in the 1980s its obligation to be upfront and not to try to ignore the possible hazards of a chemical called PCB, used in transformer cooling oil, which has the image of being harmful. That company's $50–60 million program to eliminate all of the network transformers and PCB, especially out of the core cities—San Francisco, Oakland and San Jose—was sped up and completed in three and a half years instead of the planned-on five years.

In Akron, Goodyear's chairman & CEO, Robert Mercer, learned of a tank containing methlyisocyanate at a company plant (the same chemical that caused the deaths of thousands in Bhopal India). His reaction was swift and firm. "Get rid of it!"

"But," came the response from the plant, "we need it to make the accelerator (for one of our most profitable products)."

Mercer stood firm, "It's gone. Shut it down. Bail that stuff out of there and get rid of it."

"But," plant personnel persisted, "if that happens, we'll have to close the plant."

Mercer would not retreat. "Close it! There's no appeal to it. We're not going to have that stuff in the middle of a residential area."

Citizenship encompasses more than just not being a nuisance; a good citizen is also supportive of his government and community's interests and causes. This involves doing one's part in a constructive manner. For example, when California-based Security Pacific purchased banks in Arizona after that state's legislature passed a law which permitted it, Security Pacific Corporation assured the people of Arizona that just because it was a California-based bank, it was not going to abandon the causes that the formerly Arizona-owned banks had supported.

When the government imposed rigid controls and restrictions during World War II, the obligation of doing one's part to help the nation constructively was demonstrated during a meeting. When an affluent vice president of one firm vehemently protested what he felt was an inadequate profit margin on one of his products, Paul V. Galvin, the founder and chairman of Motorola, flared, "Don't you understand that men who make less in a year than you make in a week are dying while you carp about profits?"[5]

After the San Francisco earthquake of 1906, the first business decision Levi Strauss made was to revive the policy of extending credit to retail merchants who were wiped out. Levi Strauss & Co. served as a low- or no-interest bank for its hard pressed customers.

TRUST

Trust makes sound and satisfying relationships possible; business could not flourish without it. Virtually every move made in business—every decision, every deal, every action—rests on trust. All the lawyers and all the airtight contracts they draft cannot assure the same degree of confidence and peace of mind that trust produces. There are loopholes to be found in even the most carefully worded contract; and sneaky people can always find them. The cost of protecting oneself in every situation, policing each transaction, and eliminating all possibilities of being taken advantage of is prohibitively expensive and time consuming. Trust is a sine qua non for business performance.

Jack Peters, of J. Walter Thompson, explains the importance of trust in his business, which is advertising. "There is one thing that drives our business and I think most companies: it's trust. If our employees don't trust us, they really aren't going to give us their best. And they are going to look around, and they're going to feel, eventually, that they would really rather work someplace else. If our clients don't trust us, they're going to find somebody else. If consumers don't trust the client, or his product or service, they are going to buy something else. Trust really does drive this industry and a lot of businesses. If you cheat a consumer, not only will he not forget it but he'll "trash" you every chance he gets. Now, if it is a toothpaste that didn't turn out to be what he's looking for, he's not going to say very much. If it's a big purchase, if he bought a car and it didn't perform, I tell you, the first chance he gets to buy a different one he's going to buy it. And the first chance he gets to "bad mouth" the poorly performing product, he will. Trust does work in our business, and it works in our clients'. "

A perception exists that many large-scale business organizations are filled with untrustworthy individuals who conspire to cheat the public. It would be foolish to argue that despicable actions have never been a part of the business scene; history suggests otherwise. But it is equally foolish to think that people who are dishonest enough to behave unethically with those outside their circle are not inclined to behave unethically within it, and thus jeopardize its long-term stability. This point deserves to be explored.

The realities of organizational dynamics require trust, and hence trustworthy people, for long-term survival and the effective performance of organizations. Well-run organizations are made that way because this reality is generally recognized and respected. Donald D. Lennox, of Navistar, captures succinctly what top-level business leaders typically think: "We can tolerate a mistake. We can tolerate occasional use of bad judgment in making a decision. But, I, personally, in no way, can tolerate a lack of trust. And my feeling is if I can't trust an individual, then I don't want to work with him."

Trustworthiness is very often revealed by little things. One CEO, an avid tennis player, says he gets some indication of another person's integrity by how fairly that person plays the game—whether he tries to hedge on calls or twist the rules to his advantage. And William Walton, Sr., of Holiday Inns, writes, "A man who is known to be cheating on his wife, to whom he has made one of life's most solemn, if not holy, commitments, can hardly be counted on with any certainty to keep the terms of a business deal."[6]

Trust is achieved by many sorts of actions. Principally, these include: a clear commitment to high ethical standards, thorough and consistent honesty and honest dealings, open dealings, placing a cause or standard ahead of self, and consistency in action and steadiness in living up to commitments.

A Clear Commitment

A tendency which even the best of us can easily slip into is to approach others and situations with the attitude, "Everything is relative; nothing is black or white. What is true, or honest, or right is really just a matter of opinion!" Theoretically there is some amount of truth to this perspective. But we should also consider the great danger it poses to integrity and to the furtherance of trust. This perspective not only permits but actually invites people to hedge on standards. Indeed it removes standards from consideration altogether.

As a result, people are encouraged to concoct whatever line of reasoning is needed to support the schemes they think will gain advantages for themselves. Joseph L. Jones, of Armstrong World Industries, suggests we approach situations with these questions: "In every dealing with each other, are you going to be devious, or are you going to be straightforward? Are you going to tell the truth, or are you going to lie? Are you going to treat one customer like the other one, or are you going to treat customers differently? . . . It's not a gray area. It's either black or white. It really doesn't leave itself much room for interpretation."

Consistent Honesty

One bloom doesn't make a spring. A little stupidity can cancel out a mountain of virtues. It is much better to think of honesty as a pattern rather than an event; it has to be a consistent and settled habit before it becomes noticed. Even the perception of lying, or of not telling the whole truth readily and willingly, can cast doubts on one's motives and character, thereby destroying others' trust. Much of what causes people to lie is not evil deeds that they wish to hide but much lesser failures and shortcomings that they fear would be damaging to their egos. People tend to lie mostly about silly things: their own minor shortcomings.

Tragically, the result of this lying is detrimental to these otherwise decent people. If found out, lies only multiply the damage to an individual beyond the shortcoming he tries to keep hidden. The loss of trust caused by lying is far worse than a small failure; it indicates not only a competency failure but a character failure. Gerald B. Mitchell, of Dana Corporation, says, "Every time that you break your word or are proven to be dishonest or somebody you can't trust, the hurt is magnified a million times. So you must never, never let it happen. It'll happen accidentally enough times to hurt you, so that in business the relationship is never the way it's portrayed—of being sharp or nasty. You can be tough because they expect you to be tough, but you must be honest. The most important single ingredient is honesty. I don't want to deal with anybody I don't think is honest, and I don't expect them to deal with me if they don't think I'm honest. Out of that stems a trust. You trust people or you don't trust them. If you don't trust them, you won't do business with them no matter what the price is. . . . There is no way you can do business on an ongoing relationship if you don't have that trust."

The truth usually has a way of getting out, of becoming known; it is rarely kept hidden for very long. Coverup efforts are ill-advised, and in the longer span of events, they bring little or no advantage. It is abundantly clear, from what experience shows, that lying is incalculably stupid. "You can do it for a while," observes John McConnell, of Worthington Industries, "but eventually its going to catch up to you and you're going to get caught. I've always told our salespeople, 'Do not lie . . . to a customer, because if you lie, you'd better have a great memory, because you're going to forget what you told them eventually and you're going to have a big collapse. If you are late on an order, you call and tell them and tell them why, [and] when you'll make the delivery. But do not call and say, We've got a machine down and we can't make the order. In other words, [don't] shift the blame to something else that isn't true.' "

Openness and Above Board Dealings

When Richard W. Sears began his mailorder business, he immediately set about to build trust with his new customers. He knew that country people were suspicious of city people. If he were to become successful, he reasoned, it would depend on his customers' trust in him, and not the other way around. His "send no money" policy accepted their sincerely held doubts. His policy was based on the point of view that said, "You are perfectly right in doubting the sense of sending money to a firm you don't know. So don't. You send us your order, and if you are satisfied with our merchandise, we'll do business." Sears even offered bank references. In a sense, he invited the farmer to question him. The 1894 Sears catalog stated, "We refer you to The Union National Bank of Minneapolis, and you are at liberty, if you choose, to send your money to them with instructions not to turn it over to us unless they know us to be perfectly reliable."[7]

Honesty, obviously, involves not lying. But this alone will not generate trust; it merely eliminates one thing that might prevent it. How one makes the truth known can be just as important as the fact that it is told. People develop suspicions where they feel they are not getting full and straightforward answers; they do not trust people who appear to act in devious ways—those who act as though they are holding something back.

Openness is the full expression of what one knows, believes, feels, and intends to do. It involves a willingness to do everything aboveboard, in full view, and quells suspicions because it makes it obvious that the person who acts this way feels there is nothing he needs to hide. William T. Creson, of Crown Zellerbach, observes, "To me an important . . . behavior is being willing to take a personal risk of being open and being transparent so that people have a reasonable idea of what's going on inside of you as well as on the surface, because they are going to constantly try to figure out what's going on inside of you anyway. And if you're willing to share that, and if you can demonstrate a reasonable degree of fairness, high degree of consistency in your behavior, [they] can come to understand how you're going to react to them, and vice versa. . . . People want to know whatever it is they [think] you don't want to tell them, and as soon as they think you'll tell them what they want to know they stop asking. . . . It all revolves around this issue of trust. And trust, in turn, flows from openness."

Complex business transactions will likely always require personal, face to face, contact. "The people who have been successful, from my experience," says Charles W. Moritz, of Dun & Bradstreet, "are those who don't lose sight of the fact that behind an awful lot of abstractions in business are human beings. . . . The test I've always used is if something is real, can I have breakfast or a cup of coffee with it? I can have breakfast with a human being."

There seems to be no substitute for personal contact, because only through it can one feel confident in the trustworthiness of another person. Achieving trust seems to demand it. Frank J. Tasco, of Marsh & McLennan, says, "I have always felt that in order to get something done, to build a partnership with your client [for example] you've got to communicate with him. You've got to talk to him and build confidence. And the only way you can do that is through personal contact. . . . That's the way you do it, and there is *no* other way to do it, in my opinion, and reach it successfully."

It was through these two important actions, openness and personal contact, that is, face-to-face meetings with questions and answers, that Donald Lennox succeeded in getting vendors to extend International Harvester 60 day terms—an important factor in saving that company (now Navistar) from collapse. Extension of credit is an act of trust that even the most severe critics would not dispute. "If they had not extended us credit," said Lennox, "it's questionable if we would have had enough cash flow to survive. . . . If we were going to ask companies and individuals to make that decision, to extend themselves beyond normal business relationships on a faith basis, then we had a responsibility, I felt, to share with them the information that justified our statement that we were going to survive this crisis. So we had a series of meetings till finally the vendors were satisfied it was necessary, where we reviewed with our vendors the kind of confidential financial data you would never review outside the office. We reviewed our cash flow, our asset sales, the items we had we thought we could sell, how much we expected to realize from the sales, when this could possibly happen; and we gave them a detailed by day, projected cash flow. We reviewed with them in detail our projected reductions schedules."

Placing a Cause or Standard Ahead of Self

Selfish impulses are treacherous. The self-serving person is rarely trusted, and even when he thinks he is, the watchful eyes of others are open, monitoring his moves carefully; his acquaintances know that this person is likely to try anything to get or to achieve what he wants. After all, to him, *he* is all that matters. To him, causes and standards are only followed as long as they serve his needs, and not because he believes in them. If he can get more or do better by another approach, he will do so. Trust requires the knowledge that one will honor standards and the demands that ideals place upon on him.

Consistency in Living up to Commitments

Words are forgotten long before actions begin to fade from one's memory. Consistency of action demonstrates dramatically what a person is all about. The mechanic who promises to have your car ready at 5:00 P.M. the next day and then doesn't, is not likely to get your repeat business. The gardener who says he'll show up at 9:00 A.M. to trim the shrubs in your yard but fails to do so, will lose your confidence.

Trust demands quality performance; it is built over time through the consistent meeting of expectations. Both quality and consistency are important. A product not shipped when it was promised, a defect in a telephone system, a part left out of a package, a rude clerk or salesperson in a store that claims to be a friendly place to shop—each of these can cause tremendous damage to a good reputation and can linger on as an unpleasant memory for years. And it may take a hundred good experiences afterwards to overcome and make up for the one or two unpleasant episodes that damaged a fine reputation.

Occasionally mistakes are made, or defective goods are sent off to customers unintentionally. What is the best way to handle these mistakes? Andrew C. Sigler, of Champion International, says, "Settle them fast and settle them well, and you've got a happier customer. Running number-one-quality paper is much more profitable than running defective. If you let that defective go . . . you'll be up to your eyeballs in trouble."

At the J. M. Smucker Company, complaints are answered within 24 hours; it's a company policy. If it's a service complaint, someone will telephone to follow up. But if it's somebody who just doesn't like the flavor of a product, they might receive a gift box. The idea is the same: follow up quickly. And that generally means within 24 hours.

FIDELITY

Fidelity encompasses far more than just meeting promises; it involves meeting implied commitments as well. Fidelity often calls individuals and firms to go beyond what is legally required of them in the fine print of contracts and documents of understanding. It involves living up to high standards of performance, even though it may be terribly inconvenient and costly to do so. Fidelity adds immeasurably to the quality of relationships by putting the actions of all parties on a higher plane than they would be if self-interest transcended honor.

Much of what is involved in business transactions is never fully written down. Each party to a transaction has a host of expectations of the others involved. Those whose aim it is to achieve fidelity in their behavior are careful to both clarify and live up to expectations. Sometimes we find individuals who believe that they should live to meet even higher standards than others might hold for them or what contractual agreements specify. They thereby give added meaning to fidelity and set a higher standard of conduct for others to try to emulate, and their own authenticity is placed beyond reproach.

In the early part of the century the Timken Roller Bearing Company entered into an agreement with what was the Ford Motor Company, at that time, for some axles. Timken bid very poorly and terribly underestimated what its costs would be. And because their bid was very low, they were awarded the contract. By the time Timken realized its error, work was underway and product had been shipped. Timken was thus faced with a decision: Go back to Ford, with which they had hoped to build a business relationship in the future, and say, "We underbid by mistake. We want to be paid 40 percent more, now that we have your business." Or they could just figure, "A deal is a deal," and that the only honorable thing to do about the situation was to take it out of their own pockets, despite the fact that Timken was a small and struggling company at the time. They did the latter; they didn't go back to Ford for more money. Ford later learned about it causing them to realize that they were dealing with an honorable firm.

When the Bell system was split up a number of years back, AT&T had to divest itself of what came to be known as the "baby Bells," the regional operating companies. These became autonomous business entities. The first several years after the divestiture would pose severe cash flow problems for AT&T. This was because a considerable amount of cash flow came from local, monthly billings for telephone service. This business would go to the operating companies. Long distance service was to go to AT&T. Another of the largest cash contributors is directory advertising. There is very little cost and a great return. AT&T's board chairman, Charles Brown, promised the American public that their telephone rates would not go up under divestiture; and when he was asked before a Senate committee what was going to happen to directory advertising, Brown said that he had already guaranteed local telephone bills would not go up. That business, therefore, should go in the local Bell operating companies. And he gave it up. There is no doubt that the cash flow of several billion dollars which AT&T gave up enabled the operating companies to be solvent in their early years and to build themselves.

TEAMWORK

During the second world war the U.S. Marines under Col. Evans F. Carlson acquired a slogan: Gung Ho. Chinese in origin, it expressed the ideas of work (gung) and harmony (ho); this serves as a good way to think about teamwork, because it emphasizes the task and the importance of people functioning together, in harmony, to achieve a common goal. There are people who are first-rate thinkers and problem solvers, and who can be very decisive, yet they are unwilling or unable to work with others because they are just too opinionated or stubborn.

In reference to a store executive who praised himself and damned his company, J. E. (Jim) Casey, founder of United Parcel Service, once remarked to a UPS employee, "That fellow will never get anywhere and will never know why."[8] He didn't.

Loners generally don't work out well in large companies; the scale of work performed and the operation of major firms is such that work must be carried out by groups. Loners, therefore, are better off left on their own. "I've had my share of geniuses working for me," says Frank Carlucci, of Sears World Trading, "and universally they cause problems. I could name you some of the brightest people I've ever worked with, for whom I have an enormous regard, but it's a tough call whether their contribution is worth the pain and suffering you have to go through."

The ability to function productively and harmoniously is a great asset. "If you can be identified early as a team player, somebody that is relatively unselfish;" says Richard Heckert, of Du Pont, "sure, you're ambitious; sure you have personal goals; of course you want to progress in the organization, but if you become labeled as somebody who works for the team in an unselfish way, you can't avoid being successful if you have the other tools."

Teamwork, as evidence indicates, is not beyond the reach of long-time adversaries. In the early 1980s Chrysler's management and the United Auto Workers got together, and after a few bumpy trial-and- error efforts settled on a view. As the Chrysler Motors chairman, Gerald Greenwald, once explained, "We'll argue every three years about how much we ought to pay and how to slice up the pie. But together, we believe that the pie will get to be bigger if we all, together, work diligently on the quality of our vehicles." One key to good teamwork is open and honest communication. This entails the fair and impartial airing of everything—every question and every concern.

Teamwork, the behavioral scientists tell us, is enhanced when there is openness and when power is shared. It means, they say, that there is involvement in meaningful ways. Rubbermaid was turned around and made a profitable and growing enterprise, in part because its chairman and CEO, Stanley Gault, ushered in the idea of teamwork in real and meaningful ways. It wasn't an easy task, and it wasn't done without points of bitterness. But, as Gault says, "Today you can't tell where management leaves off and the union begins." How was this accomplished? By working closely, talking, meeting, communicating, working together as members of the same family—that's how. As Gault explains, "We confided with them with our financial information, and we've worked as partners in this. You can't mandate that. You have to earn that respect and that trust. . . . we worked. We talked. My door is never closed. They can come and talk to me, which they do. As a result we have a fine working relationship here." For the past several years Rubbermaid has been ranked in the top of the *Fortune* list of America's most admired companies—clearly due in no small part to the emphasis given by top management to teamwork and solid working relationships.

16

Treating People the Right Way

On 26 July 1905, John Stevens set foot on the Isthmus of Panama for the first time. His task: to head construction of the Panama Canal. France had tried for ten years to build a canal there but had given up in failure in 1889, the effort ending in financial ruin for investors. The technology and science of the day had been inadequate to meet the natural challenges, and the costs had been too great for private financing. Panama was described as a death trap: malaria, typhoid fever, yellow fever, intestinal diseases, and pneumonia were rampant. Few who went there to work, survived. By the time the French left they had completed only a third of the work.

Now the United States would try. The first year of the U.S. effort had been a fiasco; $128 million had been spent with no apparent results. The *New York Times* reported that the Americans had performed with less efficiency and purpose and markedly less courage than the French. A full year had been lost. Things at Panama, Theodore Roosevelt said, were in a "devil of a mess." John Findlay Wallace, the chief engineer, had quit and returned to the United States.

President Roosevelt put that job in the hands of Stevens. His charge was made clear: do whatever it takes, but build a canal. Stevens was 52 years old, a railroad construction engineer, a frontiersman. Roosevelt wrote of him as, "a big fellow, a man of daring and good sense, and burly power." Stevens was told to report to Roosevelt directly if necessary.

Besides disease, the workers there faced horrible conditions. Local merchants had pushed food prices up to where it was nearly impossible for the men to live on their wages. Some had resorted to foraging. Living conditions were despicable, sanitation practically nonexistent, smells and filth were everywhere. Accommodations on returning ships were difficult to get and priced beyond the means of the working men there who were genuinely frightened; they were trapped in a tropical wilderness 2,000 miles from home. The U.S. medical officer, Dr. William Gorgas, found few supporters of his theory that yellow fever was carried by mosquitoes.

His annual budget of $50,000 was inadequate. He was unable even to purchase common wire screening for hospitals and living quarters.

Once there, Stevens said very little except to ask questions. It was soon discovered that anyone could talk to him. He was seen in good and bad weather, trudging about in the dirt and mud, riding a switch engine, studying the landscape. The men liked him immediately. He wore overalls and a battered old hat and smoked cigars—steadily. He began to infuse spirit into a work force whose morale was less than low.

Some thought Stevens was sent to announce that the project was to be abandoned. This was not to be. There was lost time to be made up for. There was much to do. A canal was to be constructed, but first things first.

On 1 August 1905, Stevens ordered a complete halt to all work on the Calebra Cut. It would resume when everything was ready, but first Gorgas was to have whatever he needed to do the job of making the place fit for human life. Panama City and Colon were to be cleaned up. Sewers were to be dug. Streets and sidewalks were to be paved. Commissaries, messhalls, clubhouses, barracks, houses, cold-storage facilities, schools, churches, laundries, reservoirs—entire communities were ordered built. An all out assault on pestilence of every sort was launched. It would last for two years.

"The digging is the least thing of all," Stevens told Gorgas, whose requisitions for supplies were given first priority. Stevens personally signed a $90,000 requisition for wire screening alone. Gorgas had first call for laborers, too. He would lead the largest, most concentrated cleanup and health campaign the world had ever known. Cities were fumigated, cisterns and cesspools oiled once a week, brush cleared, swamps and marshes drained, water piped in, sanitary drinking cups provided. For the first time there were fresh eggs and lettuce. And there was ice. Bakeries turned out fresh bread. By December 1905 the Isthmus of Panama was rid of the dreaded yellow fever. First things came first, before the digging.[1]

In Western culture we have inherited an ethic that has steadily elevated the value we place on the worth and dignity of each human life. Man, we believe, is not to be used for the service of things; things are to be used for the service of man. All reasonably sensitive men and women who carefully work toward ideals see there is a right way to treat people and a wrong way. And they believe that no cost is too great to prohibit doing the former nor any benefit so large or important as to justify the latter. There are values and there are ultimate values.

In an ideal society decent treatment of people supersedes all other concerns. Without it, all of humankind suffers. Civilization is built upon it. Whenever a person mistreats another, or permits himself to be mistreated by others, his humanity is diminished. A person may have many fine possessions, or wield tremendous power, or have a powerful intellect and a mind filled with vast amounts of knowledge, or accomplish tremendous feats, or give vast fortunes to worthy causes, or contribute to the betterment of the world, but if, in getting or using any of these assets or talents, he seriously mistreats others and thereby does lasting harm to them, he diminishes his own humanity. In mistreating others, a certain amount of insensitivity and callousness is called for, which cancels or crowds out the finer qualities that enrich and ennoble the human condition.

We are all aware of the great difficulty involved in deciding how to act when the right treatment of some can only occur if others are mistreated. There are 12 shipwrecked passengers and there is only one 6-person lifeboat? There is one doctor and 50 people are in need of immediate medical attention; what should be done? A factory must be closed down and 145 people thrown out of work in order to adhere to environmental or safety standards; should it be done? There simply are no right or easy answers to these sorts of questions.

The world rarely offers perfect solutions for us to select from. We all recognize that there will be tragic situations, which we are forced by the nature of things to endure. Human suffering is deplorable. In ignoring or failing to acknowledge tragedy or in trying to justify its occurrence, one sweeps aside a genuine sense of pain and shrugs off feelings of comparison. By so doing, One's humanity is diminished; it makes a person less of the feeling, caring, concerned, loving creature he is capable of being.

Unavoidable events do occur that are harmful, such as the ones just mentioned. Then there are actions or events that are merely perceived to be unavoidable because to behave otherwise would conflict with convention, habits, prejudices, or misconceptions. Much of the harmful actions that cause pain to people arise from ignorance and from adherence to beliefs and conventions that serve little useful purpose. Shameful treatment of unskilled laborers insofar as health and safety issues are concerned and unannounced mass layoffs in factories are excellent examples.

Whether these events are unavoidable or merely perceived as being unavoidable the results are still the same: they hurt. A former Gillette Company chairman and CEO, Vincent Ziegler, said in a *Nation's Business* interview, "Forrest Akers, who was my boss at Dodge Motor Company, once told me: . . . 'I just want to tell you one thing. When you stick a pin in people, they hurt. So just be sure to treat people as people.' That has been a pretty good piece of management advice."[2] There are many good examples in industry of adherence to this advice. Those who have been most successful have been so because they earned their leadership status through treating people the right way—and they treated people right because they rejected those conventions and attitudes that lead to harmful and hurtful actions, embracing instead a more humane understanding of the worth and dignity of each human being.

The Southland Corporation, which Joe C. Thompson, Jr. helped form in 1927, was as much concerned with employee loyalty as an asset as it was with its hundreds of 7-Eleven Stores, dairy plants, and ice trucks. The Southland Creed appeared in a company magazine in 1960; it summarized Thompson's philosophy:

A Southland Creed

We believe that the most important asset of Southland is its people—in every plant, office and community, wherever they work and live.

We believe that the well-being and security of the employees are dependent upon the soundness and security of Southland; that to keep our company sound and secure, the people of Southland have an obligation to make the most effective use of their skill, effort and time on their jobs.

We believe that all of the people of Southland must recognize our joint responsibility to the owners of the company, to the public we serve and to our nation as a whole.

In recognition of these beliefs, and of the company's responsibilities to employees, we pledge:

That every employee will be treated fairly, with consideration and respect, and that we expect all who supervise the work of others to treat those under their direction as they themselves want to be treated.

To pay wages and provide employee benefits that fairly reward employees for their skill, effort and time.

To weigh all decisions with full regard for their effect on the well-being of employees.

To try to provide stability of employment to the greatest possible extent.

That the complaint of any employee will be listened to and handled with fairness and promptness.

To provide employees every possible opportunity for self-improvement and advancement with the company.

To provide good working conditions—safe, clean, friendly work place and proper facilities to help the employee do his job effectively.[3]

© 1960 The Southland Corporation

LIVING WITH AN ATTITUDE THAT ORDINARY PEOPLE ARE IMPORTANT, TOO

By habit or convention there is a tendency to ascribe more importance and respect to the well-to-do; to the better educated, better mannered, nicer dressed; to the more charming and attractive; and to those who occupy positions of higher status and more responsibility. The uneducated, the unemployed, the poor, and the ignorant are oftentimes horribly mistreated, not just by events and circumstances, but by others who consciously or unconsciously seem to think these folks don't amount to much and that, therefore, they just don't count. We are familiar with the tendency to reject others who are not like ourselves. It is easy to be repulsed by their behavior, and at times there may be good cause for that reaction.

Repulsive acts may offend one's eyes and ears and sensibilities, but the person who mistreats another, no matter how repulsive that other person may be, in return, diminishes the goodness that could occupy his mind and heart. In so doing he negligently prevents the expression of decency which he is otherwise capable of achieving. When others are mistreated and their humanity diminished by demeaning acts, thoughtful and sensitive observers will see these things as repugnant. So J. Richard Munro of Time, Inc., says, "Anytime I see anybody in this building who sort of mistreats a secretary or mistreats a clerk, that causes me real concern and I will quietly find out what the problem is, because those are the kind of people who scream at waiters."

In San Francisco, A. P. Giannini built the Bank of America on the principle "that when a poor man enters the bank he must always receive the same courtesy and consideration a rich man would get."[4] The principle here is clear: treat people with dignity.

Reuben Mark, of Colgate-Palmolive, recalls a visit to a company plant in Argentina. There he met with local management. Their discussions focused on business growth. Capital additions and plant expansion were the main topics discussed. Later, in touring that plant, he walked through the employee locker rooms. Here he was outraged at what he saw. "These are people who are not paid very much," Mark later commented. "The locker rooms were terrible. You wouldn't even go in there." He demanded that the situation be changed and told the local management, "Telex me when you get these locker rooms fixed."

Conflict is no stranger to business. Everyone does not pursue the same ends, and a few will even resort to means that intelligence and decency would not abide. The passion of a battle has been known to overtake what would otherwise be tender approaches to others; as adversaries begin treating each other with disrespect and worse. Those who can rise above divisive squabbles are rare. They battle for what they believe in, but they never forget of how to treat others—with decency and respect.

In conflict situations one soon learns of a management's real attitude toward employees. A company leader may make polite speeches when there is labor peace, but who is he fooling when he speaks contemptuously and uncaringly about them when push comes to shove? It makes for good press to say warm and caring things about a plant's labor force, but few are long deceived by these words if the same management treats those employees unfairly during a labor dispute.[5]

Deep-seated feelings cannot be covered up or masked indefinitely. Sooner or later they are revealed in one's behavior, either obviously or subtly. Although these feelings are slow to change, they can be altered by preventing callousness to develop out of dislike, or indifference, or contempt, or differences, or conflict. The key, as Jack F. Reichert, of

Brunswick Corporation, says, is, "to never strip away the personal dignity of people."

John H. Bryan, Jr., of Sara Lee, suggests that it is best to respect everybody else. "If you don't threaten them, and if you . . . like them, . . . genuinely like them, you find they kind of like you. And you don't have to be a screamer and carry on to lead." Bernard M. Fauber, of Kmart, describes Harry Cunningham, the man credited with being the father of the Kmart operation, as a person who had this special touch with people, "I thought Harry Cunningham was one of the most gracious men, and I had the pleasure of working for him as his executive assistant for over a year. . . . There are people in business who are afraid to compliment you because they are afraid you're going to let down. Harry Cunningham was just the opposite. He would compliment you when you didn't deserve it, and then you would go out and break your neck to make sure you deserved it the next time it came around. He is that type person. He could be more constructively critical than any man I've ever known."

RESPECTING OTHERS

Respect is evidenced by concern for others, by taking seriously their thoughts and feelings. It is also shown by the eagerness to listen to others and by the willingness to respond in a constructive manner. The scramble to better one's lot, one's position, one's standing all too often cause attention and concern to focus on the higher-ups in an organization or on those who wield power or those who could be helpful to one's career or well being. And by catering to the likes and interests of those above, people tend to neglect those below. The ones who try to scramble to the top by pleasing just the higher-ups become like flowers; looked at from above they appear beautiful, but viewed from below they are not so attractive.

The humane organization is not a welfare state, where people are cared for to the point they become helpless and incapable of caring for themselves. Instead, it involves people in working in meaningful and challenging ways because it respects them. This is happening to a fairly great extent now. Richard J. Mahoney, of Monsanto, says, "American industry finally recognized that blue collar workers have brains and emotions and you can turn them on. It's been a long time coming."

John Hoyt Stookey, of National Distillers (now Quantum Chemical), echoes this sentiment, that employees should be involved. "I don't think you can have a humane organization where 'the word comes from on high' and there isn't sharing of the decision process. It's really driven off of treating the individual with respect, which includes hearing him."

"Any problem is important if it is important to one person," says Burnell R. Roberts, of Mead Corporation. "It is important to keep directors sensitive to issues which bother our employees. Often we uncover problems which are important to people, not thought to be important to us."

At brown bag lunches held every couple of months, Mead employees and directors have a chance to discuss concerns. At one of these meetings a woman who worked in a clerical capacity started to speak but hesitated. "This is dumb," she said.

"No, we want to hear," replied the directors.

What bothered her was the location of a file cabinet. She wanted it moved but never felt she should ask.

At a Mead Corporation paper mill in Michigan, employees revealed another irritation at one of these lunch meetings. A bridge connected the main parking lot to the plant. Next to the plant were just a few parking spaces where the managers parked. Employees had to park in the main lot and walk over the bridge to the plant, whereas the managers could drive right up to the building. They told the management, "Look, you drive, we walk. Yet we get here a lot earlier than you do." The managers had never realized this had been bothering the employees. The situation was changed. Parking was immediately made on a first-come basis.

Listening, sincere listening that is, requires a good bit of humility. Would a chairman of the board listen to people at the bottom level of an organization? The answer is yes. Why? Because most CEOs not only think it is important, but also genuinely like people. It's not something they spend full time at; where problems are found, other people are delegated to solve them. But CEOs do listen; in fact they are excellent listeners.

"If I don't understand what they [employees] believe is right," says Lewis W. Lehr, of 3M, "maybe I don't know what is right. I think I do, but I've got to also know how they feel, and so I paid attention to the organization chart but I also had lots of discussions with people who were anywhere in the organization. In fact, I think all of our people have pretty much a so-called open door policy. I was called one morning at 7:00 in my home by five people from the factory who weren't happy with what was happening there, and I said, 'Fine. You want to meet me for breakfast at a restaurant we all know or do you want to come to my office?' They wanted to come to my office. So they did and told me what they thought was wrong with that particular factory operation. And I got into it and learned a little more about it. The reason they felt they could come to me was because I had befriended an employee in that factory who was an elevator operator who had a health problem. . . . She had a weight and back problem and someone was trying to put her back in a line operation she couldn't handle. I learned about that and made a few suggestions and she stayed on the elevator, . . . and that employee passed the word around that if they thought they had a problem that they ought to talk to me. And they did. We got the situation resolved. And it was a problem area. The word was not [getting] up to me. It was filtered before it ever got to me."

HEALTH AND SAFETY

In one view, only as much money and time as is economically prudent should be devoted to employee health and safety. The idea, according to this perspective, is to balance costs saved against dollars spent. Safety and health concerns are thus seen only as being smart business; a little money spent here saves enormous sums by reducing losses, including those from compensatory damage suits and lost time. A little thought reveals two difficulties with this approach. First, it sends a subtle yet strong message to employees that they are thought of as "things" and, as such, just another cost factor to be considered. They are thereby not thought of as people by their management. Under these circumstances it is easy to see why they would fail to show commitment to the organization; they are reciprocating the lack of concern shown by management.

Second, it demonstrates an ethical lapse, because by this reasoning, if it paid in economic terms to allow working conditions to be unsafe, employers probably would permit it. Enlightened managements understand the value of people and they therefore place employees above the concerns of the ledger in deciding on health and safety matters.

At Procter & Gamble the policy is, if something cannot be done safely then it will not be done at all. "There is nothing we do," say Procter & Gamble safety engineers and plant managers, "that is worth risking someone's health and safety for."

"Every supervisor," says former chairman and CEO Irving S. Shapiro, "learns very quickly that Du Pont is not prepared to accept any predictable level of injury or illness in any manufacturing unit; he or she learns that the supervisor's job is to see to it that employees do not get hurt. . . . A supervisor learns that if he or she cannot maintain a safe shop, Du Pont will get somebody who can. Similarly, every employee quickly learns that responsibility for his or her own safety is a condition of employment and that assuming unnecessary risk is unacceptable behavior. . . . The acid test of a corporation's resolve is the financial bottom line. Talk is cheap, and anyone can make noises about a commitment to safety; the test comes when safety costs dollars in terms of lost production, potentially profitable products which are never produced, and the risk of criticism in the wake of frank disclosure."[6]

William Atteberry, the former chairman and CEO of Eagle-Picher, is even more direct. "If you are going to make money and severely damage your employees in any way, whether it's their personality, . . . their health or what, you're not successful. You're not successful at all. It is a moral imperative not to injure or cause to injure another person." To this end, at National Distillers (Quantum Chemical) says the chairman and CEO, John Hoyt Stookey, "When our divisional presidents report to our senior management or board of directors, the first thing they report, by common practice, is their safety record. That goes before the money, always."

J. E. (Jim) Casey, of United Parcel Service, is remembered by employees as a man who always believed in the importance of the individual, and this was shown by his concern for their safety and comfort. "I remember," said one UPS employee, "when we were reviewing plans for a sorting facility to be located in the basement of one of our buildings, Jim, after listening to a complete review of all the plans asked, 'How about the ventilation for the people who will be working down there?' His first thought was for the people. Fortunately we had considered the problem."[7]

Several companies, including AT&T and Digital Equipment, conducted analyses of the possibility of radiation harm to fetuses if pregnant women worked day after day in front of a work station. As Charles Marshall, of AT&T, explains, "It's remote but it's a possibility. We immediately removed pregnant women after four months or whatever time was a conservative point, found them other jobs, and paid them the same thing. And some of our competitors who make a similar product were quite upset with us. But our feeling was, if there was any possible risk at all to an employee in that kind of environment, even though we could have gotten a dozen doctors to testify that it wasn't a problem, as a corporation we had no right to put an employee in that kind of situation where they could have harm. It's so remote, but we said, 'We don't care. If it's one person, if it's one expectant mother, it's not worth it.' "

VACATIONS AND TIME OFF

The sensitive employer keeps a watchful eye on employees, not necessarily to keep them working, but often to keep them from working too much and to the point it adversely affects their family life, their morale, and their health. The Upton Machine Company, which grew to become the Whirlpool Corporation, was one of the early pioneers in American industry to give factory employees a paid vacation. On 25 July 1917 a letter went out to the more senior of the fifty or sixty people employed at the company, announcing an employee benefit virtually unheard of for factory employees at the time. The method of announcing it, a personal letter to each of the employee's wives, was as human as the gesture was humane.

Mrs. Wm. Hill
950 Wisconsin Ave.
St. Joseph, Michigan

Dear Mrs. Hill:

This year we are starting a new system—which is the giving to our men who have been with us a certain length of time, a vacation with pay. Bill has worked hard and with our interest always in his mind and we want to start showing that we appreciate it. From Wednesday, July 25th to Monday, July 30th is his vacation period and we want you to work with us and see that he gets the most good out of it.

Plan some fishing trips or picnics—take the St. Joseph river boat trip, have some beach parties and so forth. Don't let Bill clean out the basement or the chicken coop or have him do odd jobs around the house; you and the family get out in the sun and the fresh air and just have a good time. We will feel amply repaid if Bill comes back with a good tan on his face as we'll know then that he has had God's open air for a good tonic.

With best regards, we remain,
Very sincerely yours,

UPTON MACHINE COMPANY
ss/ L. C. Upton, Gen'l. Mgr.

UNBEARABLE BURDENS

Conventional thinking, from a management perspective, holds that employers are within their rights to ask employees to do pretty much anything for the good of the organization, as long as it is morally upright and within the law. If employees don't like it or cannot accept this, many believe those employees can quit. The reality, however, is that many employees are not so free to quit. "Quit and do what?" they will ask. "Who will pay my bills, feed my family? Jobs are not so easy to find." And the truth is, if their aim is to avoid substantial hardship or a major reduction in earnings for at least a few years, millions of people are stuck where they are. This can present a moral dilemma. The work to be done is oftentimes for a worthwhile and valuable cause. It, no doubt, is important. But so too are the lives and the well-being of the employees who perform the work. Conflicts will arise, and easy answers are not to be found. But this reality necessitates sober reflection on the many unavoidable conflicts between the needs of the organization and the well-being of its employees.

The key here is to think of people as not just another factor of production, but as humans, whose ability to live good lives is as worthy an end as anything else is. Some organizations exhibit this approach. Frank J. Tasco, of Marsh & McLennan, explains, "Being a service organization I am very conscious, possibly, of having the Japanese approach. If you come to work here, as far as I'm concerned, you come for life. We don't experiment with people's lives and say, 'we'll hire fifty people and try this project and if it doesn't work, fire them.' We just don't do that."

According to its chairman and CEO, Richard D. Wood, the Eli Lilly Company's management feels that it is not a good idea to move people from job to job, involving transfers across the country, which present a tremendous burden on the family. Lilly's senior management believes that family life is too important to be disrupted by too many, and sometimes unnecessary, moves. Lilly has chosen to hold down the number of times people are asked to move, so as to enrich the quality and stability of the family.

EQUALITY OF OPPORTUNITY

Justice commands that people be treated impartially except for ability—everyone should have an opportunity to compete for jobs, promotions, and for the chance to develop and move ahead. The idea is to let people move as far as their abilities and hard work and wise living will take them. These ideas are generally regarded favorably, and they are fairly widespread. Still, habit, convention, and prejudice have frustrated their full implementation.

Movement toward these ideals can be seen in the better-managed companies, whose leaders see discrimination as harmful both to those who are discriminated against and to the organizations themselves. William L. Weiss, of Ameritech, says, "Nondiscrimination in hiring and in promotions is a direct corollary of respect for people, and it is certainly good for business. I have long believed that the business sector suffered a great loss by not utilizing the talents of women and minorities sooner."

James D. Robinson III, the chairman and CEO of American Express, echoes this sentiment. "Thank God, we've got a variety of cultures and people from different backgrounds. How ever you care to describe those backgrounds, it's that difference that creates energy and that difference that gives you the opportunity to benefit from the broadest spectrum of points of view. And it's up to us to try to synthesize those ideas and viewpoints and to let that different kind of energy create a company that is substantially more resourceful than any of its competition."[8]

Although none advanced into positions of real authority, it is an interesting historical fact that Henry Ford departed from the standard practices of his time and did not refuse to hire blacks in his factories. Not surprising therefore, in his passing the *Afro-American* mourned, "We have lost a real friend."[9] Today, equal opportunity is championed far more vigorously. Efforts have been made at Kmart to elevate aspirations and expectations for advancement among qualified black employees. Somehow, blacks in that company appear to lose initiative and willingness to work the long, hard years necessary for advancement. The chairman and CEO, Bernard Fauber, says, "I think they get the idea that they have no chance. . . . They give up more quickly because they are the minority."

To overcome this, 25 blacks, men and women, were brought in for a seminar and to meet the company's two black members of the board of directors, as a way of encouraging them to believe there really are opportunities for blacks in that organization. Out of that group, a few will be advanced to jobs way beyond what they have earned at that point compared to other people. They will be watched closely and helped in order to accelerate the time when other blacks can look up in the organization and truly feel that they themselves have an opportunity.

At Honeywell the numbers and percentages of women and minority employees are very good by EEO standards. But top management found that these people were not moving into management positions, and this fact was causing frustration because good people were apparently being passed over. The company's leadership decided that the situation was due, in part, to an attitudinal problem, which it tried to tackle directly. To that end, the company's diverse work force program was established, with the aim of creating within Honeywell a diverse workforce at every level in the company. The idea is to have a diversity in the types of people employed throughout the company at all levels. The chairman of the board of Honeywell has set as a goal that every time a promotion decision is to be made, at least one woman and at least one minority candidate will be among those being considered. Two black university professors have been retained to conduct sensitivity-type training sessions to alter attitudes in support of this goal.

At Chrysler Motors there are several forms of affirmative action programs throughout the corporation: minority suppliers, minority dealers, hiring and development programs inside the company, and efforts to go outside the company to recruit women. When he was the chairman, Gerald Greenwald, would sit with senior management every 90 days to review affirmative action progress. One of the measures that continues to be used for executive bonuses is progress made in hiring women and minorities. As Gerald Greenwald said, "The auto industry was about as male dominated as any you could find. . . . I never thought I'd see the day where I'd see women mix with the men on the line in our assembly plants as supervisors. . . . I think we've come a long way."

At Bristol-Myers Squibb, the chairman and CEO, Richard L. Gelb, believes that television commercials for their products are one way to emphasize equal opportunity. At last tally, 42 percent of the Bristol-Myers Squibb commercials had minority representation. In the 1970s that number was about 10 percent.

When Peter Ueberroth became the commissioner of Major League Baseball he found that, unlike the 1984 Olympic Games, which he had organized in Los Angeles, where all races, colors, and creeds and both men and women were involved, the administrative and management side of baseball was not totally fair. "There were about 20 people in all of Major League Baseball that were minorities in any kind of position off the field. It wasn't fair. It wasn't right," observed Ueberroth.

He and the owners of baseball clubs carried out a project aimed at changing the situation. "We chose the method to change it by honoring Jackie Robinson's 40th anniversary of his entry into major league baseball," says Ueberroth. "Basically, we have a real success story on our hands, where we have gone from a little over 1 percent minority involvement in Major League Baseball, in over one year to over 10 percent. And, that's across the board kinds of positions. . . . I think this institution is better off for it. So we're pleased with the results."

LOYALTY TO EMPLOYEES

At an earlier time in our country's history, back before men and women were paid very well for their manual labor and when working conditions were harsh and work days were long, back before employees were protected by strong unions and employment laws, and back before there were many caring and enlightened managements, there were a few employers who lived to reach for a higher standard. To these people the common laborer was not just a cog in a massive productive machine, to be used and discarded when he was no longer needed. These few employers felt they had an obligation to those whose labor helped produce profits. They took that obligation very seriously, and when tested, they made good on what they said they stood for—decency, fairness, and above all, loyalty to employees.

Part of the $350 million of property damaged in the San Francisco earthquake of 1906 was the factory that turned out the copper-riveted denims for Levi Strauss. The nephews of Levi Strauss, Sigmund and Abraham Stern, who were running the company then, placed an advertisement shortly after the disaster in the city's newspapers. It announced to the company's 350 employees that their salaries would be continued until further notice. It asked them to register their names at the Oakland factory. Some would be put to work there; others would not return to their jobs until the new factory opened in San Francisco in September.

Today this same decent, caring philosophy remains alive in many parts of American industry. "There are a lot of times we take something on where there is no profit at all, but we've got to maintain jobs," says the American Greetings chairman, Irving I. Stone. "We have people who depend on us. There is a responsibility to your own people and to your community. Also, there are people in here who are sick and can't work. We're not going to let them go. We're going to take care of them. There may be thirty to forty people out on medical leave; they get paid every week. You just can't be ruthless and let them go. You've got an obligation to take care of them."

At Hewlett-Packard, sluggish business conditions in the mid 1980s necessitated substantial cost reduction measures. The sensitive management at Hewlett-Packard had employees at its manufacturing and administrative facilities take unpaid time off, one or two days each month for a few months. No one was terminated. Sales and service personnel reduced their work schedules to effect a 5 percent pay reduction. Pay reductions of 10 percent were made for the 27-member Hewlett-Packard Management Council, the company's senior policy-making body, and external members of the board of directors took a 10 percent reduction in board fees.

Plant closings are particularly difficult. It once was the practice to tell people as they left for home on Friday afternoon with their pay, "Don't bother to come to work on Monday. We're closing the plant." Happily that practice is a thing of the past and unheard of among the large, well-managed companies. Yet, this problem remains a concern for corporate leaders. Hicks B. Waldron, of Avon, comments on how he has responded. "I have from time to time sat back and said, Okay let's just think a bit about, 'do unto others as you would have them do unto you' when you are really facing a difficult problem like, do you close down a plant or not? Now the closing down of a plant . . . you do it because you need to do it because in the long run it's better for everybody. But then the question becomes, what do you do with all the people? Then the issue ranges all the way from absolutely nothing to everything. Somewhere between these extremes is the right thing."

Part of the answer lies in planning, and part involves helping people through the dislocation process. At Westinghouse, the chairman and CEO, Douglas Danforth, explains how planning and relocation efforts are used. "Let's suppose we have a plant that we think may not be with us five years from now. We know the attrition statistics—people retiring and quits and changes. And so we gradually take that plant down over several years, rather than one Friday night to a Monday morning. And concurrently with that we have retraining programs. We have transfer programs. We have separation programs. All are voluntary. We set up resume writing; we set up office facilities for them. We put ads in the newspapers to locate them. We subsidize their incomes on their new job for a year or so."

One reality of business is that corporations enter new areas and new markets and expand in these, reducing their level of involvement in other areas and markets. They buy and sell portions of their businesses. As with plant reductions or closings, these additions and reductions in corporate holdings present human concerns. Good business people try to adjust their businesses to keep them profitable or to return to reasonable profit levels. But there are situations where selling a portion of a business is the only alternative. Here there are cautions to observe.

The late Joseph B. Flavin, of Singer, explained how he approached selling that firm's computer business as a last resort because Singer was on the verge of bankruptcy. "We went out and talked to all the key potential players in the United States and Europe and ended up breaking the business in two pieces, selling part of it to TRW in the United States and part of it to ICL people around Europe and Latin America. And in order to keep it a vibrant business, what we decided to do was to sell it on the basis that all the parts and equipment that we had, . . . as well as the customer reputation, we would sell to them at whatever price was necessary to assure them a fifty percent gross profit, which meant the business could survive long enough for them to do something with it if they wished to do so. And one of the outcomes of that which was very positive from our viewpoint, is, 90 percent of the people kept their jobs, and they just went on and worked there."

The best thinking in the area of human resource management holds that loyalty to employees should run in two directions: if they are performing satisfactorily, they should be recognized; but if their performance is unsatisfactory and honest measures taken to improve it have been ineffectual, they need to be told that, too. If necessary these people may have to be released. That way they can go somewhere else, where the standards and conditions are different and where they have a better chance of being successful. Flavin said, "You have a responsibility. If you're going to let people go, let them go in the first five years. . . . If you keep them ten years, then they deserve all kinds of assistance and support to make it." And if you are in management, "your job is to help them make it," says Flavin. "We put out a policy in 1976 that said if anybody had ten years with the company you could not let them go without my approval."

At Motorola the same policy applies, as the vice chairman and CEO, William J. Weisz, explains. "Anybody who has been with this company ten years or more, to be released, must have the personal approval of the chief executive. So if you've been [here for ten years or more] there is [a] real case to be made if somebody thinks you ought to be fired or laid off."

PREVENTING THE MISTREATMENT OF OTHERS

The man who holds another man's coat while this other man throws stones at a victim is part of the crime. The observer of a misdeed who does not speak out against it or does nothing to stop it is a party to it also. This is fairly well understood in an abstract or theoretical sense. Yet we are generally aware of the tendency to turn one's head so as not to see wickedness and pain and suffering. Perhaps this is because people become too worried about their own skins to step forward to the aid of others. Perhaps they reason, "It isn't any of my business, so why get involved." But whether they like it or not or whether they know it or not, if it goes on, they *are* involved.

As part of the human community, what affects one has some effect on all. The tone of an organization is altered for the good or the bad, depending on the acts of its members. A cruel deed diminishes not only the victim's quality of life but also the humanity of all who permit it to happen. Both a misdeed and the knowledge of it, if it is allowed to happen without interference or rebuke, diminishes the humanness of the perpetrator and the observers.

For many people, job mobility is really quite low . Many employees truly are dependent on their jobs. Sexual harassment is an ugly reality, and when it occurs it affects everyone, especially the victims. John M. Henske, of Olin Corporation, tells of his own reaction to it. "One of the things I'm a stickler on is sexual abuse. I think the most miserable type of thing I can think of a boss to do is to take advantage of the secretary. She may be totally financially dependent upon [her job], and he knows it. Wherever I've been, . . . that was grounds for dismissal no matter who you were. You just didn't do that. One of the fellows I did discharge when I joined this company was one who had a reputation for misusing women employees. Among the reasons I gave him was that there was just too much evidence that that might be happening and I'd think you'd be better off somewhere else. I think most companies treat it the same way we do."

One of the major influences on the Western world, the Golden Rule, introduced a radically different dimension to the body of moral thought and reasoning. Before the Golden Rule, people were commanded *not* to treat others in ways they themselves would *not* want to be treated, but the

Golden Rule instructed people to treat others as they *would* want to be treated. This was neither a minor change in the wording of an ancient maxim, nor merely a subtle shift in emphasis. The Golden Rule introduced the idea of service to others, calling our attention to what we can do for others, as opposed to merely what we ought not do to them.

A question we can raise is, "Ought we actively attempt to influence what happens to people by the actions or inactions of others?" Should a person, as a third party, intervene to halt the mistreatment of another or work to influence others to serve the welfare and betterment of other people? We all realize that what happens to others is generally not a result of just our own actions—a reality which can easily lead us to feel hopelessly insignificant and cripple our resolve to act in helpful ways, albeit indirectly. Certainly the nation or the organization that sits by idly and permits the mistreatment of any of its members by circumstances or by the hands of others ought to be judged as inhumane.

We know that we can exercise direction over our own actions, and our experiences tell us that we are capable of exercising some influence on the actions of others. We are free to act, just as we are free to think and to choose. These thoughts present us with a powerful guide for our own behavior: we ought not to sit back and permit the mistreatment of others. Even if we cannot stop it entirely, we are still compelled to abate it as much as we can. Unless we exercise our freedoms fully and appropriately, we render ourselves less than the human creatures we could be. But our guide here can be extended much further. For just as the Golden Rule enlarged our thinking to holding ourselves responsible for doing for others—serving them ourselves—it also introduces us to the possibility of actively influencing circumstances and exciting others to the service of each member of the human community, so that each one is treated as we ourselves would wish to be treated.

IV

TO SERVE FAITHFULLY

17

Rendering Useful Service

As humans we realize that we are free to live our lives doing what we like best and choosing for ourselves how we go about it. We are free to fill our days in the quest of our own interests and pleasures; we are at liberty to "do our own thing." We may live chiefly to please ourselves, pursuing our own personal wants, our own comforts, and our own aims. Those who spend their lives in self-serving pursuits, believing that these activities will yield them great happiness and lasting satisfaction, ultimately find—after it's too late—that they do not. These people never really live, because they never live for anything worthwhile; at best they merely exist.

Human experience from ages past and present tells us that it is impossible to achieve significance without making life an adventure in the quest of something grand. Living is most exciting and truly worthwhile and satisfying when one aims not to please himself primarily but instead struggles boldly in the service of something greater that has genuine merit. A careful analysis of the happiest people shows that they have succeeded in forgetting themselves while they are all-consumed in the service of something truly worthwhile. The good life is achieved not by obtaining valuables for oneself but by serving others in valuable ways.

THE IDEA OF SERVICE

The study of human motivation has brought forth theories and practices that have demonstrated themselves to be effective in increasing the levels of work motivation. However, what goes unrecognized is that such practices are potentially quite harmful in a profound way. The concept of a hierarchy of human needs has led to the practice of creating motivation toward the purposes of an organization by arranging working conditions so that employees can satisfy their unmet needs by performing their work roles. Indeed, this approach does produce better-motivated employees, but adherents to this theory overlook an important ethical issue. It ought to be asked whether the people being led by this motivation technique are managed in ways that enable them to live better lives.

Many motivation theories exploit the fact that most people do live primarily to satisfy their own needs—physiological, security, social, self-esteem and self-actualization. But, ought people to live for themselves primarily, if the aim for each person is to live a good life—a worthy, satisfying life? The proposition that the ultimate in the human experience can be sought as an end in itself ought to be questioned.

Self-actualization, the pinnacle of the human-needs hierarchy, involves "the desire to develop one's true potential as an individual to the fullest extent and to express one's skills, talents and emotions in a manner that is most personally fulfilling."[1] But is self-actualization, as the theory suggests, really the ultimate in the human experience? How can it be, when by definition its aim is to please the self and when it is deliberately pursued as such? This motivation theory collides head-on with the reality that genuine satisfaction is achieved when one lives for something outside of oneself instead of doing what one merely enjoys or doing things that might produce recognition and praise or a sense of self-confidence, or affection and companionship.

The tragedy of this theory of motivation is that it condones and encourages self-serving behavior. It levels people downward, where self-centeredness is the primary pursuit and self-awareness is ever present. By using this theory, people are led to feel right and good about asking, Which of my needs can I satisfy next? Those who make lasting contributions to the world, as history reveals, are not the ones who seek happiness for themselves, nor are they the ones who make self-actualization their life's quest. The genuine fulfillment a person derives from his efforts is not something he can find by pursuing it directly. Instead, *it finds him.* A sense of fulfillment comes unexpectedly, through sacrifices in the service of others or in some great cause. Instead of lifting people toward living good lives, many motivation theories tend to push people toward less meaningful lives than what they are capable of living, because these theories make the primary concern of the person the satisfaction of his own appetites.

Governments never really amounted to anything noble or lasting or worthwhile until they started to serve more than just those who governed. The Roman Empire was not great because it was large and powerful; it was great because many of its leaders, like Tiberius, were first-rate administrators who built roads and bridges and aqueducts and cities. They produced and carefully administered a system of government and laws. Their armies protected and maintained a stable empire. By and large, the great purposes of peace, stability, knowledge and reason, and improved prosperity for the masses were sought and the human condition was bettered.

When people decided they ought to govern themselves, the democratic countries produced wonders—wonders that can only be explained by the fact that they exist primarily to serve the governed and not those who govern. It is through man serving mankind, and not man serving himself, that man accomplishes anything of genuine value from which he can derive lasting satisfaction. It is through leaving something of lasting value that a man can cheat death out of its sting and its threat to erase any hint that he was once here. When we search to find what it is that elevates mankind and allows a person to find within himself and in his life's experiences something worthy of his own respect, we discover that it is loyally serving some great calling, boldly and without hesitation or calculation. When we see lives that are led in this way we know immediately that they are good.

The idea of service holds enormous possibilities for each human life. Working in one's calling to serve others or a great cause, first and ahead of self, has produced remarkable results and achievements for mankind, and also it has changes dramatically those who chose to do so. We are struck by the accounts of the lives of those who have been enriched and elevated through serving, and our ability to wonder prods us to try to understand this phenomenon and what it might imply for ourselves.

It is not uncommon to learn of wealthy and successful people in business who sought neither money nor position, yet these things came to them. One CEO put into words his experience. "I have never had the desire to be rich. If I had ten goals it wouldn't make the top ten. Yet the harder I tried and worked at what I believed in, the richer I became." Another CEO said, "The goal I had in mind was never to be the chairman and CEO. . . . I was involved in new businesses, interested in building them. And as the businesses grew, my job grew with the businesses and all of a sudden the business was pretty big and I was moved to another business which was pretty big. And from there I was moved to the presidency, and it just seemed to come sort of naturally, and it didn't ever really impress me as anything that I had to go out and fight for or really work for because I just worked to do what I was doing and it occurred."

We are confronted by the same phenomenon in the lives of people who are extremely generous. Some of them give tithes to their churches, while others give similarly large portions of their earnings and time to charitable organizations. Surprisingly, instead of living less well off, more wealth and income than they would have ever dreamed possible seems to come to them. One highly successful business leader expressed his experiences with this phenomenon, saying, "I'm a tither to my church and have been for about 25 years. And the more I give the more comes back to me. I don't give because I get. But the more I give, it seems the more I get. The more I'm willing to serve, the luckier I become. My management philosophy is that one leads by serving."

Without careful consideration we might think this sounds odd, backward in fact. Some doubters might choose to discount it or dismiss it out of hand as nonsense. But to others, whose minds regularly question and whose curiosity is challenged to think further about this, will find a hint of explanation through examining statements like the one made by Nathan Ancell, of Ethan Allen, who built a highly successful enterprise and earned a fortune in the furniture business. "Human nature," says

Ancell, "is controlled by the law of self-preservation, which leads to a feeling that you should take care of yourself first . . . and take care of feathering your own nest, first and you don't think of taking care of somebody else first. . . . But, that's the way most people try, and that's why most people fail at becoming successful, because they put their priorities backwards." We are also made aware of this idea by statements such as Rotary International's slogan, "He profits most who serves best."

Worthy of our notice here is a little-known side of John D. Rockefeller, the very Gibraltar of capitalism. While in his late teens, in Cleveland, Rockefeller worked in a commercial house and attended Folsom's Commercial College. Each month, from his weekly earnings of $3.50, he contributed $1.80 for religious purposes, which included his Baptist Sunday school and the Five Points Mission in the New York slums. Through summers and winters young Rockefeller wore the same shabby coat; his contributions continued.

We can begin to understand why service leads to a better world and to a better life than the pursuit of being served, through considering what selfless service demands of those who choose to follow that path. Living to serve demands a radical departure from customary attitudes, orientations, and habit patterns. It requires boldness to put oneself second and something greater first. It requires vigilance to monitor one's feelings and actions to maintain these priorities.

Service places three great demands on a person. Each one is a challenge, and yet each is a necessity. A life of service calls the individual to (1) obliterate himself as the central focus of his life, (2) make whatever sacrifices are necessary to shoulder his responsibilities and carry the burdens demanded by his cause, and (3) fully realize that he steadily builds his own character and that, after a while, if he has lived primarily for himself, it might become impossible to change from that pattern.

PLACING GREATER CAUSES AHEAD OF ONESELF

To some, self-denial is a masked way by which they are, in fact, consumed with themselves and their own perceived goodness. We are all aware of people who make a big to-do about how good they have been, about what they have done for others, and about how they have sacrificed and suffered as they performed worthy deeds. And perhaps they have done some wonderful things. But upon careful examination we find that all their goodness is canceled out because they have not worked for the benefit of others at all but instead, for themselves. They carry on, complaining about the pains which they feel they have endured, and they announce how good they think they have been in order to capture the applause of others and feel superior to everyone else. This reveals one of their primary aims: the approval of others. Moreover, they feel their sacrifices and their service make them better than others; to feel superior to others is another of their aims. Clearly they haven't denied themselves at all; instead they have placed themselves on a pedestal for self-worship, with the expectation of praise from others.

One does not deny himself by bemoaning his burdens and sacrifices and good deeds and clamoring for the praises of self and others. One denies himself by forgetting about himself. In fact, self-denial involves not thinking about oneself at all. The person who forgets himself dethrones his self and is thereby able to enthrone his cause. Those who cannot do this serve up troubles for themselves.

How often we encounter people who have fallen by stumbling over their own egos. Concern for one's own importance and status is not only unbearable to others but it also prevents a person from doing those many important chores—loathsome and menial—which spell the difference between great and ordinary. Worse still, the person who constantly feeds his ego with praise and compliments is under the domination of an ever-demanding tyrant—an ego that is out of control, always demanding more. If he cannot get others to sing his praises, he is left to do it himself, and he generally does.

We are all familiar with what an annoyance this person can be to others. Being dependent on their favorable opinions, the self-centered person is forever in quest of others' approval and inextricably tied to their approbation for any sense of satisfaction. He regularly resorts to anything and everything in order to win the applause of others, and he is thereby rendered untrustworthy. The big person controls his own ego and is not worried about projecting an image of importance. He is genuinely unconcerned with who gets the credit for the accomplishment of a worthwhile deed. The most successful business leaders tend to believe that there is no limit to the amount of good one can do, and no limit to the things one might accomplish with the help of others if one is unconcerned about who gets the credit.

A man who is interested more in the results than he is with himself and satisfying his own ego will let the credit go where it may, paying very little attention to it. Instead he takes satisfaction just in knowing an important job was done. Moreover, a person who is more concerned with an important cause than he is with his sense of self importance is free to act nobly and courageously and thus make possible what otherwise might not have been accomplished. John J. Riccardo, a former chairman and CEO of Chrysler, did a number of courageous things during his last few years at that corporation. They involved denying his ego.

One, he reached out and hired Lee Iacocca, promising him the CEO position within a couple of years. Two, as relations with the government deteriorated in the attempt to secure a loan guarantee for Chrysler, Riccardo accelerated Iacocca's move to the CEO position a year faster than promised. Riccardo recognized that Chrysler was having difficulty in getting a loan guarantee, so he took early retirement and stepped down, acting in the best interests of Chrysler Corporation and giving it a fighting chance for survival.

The ego starved for attention demands center stage and all the recognition it can attract, both deserved and undeserved. The healthy ego permits humility. One former chairman of the board remembers that when he was a younger man and working for his firm, he had an outstanding year, and around Christmastime he was informed by one of the firm's managers that he would receive a nice bonus.

Most young men would have immediately begun to visualize how such a windfall might be used, especially with a young family, but not this man. Instead he told the manager that he didn't feel he could accept that bonus because although he had had some success, it was largely due to the team of people that had given him the backup to get the job done, and that the only way he could accept the bonus would be on the basis that it would be shared with the group.

Denying oneself does not mean one must give up all material possessions and comforts or inflict pain and hardship on oneself, as some primitive religions are practiced. These acts, in fact, only cause a person to consider how pious and wonderful he is making himself. Instead of forgetting about himself and whatever hardships he might endure as he does something useful or serves the needs of others, he instead serves his own need for self-approval.

Use of material objects primarily to project an image of importance, instead of putting them to useful service, is also in opposition to the kind of self-denial of which we are speaking. One CEO changed corporate practices so as to make the executive prerequisites tools for service, instead of symbols of importance and privilege. "I never took the corporate plane instead of the shuttle to go to lunch [meetings out of town]. When the manifest for the plane for the previous month came around and I found a couple of my senior people doing it, I put 'Washington?' alongside of their entry and sent it to them. They stopped using it. We had previously only one company car. The chairman had full use of it. I could occasionally borrow it as president if he were out of town, but otherwise his secretary would say, 'Oh, no. That's got to be there in case the chairman suddenly decides he needs it. So you'd better rent a car if you have to have one.' When I got to be CEO I changed that, and I said, 'The car is a company tool. I have first call, but if I'm not using it, it should be scheduled for anyone who wants it in the executive group.'. . . It saved some money. My wife never used it. I made the point, this is a tool not a prerequisite."

It is possible to serve one's cause so singlemindedly that the outcome harms other worthy causes. In his book, *The Philosophy of Loyalty*, Josiah Royce introduces concept of "loyalty to loyalty"—that we ought to be loyal to causes that are not divisive of other people's loyalties. Living in a world of many needs and many worthy causes, we must, according to Royce, recognize that self-denial might require us to sacrifice doing things in the easiest fashion, so as to permit other causes to be advanced.[2]

An excellent illustration of this principle is shown in Peter Ueberroth's explanation of how the 1984 Los Angeles Olympics were organized. "Everything [was] done on a voluntary basis, not a charitable basis; we did not form a charitable corporation. We formed a not-for-profit corporation, but no tax deductions could be taken. Any surplus from this business would go to other charities across this country, because we did not want to compete with churches, synagogues, hospitals, cultural groups. . . . It would devastate a city because all the people would donate that year's budget to the Olympic movement to get tickets and other things. [That would] devastate all the other institutions that would have to live there [Los Angeles] full time. So that's why we chose not to get into any donations."

When a person has a cause that captures his full loyalty and devotion and he has forgotten himself in its pursuit, he will discover that no job to that end is beneath him. In his mind the only important thing is that the work goes forward productively; in this spirit, all the tasks that contribute toward its achievement are to be carried out cheerfully. To the dedicated, loyal person, no one is so important that he should stand on his office or sense of self-importance and refuse to perform the menial work that is necessary. This principle is found in the lives of great leaders. The leader who serves his followers, that they might perform their work, is a great leader. And the one who denies himself the temptation to rest on his position as an excuse for not pitching in when he can give assistance, often becomes an admired leader.

The incident when General Washington dismounted his horse and, in the mud and alongside his men, moved a stuck wagon, is a well-known illustration of this great idea and a good reminder of why he was so revered even in his own time. We can also catch a glimpse of this sort of person in the following anecdote about the UPS founder and former chairman of the board.

A fair-sized contingent of top UPS managers including the company's chairman, Jim Casey himself, was once staying at a motel. This group was preparing day and night for hearings on an intrastate application for operative rights. One evening during their stay, a group of the managers met in a large parlor. It was chilly and a little drafty. One of the men felt his throat grow scratchy, and he worried out loud about getting a cold. He was concerned that a sore throat and a case of the sniffles could hurt his part of the presentation the next day. He asked whether anyone had any cough drops, but no one did. Although he was not directly a part of the proceedings, Casey was in the room at the time. Moments later he disappeared. After about an hour, the chairman returned with several packages of cough drops. He had quietly slipped away and walked a mile along the main highway to the nearest store, where he had brought the cough drops. It was Casey's attitude that if there were any way he might be able to help, other than just sit around, why shouldn't he do it? In Casey's words, "Any of us who can help the company get rights ought to do it. And, if cough drops help, . . . and I can get the cough drops, I ought to be the one."[3]

WORK AS A PRIVILEGE

One indication of whether a person has forgotten about himself in the pursuit of a cause is whether he views his work as a privilege, or as a form of drudgery that makes his life uncomfortable. A teacher isn't a good teacher unless he sees teaching as a privilege. A doctor is never a great doctor until he sees his chance to help others as a privilege. Those who are concerned mostly with themselves generally see their work as a hardship. Those who are concerned mostly with serving and who have forgotten themselves in the process view their work as a privilege, and in so doing are equipped with the right attitude and mental stamina to bear up to the difficulties and hardships the work involves.

The rescue of the Chrysler Corporation from bankruptcy was a monumental task, and certainly not one for people to attempt who were primarily interested in their own comfort. Gerald Greenwald recalls, "I came into Chrysler in early 1979, shortly after Lee Iacocca arrived. We really did have a mess on our hands. It became apparent quickly that we were going to do the impossible or 600,000 jobs were going to go. . . . There are very few people in this world who are confronted or given the privilege of helping to save 600,000 jobs. I feel I have been privileged."

Every great endeavor requires great sacrifices; nothing of significance is produced through insignificant efforts. Concern for one's own safety and comfort enfeebles one's capacity to give the extraordinary efforts needed for any great undertaking. When one does not view his work as a privilege and instead sees it only as a burden and source of discomfort, what might have been a great adventure that would accomplish something of genuine significance will very likely be seen as just painful drudgery to perform. As a consequence, the tedious and difficult parts of the job are usually left undone or only partially done.

By pursuing his own comfort and by trying to make his existence safe and easy, a person can easily become unable to bear the great burdens that give life its richness and fullness of meaning. Life takes on real meaning when one does meaningful things. Most often they can only be reached through doing the difficult. By forgetting ourselves we can willingly bear great burdens, and through meaningful work we can find meaning in ourselves. Then no demand is seen as too great, no work too dirty or demeaning, no job unimportant or insignificant. Then we realize that there are big victories and small victories in life and that no one who cares about the betterment of the human condition that these victories make possible will fail to work toward them, the small as well as the big.

Those who live in this fashion do not see themselves as so important or so hungry for prestige as to attempt just the large challenges, nor so afraid of formidable challenges as to tackle only the small ones. Michael W. Wright, of Super Valu Stores, recalls, "I practiced law for a number of years, and in the kind of work I did it wasn't always the size of the deal that you felt good or bad about, it was how much you felt you helped your client, whether he's large or small. . . . Sometimes you can be more help to the little guy than you can to the big guy."

The world with its many needs calls people to abandon their personal ambitions, to sacrifice their leisure time, to forgo the comfort of the easychair and fireside in order to render useful service. And again the recipe for living and not just existing demands the answer yes when these calls are made. The late Robert Lilly was vice chairman of AT&T; before that he was president of New Jersey Bell. After the Newark riots of 1965, Governor Richard J. Hughes looked for a CEO to head the commission that would look into the riots. Four chairmen turned him down and he came to Lilly, who was reasonably new on the job, and asked him to do it. Bob said, "You're darn right I'll do it!" His committee wrote a piece that is the ultimate report on civil disturbances in an urban area.

Once a CEO of a major corporation received a letter from a long-time friend. The friend wrote, telling about himself: he had just turned 52; his business had been a huge success; his cash flow from stocks and investments would be more than he and his wife would ever need; he was going to retire and take life easy. He had made his bundle of money. The system had been good to him. And so now, in effect, this entrepreneur was going to put himself "out to pasture." And his daughter had just graduated from a prestigious university with straight A's and, by the way, she needed a job. Could he please help? The CEO wrote back to this friend:

> It's a pleasure to read the American success story. The Harvard MBA, entrepreneur, business success allows retirement at age fifty-two. Congratulations! Now my advice. There is another chapter yet to be written once you've had your fill of travel and mountain climbing. It's called the pay back. In most major corporations the sense among senior officials is that they owe something to the system in part payment for their own success. This senior executive is spending untold hours lobbying for things at the government level well beyond the narrow corporate interest. This senior executive sees weekends and evenings often filled with public service in charity, education and other matters. The entrepreneurs too often take the money and run, assuming that someone will keep the system going for the next guy. The "I've got mine" attitude is all too common. Let me, at the risk of sounding "preachy" suggest testifying in Washington as an entrepreneur in favor of the the same investment tax credit that probably made your leases work, or getting active on the subject of federal R & D cuts, the same grants that helped support your daughter's education, and any number of other ideas would be a useful pay back. Maybe you could marshall some of your other "got-it-made associates" to do some local fundraising where they are virtually non-existent and always too busy. Since you don't pay me for advice you don't have to listen. But consider the advantages of the "system" and you might well consider its renewal important enough to contribute to it.

There are many ways by which people can contribute to the betterment of the nation and "repay," so to speak, the economic system that has been good to them. "Lee Iacocca had hundreds of nice job offers after he left Ford," recalls William G. McGagh who once worked at Chrysler.

"But instead of taking an easy one he believed that he owed the auto industry because it had done a lot for him. This is one of the important reasons why he went with Chrysler."

Rubbermaid's chairman and CEO, Stanley Gault, serves as chairman of the 13,500-member National Association of Manufacturers, a post that consumes 10–15 percent of his time. Why would he take that job, as busy as he is? "The country has been good to me, certainly," says Gault. "This is one way to put back something. . . . Plus the fact this is the great critical time in the history of America from a manufacturer's standpoint. This is one of the basic sectors of our economy. A tremendous amount of our families are tied to the success of manufacturing, directly and indirectly."

There are those who worry about the future and about others, and there are those who do not. The burdens that one finds are an indication of his sensitivity, but the burdens which he attempts to shoulder reveal his character. Those who see only their own troubles make a practice of leaning on others. Happily, there are those who step forward as lifters to ease other's loads. Their concerns include others and the generations to come. Their load involves living today in ways that make it possible for others to live better lives tomorrow. An example of this is concern for the environment. Most of us know by now that quality of life is dependent on the quality of our earth's fragile ecological systems and their ability to provide life, and we realize that it is easy to live well today by spoiling irreplaceable natural resources and harming the wildlife that the earth provides. But we also know that this is as insane as suicide, because ultimately that is exactly what it is.

Over a century ago in Chicago, a businessman concerned himself with environmental beauty. Aaron Montgomery Ward—he did not use his first name—built a solid business selling useful things to Granger members by mail. But his other interest, one that placed beauty ahead of private gain, was the shoreline of Lake Michigan, which wrapped around the east side of the burgeoning city. Ward, like a watchdog, acted to keep structures of any size from being built along the lakefront. Thanks to his efforts, Grant Park and the open areas along the shore have provided beauty and recreation for the citizens and visitors of that great city.

When the Procter & Gamble Company decided to build a paper plant along the Susquehanna River in Mehoopany, Pennsylvania, the plan included environmental control measures. Seventy five million dollars were to be spent on pollution control during the first five years. The plant was originally intended to be located on the banks of the Susquehanna for easy access to needed water supplies but Edward G. Harness, the manager of the Paper Products Division at the time—He later served as chairman of Procter & Gamble—insisted that the plant be located away from the river, where its buildings and equipment would not mar the beauty of the shoreline. The company worked to make sure the Susquehanna's water quality would not be harmed by the new plant. It commissioned an internationally known fresh water biologist to study the possible toxicity of plant wastes. She and a team of eight scientists conducted a bioassay of the river, examining the state of fish and plant life upstream and downstream from the proposed site. Special waste treatment facilities were incorporated. Several years later, after production began, a second survey of the river's water quality showed it was in the same healthy condition as before construction.[4]

The Pacific Gas & Electric chairman, Richard A. Clarke, explains how environmental concerns are very much a part of his company's decision making processes and one of the ways it responded to a wildlife threat. "We have a huge hydro system all up through the Sierra here, where all our water-generated power is. We manage that, in order to assure that fish life is preserved. . . . I think there are only six or eight bald eagles in the northern part of California, and they all happen to be situated along the river where we have a string of dams. The bald eagles feed on the fish that are in the river. If we let the water out too fast, the bald eagles can't find the fish and they're deprived of some of their normal feed. So we worked with the Department of Forestry and Fish and Game to manage the water flows so that the bald eagles would be assured of getting the fish that they need in order to survive. In doing this, we made a very extensive study as to the habit of the bald eagle, and we have a couple of people up in the northern part of our service territory who are probably the foremost experts in the state on the bald eagle, . . . where does it live, how does it mate, what does it eat, what are its patterns? We get very involved in animal and fish life."

BUILDING ONE'S CHARACTER

The world owes everything to those people who have spent their lives without fear, hesitation, or expectation of personal gain and comfort. If they had not been willing to neglect their own safety and security and their own self-gain and self-advancement, the world would have lost out. The value of living is not found by clinging to things and saving oneself from harm or hardships, but by wisely spending time on what is truly worthwhile. The point is this: life takes on meaning only as it is spent. Only through service do people achieve greatness. The great difficulty for anyone is to make himself into the kind of person who is able to give up what he thinks he owns, and thus clings to, in order that he become able to spend his life in worthwhile ways.

What's at stake here is putting an important idea into practice. Part of man's nature can lead him into playing very mean tricks on himself. Among the cruelest of these is procrastination. Many a life has been diminished not by lack of knowledge but by lack of will. Man, no doubt, is a document that can be revised. But the speed and the difficulty of his revision is made longer or shorter, larger or lesser, depending on the delay he makes in changing. For in a very real sense delay is self-deceptive and destructive. It is a sad day when a man's mind knows and his heart wants but his will is incapable of delivering. This is self-deceptive. His mind tells him he understands a truth, but by his actions he mocks it.

At the very least, delay destroys what could have been. At the extreme, it destroys even the will to change. There is much to be said for acting without delay, once he knows he ought to act and while he can act—while it is day and he is free to act.

We can observe people who will try to hold onto their old ways, where self is center stage, just a little while longer. Many believe that eventually they will change and serve at a later time. Others try to wait until just the right cause or need comes their way, believing that when it does they will then serve. Still others believe that they must prepare themselves first: to educate themselves first, to get their own affairs in order first, to arrange other matters more important in their own lives first, and to do any number of other things first before they are ready to serve. These in reality are all just excuses to serve oneself. If a person is to act, he must act at the moment, while he is still free to act and while he can still learn to serve. One really does not need to look very far to find opportunities for service and generosity. They are everywhere. The trick is to seize them without hesitation.

There is just one way to learn how to serve, and that is by serving. Generosity is not something people are born with; it is a quality they develop through their actions—by being generous. One does not fully understand the significance of service and appreciate the internal satisfaction that comes through serving and being generous when he deals with it only as abstract, theoretical concept. But one can grasp its full meaning by actually serving and by being generous himself. If it is tried and repeated, its value becomes apparent rather quickly, so profound is its significance.

Service can become a permanent and distinguishing part of anyone's character. In some families youngsters are taught these lessons early on. Irving I. Stone, of American Greetings, recalls, "Our family was brought up with the belief we ought to help take care of our neighbors. That's one of our principles. I remember in 1918 there was an influenza epidemic. My grandmother was making soup. All the neighbors were sick. I was a kid, 9 years old, taking pots of soup to everyone. We were drilled with that sort of belief. If anybody ever came to the door for help, we never turned anybody down. You don't live for yourself."

Generally, we most admire and most willingly follow those who are most concerned about others and least concerned about themselves. It isn't that we like these people because we get something, we value the persons they have become as a result of their generosity. They are prized more for who they are, than for their gifts of service or for the material objects which they have given. They are generous people, and that quality permeates their every action. There are many people who have fashioned themselves so, whose primary aim is to do for others, quietly, privately, anonymously. And it is uplifting to realize that anyone can choose to be a part of that company.

By giving and serving with stealth, one can keep his self from center stage, a self that is ever eager to purchase a reputation for goodness and magnificence for its own aggrandizement. The purposely anonymous examples that follow are a testimony to the fact that kindness and generosity are very much alive and can be a part of anyone's character who is willing to let go of what he clings to and say yes to really living.

A young man in his early thirties, a few years out of college, married, with four children ranging in age from 6 months to 7 years, is distraught because his wife is diagnosed to have terminal cancer. Nobody who has just paid off college education loans and has four young children has any money to speak of, and this man has no idea how he's going to deal with this nightmare. Working for a large corporation, he has basic medical insurance, but that in no way can cover the myriad of costs he'll incur—care for the children, hospitalization, and so on.

One day he gets a call. A senior vice president and director of the company, five levels above him, summons him to his office. He barely knows the man who calls him to his office. He goes there at the appointed hour, he is greeted, and he sits down. Few words are spoken. The director pushes an envelope across the table to the young man and says, "I put some cash in there. You know I make a hell of a lot more money than you do. I don't want you to sign a note. If you get in a position at some point that you can repay it or do the same thing for somebody else, you go do that. I don't want any obligation, but I want you to use it, and I want you to use it for the benefit of your wife and your kids, and I don't want you to have any worries about it because I'm never going to miss it." Over the years, other stories about this generous man somehow came to the surface. The pattern was the same. He saw a crying need where someone was going through a difficult time, and he got personally involved and helped however he could.

The wife of a large corporation's board chairman develops cancer. Her doctors give her little hope. In pain and desperation she travels out of the country to a clinic. There she receives a treatment neither endorsed nor practiced by American physicians. Yet it is her only hope. It seems to work for a time. In another part of this company a secretary is diagnosed to have the same type of cancer. Doctors give her the same, grim prognosis. Somehow, through the company's grapevine the secretary learns about the chairman's wife. The secretary is told of the seeming success the chairman's wife is having with the controversial treatment. She manages to talk with him about it. But her hopes are crushed when she learns that the company's medical insurance will not pay for this treatment. She is not to be left without hope.

The chairman encourages her to go on and do this thing saying he will find a way to see that the insurance covers it—just send her bills to his office. Her bills are sent there but that's as far as they get. He quietly pays them himself, out of his own pocket, never telling the secretary. He knew all along that he was the only one who could help. Neither the company nor its insurance could cover her expenses, legally or legitimately.

Each person's character is an unfinished product. What nature gives, in the form of aptitudes and abilities, is only a start. It is each person's opportunity to finish the job. Slowly and imperceptibly each person's character is shaped by himself through his own actions and habits. Character is shaped both by how one thinks and by how one acts. To become the kind of person one would like to become, each person must immediately begin acting that way, without hesitation and without calculating the cost.

There will be many situations where the costs will be high and the difficulties will be great. In the process of forming one's own character, it is better not to calculate the costs that the sacrifices of generosity and service demand. But if one must and finds the costs too great, before dismissing the sacrifices as too expensive, too demanding, and too difficult, one would be wise to calculate the cost of not paying the price a prized character exacts. Is it really a bargain to live with who he is when he considers what, for a hefty price, the person he could become?

THE PERSON ONE MIGHT BECOME

The person who turns from primarily living for himself to serving something worthwhile, makes a radical change. His interests and abilities broaden. He becomes a deeper person. Dickinson C. Ross, of Johnson & Higgins of California, says, "The individual . . . whose daily routine is on the basis of just business achievement, . . . before long he gets to be a very boring individual, because all he really can relate to is his personal achievements on a day-to-day basis. Then that same individual, who has the opportunity to broaden his track and become a part of the community [through service] . . . becomes a very interesting person. He's somebody that you want to be with, somebody who really wants to share his ideas and experiences with you, and he becomes a totally different character. But the person who wants to put himself first, who wants to get all the credit himself, he's short lived. . . . The self-centered individual, . . . 'me first' and 'get me just exactly what I can get as quickly as I can get it,' . . . and a major problem arises, there is nobody there to support him and finally he falls by his own weight."

It is extremely difficult to imagine anyone who wants to work for a person like this. Practically everyone wants to work for or alongside this person's opposite. In a radio address following his coronation in 1936, King George VI of Great Britain said, "The highest of distinctions is the service of others." He saw his role not in terms of power but in terms of what it would enable him to do for others. The enabling leader lifts up and thereby is strengthened both because he has more able followers and because he is valued by them for his contribution to their betterment.

The way a person lives from day to day carries over into the way he conducts his business affairs. If a man with something to sell lives on the basis of serving, his actions generally invite a large number of customers, who are eager to trade with him. They see him as someone who they know will treat them fairly and give them good value for the prices they pay. By being generous, by donating what one has in terms of material wealth, or time and talents, anonymously and gladly, a person pushes aside his self-centeredness and comforts and thereby frees himself to concentrate on important matters.

The person who serves becomes less self-centered and more concerned with purposes that others will be willing to follow. This attracts followers. He is also able to work harder and live with the drudgery of menial details, which, when attended to systematically and thoroughly, often spell the difference between mediocre performance and extraordinary accomplishment. This person becomes an attractive human being who attracts many more opportunities than usually flow to ordinary people. But perhaps most importantly, this person is free to really concentrate his best efforts on doing those things that truly do make a real and lasting difference in the world. This is man at his finest.

18

Answering Calls for Kindness

In the early years of the century, travel across the country by automobile was an adventure more for intrepid pioneers willing to bear the annoyance and discomfort of sinking into mud, or choking on dust, or running out of gasoline, or getting lost. Roads were poor; signs to mark the way were sparse; and there were many miles between filling stations. But in 1915 W. K. Kellogg, together with his chauffeur Henry Johnson, set out for San Francisco.

West of Omaha, Nebraska, Kellogg's Franklin roadster became stuck in thick mud. Seeing their plight, a farmboy tried to assist, but it was more than his team of horses could handle. A little while later the boy's father came along, and with a second team the car was pulled to safety.

Grateful to his rescuers, Kellogg asked the farmer, "What do I owe you?" The farmer just looked at him, saying nothing. A bit puzzled by the silence, Kellogg turned to the boy. "Doesn't your father hear well?" he asked. "Oh, I hear all right," the farmer spoke, "but what I am trying to do is recall where I've seen you before. . . . Now, I remember. About twenty-five years ago, my wife was very ill and our local doctor advised me to take her to the Battle Creek sanatorium. She was there quite a while, and I began to run out of money. In desperation I went up to your office, and you assured me that my wife would not lack for treatment simply because I had run out of money. That's why, Mr. Will Kellogg of Battle Creek, you don't owe me a penny."[1]

An infrequently proclaimed quality of humans is their ability to extend acts of kindness to one another. Kindness is a sign of an advanced level of civilization. That it can be cultivated in the human character is a cause for optimism when considering the future of mankind. The greatest teachings of the world that have to do with how to live together instruct people that they should love one another. This goes far beyond calling on people just to tolerate others or merely to be decent to them. It includes both feeling and acting; that is, it includes a deeply felt compassion and regard for others that becomes expressed regularly in concrete actions. Without the former there is little hope for much of the latter.

ABSTRACTIONS AND REALITIES

Opportunities to extend kindness to others do not always present themselves like a caller who knocks on one's door announcing his presence. The needs that cry out for a human touch and tender actions are perceived better if we have greater sensitivity, and the felt urgency to act is intensified by greater compassion. Sensitivity and compassion can be learned. Man's heart can be stirred to feel, just as his mind can be awakened to think. There are difficulties and obstacles to both. Hearts frozen in indifference and hatred are as difficult to awaken as minds which are mired in ignorance and superstition.

The world of business is filled with many abstractions, things that represent something else. On paper, managers daily touch and live with these abstractions—operating reports, budgets, production statistics, cost estimates, balance sheets, profit statements, all dealing with the cold realities of what has occurred and what could occur. Yet behind these abstractions is a reality—people who have nerves and feelings. And it is these people who make the enterprise go. It is easy, sometimes even convenient, to turn away from this reality by shutting off one's feelings and one's understanding of the human engine that puts life into the inert structure of a business organization.

Buildings and machinery and equipment and materials and money are all needed in business, but they themselves do not produce until people make them produce. It can be tempting to convince oneself that objectivity must be maintained at all costs in making decisions, so that these decisions are logical from a rational, business perspective, despite their impact on the lives of others. But it is really a cop-out to ignore the living, breathing people who put life into a business and cause it to produce and grow.

It is tempting to deal with just the abstractions and ignore the realities. Hicks B. Waldron, of Avon, recalls an experience that amply illustrates this idea. "We decided to sell Tiffany three years ago, [1984] and one of the bidders for Tiffany's was Donald Trump. The other bidder was an LBO [leveraged buyout] of the management. I clearly would have preferred the LBO of the management team, and ultimately that's the way it went. But as CEO of a publicly held company I had to be concerned with how much I was offered for this business. And I could lean a little in one direction but not too much. Trump came in with the highest bid and insisted that we move forward. So I called him over here one day. He sat here, and we talked for about an hour and a half. And I found myself lecturing this character on the difference between Tiffany's and a skyscraper for which he is famous. And I said, 'One of the concerns I have, Donald, is that you will treat this business as a piece of property. It is not a piece of property. All you've done is sit here and talk about that building over there.' He was going to cut a hole so you could get into Tiffany's from the first floor of Trump Tower. I said, 'If that's what you want to do, fine. But what you haven't said anything about yet and what I want to talk to you about this afternoon is the entity, the organization called Tiffany. And it's alive with terrific people, whose hearts beat and throb and who have a plan in place, whose livelihoods depend upon how well that institution does, which means, therefore, how well you do owning that institution.' Donald sat there and listened to this whole thing, and I think maybe heard it as well. As it turned out he wasn't as serious about buying it as we all thought he was, so the LBO worked out very well."

There is a vast difference between people who can see the realities that lie behind the abstractions in business, and those who can not. They approach their work from entirely different perspectives, oftentimes arriving at completely different conclusions and making vastly different decisions. The capacity to see and feel and hence value the human dimension is generally the single greatest determinant of one's success, because it is the one factor, above all others, that will earn respect and trust and hence the loyalty leaders need if they are to be effective. The leader whose abiding concerns embrace the human reality, who is sensitive to needs and feelings, is thereby able to decide and act in ways that invite cooperation and dedication from employees instead, of inciting them to bitterness and apathy.

In making business decisions it is tempting to choose to do only what is demanded by the abstractions—the numbers that measure performance. It is somewhat rare to find a sensitive person, one who sees a human need and responds to it, spontaneously and freely. Paul V. Galvin, of Motorola, regularly demonstrated this concern for people. During one of his walks through a shop, he once saw a group of women working on a production line bundled up in overcoats. He asked the shop foreman as to the reason for it and was informed that because they were running production on a single line and the remainder of the shop was idle, they were cutting costs by conserving fuel and heat. "I don't care if there is one girl working, or ten, or one hundred," Galvin said sternly, "you treat them all alike and don't save money by abusing anyone."[2]

The abstractions—the reports, the statistics, the accounting statements, the measures of goal attainment—these things have a way of obscuring many of the realities of business. They do not reveal the attitude and morale of the people employed, or the pace of modernization, or the dedication to and advancement of new or improved technology, or the impact of the firm and its operations on communities. These are not so easily measured, but they are felt, assessed, and given the importance they deserve by perceptive and sensitive leaders, even though they are not captured in statistical measures and computer printouts.

Production schedules, cost containment measures, and the like can easily come to dominate a management's concerns, leaving less attention and emphasis for employee morale and motivation. Wherever this occurs, experience shows, problems soon arise. Successful people learn to assure a balance: both the logical and rational as well as the emotional and sensitivity issues ought to be addressed. Production concerns ought to be balanced with people concerns. Douglas D. Danforth, of Westinghouse, expresses it this way: "If you are not very mindful of the humanistic side of your employees, you're not going to be as productive as you should be. You're not going to produce the quality products you should, and you're not going to have the customers you need to pay the bills."

The most skillful leaders seem to be able to address human concerns in balance with the quantitative measures that indicate business performance. Excellent examples of sensitivity to people can be observed in many parts of corporate America. Atlantic Richfield undertook a major shift in strategy that included heavy emphasis on the human dimension. Top management saw for several years that the industrial environment of America and the business environment of oil had been changing. They therefore had to reassess their corporate culture, strategy, and financial structure in order to be able to adapt to this new world.

They found that they had to restructure Atlantic Richfield both operationally and financially. A question addressed was, which business areas were still appropriate, and which assets were still appropriate? They had to decide what Atlantic Richfield was going to be. They concluded that Atlantic Richfield should not remain a diversified petroleum company but instead should become a hydrocarbon company, which does things with oil, gas, and coal. Operationally, Atlantic Richfield would find, produce, transport, and make valuable fuels and chemicals.

The metals business was sold. The mining business was shut down. Major write-downs were taken. The company was slimmed down in order to be able to deal with the future energy business and the crises it might contain. Decisions were made as to which businesses to keep and which not to keep. In seeing the "crown jewels" that were left, management decided to repurchase Atlantic Richfield stock, because they could not wisely invest the money gotten from the sale of assets in other places. Costs were reduced and earnings per share increased. Stock dividends were raised. This was well received on Wall Street.

In recalling these strategic moves, the Atlantic Richfield president and CEO, William Kieschnick, said, "We had to prepare people culturally and personally for this. We knew we were in for some culture shakes. Change is stressful, especially if it's rapid. We felt obliged to prepare employees for changes ahead and especially to get the management team below the senior level to get inputs from all employees. We needed to get our company's culture in sync with the changes we were to make. We spent years in analysis, talking about reshaping the company's culture. We involved our people, to see and consider the world we were in and to reaffirm, debate, talk about, and to define our business values, versus just writing them down for public release and sending them down through the organization. I started management talking, too, either by invitation or dictate, to rethink our corporate values. These were not published P R materials, but ideas which could be talked about and tested.

"Our perception of the environment five to ten years from now tells us that we'd better have an organizational style which is deeply permeated in personnel. In the 1970s we were in an environment that demanded we get fuel out [of the ground], get the job done, and produce at any cost. Now we need to be efficient and search for new opportunities. This means innovation and productivity. The way to achieve these things is through people. We've had a long standing respect for individuals, but we've added the twist of expectations. We expect and help people to perform. The point is, if our company goes through racking change as we adapt to a new environment, we don't just behave differently, but do it with participation and as much understanding as possible. We must never forget the role and the impact of the individual. This got tested when we decided that we had 5,000 excess employees. First we had to face the reality. If we kept people on board who would not be useful, we would be wasteful. Some must be released. How do we treat these people? One thing was to design an early retirement system—a rich package of benefits to the retiree. This gave individuals a chance to a bridge to a new career or a new change within the company. We had 6,000 takers. This left us with fewer to let go. Our style has been to bring individuals into action, [hold] work councils, and increase the amount of delegation. We adapted to a new world and did so without needless expense to the employee, but instead with an enhanced role of the individual. When we had to do something which was painful, we did so humanely and with sensitivity."

The experience Bethlehem Steel had when it was about to close one of its outdated plants is another instance of where corporate leaders took a balanced approach and chose not to neglect the human dimension and the welfare of a community. Donald H. Trautlein recounts his involvement in this situation. "When I first joined Bethlehem Steel, which was on January 1, 1977, the steel industry, even at that time, was suffering from overcapacity, [and] from a capacity . . . which wasn't as modern as it should be. It was clear that there was going to have to be some reduction in capacity. The question was, how to do that and how to do it, both from an economic and a social standpoint, most effectively? At any rate, I was part of a three-man team that had studied what we ought to do and we just about had reached a decision to close down one of our oldest plants pretty much entirely. The plant was located in Johnstown [Pennsylvania]; and the facilities were, for the most part, old and in need of updating, and the market moved away from that area. The raison d'être for the mill being there originally had been the fact that there was some coal there and some iron ore there, but the iron ore was no longer a product that could be used. They didn't use coal anymore . . . so we had pretty much decided we would have to close that mill down, probably entirely. We knew that it was going to be a tremendous blow to the community, because it was the major employer in the community. Nevertheless, it appeared that was what we were going to do.

"We were just about to announce that decision, which would have been implemented over a period of not less than six months and maybe as much as two years, when the second Johnstown flood hit in June of

1977. The flood really devastated the plant and the community. Quite a few lives were lost in the flood. And of course, the town itself was really in terrible shape. We then went back and rethought the proposition, and we figured that by spending about $50 million we could clean up the plant and run most of it, at least for a period of several years longer, and we went and made that decision.

"I was not the chairman at that time; I had just come aboard. I think I was a member of senior management that made that decision—it was made by, of course, by the chairman's recommendation to the board. I think it was a case where both the management and the board were sensitive to what was happening to a community, and that double blow of closing the plant on top of the natural disaster that they had suffered would just be too much. I'm pleased to say that parts of that plant are still running. There are still at least 2,000 people employed there. Considerable investment was made after that, and a point of fact, no money has been made at that plant, although I think it's now reached a break-even stage in terms of cash flow. So I think that was a case where a company really went quite far to keep a community from really being ravished."

COMPASSION: A FEELING FOR OTHERS

The loyal friend, the trusted confidant, the neighbor who assists in time of need—people who reach out to share life's burdens and tragedies as well as its happy moments—are treasured allies in the human adventure. They listen attentively; they see the emotional side in every situation; they are present when needed; they are the perfect tonic for every occasion.

To many minds, the roots of compassion are a deep mystery, and indeed there are various psychological reasons why some individuals develop a deep sense of compassion: some because they cannot abide strife and don't feel settled unless everything around them is serene; some because they need to feel genuine and authentic, and showing concern is their way of reassuring themselves they are the kind of person they believe themselves to be; some because they experience the world through the experiences of others and need to share others' experiences to do this; and others still because they fear so much that they themselves might suffer a disaster, that they try to protect everyone else.

The internal forces acting on each of us are not completely under our control. But each person does control his behavior, and by acting in compassionate ways it is possible for him to enrich his life by heightening his level of sensitivity to others and increasing his ability to serve their needs. In compassionate people we can observe several tendencies and characteristic behaviors. One is their willingness to assist in time of need; sometimes at real inconvenience to themselves. William H. Danforth, the founder of Ralston Purina, was never too busy to be available when a company employee needed help. Once he sat up all night with a mill worker who had fallen and had been seriously injured and was not expected to live. The worker did live, and years later rose to be a superintendent of a mill in St. Louis. He later told many people that Danforth's interest and concern had helped him pull through.[3]

Another quality compassionate people display is being approachable. It's easy to talk to them. Charles S. Mechem, Jr., of Taft Broadcasting, remembers a former boss at a law firm who would act as if he had nothing else to do but talk to people who came to see him. Although he really was a very busy person, he had a knack of pushing everything aside if someone needed to talk to him.

John A. Young, of Hewlett-Packard, displayed this approachable presence, as the following anecdote shows. In the corporate offices, a coffeepot handler—a man who drives a handcart around to work stations and offices with thermos bottles on it—called Young and said, "I've got a really big problem. I'm an émigré from Colombia, and my son is a doctor now, and I can't get him into this country." The man's son wanted to requalify as a doctor in America. The man asked Mr. Young, "Can you get him a job or anything, because he has to have a job guaranteed to even get in the country and get started?"

A short while later the man came to Young's office. As Young recalls, "We talked about this thing, and so we arranged to give his son, sight unseen, a guarantee of a job as a material handler, which of course had nothing to do with being a medical doctor. So we got him up here and he did that. . . . He started doing his nighttime qualifications. And about two years later, [the father] and his wife showed up with his son, the doctor. He had his license and was ready to practice."

Another characteristic of compassionate people is the ability to listen. They are not only good listeners but go out of their way to listen. James McKnight, who is regarded as the founder of 3M, is a good example of this type of person. Lewis W. Lehr, of 3M, recalls one incident which occurred many years ago. "He [McKnight] got word in his office that . . . some of the technical people in this research center, . . . probably five miles from his office, . . . were not very happy. Just like that, he was in his car,. . . out there to that center to sit down with the director to talk . . . to see what the problem was really about. . . . He was pretty old then. . . . He didn't go through the vice president to get there. He did it. That made an impression on me. . . . He was a person of tremendous integrity and feeling for people, and treated people well."

Good listeners who are available when people need help, like Robert E. Fomon, of E. F. Hutton, who socializes and listens to employees' problems, are helpful allies in facing life's struggles. As Fomon recalls, "I was really kind of the in-house psychiatrist, I think. I've been involved with some very tragic situations, such as malformed babies. What can you really do other than listen? I've been through divorces with guys. I've spent a lot of my time on personal problems of employees."

Compassion requires the utmost in delicacy. It is displayed by saying the right thing, in the right way, at the right moment, and above all with the right interest for the other person at heart. Mildness is not always the best approach. Harsh honesty and a strong dose of reality, aimed at helping by correcting a self-destructive pattern, may be needed to do the trick.

William S. Anderson, of NCR, recalls such a situation in which one executive, rather late in life, fell madly in love with a much younger woman and he just "lost his mind." Anderson knew this was going on and at first tried to kid him, saying, "Behave yourself. Don't be such a damn fool." Later it was discovered that his wife knew about it, the marriage was in jeopardy. Even though the man was older than Anderson, he was the man's boss. Anderson called him in and said, "You've got to shape up or I'm going to ship you out." By that harsh dose of reality, by getting the man to realize that his whole career—which was thought to be absolutely secure—was really at stake and he had to do something about it, Anderson woke the man up, causing him to do the right thing. Both career and marriage were saved.

Still another characteristic is this: They reach out in concrete ways to give a helping hand. Richard W. Sears, whose company grew to be world's largest retailer, is another person who displayed compassion for his employees in many little ways. Sears often assumed a personal responsibility for his employees. If they were ill he would often take care of their expenses. If they were hospitalized or at home recovering from an injury, he'd write them encouraging words: "We all hope to see you back in the harness. . . . Never mind the expense. Avail yourself to all possible treatment and comfort and let me know when you need more money."[4]

THE BARRIERS AND GATEWAYS

While most of us realize that it is easy to ignore human needs or pretend that they do not exist, little effort goes into asking why this is done or what the consequences of it may be. One of the more frequently relied-on reasons for holding back sympathy for another's circumstances is the tendency to blame others for having their own problems. How often we hear it said, "Those people just cause their own troubles." Their frailties not only stand out in the minds of those who are looking for some reason to find fault but also these frailties are used as an excuse for not helping. The tragedy of focusing attention on human frailties is that it hardens one's own heart. It leads the one who sees only the shortcomings in others to act toward them without feeling or compassion. This eventually renders one to become judgmental and self-righteous. He makes himself in the process incapable of any kind of tenderness, or concern, or love for anyone but himself.

The tendency to deny the cries for help and the need for understanding and compassion of his fellow creatures can be seen when someone pretends he does not see or hear these pleas. Experience shows us that people see what they want to see. They see what they believe to be important to themselves. If they believe that what is required for their own success in business is to perform well as measured by the numbers in business reports, then that is all they will see; the abstractions of business will be their foremost concern. As a result they are aware of the production statistics, but not the performers who produce. They are concerned only with what they call the logical and the rational, and are thereby rendered blind to the feelings, the expectations, and the meaningful events in the lives of those who work for and alongside themselves. But from time to time, blinders have a way of coming loose.

Cries for help, expressions of feelings, clamors for assistance sometimes grow too loud to be ignored. When it is impossible to deny these cries because of their obvious presence, another barrier to compassion can reveal itself: judgment. By being judgmental a person denies himself the opportunity to feel. Those who are most judgmental look upon troubled persons as morally weak. They may even label them wicked. They assume that the troubled person has invited his own difficulties. "Why would I," they ask themselves, "try to help someone who has brought his troubles upon himself?" And they know the answer to their own question even before they ask it. So they turn away, giving themselves a nice-sounding excuse: "I'm too busy. I can't help. I have troubles of my own. I don't want to meddle in affairs that are not of my own doing. I just don't want to get involved with that 'type' of person." To hardened hearts, each of those reasons for not helping suffices as a logical and legitimate excuse.

The tendency to evaluate others is a major barrier to compassion. The alcoholic is seen as weak. The person who falsifies an expense report is morally deficient. The person with a troubled marriage is lacking in some quality or other. Whatever the troubled person's problem is, that person is judged to be weak or corrupt or lacking in some fashion that causes the trouble. The judgmental person seems to be able to blame others for their frailties but is unable to understand and is unwilling to help.

However, when one deeply considers the attitudes and actions of those who are the most virtuous, those who truly live upright lives, those who are admired most by others for their character and high principles, he finds that they are the least likely to stand in judgment of others. Perhaps these people tend to be the least judgmental because they, in working as hard as they have to live decently themselves, know better than those who do not try as hard how difficult that is to do. Because of their own struggle, they know how very difficult it is to continually aspire toward and actually live up to high principles and exemplary standards. A summary of the matter is this: The gateway to compassion involves removing one's blind spots and coming into close contact with others who need a human touch of caring and tenderness. It is heightened through extending a helping hand and through avoiding the practice of judging others.

It is strange what a strong measure of honesty can do for a person. Someone who is totally honest with himself about what he sees is capable of remarkable things—even a change of heart. A dose of honesty is a good way to remove blind spots, to see behind the abstractions and perceive the realities that before were obscured. Richard A. Clarke, of Pacific Gas & Electric, tells of such a change that occurred in himself when, years ago, he was an attorney responsible for arguing a rate case before the California State Legislature. "I went up to the legislature with all my empirical data and arguments as to how it would be terrible to depart from cost-based rates," explains Clarke. "You know, rates should be based on the cost of serving particular customers. This 'lifeline' concept was going to add a social dimension to rate-making. You were going to give people energy below the cost of providing that energy. I went up trying to argue to the legislature how irrational that was, and what the consequences would be. But the people who were supporting these programs, they brought up busload after busload of senior citizens, of clergy, and the hearing rooms would be packed with these lovely little old ladies that could be my grandmother. . . . These fine people just sat there. And they would grimace and grunt when I would be saying these things, because they had a need and they needed a solution to that particular need. The legislature, of course, didn't respond to my eloquent rhetoric; but they responded really more to the feelings, the sense that these people conveyed, that there was a definite need and something had to be done about meeting that need. That, more than any event that I can think of, really underscored to me the importance of dealing with needs and feelings and that you can't rationally persuade or discount feelings and sensitivities. They're as much a part of the equation as the intellectual side is. And also, it just drove home the fact that as a company, we have to be caring."

The act of serving, of addressing a human need, of helping others, can have an amazing impact on a person. These experiences can dramatically alter any ordinary life. In New York City, as in other parts of the country, companies have involved themselves with what are called adopt-a-school programs. Managers and executives spend time at a high school or grade school helping with the educational process in various and creative ways.

William Woodside, of American Can (now Primerica Corporation), tells of some of the impact involvement in this program had on the people of that corporation. "Corporate top executives are great for easing their social conscience by writing checks for various worthy causes and never dabbling a toe in the water, so that it's never a *real* problem. It's a charitable contribution they are making. This has really made them face to face with what it's like to be a black, or a Hispanic, or from Southeast Asia, dealing in New York's world. And it has done amazing things for them in terms of a sense of personal commitment to social issues in the United States. So I find that almost more valuable in the long run than what we're doing for this individual group of students."

PREVENTING TROUBLE

Sensitivity and compassionate action, intelligently applied, can rescue people from trouble long before it begins, or at least while it is at an early enough stage to keep it from doing lasting and serious damage. Each human is laden with various frailties or vices, and under ordinary circumstances is able to keep the upper hand on them. But, sometimes ordinarily good people get themselves into situations that cause them to go wrong. As Robert Wilhelm, of Emporium Stores, explains, "A good way we found to detect if an employee was headed for trouble was to watch the charge accounts. We found that this was a pretty good indicator of some sort of trouble. If employees ran up heavily into debt, we'd call them in and ask, 'What can we do to help you?' Oftentimes we found there was a problem like a divorce or some personal problem. Once people get themselves into tremendous debt, they can turn to stealing. These aren't bad people. They are just desperate. We think we stopped a number of ordinarily good people from becoming bad."

Companies themselves can be the source of trouble, leading people into situations where their inabilities or frailties get the better of them. It would be easy to simply condemn these people and write them off as weak; it is a temptation to judge and discard people after having a hand in their destruction. But it certainly is not kind or praiseworthy. Responsible managements will address these situations honestly, accept their share of the blame, and work positively for good solutions.

Frank J. Tasco, of Marsh & McLennan, tells how this type of situation is addressed by his organization. "This business encourages a lot of entertainment. As a result we get a lot of people who can't handle it and end up with problems—mainly drinking. In the company I came from we had at least ten cases—close, high-level colleagues. We worked with and salvaged [them] through setting the way, preserving their jobs, preserving their incomes, taking all the pressure off them so they could get their lives back in order. And all my partners and all the people in this company subscribe to that uniformly. We are great believers in human beings and their contribution to this company. And if someone gets off the track we are all going to pitch in."

HAVING A HEART

Is it possible for big corporations to have a heart? Can they *afford* to have one? They can cleverly capture new markets. They can develop new products and manufacture them successfully. They can make goods and services available that are of high quality, and priced so the ordinary citizen can purchase and enjoy them. They can grow and expand and return profit for their owners. But can they take care of their producers—the men and women who have served their purposes skillfully and faithfully? The answer is not only, "yes, they can," but also "yes, they do." In situations where they have been under no legal obligation, and some might even say they are under no moral obligation either, they have stepped forward to assist, because their leaders recognized that if they did not help no one else would. Even at a huge cost to themselves, they have put what they felt was an obligation to people ahead of immediate gain. Business is business; it is concerned with profits and costs and productivity. Yet well managed businesses also seem to take good care of their people when they are in need. The best firms go to great lengths to extend sympathetic and helping hands, as these illustrations indicate.

A manager who has only been employed by one particular firm for two years learns that he has cancer. For over two years he is unable to work. Yet he remains on the company payroll. He receives increases in pay and never loses a day's pay. All his medical expenses are covered. He even receives a promotion during this time period; management knows he only has months to live. Employees visit him in the hospital offering anything they can possibly do—whatever it is. His wife is given his company car after he dies because they didn't really own a car.

At another company, on a Friday afternoon, a sales representative tells his boss that he is leaving the company that day because he has another job to start on Monday with a competitor. The company's management is annoyed at not having any notice. The competitor's offer is subject to a physical, examination which the man takes on Saturday, whereupon they discover cancer. The competitor refuses to hire him. He is rehired by the firm he just left and kept on the payroll for about three years before he dies.

At still another firm an executive leaves to join another small firm in the same town and develops a brain tumor shortly thereafter. Soon he becomes unable to function in this new role. The first employer brings him back and installs him in a job that gives him a sense of meaning and a role to play—even though a reduced role. He has a reason to keep fighting and because of that lives seven years. Everyone is sure the job kept him alive.

There are countless examples of situations where people in companies have reached out to the aid of their coworkers in time of need, not just by sending greeting cards and flowers to express sympathy, but by acting in concrete ways. Consider the following true accounts of kindness and generosity. The individuals and companies responsible for these acts of kindness are not disclosed here because they wish to remain anonymous.

1. A painter working for a large paper company went into the hospital for removal of what was thought to be a benign growth on his forehead. It turned out to be inoperable cancer. Maintenance people from work went to his home and built ramps in his house for his wheelchair. Other employees raised money to help his wife and young family pay medical expenses.

2 A manufacturing company is forced to lay off people during a severe recession. Unemployment benefits begin to run out after several months, and a number of people, unable to keep up with payments, risk losing their homes. Food stamps are not adequate to feed their growing families. Through the United Way, money is provided by the company's owners to people in real need. They never learn that their benefactors are the owners of the firm where they work.

3. A man working for an industrial firm is experiencing trouble. His 25 year old son has a drug habit. The police arrest the son for steal-

ing. The father's coworkers approach management to see if they will hire the son, give him responsibilities, try to work him through his problem. He is hired but soon is missing work and causing trouble. He is fired. Yet these people tried.

4. A child of an insurance company's employee needs a liver transplant in the middle of the night. On their own, other employees arrange for the company plane to be made available to fly the child and his parents from Hartford, Connecticut, to Dallas, Texas, where the operation is performed.

5. The brother of an employee of a large pharmaceutical firm needs a liver transplant, but a suitable organ cannot be found. Employees write letters and make calls to locate one. The chairman of the board calls board members affiliated with major hospitals all over the country. A donor liver is located, and the transplant is successfully accomplished.

6. A man working for a large food company dies. Word reaches company headquarters on a Monday morning. A check for three months' salary is written, and that evening one of the senior-level people departs the West Coast with check in hand to carry to the widow in the East. The deceased man, it is found out, has failed to make adequate preparations for this event; and all his assets are to be frozen for several months, so the money is a blessing. Through company connections, three reliable people in the community are identified for the wife to go to for financial and legal advice, to protect her and her family from fast-talking swindlers.

HELPING PEOPLE IN TROUBLE

Within any large group of people there will be individuals with problems: alcohol abuse, drug abuse, child and wife abuse, suicide threats, unwanted pregnancies, and a multitude of other situations related to psychological disorders. The pressures of modern life give rise to the need to help people who have troubled lives. Chevron has tried to provide help for its employees and their families with crisis lines. Volunteers from the company, who have received over 30 hours of training in crisis prevention, are available at any hour to take telephone calls from those in need of help. Callers are put in contact with trained professionals for appropriate counseling or assistance, on a highly confidential basis.

Throughout American industry, efforts are made to spot substance abuse and to get help immediately for those with alcohol and drug problems. At Chrysler, top management and the UAW representatives have worked on finding ways to have employees who work together identify and get help for those who need it. The Chrysler Motors chairman, Gerald Greenwald, says, "Any ten people who work together eight hours a day . . . know who among them has a problem. The fundamental is, that person doesn't want to admit to himself that he has got a problem and the other nine don't want to tell him. What we're trying to do is find some kind of environment in which people will say to that guy, 'Hey, you're going to kill yourself, . . . and you might kill me too. Or, at least the quality of the car you are helping build isn't going to be as good. You need help, you need help for self, for us, and for your family.' We want to find the rehab programs that will be constructive. We don't want to lay them off. We don't want to fire them. We want to make them want to have help."

In the distant past alcoholics were either "put on the shelf" or fired. Most firms follow a different approach today. They try to get these people into programs that will help them overcome their alcohol or drug problems and stay off of these substances once back at work. Roy A. Anderson, of Lockheed, explains what that company does. "We've had several instances now where we have taken an individual like that, referred him to this doctor who works with him. He doesn't have to report to us what's going on; he works with him, gets him into the right program on the outside, and we always bear the expense of it. They try to bring the guy back out of that and make him proud of himself. . . . There's an awful lot of that going on, a lot of that illness that's prevalent in . . . industry . . . It's the saddest thing in the world, because many times it affects those who are very talented . . . and they just waste themselves away."

Cigna was one of the early companies to create an employee assistance program, not only for the usual things like alcohol and drug abuse, but also for people who just plain have problems. Confidential help has been extended not only to employees but to their families. "I even know of instances," says the Cigna Chairman, Robert D. Kilpatrick, "where we got parents of our employees involved in alcohol or drug abuse or just general counseling. A lot of people could point to that and say, 'Well, that saves money.' I don't know whether it does or not. We felt an obligation that we may be some of the source of pressures on some of our employees and their families, and we ought to make sure that they have access, totally free, to the best kind of facilities that we could get."

19

Elevating People's Thinking and Standards

Each person is capable of making a tremendous difference in the lives of others. When all of the ways in which one person can be of help to others are considered, the one generally regarded as being of greatest benefit is the introduction of new and useful ideas—the giving of thoughts and standards that elevate others' thinking and thereby permit them to live richer, better, more productive lives. We are all capable of adding many different and marvelous things to the lives of others, but most of these lose their impact once we depart. Great ideas, however, do remain, and once they are a part of a person's knowledge and understanding they can have a profound influence on how he lives.

Much of what we observe people doing for others is done to some degree so that the doers can feel good about themselves. This, of course, is not only selfish but ultimately not very helpful, because it makes the recipient dependent upon the giver. The ultimate gift is one that produces freedom—freedom to see more, freedom to think more skillfully, freedom to do more, and freedom to become more through one's own choosing and efforts. The one gift that requires the most and the highest form of love on the part of the giver is the gift of freedom.

There are many forms of freedom: freedom from oppression, freedom from privation, freedom from illness, freedom from hunger, and so on. But none of these freedoms is so long lasting as freedom from ignorance. Ideas last. No doubt people forget some things, and their skills can grow dull though inactivity and disuse, but the knowledge that a great idea exists will continue even through various particulars of it may have slipped from one's immediate recall.

We all can be sure of one thing: man was made to think. Through rigorous thinking, he adds immeasurably to life's meaning and thus to his own dignity. Rational thought is the chief source of man's freedom. Thinking and the improvement of the mind through learning are seen by many philosophers as one of man's chief duties.

Modern man is a man of science; from that there can be no escape. By science we mean a process of free inquiry according to a method by which man can gain a more accurate understanding of himself and his world, thus freeing himself of the shackles of ignorance and superstition. We can all develop the ability to think more rationally with the aid of a scientific method of inquiry, even though there are limits to it. And there are tremendous opportunities for people to share their knowledge with their fellow creatures, which not only adds positively to their own, but also to the thinking skills and the minds of others.

Some delicacy is required in finding and seizing these opportunities. A clear difference exists between helping and meddling, between instructing and intruding, between persuading and pestering, and between bettering and butting in. There can be little doubt that there is an appropriate time and place for helping others just as there is a time and place for holding off helping. But when it is invited, when it is wanted, when it is needed and certainly when asked, there arises a tremendous opportunity to contribute to another's knowledge and understanding.

Just as a life is made less well off because of ignorance, a person can diminish his own well-being when he fails to apply the knowledge he does possess. When someone holds back a useful thought that could add understanding or knowledge to another person and could shelter him from harm, the one who has failed to inform must share some responsibility for the diminution in that other person's existence. It would not be logical to believe that the person with the knowledge to give is responsible for making the ignorant person accept it. Each human is free to determine for himself what he will put into his own mind and what he has in his mind that he will put to use. The issue then is not whether the ill-informed person uses the opportunity to learn but whether he has it to use in the first place.

Once a person becomes unshackled from ignorance, it is up to him to choose to use the knowledge that liberated him. The occasions a person may have to unshackle others from ignorance are greatly increased by his own knowledge, thinking skills, and ability to relate with others in such a way that they seek his liberating assistance.

STRETCHING OTHERS' THINKING

Stretching of minds does not always occur through seminars, or lectures, or debates. Much of it occurs by other means. Sometimes it occurs because a person tries out an idea that he feels is appropriate and others are free to view the results and learn along with the experimenter. Often it occurs through casual conversation. But it can be brought about through more deliberate means.

In business, mind stretching can take many forms. Fletcher Byrom, when he headed Koppers, used to gather a group of younger managers together for breakfast meetings. As chairman of the board, Byrom was interested in getting the company's future leaders to grapple with the difficult issues confronting the world, the nation, and the economy; by this method he hoped they would be developed for leadership roles. He would assign a current, best-selling book and have round-table discussions on it at breakfast meetings, as a way of furthering the intellectual development and thinking skills of younger managers.

Walter Peake, of the Container Corporation, connected himself with design when he headed that organization. He sought to improve the quality of design of a package, believing a package could have an aesthetic as well as a functional value. His interest in developing minds led him to found the Aspen Institute, which is a unique approach to management development that places business people in contact with great minds at seminars and retreats.

Joyce Hall never completed high school. He always referred to himself as a simple man, and he believed in simple people. Hall's company used to sponsor a high-quality radio program, "The Hallmark Radio Hour." Lionel Barrymore would frequently star in dramas of literature on this program. When television became popular, the networks came to Hall and tried to interest him in sponsoring a variety show, but he said no he wouldn't hear of it. He wanted to give people Shakespeare and Shaw. He went on and gave the media leaders a lecture. He wanted to use his money and influence to talk up to people, he told them. He said they underestimated the people's taste. He wanted to improve the thinking and attitudes of Americans and to show people the beauty of literature. He believed that when you talk up to people you get 110 percent. He was adamant that people deserve better than they might choose for themselves. He sold cards by using the slogan, "When you care enough to send the very best."

Bristol-Myers Squibb is cautious about the television programs it sponsors. Although it doesn't insist on cultural performances it does reject violence and sex on the screen. Its chairman and CEO, Richard L. Gelb, explains, "We have a group out in California and here as well [New York] which literally looks at every script of every program that we are going to be in. We have gotten our proscribed list—certain programs that are considered by us to be too violent, so we don't go in those. We may have a program that is perfectly appropriate, except one segment of it comes along and suddenly we discover something we think is offensive for whatever reason it might be. So we're constantly looking at that and taking our commercials out of those regardless of the numbers of viewers."

When he was chairman of the board of the Times-Mirror in Los Angeles, Franklin D. Murphy was instrumental in putting art in the offices. The company (Times Mirror) owns the Harry Abrams Co., which publishes art books. Times has a store where employees are entitled to get products at cost. As Murphy explains, "In the beginning [many] of our employees found art forms to be bizarre and curious. Over the years the sale of books has increased, so has art in the building. The art has rubbed off, stretching the minds of employees."

IMPROVING HABITS

Much of what people do is habitual, so it is not preceded by any significant amount of forethought. This is commonly understood. But what is oftentimes unrecognized is that few people ever consciously assay their own habits to determine which ones should be kept and which ones dropped, and which new ones they might choose to develop. People are usually fairly good at observing other people's behaviors and probably more aware of their habits than the other people are themselves. Thus they are often in an excellent position to help others reflect on their habit patterns and to help them consider seriously which ones are in their best interest to maintain. Here again the issue of meddling arises, and it must be weighed against the help that can come from a well meaning associate.

For many reasons, and not the least of which is their effectiveness and good health, business is concerned with habit patterns of employees. The workaholic, the heavy smoker, the overweight and underexercised employee are all disasters waiting to happen. Large corporations, such as Procter & Gamble, work with employees to help them improve their lifestyle habits. This effort promotes a sensible diet, weight reduction, exercise, nonsmoking, stress reduction, and general mental and emotional health. The program is intended largely to combat rising health care costs, and it is a cost effective method of reducing the incidence of cancer, heart attacks, strokes, back problems, and so on. But it also enriches lives and spares them the tragedies of serious health problems. Lockheed, too, has health programs for its employees: diet programs, fitness programs, stop smoking programs, which have produced dramatic results including fewer days missed due to illness.

Strictly voluntary, the Procter & Gamble Lifestyles Program has caught on in popularity. People today are generally well read on health issues and exposed to news reports relating certain habits to health problems. The Procter & Gamble effort is just the encouragement the employees need to get them to do what they already feel they should do.

Many people know that they should break particular habits and they genuinely want to. But somehow they just cannot seem to push themselves to do so. A little friendly, unsolicited interference may offend a few—they really are not harmed—but it might encourage many others to change in ways that help themselves, who later will appreciate the "interference." Paul F. Oreffice, of Dow Chemical, says, "I'm big on certain things like health, and I'm not beyond tapping somebody in the midsection and saying, 'Aren't you a bit overweight?' or 'Smoking is banned in any public place!' "

At Colgate-Palmolive people are recognized for quitting smoking. The board chairman and CEO, Reuben Mark, explains, "We have a clean air award. It's a little plastic thing with their name, my signature, and a medal. And they get their picture taken with me. It's a big deal. It makes it that much harder for them to restart smoking."

Ethical treatment of people demands honesty, and this involves letting them know where they measure up and where they do not. Their true character will reveal itself in the way they respond to an appraisal. It may be difficult to believe that people can actually find value in being awakened to their mistakes and shortcomings. We all have noticed the annoyance expressed by at least a few individuals who are angered at being corrected. However, we should remind ourselves of this: The intelligent person wants to learn, and because his love for knowledge is preeminent, he does not mind being told when he is wrong. Stupid people are satisfied with ignorance, and dislike being corrected.

We underestimate people when we think they will only respond negatively to criticism. A few might, but most are intelligent enough not to. A person who wants to do what is right for people will have to risk an occasional rebuff or angry response when he, however honestly and kindly, calls appropriate information to their attention. Successful people nearly always find good advice useful, and, because they are intelligent, they will heed it. Charles Marshall, of AT&T, recalls an occasion when he received criticism as a young man starting out with that company. "I was an assistant manager in a little town of 80,000 called Decatur, Illinois, and I had a boss named Whit Sapp. He was the manager, and he was a tough guy. He had size 15 shoes, [stood] six feet five inches, and every six months we had an appraisal. This is part of the ethics of this corporation. If you appraise an employee at the end of six months you really owe it to the employee to tell him or her not only the things that you can applaud but to tell them the things that they can do better and that you quietly think they can improve upon. If you don't, you cheat them of their heritage. I will never forget Whit Sapp. At the end of six months, I thought I was pretty good. He criticized my clothing, and he was correct. I could have shined my shoes a little better. I could have selected my ties better to match my suits. And he criticized me also because he thought that I was working at the office later than I needed to at night and I had a wife and a couple of children at home. It was good criticism. He told me, 'Chuck, if we have to talk about this again in six months, I don't think you're going to go up in this business, because,' he said, 'either of those are problems that will finally catch up with you.' It shocked me to have somebody be so candid."

Serious debate exists on how hard employees should be pushed at work. In many firms extreme pressure to produce causes them to give up weekends and evenings just to get their assignments completed. Moreover, the scramble to move ahead is tremendous. However, leaders in some firms encourage employees to live more balanced lives. "I don't believe in workaholics," says Paul Oreffice of Dow Chemical. "I believe in people working hard, but not in workaholics. I believe very strongly that you need to balance your family life, your company life, your community life. A good person is really one who manages to do all of those things. . . . this is a subject that I never fail to address when I talk to our young people particularly. . . . I try to emphasize that while I expect them to work hard, they need to lead a balanced life. That emphasis on a balanced life, I think, helps make for happier people."

At Du Pont, board chairman and CEO, Richard E. Heckert, tells young people, "There are very few companies left that think you ought to be a slave to your job. That's simply stupid. Most of us believe our best employees have plenty of time for their families, and we like people who value friendship and normal kinds of social intercourse—whole people, not just slaves to the work situation. . . . You can work fifty or sixty hours a week and still have a very fine private life, . . . it's just a question of management. . . . I leave my home a little before seven . . . and get home a little after six, normally; . . . there's eleven hours every day committed to that part of my life at a minimum. Sometimes I have homework but not very often. I've learned to save the evenings and the weekends for myself and for my family. And I'm able to do that by working hard, but in the regular work day."

THE CONTAGION OF GOODNESS

The quality which people generally remember most in others is their goodness—the quality of their character. Some human qualities fade in our minds. Physical beauty, a charming personality, and the ability to accomplish remarkable feats are all appealing qualities upon first sight, but the strength of their attraction lessens with repeated exposure. Other qualities are viewed as desirable but can be tolerated only in small doses: cleverness is intriguing, intelligence is fascinating, and humor is amusing. But we grow weary of those who impress us with their knowledge, we develop suspicions about the slippery and sharp-minded, and we tire quickly of the shallow antics of the clown.

The importance of goodness is made strikingly evident when we consider what sort of person we would most prefer for steady companionship, for it is goodness that most affects the nature and quality of relationships. The person of excellent character wears well in all circumstances. His goodness is genuine and he can be relied upon. His trustworthiness is never doubted. Of all human qualities, goodness is the only one that produces lasting satisfaction. We never tire of goodness; it cannot be overdone. People with excellence of character do not make a show of their good acts to impress others, trying to win their favor. They are not self-centered individuals who announce and boast of their piety hoping to purchase a good reputation. Instead their actions are genuine. They behave as they do because of the kind of people that they are.[1]

Although no one can define exactly what goodness is or which precise behaviors constitute goodness we have no difficulty recognizing it when we see it. Most people have an inner sense that signals whether another person is ethical. Their goodness is readily apparent, and many of us can quickly spot it in another person, just as Jack Peters, of J. Walter Thompson, describes. "You can tell it. You can smell it in a guy. I can go into an office and get some sort of feel for a guy's moral fiber." And goodness is so attractive it outshines all other qualities in a person.

Richard Heckert, of Du Pont, recalls a high school teacher who later went on to become a well respected professional football coach. "Who can forget a high school coach like Weeb Ewbank? . . . He was extraordinary. I had that wonderful experience. And Weeb was a tremendous influence on the life of every kid who ever played for him. And what was that influence? Well, it wasn't just winning, although he did that very well. The team did [win]. But above all, it was integrity. It was 'hard work produces good results,' 'honesty is the only acceptable policy,' . . . He had no stomach for people who couldn't tell the truth and accept the reality of both winning and losing."

William R. Howell, of J. C. Penney, saw the quality being discussed here in two J. C. Penney store managers he worked with in Oklahoma. What Howell remembers most is, their goodness. "They stood for the principles of this company. . . . They focused their attention and their time and their talents on the people within those stores. . . . I never saw them cutting corners or being dishonest. They were just upright, fair in every respect with the business and with the people.".

The person who makes it his life's ambition to achieve a high-quality character is likely to respond to these realizations about goodness with this question: How might I acquire this prized characteristic? To that end it is helpful to identify sources that are commonly thought to lead to goodness but that in fact do not. Education, for instance, is thought to be the answer to practically every evil and ailment which plagues us. But education without a moral dimension to it is insufficient to the task of developing goodness. Some of the highest-principled people who have lived never went beyond grade school. At great universities, populated by highly accomplished academicians and scholars, we can find the most loathsome backbiting, pettiness, and cruelty imaginable. We see goodness both inside and outside of circles of learning.

Churches and involvement in church activities are also frequently thought to be the source of excellence of character. And although churches do a great service to society in reminding their congregations of the importance of morality and useful service, we find story after story of littleness and narrow-mindedness among leaders and congregations in all churches. And we find, again, goodness in people who have lived their entire lives as active church goers, but we also find it in people who won't have anything to do with organized religion.

Goodness is to be found among the wealthy and among the poor, in all age groups, occupations, and walks of life. It isn't within the exclusive domain of any group. Yet it isn't everywhere, either. It doesn't permeate all lives equally. How then is it achieved?

Goodness is contagious. We often think of evil, as we do of disease, as being something that can be caught, like an unwanted germ. And, indeed, like a disease, evil can be caught—but so too can goodness. In fact, it is far more effectively propagated by example than it is by argument, for in the sight of true goodness, all doubts and suspicions and uncertainties melt away because of its obvious truth and clarity. It is so genuinely attractive and powerful that the critics and cynics are left without a rebuttal. To the person whose mind is alive and growing, goodness makes a statement that cannot help but move and inspire that person to a higher plane.

Goodness is propagated by acts of goodness. The person who says yes to the right things and no to the wrong ones is more than a leader in the battle of good versus bad; he is an important inspiration to others. Douglas D. Danforth, of Westinghouse spent eleven years of his career in Latin America, managing plants and starting plants in Argentina, Brazil and in Mexico. His boss in Mexico was a man by the name of Romero Allatori, a very distinguished Mexican. Danforth, quite young at the time, found Allatori had a very major influence on his style of managing—how to deal with people, how to handle situations in a crisis. Recalls Danforth, "Romero Allatori was a man of great integrity who believed, and convinced me and we did this, you could do business in Latin America without resorting to bribery. Latin America has a very tainted reputation that you've got to do this [bribe]. Not true. And we were very successful. And to the best of my knowledge we never did anything like that."

Cornell C. Maier, of Kaiser Aluminum & Chemical, remembers a vice president of that organization whose example had a major influence on him. "He had an influence on my life and I think all of us who became close to him. He was a very good businessman. But I think that wasn't the real influence he had. He was a man of absolutely impeccable standards, very high character, completely honest. I don't think he could have pulled a fib even if it would have been necessary to save his life or his family's life. And his ethical standards were so high that he just had a great influence on my life and, I think, all of us who came in contact with him."

There is no question about it, an ethical stand can have a tremendous impact on the lives of others. The knowledge that a person has behaved honorably gives others the courage to try to act honorably themselves. Robert S. McNamara recalls an encounter he had at a state dinner. "I was at a round table. . . . There was a woman on either side of me, and a man on the left of the woman on my left, leaned across her and said, 'Bob, I'd like your help.' I didn't recognize who this person was when he first spoke. He said, 'I've got to decide this afternoon whether to pay $2 million to the Shah's sister. They've sent us two billion dollar orders. Bob, what should I do?' Well, in the first place I didn't recognize him. Secondly, I'm certainly not going to speak in front of this woman, whom I didn't know either. So, I said I was terribly sorry, it's outside my experience. So he got up afterwards, and he repeated what he said, and I recognized him. He was a president of a company that, I knew because the Shah had told me, was in competition for orders that might well have been worth $2 billion. So I said to him, 'At Ford I came across this situation, we never paid a dime to my knowledge. I'd tell him to go to hell . . . and frankly I hope that's what you'll do.' "

We may be optimistic for the human condition not only because goodness can be contagious but also because most people prefer to behave ethically. As Sanford N. McDonnell, of McDonnell Douglas, observes,

"I think basically most people want to do what's right. . . . I think the large majority of them do." Acquiring excellence of character involves coming into regular contact with highly principled people on a regular basis and disciplining oneself to make personal choices in an ethical fashion.

Open minds and hearts can be greatly influenced by goodness in very ordinary circumstances. One might catch goodness from acquaintances as well as from superiors in the workplace. Richard Heckert, of Du Pont, recalls, "I had a plant manager that I was fortunate enough to be in a car pool with when I was a superintendent—a technical superintendent in his operation. You can learn more from people in a car pool experience sometimes than you can working for them in the office for eight hours a day or ten hours, whatever it turns out to be. And hearing him talk about his decision-making process and the trade offs that he was faced with and learning that he made lots of hard calls, but very honest calls, was very motivating. You know, it told me that you can be a completely honest human being and do what is right to the best of your ability and not in any way negatively influence your performance with the company. People don't always believe that. They think sometimes in order to get ahead you've got to shave the truth or do something less than be totally forthcoming. I say that is exactly wrong. In our company, we admire those who have the ability to tell the truth every single time, have the courage to do it whether the news is good or bad. They're the ones we look for to take on the positions of great responsibility."

Charles Lazarus, founder of Toys "R" Us, describes an experience in which a superior's adherence to high ethical standards had a profound impact on himself. "If you're an employee [at Toys "R" Us] you have no discount. I pay the same price, and I pay it very ostentatiously, and I buy everything, and everyone in the company knows it. Every officer buys everything at full price. There are no discounts. . . . I learned that years ago working at Giant Food in Washington . . . from a man, a genius I'd have to call him. . . . When I was a young kid, I used to carry packages and I used to eat lunch with him occasionally. I must have been 12, . . . and when he would go next door to the luncheonette he would buy a half dozen eggs. I said, 'Mr. Cohen, why did you buy those? They're yours.' And he said, 'That's exactly why I bought them. Everyone should see that everything that goes out of this store is paid for, no matter what.' "

In business organizations there is a tremendous challenge for leaders, particularly at the highest levels, to set a good example. This principle applies to everyone in the organization no matter what his role or assignment is. William B. Walton, Sr., cofounder of Holiday Inns, says, "Many executives touch and influence the lives of thousands of people, both inside and outside the company. Their touch can be a blight or a blessing. Their influence can build up a person or tear down. To have a positive impact, they need to set the prime example of honesty, loyalty, dedication, and sincere caring."[2]

Stated more pointedly, Willard C. Butcher, the chairman and CEO of Chase Manhattan, says, "Business leaders today cannot shrink from their obligation to set a moral example for those they lead. They must draw the line between on the one hand, the perpetual push for higher profits and on the other, actions antagonistic to the values of the larger society."[3]

Both high standards and low standards of conduct can be spread throughout an organization. And, unfortunately, it is more difficult to raise standards than to allow them to drop. Unethical behavior, as Jack Peters, of J. Walter Thompson, says, "spreads down throughout [a] company like wildfire. . . . I think it's harder to get the standards raised." This is why discipline is the other necessity in the equation. And the higher one ascends the organizational ladder, the greater is the need to watch one's own behavior, because people take their cues from those at the top.

Burnell R. Roberts, of the Mead Corporation, puts it this way. "I have to set an example myself for the people at Mead. If any shortcuts are taken, they suddenly would begin to think they can take shortcuts too. I'm an example and I can't be flippant about it."

Michael W. Wright, of Super Valu Stores, shares this point of view and cautions people to watch everything they do to set the right tone. "I think," says Wright, "that in general you set the tone of the organization in so many areas. If you cheat on your expense accounts, believe me, everybody else in the organization will know it and start cheating on their expense accounts. . . . You probably lead more by example than you do by what you say. People watch everything you do. You hate to think of it that way but they do . . . watch you all the time."

It is important, therefore, to discipline oneself by: (1) surrounding oneself with other highly principled people, (2) being consistent and not having double standards, (3) being totally honest and ethical in all situations, (4) paying attention to what might seem to be little things but that actually send big signals, and (5) being a kind and caring person who serves others, as well as being an ethical person who is totally upright.

Keeping the Right Company

It is much easier to discipline oneself when there are other high-minded people nearby. Group forces can be a strong ally in elevating and maintaining exemplary standards. "Henry Kaiser," as Cornell Maier recalls, "had very high standards and that was obvious to all the people. And he insisted on surrounding himself with people who had those same standards. And that was carried through Edgar Kaiser, his son. . . . And he and Edgar had very high standards. They insisted that he surround himself with those kinds of people."

Robert C. Williams, of James River Corporation, and his partners who formed that company were highly interested in being role models and tolerating nothing but the highest standards in how they dealt with suppliers and customers and employees. "Back in the early years," recalls Williams, "we were known, somewhat laughingly, as the All American Boys."

No Double Standards

If goodness is to have a hope of spreading, it must never be compromised. There are at least two reasons for this. One reason is that the person who always acts in highly principled ways is far more believable and far more convincing than the one who is not so steady in his conduct. If a person cannot display honesty in one area of his life, others will with good reason doubt his honesty in other areas. Trust rests on one's predictability, and the person who lives for the sake of expediencies—trying to get just what he wants at the moment—is seen as not only unpredictable but also treacherous.

Douglas Danforth, of Westinghouse, adds the thought, "If the leader of an organization is a little casual about these things, his organization is going to be a bit casual." The other reason for it is that people might believe that the occasional ethical action was not taken so much because of its own merits and as being the right or a good thing to do, but because it was more expedient than a dishonorable move. There is always a temptation to succumb to the pressures and forces that seem expedient but that have shades of wrong. These are oftentimes referred to as "gray areas." While it makes some sense, intellectually, to look at issues and decisions involving ethics as gray areas, and in so doing realizing that there are really no perfect choices—every action has some degree of imperfection—it must also be realized that this very viewpoint opens the door a crack, to allow us to talk ourselves into a less than honorable course because it is expedient. Those whom we honor most when it comes to ethical conduct tend to be those who look at things in terms of black and white, as being either right or wrong, and they are darn clear about which is which. They may see gray areas, but once they make up their minds and take a stand, the issues are cast in terms of black or white.

While we have seen how goodness can propagate goodness, we do well to recognize that the same can be the case with wrongdoing. Double standards permit the spread of unethical actions throughout an enterprise. To allow one set of standards for operations in one culture and a different set elsewhere is seen as unwise by top-level leaders. Robert F. Froehlke, former head of Equitable Life, now of IDS Mutual Fund Group, observes, "On the boards on which I've served, the boards have been absolutely adamant, saying that you can't have two sets of standards, because no matter how far out this appendage is, it is an appendage. The circulatory system does come back. And if you allow something to happen in Bahrain that you wouldn't allow in San Francisco, inevitably it's going to come back. So therefore, so far as legality and ethics are concerned, you've got to have one code. Admittedly this really puts you at a disadvantage, because the payoff is accepted in [places like] Korea. When I was Secretary of the Army I went to Korea. . . . So much more gasoline was being used than we used for military purposes that it was clear the civilians were taking it for themselves in payoffs. And I raised the issue and was very discouraged by the answer, 'That's the way we do it over here.' The problem was that we had an awful lot of civilians . . . who had been there for 15 or 20 years, married Korean women, and they weren't bad people, but they had been over there too long. And, they thought in the culture of Korea. Well, we changed it and said, 'You aren't to do it.' But they kept on doing it. We moved in and we convicted certain people."

Burnell R. Roberts, of the Mead Corporation, finds the same thing when it comes to double standards: Don't permit them. He explains, "In Italy we discovered that one of our subsidiaries kept two sets of books. We decided immediately to sell that company. It just isn't right. When it comes to ethical decisions you just have to draw the line. Otherwise, where do you stop? You can't have double standards. You'd better draw the lines pretty fast in setting the example." In drawing the line quickly and clearly, a position is immediately staked out, a stand is made. And that sends a powerful message throughout the organization and beyond.

Charles Lazarus, of Toys "R" Us, recalls how he came to the conclusion that "honesty is the only policy." "I came to that conclusion," says Lazarus, "when we got into merchandise. In the first little receiving area that we had I noticed that occasionally we would be short cartons and we'd be over cartons. And we made a big to-do about being short three cartons out of a shipment while we didn't seem to make a big to-do about being over cartons. And since I was directly involved, hands on, I looked at it and I made an immediate decision: the over cartons went back; and that we never accepted an over carton that was not ours. And, if we did accept it, we would log it in and then pay for it, particularly if it came out of a railroad car. That policy really paid off. The reason for the policy is, I decided that if the company took three cartons, why shouldn't the worker take three pieces? It didn't cost them anything . . . why not take it? I knew that that would end up killing them. You started out and the morality would be very low. It's kind of like taking home office supplies, which is looked on benevolently to a certain degree if you take home a couple of pads or something. But the question is, how far does it go? My answer is, it doesn't go anywhere."

Being Ethical in All Situations

Goodness has a tremendous power of influence on people. Its effects are both subtle and profound. Goodness oftentimes sends a signal of what a person will stand for and what he will not stand for and it can help cause others to accept a higher standard for their own lives. It may also encourage less ethical people to stay away. Honest people and ethical companies who conduct themselves only in honorable ways thus have a tremendous ally—their goodness tends to keep trouble away. Moreover, honesty in one area is contagious to honesty in other areas.

Nearly thirty years ago the managing director of Caterpillar's European operations in Granoble, France, was desperately looking for a suitable apartment. The housing there for Americans was very hard to come by. The city was bulging. Decent accommodations were not to be found. He persisted to look for an apartment to buy. One was finally located—A brand new, seven room suite on the sixth floor of the Park Hotel. When they finally got down to negotiating for the final price, which had previously been agreed to and determined, the negotiator for the seller said, "Well, of course there's the accommodating payment to give you priority to get this apartment." It was the first time anything like that got into the issue. At that Wally, the managing director, merely got up and said, "The meeting's adjourned. I don't want your damned apartment." And he walked out. That particular example permeated the whole community. Every one knew from then on that whenever they dealt with Caterpillar in general or Wally in particular everything was on top of the table.

Little Things that Send Big Messages

Who will ever know if we do it? And, if they do know, what is the difference? Who really cares? Each of us knows that these and other questions are not uncommon. It might be thought that little things are not important, that nobody really pays all that much attention to them. But our experience reveals the opposite. People do pay attention to these "little things."

What's interesting about successful leaders is that they watch and discipline themselves in all matters—especially little ones. And some even suggest it is important to watch matters which are thought to lie outside of one's professional life. Douglas Danforth, of Westinghouse, says, "We have corporate aircraft. I know many corporations, and there isn't anything unethical about it—they'll do it for safety and other things—to use corporate aircraft for personal use. We absolutely never do it. I never do it, and therefore no one else does it. Because, again, it's a little thing that can feed on itself." And, James R. Eiszner, of CPC International, has the same feelings about the use of the company's limousine. "Because I do that, the other officers also don't use the chauffeurs for personal use. I think you set an example." And when it comes to personal telephone calls from the office, Reuben Mark, of Colgate-Palmolive, is scrupulously honest; he logs each one and pays for them out of his own pocket.

Acts of Kindness

There is far more to goodness than merely the avoidance of wrongdoing. Goodness involves positive actions—kindness, service, and generosity. And it is through these actions that goodness is best spread. Verbal arguments for good and kind actions are not nearly as convincing as are genuine, caring actions themselves. George Schaefer, of Caterpillar, recalls the first boss he had at that company who illustrates this idea brilliantly. "He was a Swedish fellow who was the general auditor of the company, and he was tough and he was thorough—and you would call him mean. But, boy, he was a man of high principle and a man with a heart as big as you could find. One little example: I was shipped out to our California plant and I came back here [Peoria, Illinois] for a meeting in mid-April. And, of course, it was already warm and sunny out there and I came into Peoria. And they had caught one of these April cold snaps. It was down around 25 degrees. When I walked into the office that morning without a coat on, he said, 'Where's your coat?' He went home to get me one of his coats. I'm a junior, 23-year-old, accountant, and this guy is a big wheel around the company. You know it is those kinds of things that make a lasting impression on you." Kindness is best learned when one observes and experiences it himself. If our aim is to create a kinder world, then we can best excite others toward this aim by acting in kind ways ourselves.

LESSONS FROM WRONGDOING

The ability humans have to learn from their own experiences, as well as those of others, is generally under used. Yet this capacity offers remarkable possibilities for bettering the human condition. A person stands a strong chance of improving the excellence of his character if he can become sensitive to the joy and pain around himself and if he is perceptive enough to discover its causes. The experience of a painful situation is most often seen in terms of just the pain itself. But there can be, and there usually is, a lesson to be discovered in these situations, and the lesson can provide guidance toward a higher standard. Whenever a man learns what the source of the pain he experiences is, he places himself into a good position to know what to monitor in his own behavior so as never to produce pain in the lives of others. A corollary case exists for joy.

As goal-seeking creatures, humans are keenly able to discover which behaviors work effectively. If this same interest and skill were extended to include the valuable lessons of how to avoid inflicting pain on others, the world could be greatly benefited. This is a distinct possibility, as the experiences of one business leader demonstrate: "I worked for a guy who was absolutely immoral in the way he treated his own employees. He would lie to them, and he would use them, and he would push them around vigorously and hard for his own advantage. His own personal moral qualities were miserable and I saw how it shouldn't be done. I quit. He got fired, incidentally." The person who approaches the world with the desire to learn something from the joy and pain others experience will have many teachers. Moreover, he will find many opportunities to gain valuable insights from which he can shape his own life.

20

Bringing Out the Best in Employees

After social and industrial reforms were enacted earlier this century and last, eliminating the many deplorable working conditions in this country— child labor, low pay, the 12-hour work day 6 days a week, unsafe and unhealthful working conditions—psychologists and behavioral scientists stepped forward with their techniques to increase worker performance.

At first, managers and supervisors were schooled in the importance of being nice and improving worker morale and job satisfaction. The idea behind the human relations movement, as it later became known, was to create happy workers who would respond with increased output and performance. Managements really were not concerned so much with worker happiness: it was just that by making them happy they figured they could get workers to produce better. Neither the increased happiness nor the stepped-up performance was effectively achieved. Shortly thereafter, the human resources movement took up where human relations had failed.

There is more to motivating employees than just making them happy, the psychologists and behavioral scientists concluded. Employees must be seen as a resource, to be developed and used to their full potential. The revised prescriptions for motivation included meaningful work. Job enlargement and job enrichment, responsibility, involvement, and participation in the decision making processes were to be the methods of arousing workers' motivation. And there was training and development to increase employees' talents and abilities. The results were stunning, showing clearly that believing people could perform remarkably and giving them the opportunity to perform produced high levels of output and highly committed employees. Employee participation has become a part of American business largely for one reason: it works. And because of this managers and supervisors have adopted the methods and techniques that involve people and use their talents. The exchange appears satisfactory to both parties: more meaningful and fulfilling work for employees and higher levels of performance for employers.

ETHICAL CONSIDERATIONS

Whenever we approach matters on a quid pro quo basis we can run into an ethical snare. To avoid getting into this entanglement unknowingly, we can ask ourselves, "Are we acting in ways that are expedient, that merely produce the results *we* want? Or are we acting in ways we know to be right and morally justified?" It is tempting not to raise these sorts of questions, and when we do, we must be aware of the chance that we might try to concoct moral justifications to support whatever turns out to be in our own best interest. In plain language, if mistreatment of employees were more profit producing than humane treatment there would be a great temptation to not only do that, but also to devise a justification on some moral grounds to support it.

Approaching employees on the basis of, "What must I do for you to get you to do what I want?" may produce an expedient solution enabling them to be good workers, but it may not lead to making the work environment good from an ethical perspective. There are three consequences to which the quid pro quo approach can lead.

First, in voluntarily making exchanges of material objects, each party willingly gives up something of value to obtain some other object that he values more highly. Each party thereby is convinced that his material well-being is improved. But when it comes to the treatment of people in exchange for their actions, we are in fact placing people on the same level as material objects, and in so doing we are obliged to question whether we ought to do so. Should we treat other people as objects so as to cause them to do what we want them to do in exchange for the way we treat them? Or should we treat them in ways that we believe are right and decent and morally justifiable on their own merits? Moreover, we ought to be more fully aware of the consequences of a "this for that" way of thinking. One danger is that one would tend to place oneself first and to place what one intends to get as primary in importance, putting what one does to others and the way one treats others as secondary. Expediencies can then overshadow the moral issues, and the way we choose to treat others is reduced to that of merely finding ways to most benefit ourselves.

Second, we are indebted to Douglas McGregor for calling to our attention the importance of the relationship between the perception managers have of their employees and their treatment of these employees. In his classic work, *The Human Side of Enterprise*, McGregor presents two entirely different sets of assumptions about the average human being: Theory X, which holds that people are by nature lazy, not very bright, and that they prefer to be led and told what to do; and Theory Y, which is based on the idea that behavior is caused, holds that people are not by nature irresponsible and unwilling to work, but that their experiences have caused them to become so, and that they have the potential to become hard-working, dedicated, loyal employees, provided management can arrange the work conditions in ways that bring about these behaviors. How we treat people is a consequence of our perceptions of them.[1]

Tom Peters has done a magnificent job of documenting the extraordinary results which companies have achieved by accepting the Theory Y assumptions about people and involving them as the human resources approach to leading and motivating prescribe.[2] But more significantly, Peters has again called to our attention the importance of really believing— "at a bone-deep level," as he says—that people are capable of extraordinary performance if given the opportunity. Without this deep-seated belief, something a "this for that" emphasis overlooks, managers' attempts at using employee-involvement methods will be superficial, erratic, and seen by employees as insincere and manipulative. Andrew C. Sigler, of Champion International, points out the necessity for sincerity. The person who tries to manipulate people, who uses the principles of the behavioral sciences as gimmicks merely to get something out of employees, generally won't be very successful. As Sigler says, "You can't kid the employee in the mill. The aggregate intelligence of employees is amazing. They can sniff out a phony in a minute."

Third, the methods and techniques for leading and motivating, which the behaviorists have embraced and have shown to be effective in causing people to be good producers, do not come to terms with the question of whether they also help these producers become good people. These theories and approaches are, by and large, amoral. Leaving the ethical issues untouched, they neglect any possibility that people might develop a burning concern for the significance of their efforts to the betterment of mankind; they do not address the value of this concern. And they neglect the need people may have to feel right about themselves by knowing that what they do is ethically sound and morally justifiable.

MAXIMIZING HUMAN DIGNITY AS WELL AS PERFORMANCE

The theories that the behaviorists advocate do work; they work dramatically well. And because they do work so well, more people are becoming convinced that they too should adopt them. The behaviorists argue eloquently for the implementation of their techniques, using as their chief reason, "Look at what these principles and methods will do for you." When one deeply considers the moral implications this point of view holds, its flaws become immediately obvious. Humans are capable of a much nobler concern, a concern that will not only produce better performance from a business perspective, but also better people from an ethical perspective. Managers may well concern themselves with two question: "What must we do to cause employees to produce?" and "What can we do to help our employees have better lives—giving lives genuine meaning—insofar as their jobs are concerned?"

By following the behavioral science prescriptions employees perform remarkably well, because they are developed and allowed to participate in decisions that affect them. Work is so arranged that employees can satisfy their many human needs. But the satisfaction of human needs and high levels of productive performance are not at the pinnacle of human possibilities. There is also the feeling of genuine significance within the safe boundaries of ethical standards. The possibility exists for managers to concern themselves with creating employment situations in which employees live better lives, where employees derive a sense of significance from their work and are untroubled by their consciences because they adhere to a high level of ethical conduct. This concern can add a radically different and far more encompassing dimension to the process of leading and motivating employees. It affirms and justifies on an entirely different level, beyond a simple exchange mentality, the theories and principles that the behavioral sciences offer. And it embraces additional dimensions of lasting importance to employees. Namely, it views their participation as a way of finding meaning, and not just in the enjoyment of doing what they like to do. Employees are thereby provided a greater sense of meaning through the contributions their efforts produce for others—those who depend on the employees' output. This concern also embraces the need to address the concerns people have about the ethics of what they are doing in their jobs. It can provide a safeguard that prevents them from being forced to do things that are unethical or that poison their self-respect.

BELIEFS ABOUT LEADING

There has been much thought and discussion about the roles of leaders and the art of effective leadership. One concept of leadership asserts that effective leaders serve those who follow them. They do what is necessary to help their followers produce effectively. The effective leader does not have to demand that followers take orders and do what they are told, or attempt to manipulate them with a "this for that" approach, or try to persuade them through charm and charisma. Instead, the leader sincerely serves his followers, helping them to live better lives through meaningful work by developing and involving them, and by assuring that the highest level of ethical behavior is maintained. He makes sure people are not forced to diminish their dignity as human beings by what they are required to do.

Several of the beliefs of successful leaders about the task of leadership confirm the practicality of approaching it from a perspective of serving employees, and thus freeing them to willingly perform. More specifically, several beliefs are evident.

The Value of Work and of a Good Place to Work

In our society a person's work provides the main source of meaning to his life. Without work, life can be miserable, and with dull, meaningless, demeaning work, a person's zest for living and his sense of self-respect withers. Without employment there isn't going to be a very strong family structure or adequate motivation for education. Good jobs not only provide the ability to feed and protect, but they also give meaning and dignity and the hope and motivation for family members to educate and improve themselves.

A Genuine Respect for People

Call it humility, call it love, call it a reverence for people—a deep, genuine respect for others, for their dignity, for their rights, for their feelings—this all adds up to treating others as one would want to be treated. This respect is not reserved for just a few important people worthy of respect—people who might be helpful to one's career—but all people, especially those who some might feel do not really matter very much. Where there is genuine respect, there is the honest belief that "everyone matters." At Time, Inc. (now Time Warner, Inc.), the chairman and CEO, J. Richard Munro, identifies that company's culture as one where the overly aggressive or too ambitious person won't make it no matter how smart he is. "If you try to get to the top of this company by marching over people's bodies you will not succeed because the [organization] culture will destroy you."

A Personal Interest in Others

"I think the average employee wants his boss to care for him," says William S. Anderson, of NCR. "He's happy about his company. He's happy about his particular work. But if he thinks the boss just treats him as just another piece of a chess set, that he's just a number, even though his boss may call him by his first name, I think he isn't as happy or may not be as hard working, or may not be as loyal as he would be if he thought, 'Well, my boss really is interested in me. He's interested in me as a person. He likes me. He asks after my wife. He remembers my wife's birthday. He knows my kids. He knows about the illness of my mother. Therefore, he's interested in me as a person.' The average person wants that, and if he believes that you have his interests at heart, then he also has your interests at heart." Effective leaders sincerely care how people feel, especially about their work. "The only way things happen in any human enterprise," says Reuben Mark, of Colgate-Palmolive, "is when the people who have to do the work think the people at the very top care and are looking after their welfare."

The leader who has a genuine concern for employees—the leader who genuinely wants them to have good lives—will try to make the workplace a good place to be. "I get terribly depressed," says Richard J. Mahoney, of Monsanto, "when somebody tells me that some of our people come to work on Monday thinking like they're on the assembly line in Detroit and they've just got to somehow get through the week till Friday. I find it terribly depressing. I spend a lot of time trying to get rid of bureaucracy. . . . I think it's disgraceful if we have a company where people are coming to work just trying to get through. . . . Every month I have a luncheon with middle- and lower-level managers. I go out and work in the labs. . . . [I] try to be visible [and] try to hear what's troubling them." In describing the Bank of America, Chairman of the Board Leland Prussia says, "This is not a machine that grinds out profits in the best interests of the shareholder and doesn't give a damn about the employees."

People Make the Difference

The person who continues to rely totally on himself—on his own talents and efforts alone—as he pursues success in a commercial enterprise will generally not advance very far or accomplish much. Success in these circumstances is almost always associated with effective leadership skills, which are based on the strong belief that the task of leading is primarily concerned with one thing: the just and effective handling of people. "You hear . . . statements . . . that people make the company," says William Anderson of NCR. "A lot of people say those things. But do they really mean it? I hope they do because it is absolutely true."

"You can find a lot of people that know a lot about efficiencies of operations, a lot of technicians, a lot of engineers that can help you on the fine points of operation, but the thing they should spend their time on is people," says Donald H. Hall of Hallmark Cards. "Graduates who go out in the business world . . . [had] better remember that their success, ultimately, will be judged as to how well they select and care for those people who work for them and that they will not raise to heights that they might have ambitions for unless they have that group behind them."

It's the ability to help people work productively together that makes the difference in whether a person is ultimately successful in management. If the failure side in management is examined, an inability to do this is at the top of the list of reasons for those failures. Donald E. Petersen, of Ford, says, "It's striking to me how much more important ability to work with people openly is than any other element is, in terms of being a successful manager."

Unleashing Talents and Enthusiasm

The words of the former General Electric chairman, Ralph Cordiner, captured the essence of leadership: creating climates where people can achieve the best within them. This is another way of stating the importance of estimating generously the capabilities of fully developed and highly committed employees. It involves believing that even ordinary persons have great potential. And it involves giving those employees the freedom and the responsibility to act. Donald Hall, of Hallmark, sums it up nicely: "Being able to manage people is not standing over them with a whip but being able to understand people who work for them and around them and maximizing people's potential." Seen as a vast resource ready to be unleashed, the task of leading involves creating an atmosphere in which people will become dedicated to their work.

Andrew Sigler, of Champion International, says, "I think my job is to create the atmosphere where people can enjoy what they do, where they treat each other with respect, under an umbrella that says, 'If we are not productive and profitable we're going to fail.' "

The fundamental issue is whether leaders sincerely believe that even ordinary people have talents and can develop the willingness to put these productively to the work at hand. Reuben Mark, of Colgate-Palmolive, looks upon his organization as a source of enormous talent. "We have thirty-five to thirty-six thousand people around the world, and therein lies an incredible reservoir of talent and excitement and ability to make things happen. The job of management is to unlock that talent. In my view, the way to do it is that love is a better motivator than fear."

If people are to be seriously involved in the running of a business, they must be trusted not only in terms of their competence but in terms of their willingness to work. Given the opportunity, will people accept responsibility? At Hewlett-Packard the belief is that they will; the motto is: "Everybody wants to help you do a better job and will willingly do so given the chance to participate." First, it is necessary for managers to believe that this is the case, and second, it is necessary for them to create an environment in which employees can come forward to make contributions.

Jack D. Sparks, of Whirlpool, advises, "Don't try to do everything yourself. Let other people help. It's natural for a human being to want to help somebody. The problem comes in this world when the other person involved doesn't want any help. They know it all. They can do it all. I'm a great believer in letting people help."

Lewis W. Lehr, of 3M, says, "People who have a responsibility to do a job, no matter how menial it is, want to do the job a little bit better, and if you give them the responsibility and the right to do that, they do it."

THE NEXT LEVEL: TO FEEL RIGHT ABOUT ONE'S EFFORTS

The eagerness to find ways of motivating employees effectively has led to methods and principles that work quite well. These are: believe that people have abilities and want to work; develop them and train them to be efficient and skillful; give them freedom to contribute; involve them by allowing them to participate; and recognize and reward them and appeal to their needs so that they can satisfy their needs as they produce for the organization. Businesses led by pragmatists are quick to do what is necessary to lead people to become good producers. But they can also exercise some idealism and go further to lead these producers to become good people. And here to we find encouragement to work toward this end, because the desire to be good and lead a meaningful life is a possibility for everyone. Two important possibilities exist for all normal human beings: (1) to achieve a sense of significance through knowing that their work has real meaning—that it contributes in some fashion to the betterment of mankind, and (2) to rest easy at night, feeling secure that they are ethical and are living decent, upright lives.

Managements never got very far with motivating people by standing over them and demanding good work; it was a rude awakening to many managers that the most effective way of leading was to believe that people wanted to work hard and that they would if given a chance. This same general approach will work in achieving goodness: believe that people want to be good, and free them up to work at it. To raise the level of ethics of a group, it is far more effective to raise the moral tone and commitment to good than it is to police them and scrutinize their every move with the aim of weeding out every speck of evil.

WORK AS A SOURCE OF PRIDE

In any human endeavor, if a person is willingly going to give his best efforts, he must believe in what he's doing. A doctor isn't much of a doctor unless she believes her treatments will bring relief, that her prescriptions will cure; a teacher isn't a good teacher unless he believes in the value of education, and a salesman can not really sell with genuine enthusiasm if he isn't convinced his products represent good value. On assembly lines, how can workers attach doors to automobile frames with pride and care if they really don't think the cars they build are any good? In offices, how can clerks and order processors and accountants find genuine value in their work if they know they are engaged in dishonest practices? They can not.

Unless people know that their work has value and that they are acting in honest and upright ways, they can not believe in what they are doing and hence will not give their very best efforts. If a businessman is to find genuine satisfaction and give his very best efforts, he must believe his product or service represents a solid value and that his methods are ethical. Charles W. Moritz, of Dun & Bradstreet, says, "Human beings are entitled to some meaning in their lives, and management has an obligation to provide that within . . . the work environment of the business."

If people are to realize their full potential, they need to feel that they are engaged in productive and meaningful work. All too often employees lose sight of whatever their real purposes are. In many cases, perhaps, they may never have had a glimpse of these in the first place. John A. Young, of Hewlett-Packard, recalls some excellent advice from a vice president of manufacturing he worked for. "Make sure that all of the people working for you don't fall into the category of just thinking that they do mundane jobs. Make sure that every day you think about ways to keep everybody who works for you cognizant of what it is they really do. Their work may involve assuring that a critical part of an analyzer, or some other product, works well. There are people who will use and depend on the quality of that product."

In many of America's companies the chairman of the board or president will meet with employees in informal gatherings from time to time and answer questions and explain where the business is headed. In one such company the chairman was holding a question and answer session with employees after the group had met for breakfast. There was a young man at this gathering who worked in the second shift of the computer room of one of the company's divisions and he seemed to be scared to death to ask his question. He would put up his hand and then he'd pull it down, but finally he got up enough courage to ask. He started slowly and cautiously, telling first about his work attendance. He had a good record. He also mentioned the effort he and others gave to help assure quality work. Finally he got to his real reason for speaking up, and he said, "My question is this: Where does my work go, and is it important to anybody?" As Charles Moritz, of Dun & Bradstreet, who recounted this story, commented, "What an incredibly lonely, horrible existence to be working and not knowing where one's work goes and whether it is of value to anybody!"

It is generally believed that if they are to give their best efforts day after day, people must feel their job demands are decent and honorable. If they are to feel right about themselves, that is, if they are to have self-respect, the actions that their jobs demand of them must seem praiseworthy. Here management has a moral obligation to assure that whatever they do and whatever they ask others to do is morally justifiable. We also need to recognize that part of a person's reputation is tied to what is done by the firm that employs him.

Management has an obligation to protect the name of the organization and the reputations of all employees by showing absolutely no hospitality whatsoever to those who are unwilling to abide by high standards and by identifying wrongdoers and purging them from the organization. At Whirlpool Corporation all employees are expected to live by a simple, yet comprehensive, code of ethics, the foundation of which is this: "No employee will ever be called upon to do anything that is morally, ethically or legally wrong. If an employee should come upon circumstances of which he or she cannot be personally proud, it should be that person's duty to bring it to the attention of top management if unable to correct the matter in any other way." As Whirlpool's chairman and CEO, Jack Sparks, says, "It is the responsibility of management, starting at the very top, both to set the example of personal conduct and to create an environment that not only encourages and rewards ethical behavior, but also makes anything less totally unacceptable."

AN ETHICAL ORIENTATION

The primary concern for any organization interested in high ethical standards should not be so much with searching for wrongdoers but with creating situations and work environments that do not tempt ordinarily good people to do wrong in the first place. In the course of operating businesses there are many pressures that create temptations, and these can easily lead people astray. Many firms today work hard at identifying these pressures. They look for ways to either eliminate them altogether or reduced them as far as possible. They are also trying to enlighten and encourage employees to say no to temptations that remain.

A good way to keep from getting into trouble is to avoid tempting situations. From a management perspective, this bit of advice suggests the usefulness of structuring the workplace to make it free from inviting temptations. This is an approach followed by William Woodside, of American Can. He says, "There are certain situations which are more tempting than others. We review carefully all purchasing contracts and things like that, because that's an enormous temptation for purchasing clerks or anybody else in that field. So we spend a lot of time looking at that. We're trying to make it difficult for people to accidentally fall into temptation, to yield to it."

At Ameritech, William L. Weiss explains, "We increased the auditing of the business and tried to convey to people that 'auditing is your friend, not your enemy.' What it tells us, and what it helps us do, is stay on the side of ethics, because if people largely know that there is a sound professional auditing function in the business and you advertise it and you insist on it, if somebody has the tendency to break over the line when pressure gets huge, they maybe will not do it when they might do it otherwise."

In today's world of business, managers are generally convinced of the need to set standards for production, sales, market share, earnings, and many other desirable outcomes. Performance is measured in terms of the extent to which these goals have been reached. Anything substantially short of these targets is generally regarded as unacceptable. This is called management by objectives. Harold S. Geneen, who was the CEO of ITT for 17 years, writes in *Fortune*, "The efficacy of management is quantifiable. It can be measured by the profit and loss statement. . . . we would do everything we had to that was honest and legal to bring in the results we desired."[3]

The world would be a better place if the pressures for improved performance produced only that. Unfortunately, it oftentimes yields unwanted side effects. William Woodside, of American Can, puts it this way: "You can put so much pressure on an organization for performance that you really force [people] to do unethical things. If you set impossible goals for attainment, and you criticize or penalize people heavily for not making those goals, then you are just asking for all the ethical problems that you are certainly going to be facing." As Neil Harlan, of McKesson, sees it, "Any time you put pressure on any operation to make profit, you are creating an environment in which they [employees] might think, 'Well, the most important thing to the company, and therefore the most important thing to me, is that I meet that goal, meet my budget, and therefore I will do what I have to!" These words of caution do not come from theoretical possibilities; they arise because of actual cases do occur. Examples of the problems created by too much pressure for results, described anonymously by CEOs of major corporations, are given in the following two paragraphs.

"A person who was the manager of a fairly large maintenance organization was pressed for performance to the point where he began to cheat. He would probably have been the last person that several of us would have predicted would have gone over that line, but we didn't realize how strong his pride and ego needs were to succeed. It wasn't a matter of money, it was a matter of succeeding. And he finally began to cheat. And we finally discovered that, and because of his very long and very stellar performance and without any trace of that, other than the last couple of years where he just simply went over the line because of the pressures for performance, we didn't fire him, although there was serious argument as to whether we should or not. We demoted him, moved him out into another organization, and he continued his service prior to retirement in a lesser position in the organization where he wasn't under the same pressures and where he could perform reasonably well without the implications of what had happened here being a problem to him. Had it been a younger person with less tenure with the business, he would have been fired."

"We had a case of bending the rules in [a] . . . plant where, because this was an old plant [which was] trying to compete against newer plants, . . . This is a plant where people's jobs were on the line. . . . Way up in that organization somebody began to change the numbers, the number of batches and so forth, so the efficiencies would look better than they were. Finally we tripped over this and we dismissed the plant manager and two or three other people in it. But it was done because of the quantitative system of measuring performance we had at the time. They were looking to try to get more orders to the plant and didn't feel they could unless they made the right quantitative report . . . so they fudged that report. We tried to get at the value system there: 'Why didn't that get understood up the line better? Why wasn't it addressed as a problem the way it should have been?' We ended up putting $37 million into that plant to renovate it and get it up to the way it should be. I think there are a lot of pressures [with] these quantitative systems, and they don't tell you too much about what is going on."

Surveys made in several corporations indicate that a dangerous situation exists with the bottom-line-only mentality. These studies show that a frighteningly large percentage of middle-management personnel feel strong pressure from higher ups to take short cuts and do whatever is necessary in order to make sure they meet budgets, goals, and bottom-line performance targets. In one situation a management employee of a large corporation was fired for unethical behavior. He turned around and filed suit against his employer, claiming that there was a strong implied directive from his management to take the shortcut in order to meet the goals laid out to him.

The necessity to perform well, that is, to meet set goals and standards, can become so strong that it overpowers a person and he acts unethically in order to succeed. This reality presents a formidable challenge for business leaders. But to simply remove the push for better performance is not a satisfactory solution. William Weiss, of Ameritech, says, "The answer to me, isn't less pressure. Businesses have to perform." William T. Creson, of Crown Zellerbach, says, "That kind of pressure brings out the best and it brings out the worst in people. For those people who are flawed from a character standpoint, it provides the opportunity, or the incentive, to do unethical, and in some cases illegal, acts. . . . When I've seen it as a problem, it's more often that a zealous manager wants to project his area of responsibility is performing well, or competing well with his peers or with other parts of the company. That's the down side of accountability. The up side is that it provides a positive yardstick by which people measure their accomplishments, measure themselves on a tangible basis and not only the tangible, financial awards, but the psychic income of saying, 'I met a goal or I met the commitments that I made!' "

Organizations won't perform very well if there are no standards to propel commitments into tangible actions. The trick is to get that high performance without causing people to step over the line. Five conditions are helpful in achieving this end.

1. Management must articulate its belief that both performance and ethical conduct are expected, and that employees should *never* feel compelled to do anything illegal or anything that by a reasonable person's judgment is unethical in order to meet a performance standard. Unless performance standards and the necessity for *always* taking the high ethical course are equally emphasized, a signal will surely be received by people that maybe the ends do justify the means.

The message top management sends to its employees is only as strong as management is able to demonstrate by its own exemplary conduct. Employees have to believe that if their instincts tell them a particular business relationship is wrong or that some action is unethical, even though it could produce some other desired result, their refusal to act in dishonorable ways will be supported by top management. Philip E. Lippincott, of Scott Paper, says to his people, "We do not want you to feel because of the pressure of performance and other things that you ought to bend any of [your] beliefs or principles."

2. Goals should be set intelligently and carefully and regularly updated. Impossible-to-reach budgets, sales levels, and profit targets should be identified and revised. Robert A. Schoellhorn, of Abbott Laboratories, says, "The most important way of keeping people from bending the rules or cutting corners is to establish goals that are tough but realistic."

3. Rely on qualitative as well as quantitative measures of performance. The shortcoming of managing by just the numbers is that the "hard measures" frequently obscure other, equally important, parts of a business. The numbers do not always give an accurate representation of performance. At Dow Chemical, as Paul F. Oreffice explains, bottom-line

numbers are not the *only* measure of employee performance. "Performance is not based just on numbers by any means. . . . We make safety performance of their unit a part of their performance review—part of their compensation. Safety is just as important as producing the goods. . . . They don't get judged just on bottom line."

At Deluxe Check Printers, Eugene R. Olson explains that other targets are important—things that can't be measured quantitatively. "We don't really set hard and fast numbers. . . . They are not necessarily paid more if they go out and hustle and get *x* amount of business, because that isn't really the number that we think is the most important. Treating customers well and retaining business is just as important as getting new business, and so I think, in terms of how we evaluate people, [it] has to do with how they have treated the people under them, whether or not they've been having any problems in the division, if he's losing people because they are unhappy with the organization. . . . That would be something that we'd be concerned about."

4. Involve people in setting the ethical tone of the organization. Solicit their thoughts and feelings. People want to feel they are ethical; they sleep better knowing their actions are respectable. They want to believe that top management where they work is solidly behind high standards. It is a tremendous relief to people to be reassured that their leaders are dedicated to doing what is right; they can then be proud of their company and can become better employees and people.

Throughout large organizations there are countless opportunities for unethical acts and there is absolutely no practical way to police thoroughly and stop 100 percent of these. Nor would it be sensible to try to police people excessively with the aim of weeding out every possible misdeed or chance of a misdeed. That would no doubt produce unacceptable consequences. A far more effective approach seems to lie in involving employees in the task of uncovering unethical practices and identifying problem areas that contain ethical conflicts. At United Parcel Service a program has been in place for over 20 years called "Talk, Listen, Act." Every employee of the company gets an interview with his boss once a year. The boss is then required to prepare a write-up of the conversation. Someone in personnel follows up on about 25 percent of these each year. This procedure encourages upward communication and has the dimension of acting tied to the listening. Most firms work at trying to find out what's on the employees' minds. It sets an atmosphere that encourages upward communication—something that must be stimulated if it is to occur.

If employees are to feel that it is worthwhile to voice their feelings and concerns, it is necessary to establish a climate of trust and a knowledge that their ideas are welcomed and will be taken seriously and acted upon. Then they may be willing to voice their worries or thoughts about ethical matters. To that end, some companies have a person with the title of ombudsman. The ombudsman is available, on a confidential basis, to employees who don't feel they should discuss their concerns with their superiors, for whatever reason. At Raytheon, employees may write to the company's ombudsman at a post office box outside of the company's mail system. This person reports to the chairman of the board on these matters, and each ethical issue uncovered at Raytheon is handled personally by the chairman of the board, the president, and the ombudsman.

5. Training in how to handle ethical problem areas serves to reinforce the idea that the company is serious about what it claims its stance to be on such matters and it helps people to better know what to say no to and even how to say it. Raytheon has a 25-minute videotape depicting several situations which employees might encounter on the job, pointing out what is unethical and what the company expects of them. The Ethics Resource Center in Washington, D.C., has produced a similar videotape showing six situations involving ethical choices. The aims of ethics training are to raise levels of consciousness, to express company standards and expectations, and to encourage people to do the right thing when confronted with an ethical choice.

21

Crusading for Quality

Many lives are made trivial not by lack of opportunity but by lack of character. The privilege of being in the right place at the right time to do something great comes to very few people, but each person has countless opportunities to do ordinary things extremely well and to steadily improve his own performance.

The human being has the ability to evaluate his own actions and performance, and each person has the capacity to improve. Whether he soberly inspects his own behavior and carefully works to improve it, as he ought, is a reflection of his character. For as he strives to perfect his own performance, reaching out to elevate the quality of what he does, human progress occurs and the human condition is advanced. His efforts count for something. Through striving for quality a person may escape the trap of triviality.

ACTIONS MAKE STATEMENTS

Our efforts make a statement of what we think of ourselves and determine who we eventually become. They reveal the extent to which we respect ourselves and take seriously the things we do. They reflect the level of expectation we hold for ourselves, and they also reflect what we think of others who are affected by our actions. Slowly and over time we form, in the minds of others, our reputations. What others ultimately think of us is largely a product of the quality of our performance, and that is a consequence of what we strive for and how deeply we care about what we do. A person who sincerely believes that his abilities can produce high-quality performance will, acting rationally, make quality his goal. And a person who cares deeply about the effects his actions have upon others will also make quality his goal.

What is true of individuals is also true of business organizations. The Whirlpool Corporation promise "To build and sell only good quality, honest appliances designed to give customers their money's worth . . . and . . . to stand behind them" is but one of many commitments by organizations that reflect the dedication to product quality and customer satisfaction of which we now are speaking. Such a standard, conscientiously pursued, is a running commentary on what Whirlpool personnel, from the company's founding in 1911 to the present day, think about themselves and their ability to make good quality appliances. It also reflects what they think about those they serve—their customers. This practical business philosophy has a fair number of ardent advocates. R. Gordon McGovern, of Campbell Soup, for instance, personally tests out as many of that company's products as he can, because he believes it's important to do everything possible to assure that customers are offered good products. "I eat as many of them [products] as I can, routinely at home with my family," says McGovern. "I try to get everybody doing that, so that we're all kind of [our] brothers' keeper on how well we deliver. And I try to cultivate people who criticize the food to me. We have a friend at home who comes over routinely. She's . . . a gourmet cook. She 'blasts away,' and I listen."

Most people are profoundly interested in what others think of them; they yearn for approval and will go to great lengths to try to achieve a good reputation. The approbation of people of substance is earned by substantive actions; those who fully understand quality and strive deliberately for it themselves can see the same in others and what they do. And it is the approval of these people, the ones who know and value quality, that enlightened people are glad to receive. The sort of people a person is gladdened and honored to receive recognition from is a statement of that person's standards for himself—of whether he aspires to great heights or is easily contented with mediocrity. It is deceptively easy to be contented with any applause, no matter its source. Those who are most serious about making quality a part of their lives are only affected by the recognition given by others of substance—those who have demonstrated the ability to achieve quality themselves.

The active pursuit of quality begins with high expectations for oneself and one's organization; it rests on the assurance one has about his own ability to perform, and it is frequently expressed by the weighty ideal that any performance that fails to reach the highest standards of excellence is wholly unacceptable. Our experiences tells us that the reputation a business enjoys is earned largely by its ability to attain quality standards in all that it does. At Goodyear, for example, a simple slogan has guided decision making at all levels for a long time: "Protect Our Good Name." Contained herein is a philosophy that encourages all personnel to do the right thing; in one particular situation it prompted Goodyear's chairman and CEO, Robert Mercer, to take immediate and drastic action in the quest for quality.

When visiting Goodyear's tire plant in New Delhi, India, several years ago, Mercer noticed that the products being turned out were substandard in terms of appearance and performance. Goodyear had dropped from first place to sixth place in the India tire market, despite being there over 60 years. It wasn't quality leadership, but taking a back seat and trying to do things at the least cost. This wasn't what Mercer believed Goodyear should stand for. In his words, "I said, 'What's happening here, fellows?' And they said, 'Well, what do you mean?' I said, 'That tire should not have the Goodyear name on it; it should never leave this factory because it's not up to our specifications.' And the plant manager said, 'Well, that's the best we can do with the equipment that we've got.' And they had some old machines and needed new machines."

Mercer said, "If it's going to carry our good name, it's got to start with our quality and performance level. . . . Shut down every piece of equipment you've got in this plant that is incapable of producing a product that meets our specifications." The plant manager kind of stared at him for a moment. He wanted to call somebody in Akron, Ohio, but it dawned on him that there wasn't anybody higher up in the organization than the man who had just issued the directive. The plant manager said, "Do you realize I've shut down 40 percent of the plant?" Mercer said, "Let me tell you something, my friend. I'm trying to figure out whether we ought to shut down the entire plant and get rid of it and just pull out of India as a manufacturing facility. . . . I'm just leaning this way to let this operation continue, so let's not challenge this. I want it done." The plant manager had the entire plant shut down. Mercer knew that they could get the job done if they had the right equipment, and $4 million were spent replacing faulty and worn out machines. Today that plant is turning out good-quality products, and the spirit, attitude, and pride of the people there are all high.

One of Barney Kroger's rules for success in his grocery business was, "Never sell anything except for just what it is, and don't sell it then if it isn't good." Kroger, right from the earliest days of his business, was a skillful buyer. He was no easy mark for slick-talking salesmen. His credo was, "Be particular. Never sell anything you would not want yourself." He lived by this standard, sometimes to the dismay of fast-talking salesmen whose boasts of their products could not be substantiated.

One such salesman came into Kroger's store hoping to get orders for the canned corn he was selling. He showed the 23-year-old Kroger the attractive label on the canned corn and claimed that it would increase his sales dramatically. According to the salesman, nobody could afford to pass up the opportunity to stock a very large order of this corn. But Kroger held the belief that quality was too important to be left to the word of salesmen; he tested for it himself.

In the rear of his store he kept a little stove, where he carefully brewed and tested samples of tea and coffee. As the salesman waxed on about the virtues of the label on the cans, Kroger picked up a sample and stripped the label off and dramatically threw it into the wastebasket. "My customers," said the stern-faced Kroger, "don't eat labels. They eat corn. Now show me what's inside." The corn inside was full of hulls, and the salesman stomped away without an order. It didn't take long for the word to spread among the traveling salesman that the man who ran The Great

Western Tea Company in Cincinnati was very demanding. Only those salesmen who had top-quality products or those who were new to the territory brought their wares to Kroger. That was the way he wanted it.[1]

THE DUTY TO IMPROVE

Living in a modern, industrialized nation, we see change taking place all around us. Scientific breakthroughs and advances and improvements in virtually all aspects of our world occur frequently and with increasing rapidity. In Western societies change is a way of life. Although change is part of our lives, and while we may benefit from the improvements being made daily, any one of us might be deceived to think that he had a direct hand in making those improvements. We would do well to recognize that the passenger is not necessarily the pilot, and that improvements, while they are enjoyed by many, also ought to be the direct aim of many, too. Moreover, seeing an abundance of improvements may lead people to the mistaken conclusion that the processes by which they are made to arise occur quite naturally and just as a matter of course. The reality is that although some improvements occur haphazardly, most arise because they are deliberately sought.

As humans we are obliged to think because we have the ability to think. In the same sense we are obliged to improve what we do because we *can* improve what we do. This is done through reflecting upon and critically analyzing our experiences and then setting about to apply better methods when trying again. This is never easy and therefore not to be regarded lightly. One result of special interest arising from this sort of effort is that it always adds immeasurably to one's own sense of self-worth and to the richness of one's existence.

Membership in society affords each of us a great many benefits and privileges. One point of view regarding the obligations and responsibilities membership carries is this: if one gladly accepts and enjoys these many benefits and privileges, then he is obligated to help maintain them and add to them as best he can. Socrates, for example, believed that because he enjoyed the benefits of the law and the state, he therefore had an obligation to the state and was duty bound to obey its laws. Readers who are familiar with his life will recall that he willingly went to his death because of his beliefs. Membership in society carries a price.

Our duty to improve, making it a part of our pattern of living, is revealed more clearly when we realize that our behavior has an impact, for the better or worse, on the behavior of others. In traditional societies change and improvement are practically nonexistent. Because behavior is governed by tradition, change and its resulting progress does not occur, because the social norms in these cultures prohibit any deviation from the established, prescribed behavior patterns. This demonstrates dramatically the influence that social norms can have on people. Group influences in the form of norms are profound. Most behaviors are learned. For practically all of us they are learned through observing the actions of others. Based on her many years of careful observation, the sociologist Margaret Mead concluded that most behavior is not learned from one's betters and elders but from one's peers. She called this process "lateral learning."

If this is true, then we are left with a guide for our own lives: If we wish to enjoy ongoing improvements, then we are obliged to be a part of the processes that make those improvements possible. Think of what this means. We ought to contribute to that progress by making improvements ourselves and by acting in ways that add positively to the norms that promote improvement. Improvement takes on an entirely different meaning in our individual lives when it is seen as not being an ordinary occurrence that happens naturally but a duty to be pursued deliberately.

THE CURSE OF COMPLACENCY

Anytime a person sets about to improve, he is at the same time subtly saying to himself, "What exists now is not good enough. Something better is possible, and I am going to make it a reality." Sheer laziness and an unhealthy ego make this particularly difficult, perhaps impossible, for many. A person's pride can easily block an honest self-appraisal. It takes humility to see and admit to imperfections, and it takes self-assurance and optimism to attempt to mend them. A fair measure of ambition is needed to overpower the easy path of do-nothing and the happy glide many enjoy as they ride along the groove of unthinking habit. Our challenge is to overcome complacency, a condition rooted in the belief that things are good enough already.

The sources of complacency are many. If some amount of nagging dissatisfaction could not become a part of man's character, and were it not so strong as to overpower his pride, progress through the pursuit of improvements in quality would be quite impossible. When it comes to quality, we would be wise to add to our lives a sense of constant dissatisfaction with the status quo, and to think of quality not so much as a graspable end, but more as a desirable and motivating aspiration that will ever stretch our imaginations and our best efforts.

Few would deny that progress demands a steady commitment to quality. It was by making quality "Job One" that the Ford Motor Company, for example, was turned into the most profitable automaker worldwide. The Ford chairman and CEO, Donald E. Petersen, explains it this way: "We . . . call our approach total quality excellence. . . . The whole idea is that you are truly living by the belief that you simply must approach all your activities throughout your enterprise, and each individual has to approach his or her part of that, with the idea of the final incentive to strive at all times for excellence, or you're going to fall apart, you're just not going to come together. You have to be thinking along those lines of 'integrity is never compromised'—some form of aspiring always for excellence and constant improvement. There's no such thing as 'an absolute level and then you have got it made.' "

Another automaker quick to meet the competitive challenges in that industry is Chrysler Motors. Its (now former) chairman, Gerald Greenwald, said, "The quality of our product is of fundamental importance. It is the most important factor in our company, and Number Two is a long way from Number One. . . . We feel very strongly that we should pay based on performance. For our senior management we have a bonus system. We have four measures, and we show our people where they stand every 90 days: . . . the four measures are quality, productivity, market share, and profits. Of those four, quality weighs 40 percent in the total, and the other three, equally, only 20 percent. Our basic view goes this way: if we are the world's best in quality, if we concentrate to be the lowest-cost producer and pass that on to the customer, that's productivity. Then, in many ways, market share will follow and profits will follow."

Free enterprise encourages stiff competition, making the path of complacency a prescription for ruin. The global competitive arena is filled with sophisticated and aggressive players. There is no *absolute level* of quality that assures success indefinitely. The idea, therefore, is to get ahead of the others and once in front never pause to rest. Dow Chemical has an effort underway called Quality Service and Product Performance. Paul Oreffice comments, "It's amazing how much we've improved our quality and service over the last three or four years since we've had this program. Why? Were we supplying a bad product before? No, But we got complacent. We thought we were so good we didn't have to worry about it. One day we took a look at ourselves and said, 'Hey, a lot of people that were behind us are catching up with us. They're making quality as good as ours, some even better. We want to be number one.'"

BOLDNESS: STANDING UP FOR WHAT ONE CLAIMS IS IMPORTANT

Many forces press people not to insist on high quality and not to strive continually for improvements. Each force has a certain ring of legitimacy and appears to be a permissible exception to the lofty aims that progress demands. But the most serious error one makes in deviating from the quest for quality and ongoing improvement is to fail to remember that good reputations are not made from yielding to the convenience of any one of these exceptions. Indeed, good reputations are built by always standing up for worthy aims. Boldness is a useful ally in the discipline of standing up for these aims.

High quality and ongoing improvement, if they are to mean anything to an individual or organization, have to be seen as more than just two important values among many; like integrity, they need to be seen as "ultimate values," and as such, not to be compromised for reasons of expediency, convenience, quick gains, or any of the countless other appealing excuses of the moment. The pressure to produce, to meet quotas and timetables, especially in assembly-line-type operations, presents an age-old problem to those who work in high-production situations: Does management want volume or quality? At Whirlpool, to name one firm that recognizes this peril, employees are told to opt for quality. At Whirlpool the motto is, "Quality is everybody's business."

Some parts of American industry are coming to the correct conclusion that high quality and high levels of output are not incompatible. A truth of profound significance is this: When good minds are put to the task of looking for ways to make improvements in one area, they nearly always find ways to make improvements in other areas as well. Delbert C. Staley, of NYNEX, relates his firm's experiences with this phenomenon: "We have proven to ourselves and to our people that good quality, high quality, is cheaper to provide than poor quality. We actually go at it from the standpoint of taking a particular piece of the business . . . and by improving the quality in that part of the business, we will improve the cost. You have an awful lot of people who say, 'Do you want high quality or do you want low cost?' And the truth of the matter is, they go hand in hand. . . . You get rid of the 'do-over work' and you get rid of all the errors and the going back and doing the job over again."

The time inevitably comes when the pursuit of an ideal is made difficult. For many years Zenith has been known for its quality products; their motto is, "Quality goes in before the name goes on." That company's former chairman and CEO, John Nevin, recalls a telling incident about a manufacturing problem at one of the Zenith plants when he worked for that organization: "We had a vice president of manufacturing named Jim Rooney. He was a guy who was an engineering graduate. He had come up through the plant and all. I remember having lunch with him one day and he told me that our St. Louis, Missouri, plant, which was our biggest color television plant, was down and had been down for two days. The reason was that they had a major component failure in some of the parts they were putting in the television sets. The television sets weren't meeting their quality expectations, and they just shut the plant down. That had my attention, and I said, 'How do you feel about that?' He said, 'John, I love plants. I don't get upset when a part of the manufacturing process gets out of control and you've got to shut down the plant in order to get it back under control in order to meet the standards. I don't get upset when components come into the plant that aren't worth a damn and you find out they're failing or they're not worth a damn and you've got to shut down the plant to get fresh components. That's unavoidable in American business. When I really get upset is when I find some guy who will take his mistakes and pack them in a box and ship them to our customers. If they want to shut down the plant, that's all right with me.' "

Profit pressures, as well as a host of expediencies, can encourage the business person to cut corners when it comes to quality and service. The line that separates good quality from poor is easily crossed. Profit maximization theory tells us to act according to what measurements report as being the optimum level of quality—where marginal costs equal marginal revenues. This theory does not drive all firms. We see many business leaders who approach the matter of product quality in a radically different way, so that their organizations stand for something greater than what strict economic theory advocates. John H. Bryan, Jr., of Sara Lee, says, "I just come out on the side of 'no compromise.' . . . It's dumb to make cheaper products. It really is. And, there's so much pressure on that side . . . to cut corners."

Good reputations, our experiences tell us, are not built upon cutting corners; they're built upon insistence on high standards. James R. Eiszner, of CPC International, describes a company practice used to assure that high standards are met in that organization. "When a bottle breaks in our factory, the rule is if it breaks anywhere near the filling equipment, we take a hundred jars before and a hundred jars afterward and discard them—throw them in the dump. We recall products not so much because they represent a hazard but because they represent a hazard to our image of high quality. We will throw out eleven thousand cases of a product if it isn't quite what it ought to be, regardless of whether it is satisfactory to eat."

This is costly, but top-quality producing firms are willing to pay the price that top-quality performance demands. In a talk before company employees, Eiszner once told his listeners, "We'll always have the best-quality products. That is a given in this company. It stems from the top. It always has stemmed from the top. It's repeated all down the organization. Everybody understands that if you have a question of jeopardizing a quality image, . . . you always err on the side of costing the company a little extra but protecting the quality."

Customer expectations are yet another factor to be considered in the pursuit of quality standards. At Control Data, the chairman and CEO, Robert M. Price, explains that "customer expectations and product specifications are not necessarily the same. . . . Our criterion is not simply to meet some product specification. Our criterion is to conform to customer expectation." To that end, Control Data sees the essence of quality as conforming to customer expectations, and that is reached by serving the ideal of making customers successful through the products they buy.

In spite of its maker's best efforts, a defective product may not be discovered until it is in the hands of customers or until they put that product to use, under unimaginable conditions and in ways that even the cleverest of minds could not foretell. It is impossible to foresee *all* of the ways and conditions under which products will be used and imagine all of the odd circumstances that will cause products to fail. But when failure occurs, a firm that is serious about standing up for quality will stand behind its products. The dedication to this high standard of quality has led Brunswick Corporation's top management to unusual lengths.

That firm once introduced a new, high-performance bowling ball that appeared to be an instant success. It was picked up by professionals in winning tournaments. The country's best bowlers were endorsing it. But this success was short lived; the balls proved susceptible to heat. If one was left in the trunk of a car on a hot day, the cover would soften from the intense heat and the ball would turn to the consistency of a marshmallow. (It's hard to bowl with a marshmallow.) The chairman and CEO, Jack F. Reichert, responded immediately, "Recall every ball." His managers hurried to tell him that a recall would cost the company over $1 million. Reichert persisted, "Good, recall them all, with a full cash refund to the customers." By the time all the refunds were made, the cost to Brunswick was $2.5 million. According to Reichert, "If our name means anything to a customer, when you make a mistake you've got to pay for it."

COMMITMENTS TO QUALITY

Commitments to quality generally bring substantive benefits—economic and technological—as well as a sense of pride and genuine achievement on the part of employees. These commitments also help assure a firm's future success. James D. Robinson III, of American Express, stated his belief on this matter directly, saying, "In the final analysis quality will sell. . . . I absolutely refuse, whenever I am in earshot or eyesight, to see anybody speak of productivity figures without simultaneously talking about quality assurance measures. It's easy to get productivity at the cost of quality . . . But if you do it well, quality assurance for us is just as strong as patent protection. Competition has to come fight on your turf rather than you fighting in a non-descript area where quality does not matter."[2]

Smucker's is known for high quality jams and jellies throughout the world. The board chairman, Paul H. Smucker, sees quality as one source of assurance for future growth. As Smucker observes, "We started with quality and are still probably even more dedicated to making a quality product. If we continue to do that and then come out with other products and offer food items that are basically good for the family, then I think there's no limit to what we can do as far as growth is concerned."

People who think highly of themselves and who work hard to perform well in whatever they try to do, naturally value working for a company that is supportive of those same ideals and values. This indicates the benefit to an organization that pursues quality wholeheartedly—it makes an exciting work environment, one that people having high ideals and high ability will respect, and in which they will give their best efforts. Arthur Ochs Sulzberger, of the *New York Times*, says, "People like to work for companies associated with the *New York Times* because we are always striving for quality. We don't always achieve it, but we strive. For the little papers we own, we are back redesigning, reconfiguring, enlarging the newsroom, giving them advice and expertise they couldn't conceivably have bought when they were smaller papers. The idea being, obviously, that if you give better papers, more people will buy them. We don't like to own things that are mediocre. And we get our kicks out of good products. And we're far from perfect. I think it has been the striving for some kind of quality, and I think that's what drives the *New York Times*." Quality-prone organizations are exciting because quality demands ongoing change; people in these organizations are always learning. And employees there are made to feel that they are "where it's happening"—at the vanguard of progress.

All across American industry today, people are realizing that quality begins with a commitment from the top. Quality performance is sustained by the pride all employees have in what they do. But there is more to it than just lofty aims. Inspections help, because people regard more highly those things that are checked. In practice, we find that there are savings to be had by inspecting. At Northrop there is 100 percent inspection of incoming parts, to assure quality and to save on costs. Their experience has shown them that $1 spent on incoming parts inspection saves $18 in the field. But there is more to quality than just inspections of incoming parts and quality checks on the products completed. There is the attitude dimension, which always accompanies any practice. Certain attitudes move employees to actions that are more in keeping with quality, and hence long-term improvements and success, than what would serve strictly short-term economic ends. The attitude of top management toward what is most important can permeate any organization. Northrop, for example, chooses to own its production facilities instead of using government-owned plant and facilities, because its top management believes that by so doing they are better able to assure quality and thus better serve customers. This they do despite the fact that the policy has an adverse impact on the company's return on assets.

Also important to the creation of positive attitudes toward product quality is employee involvement, as Nathan S. Ancell, of Ethan Allen, explains. "We have 6,000 people in our factories making . . . products. And the difference between having a great quality-control program and not having a great quality-control program is the pride your people have—where everybody in the factory is an inspector of his own work. We have found that that's the source of 85 percent of our quality—the pride we have been able to instill in our people."

The special urgency of pursuing quality is felt by most of us, because as consumers we prefer quality products. Buying something simply because it is cheap generally proves to be foolish. This useful idea can be extended: if a product is not a quality product, then people will not only be unable to genuinely enjoy using it, but also those who produce it will not find much in that activity to uplift their pride in themselves.

Many Americans seem to be caught in the trap of having to relearn the importance of quality. One well respected firm serves as an example for us in avoiding the peril of the cheap. AT&T came from a heritage of leasing its products, telephones. In this business environment it was important, economically, to make telephones that would not fall apart, because it cost money to repair them and it was also inconvenient for people to have a product that would go dead in the night, especially if they lived ten miles out in the country. When the transition came after deregulation and the break-up of AT&T, the market changed—a flood of cheap residence telephones came on the market. They could be bought practically everywhere.

The president of Western Electric, the manufacturing arm of AT&T, said that they could make a cheap phone better than anybody else and sell it for less, but that "we're not going to do it." Today AT&T is the dominant provider of residence telephones, but not because they made the cheapest ones. They didn't follow that route. Meanwhile, their competitors have shifted tactics to compete on the quality dimension. The AT&T vice-chairman, Charles Marshall, says, "We found the American public still has a very strong desire to have a product that will continue to work, that feels solid, and we stuck it out."

The realization that there is a profound connection between quality and business success is certainly not a new one; this very old truth seems to be rediscovered with each succeeding generation. Many of the companies we recognize today are alive because they were founded by strong adherents to the principle of providing quality to customers—men like John Deere, Oscar Mayer, and Willis Haviland Carrier. But perhaps no one has pinpointed the essential reason why quality is so important to business success any better than did W. Atlee Burpee, in an address to the French Federation of Seedsmen's Societies in Paris. He said, "Quality is long remembered after cost is forgotten."[3]

22

Serving the Customer

There are many conflicting opinions about what the principal role for business should be in society. These views range from the purely economic—earning profitable returns for owners—to the purely social—funding and championing social causes. When one begins to examine the arguments upon which these extreme positions are based, each of them turns out to be insubstantial. Profitability, as a measure of efficiency, is a social good, but it is also true that businesses ought to be good neighbors. To balance these claims, we need to see the matter more clearly.

The *primary* aim of any business, if it is to remain successful, can not be simply to earn profits, although profits are clearly necessary. It can not be to mend social ills. It can not be merely to provide jobs. And it can not only be any of the other things well-meaning people might believe that primary role should be. The primary aim of any business has got to be economic: to serve its customers by providing them goods and services in a profitable fashion. Organizations that sharply define their purposes in these terms are most likely to excite the best endeavors of their employees and flourish as a result.

At Holiday Inn's corporate headquarters in Memphis, Tennessee, many of the offices have small brass plaques with the inscription, "How Have I Served Our Customers Today?" Service is why that business, or any other business, exists; the satisfaction of the customer is preeminent. Competition demands this.

R. Gordon McGovern, of Campbell Soup, expresses the idea this way: "The customer is what you work at this business for. You've got to give value and quality to the customer. The customer is always in flux, so you're adjusting to the customer, not just once in a while but every morning you get out of bed. Every day you should be asking, 'What am I going to do for those customers? How am I going to make this business run so that they are satisfied?' "

Today's consumers are intelligent, demanding, and discriminating; they know what they want, and they are not easily fooled. The force of this reality is shown in their use of the legal system to protect their interests. What's more, there are limits to what advertising claims they will accept. Jack Peters, of J. Walter Thompson, puts it this way: "If you ever try to talk down to the consumer, if you ever forget that he's an intelligent human being, he walks away. [If, as an advertiser your claims are exaggerated or phony,] he walks away from you. He walks away from your ad. He walks away from the TV set. He walks away from your client's product so fast it would make your head spin."

The trick of success in business does not lie in fooling the customer but in outdistancing one's competitors in serving the customer. And to this end, mere words and promises are ineffectual; it is quality, reliability, and service that earn the customer's confidence and his hard-earned dollars. The best way to fight competitors is to outperform them. As Charles W. Moritz, of Dun & Bradstreet, observes, "It's only through serving the customer that profits arise. [Any business has] got to be driven first and foremost by its concern for its customers."

Customer satisfaction can not be just a nice thing that is done if it is convenient or after other more important matters are put to rest; many business failures bear painful testimony to this fact. This is underscored by an observation, made by the J. C. Penney Co. chairman and CEO, William Howell: "When you cease to fulfill a role for American consumers, you cease to exist in this business. We know that. We understand it."

There are many pressures on profit-producing organizations and on those who work in and for them. These pressures can cause anyone to lose sight of his chief role: to serve customers. Nevertheless, this aim can be made to be the master guide for any enterprise. John H. McConnell, of Worthington Industries, states the matter directly: "The customer is king and without him we have nothing." If they aim to make their organization successful, the employees of any business must work to please the customer. At J. C. Penney, for example, employees at all levels are encouraged to work as a team to satisfy customers. Chairman Howell says, "We want every one of our people to feel like that they don't work for J. C. Penney; they work for the customer."

To see to it that their best intentions do not evaporate many firms have established formal written credos. The Penney Idea, which was adopted in 1913, is an excellent example.

The Penney Idea

To serve the public as nearly as we can to its complete satisfaction.

To expect for the service we render a fair remuneration, and not all the profit the traffic will bear.

To do all in our power to pack the customer's dollar full of value, quality and satisfaction.

To continue to train ourselves and our associates so that the service we give will be more and more intelligently performed.

To improve constantly the human factor in our business.

To reward the men and women in our organization through participation in what the business produces.

To test our every policy, method and act in this wise: "Does it square with what is right and just?"

As practical creatures we fully realize that the pressure to earn healthy levels of profit is real indeed; it is a legitimate concern. Profit is a measure of performance, and as such, it is a good way of gauging how well customer wants and needs are being met commercially. Yet there are clear dangers associated with focusing attention exclusively on profit: it can lead to short-sighted and near-term thinking and actions that are detrimental to long-term success, stability, and sustained rates of growth. Pursued unthinkingly, it promotes the search for schemes to make small savings instead of encouraging larger thinking about how to serve customers better. And it fosters the attitudes of "What's in it for me?" and "How can I get something for myself?" instead of "What can we do for customers?"

If we wish to live in a world shaped more by progress and long-run prosperity than by the short-run profit squeeze, then we will keep our attention more on the ones a business must please—its customers—and less on our statements of receipts and expenses. Foresight is required if one is to accept the proposition that through serving customers well, the rewards of profit will ultimately follow.

A practical illustration of this principle is found in the history of one of America's most admired and most successful firms. At Johnson & Johnson, employees generally perceive the company's role in broader terms than profit alone. The vice chairman of the board, David Collins, noted, "It's hard for me even to think about what we do that's purely for profit, because that concept at Johnson & Johnson is so outmoded. Our people just don't think that way at all . . . we just don't think in terms of profit first. . . . We think in terms of business's other responsibilities first. The responsibility to the consumer, to begin with, is our primary responsibility. And then profit sort of comes after. It's not that we disregard profit. We like profit! We work pretty hard to get profit. [But] the idea of profit as a principal or primary objective of our business hasn't been prevalent at Johnson & Johnson for a long time."

HELPING CUSTOMERS SUCCEED

The "what's in it for me?" attitude, which we hear expressed frequently, can easily pull a person away from any serious concern for the way his product can be of benefit to customers. It can lead to the practice of "shoving product off" on buyers. There are character implications here, for no man's life is large until he comes over to the attitude of wanting to serve something greater than himself.

History shows that there have been many successful businesses built upon a concern about whether buyers are made any better off as a result of the business transacted. The leaders and employees of these firms demonstrate sincere interest in their customers, and they embrace the ideal that these customers will be helped to succeed or will enrich their existence as a result of acquiring and using their (the seller's) product. The idea here is to not succumb to the practice of merely moving merchandise in order to earn a quick profit, but instead to provide customers with goods and services that elevate their well-being.

The Ethan Allen cofounder and chairman, Nathan S. Ancell, illustrates this idea perfectly. "We are not in the furniture business. We do not sell furniture. We market a professional and practical decorating service to help people create a beautiful, warm, and inviting home environment. That's the business we're in. That's the corporate mission, the corporate objective . . . that motivates us in doing everything we do. We think . . . of our customers—the quality of their life, the home. What can we do to help create that home environment? Now that sounds like a lot of baloney to a lot of people, but that's what we've stood for in this company ever since the day we started."

The principle we are examining here is not some idealistic theory, but a practical guide that works. Cyrus H. McCormick was fundamentally an inventor, not a businessman. Yet, his customer orientation—rooted in a concern for helping the farmer succeed—proved to be the pivotal cause of his firm's early success. His attempts to license the manufacture of his reaper had been disastrous; the few that others built had not performed well because of poor workmanship.

His reputation nearly ruined, McCormick went to Chicago. There he met William Butler Ogden. With Ogden's financial backing in 1847, McCormick got a new start. He also had some novel ideas on the way customers were to be treated. Every machine would be sold, without haggling, at the fixed price of $120. For $30 down and the promise to pay the balance within six months, a farmer could have one of McCormick's labor-saving machines. The inventor refrained from the common practice in those days of hiring lawyers to collect from slow-paying farmers whose crop yields were poor or who were down on their luck. Lawyers, in that era, would use scare tactics and whatever fear-inducing methods they might concoct to force payment of accounts due. McCormick was more patient and optimistic; his competitors thought he was foolish for not trying to squeeze slow-paying farmers. "He'll get caught holding the bag," they thought. They were dead wrong;

McCormick's reapers sold as fast as he could build them. His business expanded; his competitors were cut down.

Being customer-driven involves far more than merely responding to what customers indicate they want or need. It also means studying the customers—their markets, their needs and how they can and should, as well as do, use the products sold. Robert M. Price, of Control Data, suggests an even greater involvement in understanding customers than what the simple marketing concept advises. "If you want your customer to be successful," says Price, "that means you have to understand the customers' needs maybe better than they understand their needs. . . . It's all very easy to say, 'I'll just listen to what this guy says and do what he says, and then everything will be okay.' But you and I don't always know how to achieve success for ourselves. . . . Getting close to the customer has a great deal to do with what's going on in my customers' marketplace. What kind of competitive pressures does this group or this set of customers have? What kinds of problems do they have? What is their competition? Who are they competing with? And what are the competitive factors that get into that? So studying your customers' markets and their competitive situations, not just listening to what they say, is important to really meeting a customer's true needs."

It would be the height of arrogance, not to mention a huge mistake, to follow this aforementioned advice in the extreme and leave the customer out of this process entirely—to discount the customer's ability to pinpoint his own needs. As a general principle, no one ought to do for others what they are capable of doing for themselves. Sellers can often help buyers understand better their own needs for products and show them how to use those products more advantageously. But, generally speaking, buyers should be involved in the thinking and the decision-making process.

In the 1930s Dow Chemical was selling carbon tetrachloride to the Pyrene Company for fire extinguishers. Carbon tetrachloride was a standard chemical in fire extinguishers in those days, and Dow was the exclusive supplier to Pyrene. At about that time Dow discovered a better way of making carbon tetrachloride—a process that required lower costs and yielded a product of higher purity. The quality of the carbon tetrachloride from the new process was terrific, and later Dow began shipping the product to Pyrene. About a year later Pyrene began discovering they had some leaks in their fire extinguishers, and they came back to Dow and said, "We've got some leaks. We don't know what's causing them." Every textbook in the country said that carbon tetrachloride has no corrosive impact at all on brass. And Pyrene containers were brass.

What no one knew then was that pure carbon tetrachloride would corrode brass, but a trace of sulphur in the product would protect it. The old process started with carbon bisulfide, and so there was some carbon bisulfide in the carbon tetrachloride, which acted as an inhibitor. Every corrosive test ever run had been run on impure carbon tetrachloride made by the old process. Dow did what it believed to be the right thing under these circumstances. Even though at the time it was a small company, it bought back all those fire extinguishers. Its managers felt it was the right

thing to do, because they had failed to tell Pyrene that they had changed
their process and they had failed to ask Pyrene to verify their test that the
new product was acceptable to Pyrene's uses. The larger message from
this experience points to the need to never allow a product or process to be
changed without talking to the customer. And even if a new product or
process is thought to be better, always let the customer in on decisions that
affect him.

SERVING CUSTOMER NEEDS

Discovering customer needs is never easy; it usually involves an ongoing dialogue with buyers and users, asking them many questions. But
this is not the end of it, for it also often involves a considerable number of
trial-and-error efforts to test out which ideas actually will work, not in
theory but in the practical realm of the marketplace. Firms that are good at
this process and that willingly and quickly change to meet customer
wants, usually obtain good results. One useful approach is for company
leaders to place themselves in the shoes of their customers. Peter A.
Magowan, of Safeway, affords us an excellent illustration of this. "We're
in business to serve the customer and we try to manage the company as
the customer would have us manage it," says Magowan. "We task ourselves, 'If the customer were the division manager, or the president of the
company, what would the instructions to the stores be as to how we
would manage the company? Would we raise prices or would we lower
prices? Would we add service at the front end so we could check them out
quickly, or would we cut the help to save labor cost? Would we make
check cashing simple for them, running the risk of cashing more bad
checks, or would we have the security people give the third degree to everybody writing a check in the store? Would we have an extra selection of
perishable products, knowing that because they are perishable we would
throw a lot of them away or would we reduce our selection so that we
would have no disappearance loss?' . . . We really ask ourselves, 'Would
we have a bunch of controllers running the company, accountants and
people who are good at shrinkage control and stopping bad checks and
catching dishonest customers, or would we run the company on the basis
that most people are honest and most people want to have good service
and wide selection?' We end up saying that we should run the company
as the customer would have us run it if she were in control."

In Denver, the King supermarket chain, known as King Soopers,
once held a 50 percent market share. Lloyd King's philosophy was one
of commitment to serving customers. Under his leadership King's chain
of markets responded to the changing demographics; stores moved to the
suburbs. King, himself, would frequently ask customers, "Tell me what
you don't like about our store." The "King Card" was a consumer research instrument. Within 24 hours of a complaint he had a response to
the customer. It was King's philosophy that you cannot afford to lose a
customer. He also had a philosophy of no questions asked when cus-

tomers wanted a refund. And if there were a product a customer wanted, he'd get it for that customer.

The message here is this: King's market dominance was a direct result of his willingness to listen to customers and to respond positively, in concrete ways, to what he had heard. The job for sellers is to give customers "what they want" and not "to make them want what they've got." There are examples of this aplenty. The J. M. Smucker Company has developed a line of low-sugar jams and jellies for people who do not want the calories normal jams and jellies contain or who feel sugar is harmful. They also have a line of jams and jellies made without sugar—it uses white grape juice as a sweetener agent. The Campbell Soup Company, too, sees its job as one of giving options to the consumer. To that end the company now produces low-sodium soups, low-sodium pickles, meatless frozen dinners, and low-sodium V-8 juice.

Serving customers well is neither cheap nor easy. It demands patience, a big-minded outlook, and a willingness to do for others at the expense of one's own likes or convenience. Illinois Bell, for example, would repair a person's telephone at night if it were completely out of service. That company would have preferred to wait until the next morning or wait past the weekend; nonetheless, ads were put in the newspaper that read, "If it's an emergency to you, it's an emergency to us." The public soon learned that if they wanted their phone repaired at night, they weren't going to have to argue with one of Illinois Bell's employees, who might otherwise have said, "We'll get somebody there tomorrow."

Security Pacific Bank finds that many senior citizens come to their branches every day just to check their safe deposit boxes. It is something these older people, who are alone and have little to do with their time, can do five days a week. Richard J. Flamson III, of Security Pacific, sees this as just part of the business they are in. In his view, "It doesn't make any money for us and it doesn't help our shareholders, at least so I can see a direct relationship, but I think our position is that we don't do anything to try to discourage that."

Extraordinary effort and customer service are not foreign to American business. Much gets talked about when terrible mistakes are made and customers are mistreated. But there are many instances of exceptional service too For instance, a Texas bank telephoned Deluxe Check Printers in Minneapolis on a Thursday and said that they were taking over another bank. This would necessitate new checks—in fact a whole group of checks printed in different styles with the new bank name and logo—in order to be open for business the following Monday. Deluxe employees would have rather enjoyed their weekend relaxing, but a group teamed up to work on the bank's problem instead. The bank had its checks in time to open as planned.

Frank W. Considine, of National Can, recalls a time when cyclamates in soft drinks were banned, overnight. He came to work on a Monday when a key customer, Coca Cola, was having to remove all its products from grocers' shelves. It was necessary to get new cans printed without the word "cyclamate" immediately so Coca Cola could start

putting out new product right away. Printing plates were reconfigured
and shipped from design studio to manufacturing plants on the same day,
and by Wednesday Coca Cola had the cans it needed. Considine says,
"That's how you build a reputation, and I don't think we deserve a lot of
applause for it. It's just the kind of responsiveness [that is needed] when
somebody's in trouble."

POLICIES AND PROCEDURES TO ASSURE
CUSTOMER SATISFACTION

In 1865, John Wanamaker established innovative policies on behalf
of the customers of his emporium in Philadelphia. All merchandise was to
be of good quality and honestly labeled. The new system of one fixed
price, plainly marked on every piece of merchandise, put an end to forcing
customers to haggle over the price of everything they wanted to buy. And
if they were displeased later with what they bought, Wanamaker's cus-
tomer-oriented policies also guaranteed shoppers a full refund for returned
merchandise. Wanamaker believed that if for any reason a customer was
dissatisfied with a purchase, the customer should have the right to return it
and receive his money back. Finally, he believed that customers should
be able to come into his store to browse and enjoy shopping, without being pressured into buying. A rapport was thus built between merchant
and customer, based on honesty, confidence, and mutual satisfaction.

At about the same time, in Chicago, Marshall Field built a brisk trade
on similar policies: fixed prices, cash sales, accurate representation of all
merchandise, and unusual courtesy to customers, a rule that was strictly
enforced.

Today's merchants and manufacturers are generally guided by policies aimed at honesty, fairness, and courteous treatment of customers.
Great efforts are not just made at discovering what buyers want, but also
on finding out how satisfied they have been with their purchases and with
the treatment they have been given. Chrysler tracks customer satisfaction
with a measure called the Customer Satisfaction Index—the CSI. Every
person who buys a Chrysler product, car or truck, gets a letter about thirty
days after the sale. It has a checklist with it: Were you treated right? Was
the car/truck ready? Did the dealer explain the warranty? and so on.
Every dealer has been given an objective: he has to improve from where
he was the year earlier. To this end, one of the measures Chrysler uses is
customer loyalty—the percentage of people who make a second purchase
from the same dealer. If the loyalty factor isn't high enough, or if the
customer questionnaire reflects dissatisfaction, field representatives sit
down with that dealer to work on the problems.

At Ford, until recent years dealers were recognized strictly on the
basis of high profit and high volume. That has changed, and real progress
is being made on improving the average dealer's ability and desire to treat
customers properly. According to the Ford chairman and CEO, Donald E.
Petersen, "The quality commitment performance of the dealer is now be-

coming one of the important ingredients in the overall evaluation of the individual dealers. There's a whole array of excellent programs . . . urging all dealers to take on and use to improve, very substantially, how an individual is treated from the moment they start the sales experience— walking in the sales room—through the purchase, through . . . the ongoing life of using the product for a number of services." Out of 56,000 Ford dealers, 70 won the president's award for good service. Those dealers had to be the best on customer treatment. Petersen says, "It always used to be high profit, high volume. But now you cannot be among those award winners without a high score on treating customers properly."

Measurable targets for service and customer satisfaction may include activities that are known to produce these ends. For example, some companies measure response times in filling orders and shipping them to customers. The beauty of these kinds of measurement is that they can assure execution of activities that achieve important long-term goals. These activities might be the means to important long-term ends, which otherwise might not be performed because other activities could achieve short-term results much better. Measures of customer satisfaction today may not have much of an impact on current results, but they certainly do affect results in the years ahead.

Another way to help assure that important activities are carried out is to create conditions that reward desired behaviors and penalize unwanted ones. For example, some firms pay their salespeople a salary. Although this may not be as motivating as commission pay, it can encourage salespeople to spend more time with their customers and not neglect them in order that they might be free to hunt for new ones.

By the time customer complaints start coming to the attention of management, a problem may be out of hand; it may actually be too late— the damage may have already been done. A way around this is to prevent ill-treatment in the first place. At Teledyne, top management is constantly checking on its service organizations. They will arrange for certain people to call from various parts of the country and ask for service, for example, on their swimming pool heater—a Teledyne product. Or they will damage in one way or other some Waterpiks—another Teledyne product—and send several to the service unit to see what the reaction is. In this way management not only obtains a reading on the economic effect of solving the customer's problem with a damaged product, but it also learns how the customer service is rendered—quickly and with a smile, or with a delay and a chip on the shoulder.

At Hewlett-Packard, John A. Young once began to get indications of a letdown in the attention given to customer complaints. He began hearing complaints from customers who had been shunted through the company from one person to another, to another still. Sometimes they would have had to call seven telephone numbers trying to get to the right person for help with their problem. Young began to check those complaints out for himself. "I started calling up like I had a problem," said Young, "to see what happened to me, and I began to get the same thing—'well, nobody's here. Why don't you try these? Maybe you ought to check with the factory and they'll give you some number or some division.' This . . . led me to an entire retraining of our company about customer satisfaction."

Various methods are used throughout American industry to speed answers or help to consumers. Worthington Industries has three airplanes that are used mostly to fly its engineers and service representatives to customer locations where its products are being used. If a customer has a problem, a metallurgical engineer from Worthington will be in his plant to have a firsthand look and begin to solve the problem, generally within two hours. Many companies have toll-free hot lines—Procter & Gamble claims to have set up the first one in the country for consumers, and General Electric and Whirlpool have them also. Consumers can call service representatives 24 hours a day. Whirlpool gets over 350,000 telephone calls each year. They find that 95 percent of the people receive satisfaction from the information they are given over the telephone. Most of them call to see where they can get service, and someone from Whirlpool calls back later to see if they got the service.

Retailers find that the best way to handle dissatisfied customers is to return their money. At J. C. Penney the policy is this: only the store manager can say no to the customer. Sales clerks who work in Penney stores either do what the complaining customer demands or refer the problem to the store's manager. It is a policy that aims at keeping store clerks from becoming too protective of their employer's interests and insufficiently disposed toward solving customers' problems or meeting their demands.

Penney's chairman of the board, William R. Howell, says, "The reality is that the person who is most uptight generally about a return is a customer. We found that most Americans have a little bit of anxiety about even returning something, expecting that they're going to get hassled and so forth. And we desperately try to train our people to keep that same smile and to make the customer, a real customer, out of a return situation because it's an opportune time to be different, to be unique."

At Kmart, customers dissatisfied with purchases are given their money back with no questions asked. Customers are then free to buy any other product, and they usually do so in the same store. At Safeway, customers are protected by a guarantee policy. Anytime a purchase fails to satisfy a customer, all that person needs to do is tell the people in the store, "Such and such a product failed to satisfy me," and they are refunded their money.

Chrysler Motors encourages every customer who doesn't think he has been treated right, to try first to resolve his difference of view with the dealer. If that doesn't work, Chrysler tries to get its factory people in as a third party. And if that doesn't work to the satisfaction of that customer, he or she has the right to ask for arbitration. Chrysler maintains over 50 arbitration boards around the country. Purposely, no one on those boards works for Chrysler or even has any equity (owns stock) in Chrysler. They try to have an engineer, a lawyer, a businessperson, and a maintenance person on these boards. On occasion they have a university professor or someone from the clergy. Chrysler is looking for boards to give straightforward fairness in settling disputes. The ground rule is that Chrysler will live with the arbitration results. They ask the consumer to live by the results also. However, the customer is not obliged. If he is still not satisfied after the arbitration process, he can take the matter to court. Very few cases get that far.

RESPONDING TO COMPLAINTS

There is a perception that American companies do not care about customers, that once a sale has been made their interest in the buyer ends. Actually, business leaders are profoundly interested in customers, and they work hard at earning their patronage and trust through providing quality products, fair treatment, and reliable service. And when customers are dissatisfied for any number of reasons, effective business leaders not only want to know about it, but often become personally involved in retrieving mistakes or remedying shortcomings. The most successful companies are very quick to respond to customer complaints. The best way to satisfy customers is to give them what they expect in the first place. People trust what performs. But if mistakes are made, and they are made from time to time, the sensible thing to do is to correct them immediately without arguing about them. As Joseph L. Jones, of Armstrong World Industries, says, "If we do make a mistake in our factories, and we do, we correct it. We don't argue about it; we fix it. We pay for it; we replace it, or whatever." Customers do not want hassles; they want products that work, that perform as they are supposed to perform. And when they do not perform as designed, effective leaders see that they are fixed immediately.

Litton Industries makes a piece of navigation equipment for airplanes, and some of these have been sold abroad to friendly foreign countries. On one occasion Litton's board chairman, Fred O'Green, received word that a few of these instruments were not functioning as they were designed to perform. His immediate response was to send the top technical people from the United States abroad with spare parts. O'Green's order was swift and direct: "Fix these instruments at whatever it costs." Litton's technical people were dispatched with a full understanding as to what their mission was. In due course they talked with pilots coming out of the field about the difficulty, uncovered its cause, and fixed the problem.

The special importance given to customer satisfaction is made strikingly pronounced when we learn that many heads of corporations take a special interest in customer complaints. Some become involved personally. O'Green sees every letter of complaint sent to his office and reviews not only the company's action but the consumer's response to it.

Chrysler's Gerald Greenwald says, "I read customer complaint letters. I watch and track the numbers. About every other month I go to one of our 25 zone offices and I spend time with the customer relations representative in each one of those. I ask them what is going on and what the [product] quality is. I ask, 'Are there particular kinds of complaints focused upon a given dealer, a given car, a given engine, a given product?' I come home the next morning and we go to work [on whatever problems are found]."

J. Ray Topper, of Anchor Hocking, responds to anyone who writes with a complaint. He says, "We always respond. We never question. If it's any product that's within warranty we replace it without question. We have questions many times . . . but we don't question."

At the Bank of America there is a regular procedure followed for letters and phone calls of complaint addressed to the president and chairman. "We get a lot of mail and telephone calls. . . . We look at, review those all individually, personally," says the chairman, Leland Prussia.

Letters of complaint from consumers to the chairman or president of Rubbermaid get an answer within 48 hours. The chairman, Stanley C. Gault, says, "We receive more letters of compliment than complaint. And a substantial part of our complaint letters are for products we didn't make. The wastebasket splits, or the laundry basket's handle tore off, or whatever. There's no name on it. We're the only name that they can think of, so obviously it must be ours. So they write us a nasty letter. We tell them obviously they've made a mistake. Everything that we make does have our name on it. Therefore, since you *thought* you were buying ours, and we know you will the next time, we send them a replacement . . . and then you should see what we get back. They tell all their friends and all the neighbors."

Before assuming the chairmanship at Rubbermaid, Gault headed the appliance division at General Electric. Once, just before Thanksgiving, he received a call from a couple who were distressed over their recent purchase: a GE kitchen range. As Gault recalls, "They had bought one of the new high/low ovens . . . and paid $700 for it. In shipment, the liner had become buckled and part of it dropped. You couldn't use the oven. It was the first time that his parents were coming to stay, and obviously for Thanksgiving dinner. . . . We had promised to have that range fixed that day or before, . . . and I said, 'We made the promise to you, and I'll tell you, I haven't got much time, but are your folks there yet?' He said, 'No, they're going to be here in a couple of hours.' I said, 'Well, I'll tell you what, just so you and your wife don't have to worry about this, you will use that range tomorrow morning, but you don't want to start too early. Either we will fix it or we'll have a new one. . . . The main thing is you have somebody on that telephone tonight so that whenever we call you, you can arrange for delivery.' So I called the national service manager and said, 'Take care of it.' . . . How many people they would have told over the next few weeks of that story, I have no idea. But somebody will have to talk hard and long before they convinced him not to buy GE from now on."

23

Serving to Improve Communities

An inescapable reality of American business today is the deep sense of civic responsibility held by the leaders of its largest and most successful enterprises. As a businessman, perhaps Benjamin Franklin's most impressive contribution to the ideal form of American business was the introduction of "communityism"—the recognition that business ought to become involved in community affairs in positive ways. Public service and philanthropy were legitimate concerns, he believed, because it is good business to improve the health of the communities from which wealth is derived and because public problems can benefit from private solutions. Today's leaders recognize the direct link between healthy, vibrant communities and economic progress and their businesses' success. "We have an obligation to the communities we live in and work in," says William R. Howell, "because there's no way to have a successful, healthy J. C. Penney store unless you have a healthy community."

IMPROVING SOCIETY

Long-term prosperity depends upon the environment for free enterprise in a democratic society. If communities are vibrant and healthy—if there are jobs, good education, opportunities for everyone, freedom to choose, and high levels of hope and lofty expectations for the future—the business environment will enable enterprises there to thrive and hire people and grow and make money. Robert D. Haas, the president and CEO of Levi Strauss, captured this idea when he said, "Corporations can be short-sighted and worry only about our mission, products and competitive standing. But we do it at our peril. The day will come when corporations will discover the price we pay for our indifference. We must realize that by ignoring the needs of others, we are actually ignoring our own needs in the long run. We may need the goodwill of a neighborhood to enlarge a corner store. We may need well-funded institutions of higher learning to turn out the skilled technical employees we require. We may need adequate community health care to curb absenteeism in our plants. Or we may need fair tax treatment for an industry to be able to compete in the world economy. However small or large our enterprise, we cannot isolate our business from the society around us. Nor can we function without its goodwill."[1]

David T. Kearns, of Xerox, observes, "The only way for a corporation to exist and capitalism to survive is to be part of the whole society. We depend upon a healthy environment to sell our products, to hire people, to have customers to sell to. . . . You could sit back from that and say, 'No one company is big enough to affect that whole environment. So if you don't do any of those things it really won't make any difference.' . . . You could make that argument, and that is one way to look at it. I really do think, particularly the large corporations, if they are going to survive as entities, the only way to do that is to feel a responsibility to the communities that . . . [they] operate in. Companies have to be concerned with the owners—the shareholders, the employees, and the customers. And the fourth is the communities . . . [they] operate in, whether that's the country . . . [they] operate in or a local community. Also, depending on the size of the company in a local community, when you are such an overwhelming size in a community in terms of the number of employees, then there are probably a lot of other companies and businesses that depend on you in that community. You take on additional responsibilities. For example, does the hospital work? Does the school system work? . . . I think that companies think about this a lot more today than they did before. I feel strongly that it is in the best interests of the shareholders, the employees, and the customers to make sure that the corporation does put something back, that it is well thought of. And I think the whole image of the company helps you sell products and do a whole lot of other things besides. . . . What do you put back? Well, one is money, and that may be debated as some percentage of after-tax earnings. But in addition to money there are people resources."

The expression "put something back" into the community implies that business has taken something from the community, that it has diminished the community in some way, and that now it ought to repay what it has taken. But profit does not necessarily arise at the expense of others, and communities are not harmed by honest, profitable businesses. Indeed, quite the opposite is the case. Expressions such as "put something back" or "repaying society" are misleading. It would perhaps be more accurate and appropriate to say "add to" or "improve the health and vitality of" or "contribute to the betterment of" the community that has given a business the opportunity to prosper. This refinement of expression does not diminish the level of responsibility business leaders feel they ought to assume in community affairs.

What business generally resents is the attitude that because it has earned profits, those profits somehow belong to those whose needs exceed their means and that those who risked their financial resources and worked hard to earn the profits should not be entitled to use those profits as they choose. Business resents the claim outsiders make that the profit-making entities (businesses) in society have a social responsibility to empty their deep pockets and give away their resources trying to address needs, instead of reinvesting those resources in business expansion and modernization to create more products and provide more employment opportunities—and eventually add substantially more revenues to the tax coffers. Edmund T. Pratt, Jr., of Pfizer, sees it this way: "The term social [responsibility] was coined not by us but by somebody else, and in a way we sort of backed away from it because it was sort of rammed down our throat—as though we didn't have it and [it was] something we ought to get. And we've been doing these things forever." It's not that business leaders don't see a responsibility, and it's not that they don't want to accept a fair measure of responsibility for bettering their communities. However, they do not particularly like being told by outsiders what business's responsibilities are. This is largely because many of these critics who have taken it upon themselves to define for business what its responsibilities are, have the notion that business has unlimited resources that ought to be given away.

Most business leaders feel that they do have some responsibility in these areas; each one of them sees that responsibility somewhat differently. There are a variety of reasons why they, in particular, feel that they have this responsibility. First, they are members of a community. Lewis W. Lehr, of 3M, says, "We are all part of a community. Our children, our employees' children, [in] many cases our customers' children, our shareholders children, are part of the school systems, are part of the Boy Scouts, Girl Scouts, all these other organizations, the churches. . . . I think it is necessary to also say that you, as an individual, have a responsibility within the community. And if you say that, then you also have to say we, the corporation, will help with some resources and certainly with some time, so you can play a role in the community also."

Second, someone must take that responsibility. James D. Robinson III, of American Express, says, "Somebody has to take the responsibility to see that the needs of society are met. You can not duck it. You can not hope somebody else does it and that it will go away; it won't. If you are going to be active in any kind of major business activity, you inherit a burden of responsibility to try to make change work for the betterment of society."2

Third, business has the talents that can be brought to bear on special needs and problems. Edmund Pratt says, "I think most of us feel we are that part of society which is most highly organized and experienced in moving the ball from A to B. We know how to get things done. And therefore, I believe most of us feel that since that is our basic strength, those of us who make products and get things done have a responsibility to use that capability."

THE PRIMARY TASK OF BUSINESS

In our society each institution has some primary task: labor organizations advance the pay, benefits, and working conditions of labor; hospitals provide treatment for the sick and injured and teach and research medical practices; schools provide education; governments enact and execute laws. The primary task of business is to provide high-quality goods and services at competitive prices and at a profit level that attracts needed capital for continued growth. When institutions place their priorities on performing functions that they are incapable of performing well, society suffers. The chief social responsibility of any institution must begin with performing its central task effectively.

Each entity ought to leave the primary, other responsibilities in the hands of those other institutions to do what their expertise permits them to accomplish best. This is not to say that business can ignore problems which it could help to solve. Robert A. Schoellhorn, of Abbott Laboratories, believes, "Private enterprise does have a role in addressing social problems, but that role is primarily through the conduct of the business of that enterprise. . . . We have an obligation to become involved in social issues and problems surrounding our business. I am less comfortable that private enterprise should become involved in social problems beyond its business." Robert H. Malott, of FMC, goes further to say that, "to talk about business altruistically going out and solving the world's problems is nonsense." Malott believes that "business's role . . . is . . . primarily to be successful and profitable, a good employer, and effective in its relationships with all its constituencies, not the least of which are its owners. . . . American business has a role in terms of addressing social problems, but I don't think it should be motivated by the desire to solve social problems. . . . There are problems that are in the best interest of the health of our economic system and the businesses that are part of it if they are solved. And there are some social problems that should not be our responsibility other than to support government action by the tax we pay. I do not think that you should look at business as having a primary role in life to solve social problems."

The first and foremost responsibility of a business entity is economic: to efficiently provide the quality goods and services customers want and to earn a profit. Until a business is profitable it cannot be judged as being a productive and positive force in society, because it is not performing its primary role effectively. Unprofitable businesses, as has already been mentioned, are a net drain on scarce resources. Until a business is profitable, its intentions to become involved in communities, to support worthy causes, and to fund charitable organizations are just hollow words.

In looking at any institution, a question that ought to be raised is "How can it contribute best, or contribute in the most useful ways, to society?" It is doubtful that business best contributes to society by supporting symphonies or low-cost housing for the poor; it does it best by determining the long-term social requirements of its own function and finding the best ways of meeting those requirements. By neglecting this primary responsibility, for many reasons in the postwar period the automobile makers in this country failed in some degree to fulfill a social requirement: to maintain the health and competitiveness of their industry. There was an imbalance of bargaining power between labor unions and the auto makers, partly because of antitrust regulations. Automobile companies were not permitted to bargain collectively in a way that gave them an offset to union bargaining power. After each of the Big Three automobile companies had taken, in different years, very costly strikes in the late 1940s and in the 1950s there followed a period of nearly twenty years when, under great pressure, they gave wage increases substantially in excess of productivity gains. The result was that the real cost for unit of output increased. It didn't matter then, because there was little foreign competition; but that was one factor that stimulated foreign competition bringing on the decline in the American automobile industry in the 1980s with losses in market share and in hundreds of thousands of jobs.

A distinction should be drawn between social responsibility and philanthropy. Social responsibility ought to be thought of as accountability for performing a primary task and related tasks in support of it. For a business to fulfill its social responsibility it must produce quality products that are needed and wanted by customers. This means adhering to quality standards, and it also means providing good jobs and healthful working conditions. It means honest advertising and decent and ethical treatment of suppliers and employees and customers. It means being a good neighbor and a positive influence on the quality of water and air and other natural resources. It means abiding by the letter and the spirit of the law and working within the system to educate the public and legislators to pass better laws that affect its ability to compete. And it means adding to the advancement and development of knowledge and technology.

Unprofitable businesses have little or nothing to give to philanthropic causes. They cannot even pay taxes. The importance of profit is made strikingly clear when one considers that much of that profit goes to taxes. In East Chicago, for example, Inland Steel pays over 50 percent of the tax burden of the companies in that city. The individual taxpayers, the property owners, are responsible for about 15 percent of the entire tax burden there and receive essentially 100 percent of the benefits, because the major industries take care of their own sewage, water, and all other services. In fact, Inland Steel has its own fire department, which from time to time helps the city of East Chicago with fires.

ENLIGHTENED SELF-INTEREST

A concept not to be disregarded is enlightened self-interest—a concern for doing something that benefits others as well as oneself. Some of this involves corporate image building and public relations, but those activities can be better and more economically performed by advertising than by charitable endeavors. Much of enlightened self-interest involves making communities and work places attractive so as to secure the employment of a capable and motivated work force. It also often includes contributing to educational and civic activities that benefit the long-term health and success of the firm. Robert McClements, of Sun Company, identifies several examples of enlightened self-interest shown by American companies operating abroad.

Ford Motor Company has built 128 schools in Mexico.

Champion International subsidizes 13,000 meals a day for its workers in Brazil and runs a low-price co-op supermarket for its employees.

When Bechtel built a 500-mile pipeline in Peru, it also built communities along the line to make sure the workers had clean housing, adequate food, and decent public health facilities.

Caltex constructed 590 schools in Indonesia, with enrollments of over 15,000 children. It also built 2,600 kilometers of roads and maintains them at a cost of $1 million a year.

Goodyear Tire and Rubber builds mosques near its rubber plantations to make it easier for workers to worship.
3M has opened 13 agricultural research centers in its third-world locations.

Del Monte Corporation's food processing plant in Nairobi employs 6,500 Kenyans, and another 5,000 jobs have been created to support the plant. Del Monte has built housing in Nairobi for 12,000 people.[3]

The motivations behind these actions are not claimed to be altruistic. Corporations operating anywhere recognize that they must have a healthy, intelligent, well motivated work force. In less developed countries, companies intervene to meet needs of food, housing, transportation, and education in order to survive and prosper. Frank Stranahan, of Champion Spark Plug, points out that his firm's operation in South Africa employs 100 people and 98 of them are black. "These people now," says Stranahan, "where they had nothing, have homes. Their children are going away to school. They're all dressed properly. They're all fed properly. . . . They have an expanding economy and there are a lot of other employers over there that are exactly the same way."

A company's standing in the community determines the treatment it receives from others and the degree to which it is an attractive source of employment. Good people shy away from companies with spotted reputations. Enlightened self-interest leads businesses to work hard at behaving ethically and doing things that benefit their communities. Donald H. Hall, of Hallmark Cards, observes, "I think the public at large is persuaded by a company that has done some very fine things in their community. It rubs off on the way in which employees look at their company—the pride they have in their company." Thomas H. Cruikshank, of

Halliburton, says, "We, in many ways, are benefited by the desirability of [the] . . . community. . . . Whether we're going to get the right kind of people who will live here and work here depends somewhat on the quality of life within the community." Then there is a motivation to help to improve the community, because benefits flow back to the companies in it.

COMMUNITY INVOLVEMENT

"Business," says Irving I. Stone, of American Greetings, "is more than just making a dollar. We've got to live with people. Sometimes there are problems in the communities where we have plants. We try to pitch in dollarwise or pitch in ourselves to try to help out. We help raise money or help organize an effort. We lend our personnel for a while. That's the way we operate. We have someone whose job it is to get our people to help out. She has the authority to ask people to pitch in on these things. If there is a cleanup drive, she may get fifty people to go down and help out. Every plant has a budget for projects in the community."

This attitude and commitment to community needs is typical of large American companies. They feel a need and have a strong desire to be involved in making the nation and their own communities a better place. To that end, Pfizer supported the work of doctors Jonas Salk and Albert Sabin on polio vaccines, and the company spent millions of dollars on facilities to produce the vaccines in commercial quantities and then sold the Sabin oral vaccine as a public service at near cost.

When Fort Wayne, Indiana, was inundated by flood waters in the spring of 1982, Anheuser-Busch's Columbus, Ohio, brewery packaged about 2,250 cases of 12-ounce cans of drinking water and shipped them to the disaster area. Metal Container Corporation, another Anheuser-Busch Companies subsidiary, made a special production run at its can manufacturing plant in Columbus to provide the needed quantity of white cans.

Cigna offers discounts on insurance policies to bars, taverns, and other establishments that sell liquor if their proprietors and employees go through a training program to recognize when customers are getting too intoxicated and how to say to a person that they can not serve him another drink.

In the Twin Cities, 3M employees hold "paintathons" in the spring. On a given weekend nearly a hundred company employees volunteer and paint over a dozen houses for old people who can not afford to have their homes painted. 3M provides the paint and transportation. And every Tuesday, about three hundred of 3M employees leave the offices at noon and are gone for one and a half to two hours, with pay, to teach English to Vietnamese, Cambodians, and Mexican Americans in the community.

Procter & Gamble helps mobilize its employees to meet community needs through its Volunteer Support Program. It has a full-time employee who serves as a clearinghouse, matching needs with the skills and interests of Procter & Gamble volunteers.

In Oakland, California the Clorox Corporation built and supports the East Oakland Youth Development Center which offers programs for neighborhood youth. Those include (1) arts, crafts, photography, and performing arts; (2) counseling—a full time counselor provides crisis intervention, group, individual, and family counseling; (3) education—remedial math, reading, and spelling assistance for elementary and junior high school students; (4) physical development—recreational activities and programs in basketball and track and field; (5) sewing—instruction in sewing skills to ages 8–24; and (6) Project JOY—Job Opportunities for Youth—provides job readiness and preemployment training for ages 16–24 years after which the graduates are matched with prospective employers.

Throughout America many firms are involved in join-a-school programs. Employees from these companies volunteer to teach classes, help with clubs, enlist community support, and serve as an additional resource to the schools. With about fifty people from his organization, William Woodside, of American Can, has worked with Martin Luther King, Jr., High School in New York City. To him, the join-a-school program has been one of the most satisfying activities he's been involved with. School attendance has improved; teacher, student, and parent morale has improved, absenteeism has gone down, and so on. According to Woodside, "It's encouraging to see what a little attention and concern will do for people who never have felt any kind of concern or any kind of caring by the outside world. . . . You don't get this kind of feedback by writing checks. You get it from involvement."

REVITALIZING CITIES

Urban decay is a familiar phenomenon across America. Downtown businesses leave for the suburbs or other parts of the country. Urban flight erodes a city's tax base, driving up the rates for those who remain. Small shops find it difficult to survive. With others leaving and the deterioration in neighborhoods, the costs and inconveniences of urban locations make movement to suburban areas an even more attractive option.

When Pfizer announced plans to help revitalize the area surrounding its manufacturing plant in East Williamsburg, Brooklyn, The *New York Times* described it as the "first in which a manufacturer has taken a leading role in advancing development" of a New York City neighborhood. Pfizer was formed in East Williamsburg in 1849, and for years that Brooklyn plant was its only facility. It was a pretty area, with a stream running through it. During the previous forty or fifty years the area had deteriorated badly. Most of the other businesses there moved out. Pfizer considered moving too, but its leaders felt the company had a commitment there. They had started their business there and had been successful. And there were lots of people living in the area who worked for Pfizer, reflecting the racial, and other, makeup of the area. The complex had been the only Pfizer plant until after the second world war, when Pfizer began to expand its operations both in the United States and abroad.

If local conditions were permitted to deteriorate unchecked, Pfizer would be inhibited from recruiting and retaining highly skilled employees and running multiple shifts. Something, clearly, had to be done. A thorough study was made, and with various city agencies' support, a plan was drawn up to revitalize the area. The East Williamsburg Redevelopment Project holds the promise of new industry, jobs, housing, and commercial revitalization. The 63-acre area that encompasses Pfizer's 22-acre plant site is once againa productive, secure place to live and work. The redevelopment project has nearly a half-million square feet of efficient, low-cost industrial facilities, generating nearly 1,000 new jobs and up to $50 million in new investment. The results have been a visible improvement in the area and a significant drop in crime. Industrial activity among smaller companies in the area has expanded.

In Minneapolis and St. Paul, Control Data successfully located five new plants in depressed inner-city locations. The total employment in these plants is about 1,600. Conventional measures of performance show these production facilities to be equal or better than other conventional operations—the rates of tenure, absenteeism, and profitability now are good. The first inner-city plant began in 1967. The Northside plant, at the outset, was beset with many problems. Three of these were credit for employees, a lack of daycare, and absenteeism. Control Data solved the employees' need for credit by providing loans from its Commercial Credit Company subsidiary. To deal with the problem of the lack of day-care facilities—there were none in the area—Control Data enlisted community support, and a daycare center was started in a vacant, 80-year-old school building. Monday morning production nearly always was off, because many of the work force would have been thrown in jail over any given weekend. The company responded by (1) providing extensive counseling and help to solve personal problems and (2) dispatching a lawyer to the city jail with a book of bail bonds to get employees back to work.[4]

Other corporations, at great expense and inconvenience, have rebuilt downtown corporate headquarters instead of exiting the decaying urban areas for more attractive suburban locations. In Peoria, Illinois, Caterpillar wanted to put its general office headquarters on a nice green field site adjacent to its research and engine facility. It would be attractive and convenient. The city fathers went to Caterpillar and said, "The downtown area really needs that big, attractive, multimillion dollar building. It will help renovate the downtown. We know that there are going to be all sorts of problems in picking up all the little property owners to purchase the site. But for the good of the community, we need that building downtown." Caterpillar said, "Okay, the economics don't support the choice to locate downtown, but for the betterment of the community, we'll do it."

In 1985, Whirlpool purchased Washington School in St. Joseph, Michigan, which had been closed down. Whirlpool could have built a modern office building elsewhere for much less money, but it purchased the school and spent an additional $3.5 million to renovate it for the Kitchen Aid Division's marketing and administrative headquarters. Today the property is the site of over 80 jobs, and it is on the tax roles to the benefit of the city.

Armstrong World Industries wanted to build a new office building on a 600-acre tract of land west of Lancaster, Pennsylvania. Top management realized that it was in the company's interest to maintain a vibrant, attractive city if it were to recruit good employees to work in Lancaster. Enlightened self-interest caused them to build the office complex downtown instead. The city has received national recognition for the rejuvenation of its downtown area. It was in Armstrong's best interest, management believes, to help remake a beautiful city and a pleasant place for people to live and work.

New Brunswick, New Jersey, home of Johnson & Johnson, was a classic example of an industrialized city that had been allowed to run down. All the large retail stores had fled the downtown area. Johnson & Johnson would liked to have moved out too: the spot its management had in mind was out in the country, a magnificent location. The land was very inexpensive. Buildings could be put up quickly at quite a reasonable cost. Many employees lived within relatively easy commuting distance of this area of New Jersey. Access to and from work would be easy for them. If a poll had been taken of Johnson & Johnson employees who worked in downtown New Brunswick, they would have overwhelmingly opted for the rural setting. But the board chairman and CEO, Richard Sellars, made the decision to stay in New Brunswick, where the company had been founded. He would lead an effort to revitalize the city. His decision was to complicate his personal life, not only in terms of his commuting—the new spot contemplated was near his home—but also in terms of the problems he would face inside and outside the company.

It would be a huge job. Sellars had to fight to get federal government support. A new highway had to be built that would take interstate trucks around instead of right through the city. The entire retail area downtown had to be totally rehabilitated. If a quality retail area could be built, people would be attracted, helping to revitalize the center city. The city's leadership and the local business community needed to get behind the effort. But there was division, with Republicans fighting Democrats and activists fighting conservatives. Sellars had to contend with the sentiments inside the company, which had grown to a virtually unanimous vote of, "Let's get out of here." There was crime in the city. Parking and traffic were annoyances. Sellars persisted. Today the New Brunswick experience is a model of federal, state, local, industry, and community cooperation to rebuild a city. The Johnson & Johnson headquarters was built at a huge cost; the nine acres of land purchased for the downtown site cost almost 25 times what the nearly forty acres in the country would have cost. Building costs downtown were considerably more expensive also. Nonetheless, the result is that New Brunswick is on an upward path in terms of rehabilitation.

THE TITHING OF TIME

Corporate executives, as well as all employees, give not only money but their time and skills to worthy causes. Franklin D. Murphy, of the Times-Mirror in Los Angeles, for example, devotes about a third of his time to nonprofit organizations. One CEO of a major firm located in New York City, typical of many other corporate heads across America, said, "CEOs, officers and employees of companies all over America make the whole volunteer system work. It's one thing to say, 'Let's give $50,000 to the Boys Club or $50,000 to Junior Achievement.' It's another thing for me and others to accept the job, as I did for example, to become chairman of Junior Achievement because Junior Achievement's goal is to teach kids in the elementary grades what the free enterprise system is all about. So I took that job. And it uses up a considerable amount of my time. It cuts into my personal time. Yesterday afternoon I spent two hours at a Salvation Army board meeting trying to decide on some real estate transactions for housing for kids. I spent an evening recently at a place called the Covenant House watching kids come out of the streets with dagger wounds and diseases. The compassion that exists in the business community is unbelievable. If business people stopped giving their time to outside causes tomorrow, what would happen to America? We would have a holocaust in this country, that's what. It would be a tragedy from which we would never recover."

A solid and important step toward the achievement of a sense of self-respect is getting a good job and performing well in it. For many young people, especially among urban area minorities, it is extremely difficult to qualify for a good job. Their opportunities for work, any kind of decent work, are limited. Many are never able to establish any sort of work record or learn the skills and work habits needed for employment in well paying jobs. In New York City, Delbert C. Staley, of NYNEX, started the summer jobs program in 1981. Under his leadership over 10,000 jobs for 16–19-year-olds were solicited. The second year it was run by the president of Citicorp, and the third year by the head of Philip Morris, and after that by the head if IBM. Each summer up to 40,000 youths are employed, and a fair percentage of them eventually go on and become permanent employees of the participating companies.

The National Advisory Council on Minorities in Engineering (NACME) was formed to increase the number of minority engineers. Reginald H. Jones, former chairman and CEO of General Electric, was its first chairman. The impetus for this grew out of a concern that General Electric had about being unable to integrate blacks into upper management to the degree they would like. The real problem, they realized, was qualified supply. A very small number of blacks were graduating with engineering degrees, and many of these came from schools where General Electric did not extensively recruit. If one looks at the demographics of this country, one finds that the under-25-year-old population will be shrinking until about the year 2000 and that there is an increasing percentage of minorities in that population. During Jones's chairmanship, of

NACME, 35 large corporations joined the national effort. In his words, "Without any government help, we have been able to triple the number of black engineering graduates and also show significant increases for other minority groups in the technical professions. This accomplishment was one of the most heartwarming experiences of my tenure as a chief executive officer. I was truly encouraged that I could get so many fellow CEOs to join me in raising the necessary funds and then devoting the time to enlist the support of their associates in this endeavor. It did require a great deal of effort because we had to start back at the secondary school level and then follow these students through their university life and then on into the business world."[5]

Fund-raising efforts involve much more than just collecting monetary donations. They involve giving great amounts of time to organize and carry out the fund-raising activities themselves. The real generosity of successful business people does not lie so much in their giving of money—their wealth permits that and they are glad to make contributions—but in their giving of their time to organize and motivate charitable fund raising activities. Perhaps the best known community fund raising effort is the United Way, or the United Foundation—it has different names in different cities. The United Foundation Community Fund system really got started in Detroit. Henry Ford II, Walter Reuther, and other business and labor leaders decided that there could be much more effective community service if the unions and the companies got together to cooperate in a single campaign. This would minimize fund-raising costs, and respected members of the community could, together, get behind a single effort of raising and allocating money.

After the Detroit riots there arose a strong feeling in the black community in Detroit that it was apart from the rest of the city. They felt that black charities weren't being adequately recognized by the United Foundation; they saw money going to suburban Boy Scout groups and that kind of thing. So in 1969 a new funding mechanism was set up to deal with inner-city problems in Detroit, apart from the United Foundation campaign. It was called New Detroit.

In 1970 John Nevin, then with Ford, was made chairman of both the New Detroit and United Foundation campaigns. As Nevin recalls, "I found . . . in 1970, . . . a difficult economic [situation] . . . General Motors was out on strike, and when General Motors goes out on strike in Detroit a lot of other industry goes down with it. So it was going to be a tough campaign, and I found that a number of the large corporations that had been funding New Detroit were really thinking about whether or not they could contribute that money a second year in a row. I talked with Henry Ford about it. I told them we were going to try to get more companies involved, and I said, 'You've got me in an impossible position. The ten largest companies in Detroit contributed 65 percent of the money for New Detroit last year. If the word gets out that they're reducing their funding, my chances of going to mid-size companies and getting more are just nil. I have to know where we are on the base.' So Ford said, 'Well, what do you want me to do?' I said, 'I need some way of finding out what kind of support we're going to get from this group." And Henry Ford said, 'Well, I'll get the senior people of those companies together.'

"With Henry Ford's clout, a week later he's got a meeting at five o'clock in the afternoon, or something like that, of what really is the business leadership of Detroit, the people who have been funding New Detroit. . . . He walked in and said, 'John's got the responsibility to run this drive. He's got to run the New Detroit drive as well as the basic drive. We know this is a tough time and some of you fellows are talking about backing off and he, understandably, is concerned that . . . you [might] back off. He's saying that if he can get this amount of money from the companies who supported last year, he'll take responsibility for going to other companies and getting the rest of his quota. There's no way he can do that if he asks other companies to make up for Ford backing off and General Motors backing off.'

"Mr. Ford wears half-glasses and when he's very serious . . . about the company, he'll pull the half-glasses down and look over them. Among PR guys at Ford, that's a moment of terror, because that says Henry Ford's about to say what he means instead of what somebody wrote for him. He pulled these damn glasses down and says, 'Now we've had a meeting in our company. We've talked about this, and as you know, we're going through tough times too. Our conclusion is that we've got no choice but to fund New Detroit for exactly the same amount of money as we funded last year and that's what we're going to do. What I want to find out today is what you guys are going to do.' Oh my God, I walked out of there with 95 percent of the quota for those six or seven companies.

"I was in Henry Ford's office when we discussed this thing, and he looked out the window of the office. He lives in Grosse Pointe, and if you're sitting in his corner office and looking at Grosse Pointe, you look right over the part of Detroit that burned a year before. He said to me something that I'll never forget. He stood at the window and he said, 'You know, John, I stood here just a few short months ago and watched this city burning between my office and my house and we've got to make sure that never happens again.'

"I don't believe he's a saint or anything like that, but in the gutty decisions that counted, that guy has a social conscience that's just extraordinary. There is an example of a guy using his clout . . . to get something done."

V
PERSPECTIVES

24

Measures of Success

In 1917, When B. C. Forbes introduced to America a new magazine that bore his name, he included a sharply worded editorial in the first issue. "Business," he wrote, "was originated to produce happiness, not to pile up millions." Forbes questioned the commonly held perception of success. "To the business man, success heretofore too often has been merely to become rich," wrote Forbes. "That is not a high standard. It is a standard, happily, that is passing. . . . More and more men of achievement and wealth are becoming increasingly concerned over their reputation, over the regard in which they are held by their fellow men. They are more anxious to enhance their standing in public opinion than in Bradstreet's." More than this, Forbes also pointed to the dangers of living solely to succeed in business; it is a grave mistake to pursue only the material and to neglect the enjoyment of the nonmaterial, the ideal, the spiritual. "What profiteth it a man to gain uncounted riches," asked Forbes, "if he thereby sacrifices his better self, his nobler qualities of manhood? . . . The man who depends on his bank account to insure him a happy life reaps disappointment. Success is, or should be, the ambition of each of us. But success need not necessarily be measured by dollars."[1]

ACHIEVEMENTS

Success is less a matter of what one acquires and more a matter of what one achieves. It embraces achievements in making genuine contributions to the welfare and happiness of others, as well as the perfection of qualities one develops within oneself. Instead of concerning oneself with getting valuables, it is important to work at becoming a valued person. The kinds of things we ultimately achieve depend upon the kinds of people we have fashioned ourselves into. People who develop their minds and skills and standards—informed, intelligent, caring, and ethical people—see more opportunities, and they invite and attract more opportunities than people who do not develop themselves.

Through focusing his attention wholly upon getting, a person is apt to miss out on involving himself wholeheartedly with the important tasks of achieving. Success is elusive. Those who pursue the commonly held measures of success—wealth, power, and prestige—usually fail to achieve success itself. This is because they fail to prepare themselves to be able to accomplish anything of genuine merit and because they are unable and unwilling to work hard enough at contributing anything of real benefit to the world. Again, a sure way to fail to be successful is to work primarily to obtain what most people see as marks of success. Any achievement of substance demands substantial effort and sacrifice; it nearly always requires sustained, dedicated effort. It is often said of such an effort, "It was a labor of love." And indeed it is. Love of a great cause, love of the difficult, and love of fulfilling some lofty aim—these loves—lead people to succeed. The person who is primarily out for his own comfort, who is merely calculating what can be gotten for himself, won't pay the price that achievement of genuine contributions exact; at best, this person will endure a miserable existence.

CHARACTER

To be sure, the path to earning success begins with the self. In the world of business this involves making oneself into a worthwhile human being: a kind, decent, ethical person who always plays it straight. Readers who are familiar with Sloan Wilson's novel, *The Man in the Gray Flannel Suit*, may recall the description of a situation in which one of the characters, Tony Bugala, briefly contemplates a shady scheme. "No—that wouldn't work," Tony thinks to himself. "In the long-run it never paid to try that stuff, not if you planned on getting big. If you wanted to become really tops in the business, you had to forget that small-time cleverness and play it straight."[2] Here Wilson is telling us something about human nature and something about our world: There are many temptations, but in the long run these shortcuts do not lead to success.

To succeed in our respective fields, whatever they may be, we must first succeed at being good human beings: a reality enunciated by many highly successful people.

William R. Timken, Jr., of the Timken Company: "If you want to be in business for the long-run you can't chisel, cheat and do the things that are illegal and immoral, or they'll catch up with you."

Robert A. Schoellhorn, of Abbott Laboratories: "Word travels fast in this business, and if we weren't being fair, we wouldn't be growing."

Barron Hilton, of Hilton Hotels: "Honesty is a very important aspect of any successful business career. A person's reputation is built on his being honest. And when a person gets a bad reputation, it affects his ability to deal with people and, more importantly, particularly the lenders and the financial people that have to be a part of your ability to go out and develop a system of hotel properties. You have to have the financial world behind you, and you're judged by them by your honesty and integrity."

John M. Henske, of Olin Corporation: "It's better to work with people honestly, openly, fairly—not try to get ahead by cheating or gouging or lying. . . . You'll see unethical behavior and it may not get punished, or in fact, it may actually get rewarded for a while. . . . I can think back over my career, of people that I thought were getting ahead improperly—who got ahead so far and then their careers just stopped. Somehow or other it caught up with them. And they don't go any further and usually they go down. And you see enough of that to say, 'It just doesn't pay off to get ahead by cheating or hurting somebody else.' "

MORAL COURAGE

The greatest strength of business in a free economy is its ability to change, to adapt to the moving targets of ever-changing markets. Business is quick to adopt new products and methods in the fast pace of technological advancements. A competitor must change, or it will be replaced by a better one. Competition promotes change—something cheaper, something with greater ability to perform, something more efficient, something more attractive to consumers. And because of the power of the market mechanism to allocate resources swiftly and effectively, business people learn that survival demands adaptability; success often dictates that one be ever alert and quick to change. The free-enterprise, market economy of the West makes business the most change oriented of all institutions.

As a result, business people tend to be pragmatic. They do what works best. They are constantly drawn away from old methods that time and circumstance have rendered obsolete, to change to new methods that will work. Thus business, because of its orientation toward doing whatever is required in order to survive and flourish, is particularly susceptible to honoring the view that "good ethics is good business," largely because of its pragmatic appeal.

There is undeniable evidence that good ethics really is good business. For instance, good citizenship in the community helps to win community support for projects and business expansion. Also, a company that produces or markets shoddy goods will lose clients and customers. Fair treatment of suppliers nets a company loyal service, good attention to quality, and timely delivery of supplies. Fair and respectful treatment of employees is also good for business, because when an organization mistreats its employees everyone can usually see it, and the better people will refuse to work for that organization. And those who must work for that employer out of the necessity of their own circumstances, will most likely not give it their full loyalty and best efforts.

These are all reasons why abiding by high ethical standards is good for business; however, this position is conspicuously lacking in character. If the best reason someone can muster for acting ethically is to be able to further his own private gain, we can conclude with fair certainty that ethics and morality will be early and swift causalities whenever conditions are reversed—and surely this will occur. The ethical approach is superior on all counts to the unethical path; but, to justify ethical behavior with the pathetic reason that it is simply good business actually denies one's authentic commitment to lofty ideals and reveals a person who is little more than a crude materialist, a vulgarian of money.

True leaders do not gain their influence because of clever, pragmatic schemes to achieve established aims. They derive their appeal to others, and thereby earn leadership status, because of their authentic commitment to lofty ideals and standards. Methods that are insincere and self-serving are disquieting to others' sense of what is right and a leader who uses them is thereby likely to lose their support. In large measure, true leaders derive their power to influence from their adherence to the view that being on the wrong side of the highest standards of conduct is unacceptable. People follow leaders who believe in things that good people are proud to follow. And because they are unshakably loyal to clear standards and patterns of conduct, these leaders are able to evoke unremitting loyalty to those same ideals among their followers.

Integrity is destroyed whenever a person follows ideals merely because he expects something in return. As the view "good ethics is good business" percolates through an organization the highest kind of idealism is destroyed; people's loyalties are jolted away from what is right to what is expedient, and an unsuitable atmosphere grows up in which ideals are disowned and a sort of fragmented morality blossoms forth. Lofty ideals and standards are thrown aside, and schemes are devised and implemented primarily because they are expected to work—rationalizations are concocted to justify them afterwards. Thereby, both character and stability are diminished. Here, moral courage is called for. Whenever pragmatism is given as the chief justification for morality, it is abundantly clear what remains uppermost in that person's heart. It is wise, therefore, to justify ethical behavior wholly on moral grounds and to leave the processes of business change to be justified on the pragmatic bases of survival and business success.

CONCEPTS OF SUCCESS

Success, like love, is defined and measured in many ways, and each person will define it differently. Still, there are recurring themes in what the nation's business leaders see as being success.

1. It isn't accumulation of wealth. "Success," says Timm F. Crull, of Carnation, "certainly isn't being able to drive a Cadillac or a Mercedes, or having a big bank account." Money and property may be an indication of success, but they aren't the chief aim of those who have been successful; they are a result of success, a by-product of accomplishing something of value. Wealth, in and of itself, is not the focal point of those who are most successful in business. Instead of having, business leaders see success more in terms of accomplishing, of being useful to the world. Nathan S. Ancell, of Ethan Allen, says, "You've got to live a constructive life. You've got to fulfill yourself. And you've got to have a reason for being on earth. You must have done something before you die, and making money is not doing a thing except maybe to fill your mouth and give you 45 suits and six houses. But that isn't it; that's not where it's at."

The chief purpose of business is to create value with limited resources, and successful business leaders see this as an exciting adventure. John E. Swearingen, chairman and CEO of Continental Illinois and former Chairman and CEO of Amoco, says, "I put money down toward the bottom. Sometimes I think that people who are successful in the business world work for a hell of a lot less than they work for just for the sheer pleasure of doing the kinds of things they do and building things that they're trying to build, and what they're able to achieve."

And even when a person acquires wealth, the question arises: What does he do with it? Roy A. Anderson, of Lockheed, has another measure of success. "I don't measure it in terms of money," says Anderson. "I just don't. I just don't think that's important, because beyond a certain point you've got a satisfactory income, you can do practically anything that you want to do that's sensible, or whatever you want. And those who are fortunate enough to accumulate considerable wealth, what do they do with it? . . . What does he do with his spare time? . . . If he is fortunate enough to move up in the corporate body, he usually has quite a bit of resources available to him. What does he do with them? I think a measure of success is just that. What does he do with that? Does he let others share in his material things, such as working in United Way, working in community activities, working in church activities?"

Andrew Carnegie believed that the life story of a rich man should have two periods; the first, of acquiring wealth, and the second, of distributing wealth for the improvement of mankind. He rejected the word "philanthropist." It was Carnegie's belief that the rich man who really died disgraced was the one who died wealthy; he might have distributed that wealth sensibly for the public good.

2. It isn't living for oneself. Success is adding to the lives of others, to the betterment of other groups. William R. Timken, Jr. sees success as providing benefits to the constituent groups he serves—the shareholders, the employees, the customers and the communities. To Timken it is important to be a builder and creator of jobs and opportunities in the company rather than a destroyer—particularly for a short-term gain. He says, "When they carve . . . on [my] tombstone I'd like them to say

that he put in more than he took out." Not living just for oneself begins with the idea that there is a responsibility to others, and success involves meeting that responsibility.

To John H. Bryan, Jr., of Sara Lee, success includes "taking care of those who depend on you." He says, "You can't get away with just being happy yourself. You've got some responsibility to take care of [others who] depend on you." In a well run organization, top leaders derive great personal satisfaction from seeing others succeed in accomplishing worthwhile aims.

Robert Williams, of the James River Corporation, says, "The greatest satisfaction over the years has been to see people heavily involved in turning losing businesses into winning businesses. To see the frown and trust and confidence problems disappear and turn into smiles and an atmosphere of openness and trust, where people are having a good time, pushing ahead, ensuring their futures, and sharing in their own success."

3. It's making the most of what you've got. A motto that H. J. Heinz, himself, had placed in offices, halls, waiting rooms, and work areas in every Heinz installation was, "Do the best you can, where you are, with what you have today."[3] Success, as Theodore Roosevelt observed is, "doing one's duty well in the path where one's life is led."

Each person has different talents and encounters different opportunities. The question is, What do we do with them? Are they seized and used, or are they allowed to pass by as if they never existed? Cornell C. Maier, of Kaiser Aluminum & Chemical, states it this way: "Success is . . . making the most of the facilities and opportunities you have. You might be doing very well, but maybe circumstances are such that it's easy to do well. You might not be doing very well, but maybe under the circumstances you are doing extremely well." The important idea here is not, What can I get with what I've got? Instead it is, What can I do with what I've got?

Success is accomplishing something with talents and scarce resources. And it is giving one's best efforts, or as Jack D. Sparks, of Whirlpool, says, it is a sense that "you've given it your best shot." All people will not end up at the top of an organization, but that does not mean each person can not be successful. Success is not a matter of achieving distinction by virtue of one's position; it is better seen as a well fought fight, a well traveled journey, a well lived adventure; it's doing the best under the circumstances. R. Gordon McGovern, of Campbell Soup, says, "My definition of success is rather simplistic. It is to take what God gave you in the way of talent and to maximize it over as much time as God gives you to have. The real exercise is to find out who you are and then to look around in the world today and say, 'Okay, that kind of talent can best be used here.' And then you go do it up to the very utmost of your ability. In other words, don't let 40 percent go by the board, and don't sit doing A when you really should be doing B. Match up your talent where you can put it to work. If you are a salesman, be a salesman. Don't be afraid of that job just because people think Willy Lohman was a despicable character. . . . It requires integrity and it requires virtue. . . . And there's nothing wrong with any job as long as you're doing . . . the best you possibly can. And I think the only way to get at that is to try."

4. It's adding to human progress. Material progress and human progress are not poles apart, as many believe. The former need not occur at the expense of the latter. There are, to be sure, situations where material gain has been reached at a terrible price in human terms. But it does not follow that material progress must and always will trample upon human dignity. Much of the human condition is unquestionably improved through material progress—adding to the abundance and to the widespread distribution and consumption of material goods.

Business need not apologize for its role in feeding, clothing, housing, transporting, healing, and easing the burdens of humans. And persons who contribute to these and other ends having to do with adding to an economy's abundance can rightfully take pride and satisfaction in their achievements. In the biographical materials on George Westinghouse, it is reported that his greatest satisfaction in life came from the knowledge that what he had accomplished as an inventor and a businessman had contributed so largely to the benefit and comfort of others. He is not alone in this. Robert A. Schoellhorn, of Abbott Laboratories, says, "I want to know that people are living better and healthier lives as a result of the products we developed." Of all the kinds of human satisfaction, none compare to the satisfaction derived from knowing that others are better off because of something we have done. Success is contributing to that end in meaningful ways. It is the creation of value in whatever field. Robert S. McNamara defines success as "contributing to [the] welfare of the society you are associated with. . . . . It's a society [which] goes beyond national boundaries. And Richard L. Gelb, of Bristol-Myers Squibb, says, "Everything we do, in one way or other, makes people healthier and happier. I think I've gotten a great deal of satisfaction out of that."

5. It's building something worthwhile. The knowledge that he will not remain alive forever is disquieting to each man. And so, to cheat death of its inevitable sting, he spends the intervening years between his birth and his passing, trying to build something of enduring value—something as a reminder that he was alive, and something that carries on to help better the lives of others who follow. He plants orchards whose fruit he knows he will never eat; but, his mind rests, eased with the knowledge that those who follow will be better fed. Success is seen by many as building a lasting structure—an organization, a movement, a way of thinking, almost anything, that lives on and serves others. A failure is a person who leaves a mess for others to repair; he is delinquent in assuring a better condition for future generations.

A Business leader who is a thinking, caring individual, and there are many, sees his role as a steward of his enterprise. His responsibility lies in leaving it in a better condition to perform effectively in the future than when he assumed charge of its leadership.

Robert B. Shetterly, of Clorox: "The most successful business executive is the guy who plays a part in the building of something . . . of enduring value."

Cornell C. Maier, of Kaiser Aluminum & Chemical: "I hope . . . I've left behind a good company which provides opportunities for all people regardless of sex or race or creed, . . . and it does provide real opportunities for people to develop their own talents and skills to the best of their abilities. . . . And I hope I also leave behind a legacy of a company that Henry Kaiser started—one that was concerned and was involved in the communities."

Frank W. Luerssen, of Inland Steel: "I think it's my job to get the company restructured and to return it to profitability and to set a course for the future that has substantially more assurance of continued success."

Philip E. Lippincott, of Scott Paper: "I have a strong desire to leave this business feeling both the individual that succeeds me and the fortunes of the business are going to be even better and more secure in looking forward toward the future than they were when I was here."

6. It's developing people and watching them grow and accomplish things. Little ever gets accomplished in business by one person; accomplishments involve the dedicated efforts of many skilled people. The job of the manager is to provide growth and vision to personnel, to train and develop people. Top-level people are usually where they are because they realize the importance of developing subordinates, and they succeed because they are good at it. In our time it is inconceivable that a manager could be counted successful who is incapable or unwilling to develop personnel. The development of people is not only a mark of success, but also a source of genuine satisfaction. "The greatest satisfaction is to see young people, especially, move up the ladder and develop and to get promoted and develop a sense of pride and loyalty with the company," says Eugene R. Olson, of Deluxe Check Printers. "That gives me a real sense of satisfaction, especially if I've had anything to do with them."

John H. McConnell, of Worthington Industries, says, "The biggest enjoyment I get is watching people, like . . . our president, grow from a raw 19-year-old kid and develop up through the years. . . . I've got many plant superintendents, foremen, all through the company that you watch develop and grow. And that's enjoyment for me. I see this happen, and you watch it, and it makes it all worthwhile." In the pursuit for success, it is easy to neglect the opportunities to extend a hand of help or give a word of encouragement to others. Pressures to succeed and move ahead can easily crowd out one's efforts to make it possible for peers and subordinates to perform better or expand their capabilities through training and development. When eyes are fixed on the profit and loss statements there is a tendency to forget about the human assets on the balance sheet—the personnel, who produce the profits.

Charles S. Mechem, Jr., of Taft Broadcasting, sees a successful person, in part, as being one who can look at his "human balance sheet" and see on it people who he has helped and who are now successful. Success, too, includes building a satisfying place of employment for those who work there. It is unthinkable to consider someone successful who runs a profitable enterprise dollarwise that is a source of misery for all who work there.

Robert C. Williams, of the James River Corporation, believes that a measure of a manager's success is "happy, satisfied employees who share in the success of the company."

George A. Schaefer, of Caterpillar, phrases this idea of success as, "getting people to perform at their maximum capabilities and having them enjoy every minute of it."

7. It's earning the respect of others. Although the approbation of others ought not to be an end in itself—that is destructive to integrity—it is often a by-product of a job well done, a life well lived, and a measure of one's success at achieving worthy ideals and aims.

Socrates pointed out that we should not regard all men's opinions equally. Those of intelligence and virtue should command our respect and attention. It is important to assess the nature of praise one receives; if it is only for accomplishments that have been made at the expense of higher values, that success ought to be soberly questioned. George A. Roberts, of Teledyne, says, "The community has to accept the fact that you are indeed a worthy and successful man. And, worthiness, I think, is equally important. . . . I don't have any respect for businessmen who flaunt the law, get into trouble, . . . hire a very good lawyer, and escape some kind of verdict. . . . No matter how much money they make or how many leadership jobs they've had, they're not very successful unless they can measure up in [an] ethical way and not have *any* kind . . . of a bad stamp on [them]." Recognition can be enormously satisfying. It ought not be pursued as an end; but when it comes from respected friends and colleagues or from peers, it is a welcomed assurance that the recipient is reasonably "in tune" with credible critics.

8. It's enjoying one's work. An indirect measure of success is the degree of enjoyment one experiences in performing life's tasks. Every moment may not be enjoyable, and there are unpleasant times, but overall, it is enjoyed. There are exceptions, of course. Who could say he enjoyed a war effort? Yet there, too, some enjoyment or satisfaction may be had through contributing to a worthy cause, however disagreeable the circumstances and tasks may be. The ultimate issue at stake here, and the factor that leads to enjoyment, is whether the endeavor is perceived as worthwhile. Our best efforts are usually reserved for the most worthwhile quests. And if what we do is worthwhile and we recognize that it is, we will tend to extend ourselves fully and render our highest level of effort. From this, some measure of enjoyment is bound to arise. A fair measure of whether a job is worthwhile is gotten by the extent to which we find it enjoyable, particularly if we are not shallow people.

Another reason enjoyment of work is important is that great accomplishments demand great sacrifices, and a person is not willing to give much of himself to things he little believes in or little enjoys. The trick is to engage oneself in the right tasks, matching self with work. An important ingredient leading to success, as Thomas H. Cruikshank, of Halliburton, observes is "to be doing something you enjoy doing." The ultimate is to find the perfect match, where work isn't seen as unpleasant. "You ought to enjoy your work," says David T. Kimball, of General Signal. "I think if you don't you ought to question that."

There is a decision some people face, whether to work at a job they dislike because of pay or convenience factors or to work at a job they enjoy but that carries less prestige or less financial rewards. Obviously, many people are lodged in unpleasant predicaments and do not have the luxury to choose. The single parent trying to raise a family is beset with the realities of everyday expenses and may not have flexibility. But there are others who are free to choose and nevertheless opt for the wrong things and end up quite unhappy. Richard J. Flamson III, of Security Pacific, says, "I . . . think that the most unsuccessful person could be the person who made a lot of money but hated it all the while and was tormented by the responsibility and had to force himself to do all the things that you want to be able to do easily. I would think that success is having the job that isn't work." James R. Eiszner, of CPC International, adds to that with the idea, "I think if you don't enjoy your job, you are ruining your life. And there's another job around the corner. It may not be paying as well as the one you have now, or it may not be situated with as nice an office for you, . . . but that's not important. What's more important is enjoying what you do."

9. It's a well-rounded existence. The human creature is far too complex and multifaceted to be described, measured, or understood from only one perspective or measured by a single standard. This is a fancy way of saying that there is much more to life than just one's bank balance. A successful person is one who is reasonably well rounded. He is one who has not sacrificed all of the other parts of his life, leaving them in ruin, in order to achieve in one narrow arena. In fact, that practice could be risky. Bruce Smart, of the Continental Group, observes that it is better to diversify one's life, much as one seeks diversity in an investment portfolio. "You ought not to be in a position where if any one element of your life collapses on you, for whatever reason, . . . that you don't have something else left to hang onto," says Smart.

The road to a successful business career makes many demands of the individual along the way. It puts pressures and burdens on one's time and freedom. It demands sacrifices. In looking back on their careers, particularly during the years when they were younger and had small children at home, some very successful people regret that they didn't make more time for their families. They feel now that their lives would have been richer and hence even more successful had they done that. One CEO, typical of those who have this feeling, expressed his regret in these words: "I think I'd have to find a better balance, let's say between family and work. I unquestionably neglected my family during my early years of my working career for the sake of the business. Now, I've heard it said, that you can't be a good family man and a good CEO at the same time. I disagree with that. I think you can. I think it's hard. It's easier to bury yourself in your work and do nothing else. It's a lot harder to pull yourself away from it." "Don't let the driving for business success screw up your life," recommends Andrew C. Sigler, of Champion International. "[It's] better [to] lead a broad, general existence than think [entirely] about the attainment of position, because if you keep running that road you're going to turn around someday and find out that you don't have anything else."

Another CEO recommended that people "Be able to find the right balance between business life and home life. The man who's all over the business and ignores his wife and children is not successful in my opinion. You've got to be equally as successful in developing your own children and maintaining a kind of a healthy, respected home life. That goes in my mind with total satisfaction." Frank W. Considine, of National Can, tells his people, "If you're having a problem spending time at home I can show you how you can get that 6:00 o'clock airplane in the morning and get to New York in time for your meeting or get to the West Coast and you get credit for being home the night before with the family. . . . If a person really wants to be home they can find ways generally, unless they're on an unusual assignment like going overseas for a couple of months." And William B. Walton, Sr., of Holiday Inns, writes, "Is there anything finer, really, for growing boys and girls than a parent's attention and affection, counsel and comradeship? What is a horse or a boat or a trip compared to the warm security of belonging in someone else's heart? The so-called advantages people think they are providing for their families through material goods are misleading if they are produced at the expense of close relationships."[4]

10. It's a clear conscience. A successful person can live with himself. He can face his reflection in the mirror and feel comfortable with the person looking back. Sleeping well at night, resting with a clear conscience, is knowing that he has done his very best, honestly and conscientiously. It's being reasonably sure that when others see him they will say, "He's an honest guy." We all know that to obtain the internal satisfaction a clear conscience gives, a person must be scrupulously honest with himself; there is no room for hedging or rationalizing to try to make wrong appear right in one's mind. Success ultimately involves strict adherence to the truth and to what is good and noble and genuine. Success then, is mastering the self, and a clear conscience is a reasonably good indication that that is occurring.

THE FINAL MEASURE

Herodotus, in his accounts of the Persian Wars, tells of when Croesus, King of the Lydian Empire at the height of its prosperity, was visited by Solon the Athenian.[5] On the third or fourth day, and after his servants had shown Solon his vast and glorious treasures, Croesus asked the wise and much traveled Athenian a leading question: "Whom, of all men that you have seen, do you consider the most happy?" Croesus believed himself the happiest of all mortals, but he wanted yet another man's praise and assurance that he really did "have it all." Perhaps he had faintly begun to wonder if there just might be more to living than mere getting. And surely Solon must have seen before him, clothed in purple and gold and decked in rare ornaments and jewels, and making a grand spectacle of himself, a hollow, pathetic figure of a man who, after acquiring more wealth than anyone else of his time, still needed praise and also just might be wondering, "Is this really all there is?"

Unawed by the gaudiness and petty ostentation he saw, Solon must have shocked Croesus when he answered, "Tellus of Athens."

"But who, after Tellus," Croesus persisted, "seemed the happiest?"

And we are told that when Solon answered, "Cleobis and Bito," Croesus was angered. Didn't his treasuries filled with gold and silver bricks count for more than these other men's honor and public admiration? He could not understand why Solon valued his happiness so little. Solon acknowledged what was obvious, saying to Croesus, "I see that you are wonderfully rich and the lord of many nations;" but he cautioned against saluting as happy one who is still in the midst of life and hazards and believes his possessions can be a fortress for safety and comfort. And he went on to explain to Croesus that just as it is not sensible to crown and proclaim as victorious the wrestler who has yet to enter the ring, with respect to the matter of Croesus's happiness he could not give an answer until he learned that Croesus had ended his life happily.

At the time Croesus thought Solon was ill-bred and a fool for calling into doubt the obvious measure of one's success. But surely Solon's words must have tormented Croesus in the years that followed, as when he learned of the untimely death of his most favored son, and later when he was stripped of wealth and power, and again when he was about to be burned at the stake.[6]

The story of mankind is the story of a struggle. Each of us hungers to succeed, to be loved and recognized, to count for something. Many of us want to leave behind something of lasting significance as a reminder that we were once here. Most people want to be good; they want to live good lives. They want to make a difference. But each man is caught in a web of good and evil, and hence each man must struggle to make his own way through life, facing his own urges and having to make choices along the way. Each human is a mixture of avarice and generosity, cruelty and kindness, indifference and compassion, neglect and reason, self-centeredness and service. And because we have a mixture of strengths and frailties, good sense and foolishness, our characters are both sound and flawed; each life holds both noble and unpardonable motives and deeds. Each man's days are filled with a fragmented array of unspeakable wrongs and praiseworthy acts of good.

But after a man dies, and after his wealth and possessions and power are gone—he really only had the use of them for a few decades—all that remains then are the results of his adventures. His actions are imprinted on the lives of others, on those who lived alongside of him and on those who come after that. And in the end, and after each action and its consequence has been dusted off and inspected and sorted into one side of the ledger or another, each man will know whether, on balance, his life was well lived or ill spent. And each man will learn, after all things are considered, whether he brought more joy or pain to the world through how he lived. He will have left only one question: Did I do well or ill while I was here?

Will he die happily? That depends on how others view his death. Will those who remain rejoice at his passing, or will they be saddened and feel his death as a tragic loss?

Each generation has produced its share of men wholly engrossed in money and furthering their own advancement and welfare at the expense of others. Some of these people succeed in attaining wealth and positions of influence. And to those ends they use others without regard to principle or feeling. They grind up employees, cheat partners, lie to regulatory bodies and the public, and swindle customers. Yet they genuinely believe that they are successful because of what they hold title to. And they laugh at the humility and the lack of aggressiveness in others, thinking them naive for not applauding or for not using their methods of getting ahead. But when each one dies, despite the fact that many try to repair the damage they have caused by purchasing themselves a good name through their philanthropy, those who know them or have been affected by them felt relieved, and may even mutter to themselves, "Good. That rotten snake is dead. We can all sleep a little more soundly knowing that he's gone."

And in each generation there have also been men wholly different—men who have worked tirelessly and sincerely, not just to better themselves as whole persons but primarily to improve the lot of others. Samuel Milton Jones was one such man.[7] Born in Wales in 1846, he emigrated with his parents to the United States in 1849. His formal education lasted scarcely three years. He worked in the Pennsylvania oil fields for twenty-one years and then moved to Ohio, where he pioneered the development of newly developed oil fields. Six years later he began inventing improvements for oil field appliances. In 1894 he organized his own company, the Acme Sucker Rod Company, which earned him a tidy fortune. He was worth a half a million dollars—a good-sized sum in his time. While in industry he saw clearly the social and economic problems that arose from industrial organization. He felt that labor had fallen to a level of slavery. Factories lacked humane treatment of employees. This, he worked to change. He hung a placard bearing the Golden Rule in his factory, an act that brought about his nickname, "Golden Rule Jones." In his own factory Jones pioneered labor reforms: the eight-hour workday, a minimum wage, paid vacations, no timekeeper, no overtime, no child labor, no piecework, and a cash bonus at Christmas. He advocated trade unionism for his men. He suggested a cooperative insurance plan for worker illness and injuries. He built Golden Rule Park and Playground, and then added to that complex, Golden Rule Hall.

In 1887 Jones was elected mayor of Toledo, running as a Republican. His platform was for a better social order and municipal reform. As mayor he refused to follow the party's dictates—he would not grant special favors to political and business interests. He ran for reelection three more times but now as an independent, winning by large majorities, and he served as mayor until his death in 1904. Jones established civil service in the police and water department and an eight-hour day and minimum wage for city workers.

Kindergartens were established during his administration. There were free public concerts. He opened public playgrounds, too, and golf courses. He fought against private profit at the public's expense; he replaced police clubs with light canes; and he put a stop to arresting on suspicion and holding without charge.

All the newspapers were against him. The town's clergy opposed him, as did the chamber of commerce, the political parties, and the anti-saloon league. And, too, institutional voices of Toledo, the pulpit, and the press all thundered his condemnation. But the people kept reelecting him, each time by an overwhelming margin. The big, sandy-complexioned Welsh immigrant believed that working people and the poor and outcasts were entitled to some of his service. He was simple and honest. He had a great reliance on the plain truth and the power of ordinary reasonableness. Jones was above trying to even scores. When he died, the only wounds he left were in the hearts of those who knew him. His progressive policies were carried forward by his close friend, Brand Whitlock, who was elected mayor in 1905 and served until 1913.

Thousands were on hand to bid farewell. From the veranda of his home where his funeral service was held, one could see the throng standing on the lawns outside. The mass of humanity extended across streets and into yards. People stood packed to the street corners and into the side streets. The lines extended all the way to the cemetery. In the crowd were all sorts—a cross-section of humanity. There were judges and meat cutters; shopkeepers and school children; ladies of prominence and other women of questionable virtue; prizefighters, teachers and saloon keepers; men of letters and uneducated immigrants. And they all stood solemnly, and reverently, each in his own thoughts, and tears streaming down each of their faces.

Appendix: Business Leaders Interviewed

The following business leaders generously contributed their time and thoughts to this study through personal interviews from 1985 to 1988.
The titles given reflect the individual's position and organization at the time of the interview.   * Indicates participation by mail.

Nathan S. Ancell
Chairman of the Board
Ethan Allen

Roy A. Anderson
Chairman & CEO
Lockheed

William S. Anderson
Former Chairman & CEO
NCR

William Atteberry
Former Chairman & CEO
Eagle-Picher

J. David Barnes
Chairman & CEO
Mellon Bank

Robert L. Barney
Chairman & CEO
Wendy's International

Michel L. Besson
President & CEO
CertainTeed

Theodore F. Brophy
Chairman & CEO
GTE

John H. Bryan, Jr.
Chairman & CEO
Sara Lee

Waldo H. Burnside
President
Carter, Hawley, Hale Stores

Frank Carlucci
Chairman of the Board
Sears World Trading

Richard A. Clarke
Chairman & CEO
Pacific Gas & Electric

David E. Collins
Vice Chairman
Johnson & Johnson

Joseph E. Connor
Chairman & Senior Partner
Price Waterhouse

Frank W. Considine
Chairman & CEO
National Can

William T. Creson
Chairman & CEO
Crown Zellerbach

Thomas H. Cruikshank
President & CEO
Halliburton

Timm F. Crull
President & CEO
Carnation

Douglas D. Danforth
Chairman & CEO
Westinghouse

James R. Eiszner
President & CEO
CPC International

Lyle Everingham
Chairman & CEO
Kroger

Bernard M. Fauber
Chairman & CEO
Kmart

John W. Fisher
Chairman of the Board
Ball

Richard J. Flamson, III
Chairman & CEO
Security Pacific

Joseph B. Flavin
Chairman & CEO
Singer

Robert E. Fomon
Former Chairman & CEO
E. F. Hutton Group

Robert F. Froehlke
Chairman, IDS Mutual Fund
Former Chairman & CEO
Equitable Life Assurance

Stanley C. Gault
Chairman & CEO
Rubbermaid

Richard L. Gelb
Chairman & CEO
Bristol-Myers Squibb

Gerald Greenwald
Chairman
Chrysler Motors

Walter A. Haas, Jr.
Former Chairman & CEO
Levi Strauss

Donald H. Hall
Chairman of the Board
Hallmark Cards

Philip M. Hampton
Vice Chairman
Bankers Trust of New York

Neil Harlan
Chairman & CEO
McKesson

Richard E. Heckert
Chairman & CEO
E. I. Du Pont de Nemours

John M. Henske
Chairman & Former CEO
Olin

Barron Hilton
Chairman & CEO
Hilton Hotels

William R. Howell
Chairman & CEO
J. C. Penney

Joseph L. Jones
President, Chairman & CEO
Armstrong World Industries

Reginald H. Jones*
Former Chairman & CEO
General Electric

David T. Kearns
Chairman & CEO
Xerox

William Kieschnick
President & CEO
Atlantic Richfield (ARCO)

Robert D. Kilpatrick
Chairman & CEO
Cigna

David T. Kimball
Chairman & CEO
General Signal

Duane R. Kullberg
Managing Partner & CEO
Arthur Andersen

Thomas Laco
Vice Chairman
Procter & Gamble

Charles Lazarus
Chairman & CEO
Toys "R" Us

Lewis W. Lehr
Former Chairman & CEO
Minnesota Mining and
  Manufacturing

Donald D. Lennox
Chairman & CEO
Navistar International

Philip E. Lippincott
Chairman & CEO
Scott Paper

Frank W. Luerssen
Chairman & CEO
Inland Steel

Richard Madden
Chairman & CEO
Potlatch

Peter A. Magowan
Chairman & CEO
Safeway Stores

Richard J. Mahoney
President & CEO
Monsanto

Cornell C. Maier
Chairman & CEO
Kaiser Aluminum & Chemical

Robert H. Malott
Chairman & CEO
FMC

Reuben Mark
Chairman & CEO
Colgate-Palmolive

Charles Marshall
Vice Chairman
AT&T

John H. McConnell
Chairman & CEO
Worthington Industries

Sanford N. McDonnell
Chairman & CEO
McDonnell Douglas

John G. McElwee
Former Chairman & CEO
John Hancock Life Insurance

William G. McGagh
Senior Vice President-Finance
Northrop

R. Gordon McGovern
President & CEO
Campbell Soup

Donald T. McKone
Chairman & CEO
Libby-Owens-Ford

Robert S. McNamara
Former President, Ford Motor
Former U.S. Secretary of Defense
Former President, World Bank

Charles S. Mechem, Jr.
Chairman of the Board
Taft Broadcasting Co.

Robert E. Mercer
Chairman & CEO
Goodyear Tire & Rubber

Gerald B. Mitchell
Chairman & CEO
Dana

Charles W. Moritz
Chairman & CEO
Dun & Bradstreet

Richard M. Morrow
Chairman & CEO
Amoco

J. Richard Munro
Chairman & CEO
Time (Time Warner)

Franklin D. Murphy
Chairman, Executive Committee
Times Mirror

John J. Nevin
Former Chairman, Zenith
Chairman, President & CEO
Firestone Tire & Rubber

Fred O'Green
Chairman & CEO
Litton Industries

Eugene R. Olson
Chairman & CEO
Deluxe Check Printers

Paul F. Oreffice
President & CEO
Dow Chemical

Stanley C. Pace
Chairman & CEO
General Dynamics

Charles W. Parry
Former Chairman & CEO
Alcoa

John E. Peters
President & COO
J. Walter Thompson U.S.A.

Donald E. Petersen
Chairman & CEO
Ford Motor

Thomas L. Phillips
Chairman & CEO
Raytheon

Edmund T. Pratt, Jr.
Chairman & CEO
Pfizer

Robert M. Price
Chairman & CEO
Control Data

Leland Prussia
Chairman of the Board
Bank of America

Charles R. Pullin
Chairman & CEO
Koppers

Jack F. Reichert
Chairman, President & CEO
Brunswick

Burnell R. Roberts
Chairman & CEO
Mead

George A. Roberts
President & CEO
Teledyne

John W. Rogers
Chairman & CEO
United Parcel Service

Michael D. Rose
Chairman & CEO
Holiday Inns

Dickinson C. Ross
Former Chairman of the Board
Johnson & Higgins of
California

Ted J. Saenger
President
Pacific Bell

George A. Schaefer
Chairman & CEO
Caterpillar Tractor

Robert A. Schoellhorn*
Chairman & CEO
Abbott Laboratories

Texas Schramm
President & General Manager
The Dallas Cowboys

Robert B. Shetterly
Former Chairman of the Board
Clorox

Andrew C. Sigler
Chairman & CEO
Champion International

Bruce Smart
Deputy Secretary of Commerce
Former Chairman & CEO
Continental Group

Fredrick W. Smith*
Chairman & CEO
Federal Express

William D. Smithburg
Chairman & CEO
Quaker Oats

Paul H. Smucker
Chairman & CEO
J. M. Smucker

Jack D. Sparks
Chairman, President & CEO
Whirlpool

Edson W. Spencer
Chairman & CEO
Honeywell

Delbert C. Staley
Chairman & CEO
NYNEX

Irving I. Stone
Chairman & CEO
American Greetings

John H. Stookey
Chairman & CEO
National Distillers & Chemical

Robert A. Stranahan, Jr.
Chairman & CEO
Champion Spark Plug

Arthur Ochs Sulzberger
Chairman & CEO
New York Times

John E. Swearingen
Former Chairman & CEO
    Amoco
Chairman & CEO
Continental Illinois

James R. Sylla
President
Chevron USA

Frank J. Tasco
Chairman & CEO
Marsh & McLennan

William R. Timken, Jr.
Chairman of the Board
Timken

J. Ray Topper
President & CEO
Anchor Hocking

Donald H. Trautlein
Former Chairman & CEO
Bethlehem Steel

Peter V. Ueberroth
Commissioner
Major League Baseball

C. William Verity
Former Chairman & CEO
Armco Steel

Hicks B. Waldron
Chairman & CEO
Avon Products

William L. Weiss
Chairman & CEO
Ameritech

William J. Weisz
Vice Chairman & CEO
Motorola

Ben Wattenberg
Senior Fellow
American Enterprise Institute

Robert Wilhelm
Former Chairman of the Board
Emporium Stores

Robert C. Williams
President & COO
James River

Richard D. Wood
Chairman & CEO
Eli Lilly Company

William Woodside
Former Chairman & CEO
American Can (Primerica)

Michael W. Wright
Chairman & CEO
Super Valu Stores

John A. Young
President & CEO
Hewlett-Packard

Notes

CHAPTER 1

1. Sigmund Diamond, *The Reputation of the American Businessman* (New York: Harper Colophon, 1955), pp. 107–41.
2. Ibid., p. 157.
3. "Businessmen Go to Washington: It Costs them Plenty to Serve in Government," *U.S. News and World Report*, 6 February 1953, p. 86.
4. Paul R. Waddell and Robert F. Niven, *Sign of the 76* (Los Angeles: Union Oil Company of California, 1977), p. 386.
5. Stewart H. Holbrook, *The Age of the Moguls* (Garden City, N.J.: Doubleday, 1953), p. 95.
6. Arthur D. Howden Smith, *Commodore Vanderbilt: An Epic of American Achievement* (New York: McBride, 1927), pp. 258–59.
7. Thomas R. Horton, "Villainy & Heroism in the Executive Suite," *Management Review*, September 1987, p. 5.
8. "Hollywood's Favorite Heavy," PBS television documentary, 1984.
9. Josephson Institute of Ethics, *The Ethics of Youth: A Warning and a Call to Action* (Marina del Rey, Calif.: Josephson, 1990)
10. Louis E. Asher and Edith Heal, *Send No Money* (Chicago: Argus, 1942), p. 15.
11. John M. Henske, Olin Corp., Remarks made at Fairfield University, Fairfield, Conn., 1984.
12. Thornton Bradshaw and David Vogel, *Corporations and Their Critics* (New York: McGraw–Hill, 1981), p. 93.
13. John J. Nevin, "Product Quality, Corporate Competitivity and Consumerism," in *Advances in Applied Business Strategy*, edited by Robert Lamb (Greenwich,Conn.: JAI,1984)
14. Smith, *Commodore Vanderbilt*, pp. 229–30, 242, 253.
15. Korn Ferry International, *Executive Profile: A Decade of Change in Corporate Leadership* (New York: Korn Ferry International, 1990)
16. Diamond, *Reputation*, p. 125.
17. Horace B. Powell, *The Original Has This Signature: W. K. Kellogg* (Englewood Cliffs, N.J.: Prentice–Hall, 1956), pp. 303–4.

18. Ben H. Bagdikian, *Media Monopoly* (Boston: Beacon, 1983), pp. 158–60.
19. "President's Citation: Programs for Private Sector Initiatives," Private Sector Initiatives, 1987.
20. Ibid.
21. Anheuser Busch, *Fact Book*, undated.
22. Muncie, Indiana, *Press*, 2 May 1986.

CHAPTER 2

1. This thought came from Charles Kuralt's Sunday morning television program, CBS, 1988.
2. Forbes, 5 October 1987, cover.
3. Fortune, 11 September 1989, cover.
4. Eric Fromm, *The Art of Loving* (New York: Harper, 1956)
5. D. Elton Trueblood, *The Life We Prize* (Dublin, Ind.: Prinit, 1981), p. 45.
6. J. C. Penney, *View from the Ninth Decade* (New York: Nelson, 1960), p. 135.

CHAPTER 3

1. Robert McClements, "Every Cloud Has a Zip-Out Lining," Speech made at Bentley College, Conference on Business Ethics, Boston, 10 October 1985.
2. Willard C. Butcher, "The Need for Ethical Leadership," Commencement Address, Tulane University, 15 May 1987.

CHAPTER 4

1. Margaret Ingels, *Willis Haviland Carrier: Father of Air Conditioning* (Garden City, N.J.: Country Life Press, 1952), foreword.
2. Blaise Pascal, *Pensées*, translated by A. J. Krailsheimer (New York: Viking Penguin, 1966), p. 235.
3. Harry Mark Petrakis, *The Founder's Touch* (New York: McGraw–Hill, 1965), p. 111.
4. United Parcel Service, *Our Partnership Legacy* (Greenwich, Conn.: UPS, 1985), p. 7.
5. Ibid., p. 7.
6. Robert J. Haft, "Business Decisions by the New Board," *Michigan Law Review*, November 1981, p. 35.
7. Ibid., p. 35.
8. Plato, *Apology*, in The Works of Plato, edited by Irwin Edman (New York: Modern Library College, 1927), p.64.
9. Charles E. Watson, *Management Development through Training* (Reading, Mass: Addison–Wesley, 1979), p. 332.

CHAPTER 5

1. Many of the ideas expressed in this chapter were put into my mind by D. Elton Trueblood during the course of several personal conversations we had in 1986, 1987, and 1988.
2. William Shakespeare, *King Henry V*, act 2, scene 4
3. J. C. Penney, *View from the Ninth Decade* (New York: Nelson, 1960) p. 73.

CHAPTER 6

1. Penney, *View*, p. 129.
2. Diamond, *Reputation*, p. 130.

CHAPTER 7

1. Julian Dana, *A. P. Giannini: Giant in the West* (New York: Prentice–Hall, 1947), p. 45.
2. Conrad Hilton, *Be My Guest* (Englewood Cliffs, N.J.: Prentice–Hall, 1957), p. 283.
3. George R. Parkin, *The Rhodes Scholarships* (London: Constable, 1913), pp. 6–7.
4. Trueblood, *Life we Prize*, pp. 57–58.
5. Penney, *View*, p. 137.
6. Parkin, *Rhodes Scholarships*, p. 7.
7. "A Welcome for Change," Nation's Business, February 1975, p. 46.
8. Angus A. Macdonald, *The Spirit of Service: Recollections of a Pioneer*, edited by Eleanor J. Macdonald (Houston, Texas: Macdonald, 1988)
9. "Henry Ford," John Hancock Life Insurance Company, advertisement in, *Newsweek*, 24 January 1949.
10. William B. Walton, Sr., *The New Bottom Line* (San Francisco: Harper & Row, 1986), p. 16.

CHAPTER 8

1. Several of the ideas expressed about the nature of profit came from George S. Goodell. See Goodell, "The Role of Profit in the American Economy," unpublished manuscript.
2. Reginald H. Jones, "Meeting Our Social Responsibilities," an essay prepared for publication by the U. S. Department of Commerce, December, 1980.
3. McClements, "Every Cloud."
4. United Parcel Service, *Partnership Legacy*, p. 4.
5. "John Wooden on Staying Power," advertisement by Panhandle Eastern Corp., in the *Wall Street Journal*.
6. Garet Garrett, *The Wild Wheel* (New York: Pantheon, 1952), p. 104.

CHAPTER 9

1. United Parcel Service, *Partnership Legacy*, p. 90.
2. "Roy Disney's Adventures in Tomorrowland," *Business Week*, 5 August 1985, pp. 66–67.

CHAPTER 10

1. Penney, *View*, pp. 33-34.
2. Walter Deane Fuller, "The Life and Times of Cyrus H. K. Curtis (1850–1933)" address delivered during a National Newcomen dinner,New York, N.Y., 19 February 1948.
3. Petrakis, *Founder's Touch*, p. 111.
4. Dana, *A. P. Giannini*, p. 42.
5. Diamond, *Reputation*, p. 138.

CHAPTER 12

1. Albert Henry Smyth, ed. *The Writings of Benjamin Franklin* (New York: Macmillan, 1907), vol. 5; no. 77.
2. Plato, *Apology*, p. 73.

CHAPTER 13

1. Benjamin Franklin, *Busy Body III*.
2. Asher and Heal, *Send No Money*, pp. 34–35.
3. United Parcel Service, *Partnership Legacy*, p. 89.
4. Norman Beasley, *Main Street Merchant* (New York: Whittlesey, 1948), pp. 14–15.

CHAPTER 14

1. Petrakis, *Founder's Touch*, cover page

CHAPTER 15

1. Ed Cray, *Levis'* (Boston: Houghton Mifflin, 1978), pp. 16–22.
2. Walton, *Bottom Line*, pp. 187–188.
3. Ibid., p. 188.
4. Beasley, *Main Street Merchant*, pp. 4–8.
5. Petrakis, *Founder's Touch*, p. 153.
6. Walton, *Bottom Line*, p. 202.
7. Asher and Heal, *Send No Money*, p. 7.
8. United Parcel Service, *Partnership Legacy*, p. 127.

CHAPTER 16

1. David McCullough, *The Path between the Seas* (New York: Simon & Schuster, 1977), pp. 459–89.
2. "Meeting Management Challenges with Imagination," *Nation's Business*, December 1975, p. 40.
3. Allen Liles, *Oh Thank Heaven: The Story of the Southland Corporation* (Dallas: The Southland Corp., 1977), p. 137.
4. Dana, *A. P. Giannini*, p. 49.
5. Walton, Bottom Line, p. 49.
6. Bradshaw and Vogel, Corporations, pp. 211-212.
7. United Parcel Service, *Partnership Legacy*, p. 117.
8. James D. Robinson III, remarks made at the Graduate Management Program, World Trade Center, New York, N.Y., 10 September 1984.
9. Diamond, *Reputation*, p. 153.

CHAPTER 17

1. Gary Johns, *Organizational Behavior* (Glenview, Ill.: Scott, Foresman, 1983), p. 179.
2. Josiah Royce, *The Philosophy of Loyalty* (New York: Macmillan, 1908).
3. United Parcel Service, *Partnership Legacy*, p. 115.
4. Oscar Schisgall, *Eyes on Tomorrow* (New York: Ferguson, 1981), pp. 222–23.

CHAPTER 18

1. Powell, *Original*, pp. 62–63.
2. Petrakis, *Founder's Touch*, p. 118.
3. Gordon M. Philpott, *Daring Venture: The Life Story of William H. Danforth* (New York: Random House, 1960), p. 88.
4. Asher and Heal, *Send No Money*, introduction, p. xiv.

CHAPTER 19

1. Several of the ideas on the contagion of goodness were put into my mind by D. Elton Trueblood during the course of personal conversations in 1986, 1987, and 1988.
2. Walton, *Bottom Line*, p. 52.
3. Butcher, "Need."

CHAPTER 20

1. Douglas McGregor, *The Human Side of Enterprise* (New York: McGraw–Hill, 1960.
2. Thomas J. Peters and Robert H. Waterman, Jr., *In Search of Excellence: Lessons from America's Best Run Companies* (New York: Harper & Row, 1982).

3.   Harold S. Geneen, "The Case for Managing by the Numbers," *Fortune*, 1 October 1984, pp. 78–81.

CHAPTER 21

1.   George Laycock, *The Kroger Story: A Century of Innovation* (Cincinnati: The Kroger Co., 1983), pp. 23–24.
2.   Robinson, remarks made at Graduate Management Program.
3.   "W. Atlee Burpee," *The National Cyclopedia of American Biography,* vol. 16 (New York: James T. White, 1918), p. 286.

CHAPTER 23

1.   Robert D. Haas, acceptance speech, Lawerence A. Wein Prize in Corporate Social Responsibility, Columbia University, New York, N.Y., 19 November 1984.
2.   Robinson, remarks at Graduate Management Program.
3.   McClements, "Every Cloud."
4.   James C. Worthy, *William C. Norris: Portrait of a Maverick* (Cambridge: Ballinger, 1987), pp. 107–24.
5.   Personal letter from Reginald H. Jones, 9 July 1987.

CHAPTER 24

1.   Quoted in Malcolm S. Forbes, "Fact and Comment," *Forbes*, 13 July 1987, pp. 33–34.
2.   Sloan Wilson, *The Man in the Gray Flannel Suit* (New York: Simon and Schuster, 1955), pp. 146–47.
3.   Robert C. Alberts, *The Good Provider: H. J. Heinz and His 57 Varieties* (Boston: Houghton Mifflin, 1973), pp. 139–40.
4.   Walton, *Bottom Line*, p. 202.
5.   Herodotus, *Persian Wars*, Book 1 of *The Complete and Unabridged Historical Works of Herodotuss,* edited by Francis Godolphin and Richard Borroum (New York: Random House, 1942).
6.   Plutarch, "Solon" in *The Lives of the Noble Grecians and Romans*, translated by John Dryden and revised by Arthur Clough (New York: Modern Library, undated).
7.   Brand Whitlock, *Forty Years of It* (New York: Appleton, 1930), pp. 112–40.

Bibliography

Anheuser Busch. *Fact Book*. undated.

Alberts, Robert C. *The Good Provider: H. J. Heinz and His 57 Varieties*. Boston: Houghton Mifflin, 1973.

Aristotle. *Nichomachean Ethics*. Translated by Terence Irwin. Indianapolis, Ind.: Hackett, 1985.

Asher, Louis E., and Edith Heal. *Send No Money*. Chicago: Argus, 1942.

Bagdikian, Ben H. *Media Monopoly*. Boston: Beacon, 1983.

Beasley, Norman. Main Street Merchant. New York: Whittlesey House, 1948.

Bradshaw, Thornton, and David Vogel. *Corporations and Their Critics*. New York: McGraw–Hill, 1981.

"W. Atlee Burpee." *The National Cyclopedia of American Biography*, vol. 16. New York: James T. White, 1918.

"Businessmen Go to Washington: It Costs them Plenty to Serve in Government." *U.S. News and World Report*, 6 February 1953.

Butcher, Willard C. "The Need for Ethical Leadership." Commencement address. Tulane University. 15 May 1987.

Campolo, Anthony. *Seven Deadly Sins*. Wheaton, Ill: Vista Media, 1987, audio cassette.

Carnegie, Andrew. "The Gospel of Wealth." *North American Review*, June and Dec. 1889.

Cray, Ed. *Levis'*. Boston: Houghton Mifflin, 1978.

Dana, Julian. *A. P. Giannini: Giant in the West*. New York: Prentice–Hall, 1947.

Diamond, Sigmund. *The Reputation of the American Businessman*. New York: Harper Colophon, 1955.

Forbes, Malcolm S. "Fact and Comment." *Forbes*, 13 July 1987.

Fromm, Eric. *The Art of Loving*. New York: Harper, 1956.

Fuller, Walter Deane. *The Life and Times of Cyrus H. K. Curtis: 1850–1933*. Address delivered during a National Newcomen dinner, New York, N.Y., 19 February 1948.

Garrett, Garet. *The Wild Wheel*. New York: Pantheon, 1952.

Geneen, Harold S. "The Case for Managing by the Numbers." *Fortune*, 1 October 1984.

Goodell, George S. "The Role of Profit in the American Economy." Unpublished manuscript.

Haas, Robert D. Acceptance speech, Lawerence A. Wein Prize in Corporate Social Responsibility. Columbia University, New York, N.Y., 19 November 1984.

Haft, Robert J. "Business Decisions by the New Board." *Michigan Law Review*. November 1981.

Heermance, Edgar L. *Codes of Ethics*. Burlington,VT: Free Press, 1924.

"Henry Ford." John Hancock Life Insurance Company advertisement. in *Newsweek*, 24 January 1949.

Henske, John, Olin Corp. Remarks made at Fairfield University, 1984.

Herodotus. *Persian Wars*. Book 1. *The Complete and Unabridged Historical Works of Herodotus*. Edited by Francis Godolphin and Richard Borroum. New York: Random House, 1942.

Hilton, Conrad. *Be My Guest*. Englewood Cliffs, N.J.: Prentice–Hall, 1957.

Hobbes, Thomas. *Leviathan*. New York: Dutton, 1950.

Holbrook, Stewart H. *The Age of the Moguls*. Garden City, N.J.: Doubleday, 1953.

"Hollywood's Favorite Heavy." PBS television documentary. 1984.

Horton, Thomas R. "Villainy & Heroism in the Executive Suite." *Management Review*. September 1987.

Ingels, Margaret. *Willis Haviland Carrier: Father of Air Conditioning*. Garden City, N.J.: Country Life Press. 1952.

"John Wooden on Staying Power." Advertisement by Panhandle Eastern Corp., in the *Wall Street Journal*.

Johns, Gary. Organizational Behavior. Glenview, Ill.: Scott, Foresman, 1983.

Jones, Reginald H."Meeting Our Social Responsibilities." Essay prepared for publication by the U.S. Department of Commerce. December 1980.

———. Personal correspondence. 9 July 1987.

Johnson, Gen. Robert W. *Or Forfeit Freedom*. Garden City, N.Y.: Doubleday, 1947.

Josephson Institute of Ethics. The Ethics of Youth: A Warning and a Call to Action. Marina del Rey, Calif.: Josephson, 1990.

Kleinfield, Sonny. *Staying at the Top*. New York: NAL, 1986.

Lamb, Robert, ed. *Advances in Applied Business Strategy*, vol. 1. Greenwich, Conn.: JAI, 1984.

Korn Ferry International. *Executive Profile: A Decade of Change in Corporate Leadership*. New York: Korn Ferry, 1990.

Laycock, George. *The Kroger Story: A Century of Innovation*. Cincinnati: Kroger Co., 1983.

Liles, Allen. *Oh Thank Heaven: The Story of the Southland Corporation*. Dallas: The Southland Corp., 1977.

Locke, John. Two Treatisies of Civil Government. New York: Dutton,1953.

Macdonald, Angus A. Edited by Eleanor J. Macdonald. The Spirit of Service: Recollections of a Pioneer. Houston, Texas: Macdonald, 1985.

McClements, Robert. "Every Cloud Has a Zip-Out Lining." Bentley College, Conference on Business Ethics. Boston. 10 October 1985.

McCullough, David. *The Path between the Seas*. New York: Simon & Schuster, 1977.

McGregor, Douglas. *The Human Side of Enterprise*. New York: McGraw–Hill, 1960.

"Meeting Management Challenges with Imagination." *Nation's Business*, December 1975.

Mines, Samuel. *Pfizer: An informal History*. New York: Pfizer, 1978.

Parkin, George R. *The Rhodes Scholarships*. London: Constable, 1913.

Pascal, Blaise. *Pensées*. Translated by A. J. Krailsheimer. New York: Viking Penguin, 1966.

Penney, J. C. *View from the Ninth Decade*. New York: Nelson, 1960.

Peters, Thomas J. and Robert H. Waterman, Jr. *In Search of Excellence: Lessons from America's Best Run Companies*. New York: Harper & Row, 1982.

Petrakis, Harry Mark. *The Founder's Touch*. New York: McGraw–Hill, 1965.

Philpott, Gordon M. *Daring Venture: The Life Story of William H. Danforth*. New York: Random House, 1960.

Plato. *Apology*. In *The Works of Plato*. Edited by Irwin Edman. New York: Modern Library College, 1927.

Plutarch. "Solon" In *The Lives of the Noble Grecians and Romans*. Translated by John Dryden and revised by Arthur Hugh Clough. New York: Modern Library, undated.

Powell, Horace B. *The Original Has This Signature: W. K. Kellogg*. Englewood Cliffs, N.J.: Prentice–Hall, 1956.

"President's Citation: Programs for Private Sector Initiatives." Private Sector Initiatives, Washington, D.C., 1987.

Robinson, James D., III. Remarks made at the Graduate Management Program, World Trade Center. New York, N.Y. 10 September 1984.

"Roy Disney's Adventures in Tomorrowland." *Business Week*, 5 August 1985.

Royce, Josiah. *The Philosophy of Loyalty*. New York: Macmillan, 1911.

Schisgall, Oscar. *Eyes on Tomorrow*. New York: Ferguson, 1981.

Shakespeare, William. *King Henry V*.

Sinclair, Upton. *The Jungle*. New York: Harper, 1957.

Smith, Arthur D. Howden. *Commodore Vanderbilt: An Epic of American Achievement*. New York: McBride, 1927.

Smyth, Albert Henry, ed. *The Writings of Benjamin Franklin*. New York: Macmillan, 1907.

Sutton, Francis X. Seymour E. Harris, Carl Kaysen and James Tobin. *The American Business Creed*. Cambridge, Mass.: Harvard University, 1956.

Trueblood, D. Elton. *The Life We Prize*. Dublin, Ind.: Prinit, 1981.

United Parcel Service. *J. E. Casey, Our Partnership Legacy*. Greenwich, Conn.: UPS, 1985.

Waddell, Paul R., and Robert F. Niven. *Sign of the 76*. Los Angeles: Union Oil Company of California, 1977.

Walton, William B., Sr. *The New Bottom Line*. San Francisco: Harper & Row, 1986.

Watson, Charles E. *Management Development through Training*. Reading, Mass: Addison–Wesley, 1979.

"A Welcome for Change." *Nation's Business*. February 1975.

Whitlock, Brand. *Forty Years of It*. New York: Appleton, 1930.

Wilson, Sloan. *The Man in the Gray Flannel Suit*. New York: Simon & Schuster, 1955.

Worthy, James C. *William C. Norris: Portrait of a Maverick*. Cambridge: Ballinger, 1987.

Name and Company Index

Subject Index

ABOUT THE AUTHOR

Charles E. Watson is Professor of Management at Miami University, Oxford, Ohio. He earned his B.S. in Business Administration at the University of California, his M.S. in Management and his Ph.D. in Business from the University of Illinois. Dr. Watson's past affiliations include the Anaconda Company, Temple University, and Deakin University in Australia. He has also done work for Sun Oil and Procter & Gamble. Dr. Watson is the author of three other books on management.

DATE DUE